REPORTORIAL WRITING

REPORTORIAL WRITING

Paul V. Sheehan

Chilton Book Company

Philadelphia   New York

Copyright © 1972 by Paul V. Sheehan
First Edition
All rights reserved
Published in Philadelphia by Chilton Book Company
and simultaneously in Ontario, Canada,
by Thomas Nelson & Sons, Ltd.
ISBN: 0-8019-5603-X
Library of Congress Catalog Card Number 70-187838
Designed by Margery Kronengold
Manufactured in the United States of America

To Mary Ann Sheehan,
Pamela Sheehan Kaiser
and Edgar Arnold Kaiser

Permission to reprint copyrighted material in this book has been given by The *Chicago Daily News;* The *Chicago Sun-Times;* The *Chicago Tribune;* The Christian Science Publishing Society; The *Christian Science Monitor; Editor & Publisher;* Harper & Row, Publishers; Harvard University Press; Knight Newspapers, Inc.; The *Los Angeles Times;* The *Milwaukee Journal;* The *Minneapolis Tribune;* The *New York News;* The *New York Times; Newsday;* G. P. Putnam's Sons; The *St. Louis Post-Dispatch;* The *Saturday Review;* The *Wall Street Journal;* The *Washington Post.*

PREFACE

This book stems from ideas accumulated during years of newspaper work and many hours of classroom teaching. Its purpose is to serve as a teaching tool that may help to prepare students in introductory news writing and reporting classes for more advanced courses in journalism. It is meant to meet the textual requirements of a full year's course in news writing and reporting.

The approach taken is functional. An attempt has been made to eschew rules as much as possible. Substituted for them are broad frameworks and guidelines for the different types of journalistic literature. Within those frameworks and guidelines there is much room for individuality.

Narrow conformity is not the aim of writing instruction as this author sees it. The author has deliberately avoided trying to fit different leads into niches and then classifying them accordingly. Such an approach was used a great deal in earlier education for journalism. Instead, the attempt today should be to give the student an appreciation of what constitutes a good lead. Once attained, such appreciation provides ample room for individual talents to be put to work. The student should be helped to develop within his own capabilities.

Rather than use a detailed classification of news stories which is dependent partly on the sources from which the news comes, the author has placed emphasis on some of the factors common to each of the broader types of journalism. Thus, the sections dealing with the news story have not been divided into news coming from the undertaker, the city hall, the court house, the police station, labor unions, conventions, and so forth. The teacher still has a great deal of leeway in introducing these sources. Courses dealing with the reporting of public affairs will cover some of these sources in detail for students as they progress in their education.

Nor has special emphasis been placed on electronic journalism. The fundamentals should be emphasized in introductory classes. Yet depth and breadth in news and interpretative writing have been given separate chapters because of their importance in good reporting.

No effort has been made to achieve stylistic conformity in the presentation of examples. It is important that teachers and students using this book remember that each example has been selected not for its perfection but because it illustrates particular points. Similarly, the exercises that follow some of the chapters, while not exhaustive, offer opportunity for discussions of language usage.

It would not be feasible to list the many persons who have in some way, directly or indirectly, contributed to this book. Some of the most helpful have been the following:

Professor Dayle Molen, Department of Journalism, Fresno State College, has gone over each chapter critically and has offered many suggestions.

George F. Gruner, managing editor of the Fresno (Calif.) *Bee*, has also reviewed each chapter and given the author many helpful ideas.

Appreciation is also extended to the following:

Mark F. Ethridge, former publisher of the Louisville *Courier-Journal* and vice president and editor of the Long Island *Newsday;* Raymond Spangler, publisher of the Redwood City (Calif.) *Tribune* and past national president of Sigma Delta Chi; Robert Miller, veteran United Press International foreign correspondent; and Robert Myers, former Associated Press bureau chief in San Francisco and now in public relations, for giving generously of their time for taped interviews.

Nick B. Williams, vice president and editor of the Los Angeles *Times,* and Lynn Lilliston of the Los Angeles *Times* staff for making background information available.

Roger Tatarian, vice president and editor, United Press International, for giving long-standing cooperation and for making information available.

Professor Melvin Mencher, Graduate School of Journalism, Columbia University, for favors past and present and for ever-ready cooperation.

Staff members of the Fresno *Bee* for continued cooperation, with particular acknowledgment to newsman Karl Kidder and to members of the library staff.

Dr. Serge Korff, professor of physics at New York University, for permitting an interview with a reporter to be taped.

Not to be overlooked are colleagues and newspaper associates, who unwittingly have provided ideas and information. No small amount of appreciation goes to former students, who taught the author much as he was trying to teach them. And this book could not have existed were it not for the examples provided by the Associated Press, United Press International and the many newspapers mentioned throughout.

CONTENTS

Preface *vii*

Chapter 1 News—What Is It? *1*
Chapter 2 Objectivity—A Criterion *12*
Chapter 3 Six Honest Serving Men *23*
Chapter 4 Saying It Best *42*
Chapter 5 Identification, Background, Attribution and Explanation *62*
Chapter 6 Is There an Interesting Angle? *80*
Chapter 7 The Organization of the News Story *97*
Chapter 8 Types of Journalistic Literature *117*
Chapter 9 Coverage *145*
Chapter 10 The Art of Interviewing *156*
Chapter 11 Interesting the Readers *186*
Chapter 12 Feature Writing *209*

Chapter 13 Reporting the News in Depth and in Breadth *240*
Chapter 14 The Situation Story *270*
Chapter 15 Interpretative Writing *291*
Chapter 16 The Background Story *306*
Chapter 17 The Human Interest Story *318*
Chapter 18 Related Stories *339*
Chapter 19 The Color Story *355*
Chapter 20 Ethical and Legal Considerations *367*

Appendix A Copyreading Marks *389*
Appendix B Commonly Misspelled Words *391*
Appendix C A Final Exercise *393*

Index *395*

REPORTORIAL WRITING

Chapter 1

NEWS — WHAT IS IT?

> *Mails from the North—the East—the West—the South—whence according to some curious etymologists, comes the magical word NEWS.* —De Quincey

M. Lyle Spencer, a pioneer in education for journalism, defined news in this way:

> In its final analysis, news may be defined as any accurate fact or idea that will interest a large number of readers; and of two stories the accurate one that interests the greater number of people is the better.[1]

Spencer might have refined his definition to say that news is *the communication* of any accurate fact or idea; for, if a modern Robinson Crusoe were to discover an ape that could talk, it would not be news until he could communicate his finding to others.

Some persons have been less serious in defining news. A publisher in the Pacific Northwest once defined news as gossip, and one wag said news is anything that breaks one of the Ten Commandments, and that if it breaks the fifth or the ninth it is great news.

In fact, journalists today would make little change in Spencer's defi-

---

[1] *News Writing* (Boston: D.C. Heath and Co., 1917), p. 26.

nition, and a summarization of the definitions in many textbooks would be that news is the communication of information of interest to human beings and that the greater the number of persons interested the greater the news. The word "news" comes from the Latin *nova,* which originally meant "new things" and later "new tidings." An antonym would be "humdrum." And implicit in the word "tidings" is communication. The word was once spelled "newes" and considered plural, as when Percy Bysshe Shelley said, "There are bad newes from Palermo."

An Element of Controversy

Many of today's intellectuals, including some sociologists, would take issue with Spencer's definition. They would argue that editors, in their efforts to appeal to the masses, place emphasis on the sensational rather than the significant. They would define news as the communication of information that *should be* of interest to readers.

Raymond Spangler, former publisher of the Redwood City (Calif.) *Tribune,* retorts that you can fill a newspaper with the kind of news you think persons should read, but if a newspaper is not read "it is going to die a quiet but profound and complete death." To him the big challenge is to make significant news appealing.

Mark F. Ethridge, who has been connected with newspapers for more than half a century as former publisher of the Louisville *Courier-Journal* and editor of *Newsday,* has seen a vast change in the concept of news. Murders, fires and scandals "were meat for the editors" in the old days, he conceded, but such occurrences have been played down in modern newspapering. Crime news cannot be ignored, he points out, but there has been generally less emphasis on it unless it includes unusual elements.

Interest is one factor that must be weighed, he explained, but significance is another: "If you just made up a front page of things that might be interesting or of feature stories, I think you'd give a distorted picture of the world." He added that it is unnecessary to sensationalize but important to avoid dullness. "I think you can achieve a balance. You won't get the mass circulation of the New York *Daily News,* for instance, but you can get a circulation among people who wield an influence and I think that's part of the obligation of a newspaper."

James Wechsler of the New York *Post* said not so long ago that the most serious and compelling complaint aimed at his newspaper was that "we do not always give important play to the most important news of the day—that we reach out for human interest stories at the expense of stories which may have the greatest significance for the future of humanity. . . ."

Wechsler continued:

Arthur Hays Sulzberger (New York *Times*) recently asked: "Is it more urgent to inform a thousand readers or entertain a million? Much as this generation needs a sense of humor, I'm afraid that my vote goes for the newspaper that informs."

My vote goes for the paper that both entertains and informs, that reaches a million rather than a thousand, that not only puts up a fight for the welfare of most of the people all of the time but also persuades them to read all about it.[2]

(Copyright 1950 The Saturday Review Associates, Inc.)

British newspapers represent two extremes, the quality newspaper and the popular press. Americans are more fortunate than the English because a large segment of the press in the United States achieves an important balance in news presentation.

One safe generalization is that the word "interest" is expressed or implied in almost every definition of news. It must be recognized that newspapers run varied types of news because of the different interests of their readers.

Everyone would like the newspapers he reads to cater to his particular interests.

A musician may be critical because he feels not enough space is devoted to music. An educator would like more news about the schools. The artist wants more attention paid to art. The scientist complains about the lack of science-oriented news. And a laborer, fatigued when he returns home from work, may seek something in his newspaper that will provide escape or entertainment. It is up to the editor to try to find a common denominator.

In so doing, many editors strive for a balance—something for everyone.

The World Changes

The knowledge level of the people of the United States has raised considerably since the turn of the century. More education, better communications, improved transportation, a greater awareness of social and economic problems—these are some of the factors involved.

In 1815, Andrew Jackson's forces fought the British in the battle of New Orleans two weeks after a peace treaty had been signed. The reason was a lack of speedy communications. The rapidity with which news is relayed today gives readers almost an immediate report on what is going on in other parts of the world.

With change has come a broadening of interests. No aspiring journalist today would turn back to William Randolph Hearst, Edward W.

[2] "The Techniques of Showmanship," *Saturday Review,* June 24, 1950.

Scripps or Joseph Pulitzer for a definition of news. Regardless of criticisms, some valid and some invalid, the contents of newspapers generally extend far beyond the reporting of crime, fires, disaster and death.

One news executive commented that the newspaper is a mirror and that, if persons do not like what they see, they should not break the mirror but try to change the picture it reflects.

The one certain thing is that the picture constantly changes. More and more persons have become concerned about such serious issues as education, civil rights, pollution, health, slums and narcotics abuse.

Today's newspapers have begun reporting these problems in depth through the use of detailed stories that provide ample backgrounds for the facts.

The late Arthur Brisbane, a Hearst columnist, once said that news resembles the second hand on a clock, ticking noisily, whereas history resembles the hour hand, moving slowly and unnoticeably. But, he pointed out, even though the movement of the hour hand is not as observable as that of the second hand, each of the seconds ticked off by the latter is inexorably reflected by the former.

Reward for the Reader

Journalism educators have come up with a classification of news based on the reward offered the reader. Some news is classified as offering only ephemeral satisfaction, such as stories about crime, fires, accidents or disasters. Included are human interest stories. All these, it is said, are of immediate interest but soon forgotten.

News of political, economic or social significance, on the other hand, is said to provide a future or more lasting reward because it broadens the reader's frame of reference.

One of the standards often used in evaluating a newspaper is the ratio of news offering future reward to that providing only immediate reward.

It is difficult on occasions, however, to determine which news has future reward. Crime news, for instance, undoubtedly has brought public pressure on politicians to strive for ways of preventing lawlessness. Reports on accidents, particularly traffic mishaps, have prompted legislatures to pass safety legislation.

Factors of News

Most textbooks on news writing list such news determinants as unusualness, nearness, timeliness, prominence, human interest and probable consequence.

Many marriages of persons of comparable ages take place daily. This is the usual and expected, but when a man of 90 weds a woman of 22 it is not the usual. Thousands of clergymen lead exemplary lives and, because of their calling, this is expected, but when a minister is accused of raping the vocalist in the church choir, it is not expected.

An earthquake that took five lives in Los Angeles would probably interest Americans more than earth tremors that killed 100 in Afghanistan. Los Angeles is closer and more familiar to Americans than Afghanistan. The death of the mayor of Decatur, Ill., would probably rate no space in a Los Angeles newspaper, but it would be news in Decatur and in the vicinity surrounding that city.

There is an old story that if a dog bites a man it is not news but that if a man bites a dog it is news. The latter is unusual. The story needs qualification, however, for if the man bitten by the dog were prominent, say the governor of a state, it would be news. The average citizen may suffer a leg fracture in a traffic accident and it will have little interest to a city editor. Let the mayor of a city suffer a leg fracture and it will interest the city editor in his community. President Richard M. Nixon suffered a nick on his forehead while boating and it was considered news by many newspapers.

Human interest touches the emotions of readers. A small girl, for example, who is stricken with leukemia wants to see Santa Claus before she dies, or parents with 11 children are being evicted from their home because they are unable to pay their taxes.

Some feel that the most significant news determinant is consequence or probable consequence.[3] A news report that the price of coffee will rise 25 cents a pound will interest all households in which that beverage is used. And a story indicating the danger of increased military entanglements in the Far East will cause concern in many homes.

The Influence of Newspaper Policy

The policy of a newspaper should not influence the way a story is written, but it does affect the selection of news. A publication favoring the municipal control of garbage collection, for example, may select a story depicting the success of that type of operation in another city. Another newspaper advocating the construction of a public convention center may, for policy reasons, run stories telling what has been done in this respect in other communities.

Fund-raising campaigns by civic and health organizations often receive more space than would be warranted if editors were to base their decisions strictly on reader interest. Publications supporting the issu-

---

[3] See, for example, Robert C. O'Hara, *Media for the Millions* (New York: Random House, 1961), Chapter 13.

ance of school bonds may, because of policy rather than reader interest, run a series of articles on school needs.

News Is Relative

The value of a particular story on any day hinges on the total news picture for that day. A story that might make the front or a section page one day might merit only the inside on another day when the run of news is heavier.

The relative nature of news can easily be seen in making comparisons of small town and metropolitan newspapers. In a town of 5,000, the death of any citizen might be worth a story. It is said that everyone knows everyone else in a small community. What about San Francisco, St. Louis, Minneapolis—not to mention New York City?

If a man suffers cuts and bruises in a traffic mishap in a small community it is likely to be worth space in the newspaper, but if the average person undergoes the same discomfort in a metropolitan city the newspaper is hardly likely to take notice of it.

Negativism Condemned

Once, after addressing a woman's group on the subject of news, the author was asked why it is that a couple happily married for years never makes the headlines while a couple getting a divorce does. The implication, of course, is that newspapers stress the negative rather than the positive, the bad that men do rather than the good.

Many persons are convinced that the press, through undue publicity, is helping to create confrontations on college campuses, riots in the streets, and violence in general.

"Look at the thousands of students who are orderly," these persons say. "We never hear about them—all we hear about is the few who are disorderly."

It should be noted that not all divorces, by any means, make the headlines and many anniversary celebrations do, though frequently in the society sections. Achievements in the fields of medicine, science, education, sociology and psychology frequently are reported. Let a man come up with a cure for cancer and his accomplishment will be told in newspapers throughout the world.

George Kane of the *Rocky Mountain News* in Denver lampooned critics who charge that newspapers should try to balance bad news with good news. He wrote:

—An estimated 112,376 automobiles safely made turns onto Santa Fe Drive Tuesday. One didn't. Funeral arrangements are pending for. . . .

—There are 1.1 million persons living in Metropolitan Denver, most of whom never would stoop to violence. Only about 1,000 rioted recently in Red Rocks Amphitheater. . . .

—Sen. Phil I. Buster, who last year led the move to censure one of his colleagues for allegedly pocketing campaign funds, admitted Tuesday his wife, brother, uncle, three cousins, a nephew and his prospective son-in-law are members of his Washington payroll. . . .

—A young man who has never been in trouble, who idolizes his mother and turns over one half his hard-earned paycheck to her each week, who is a high school honor graduate, fell into disfavor with Los Angeles police this week when he shot one of them during a robbery.

—The Cold Coast Railroad was to present Gary Goodheart with a watch at his retirement Tuesday. Goodheart was at the throttle of the Golden Comet racing to Miami on his last run when he hit a northbound train. Injuries totaled 57.

—A British engineering firm has won a contract from the government of the desert Kingdom of Apaba to lay water lines to every village. Unfortunately, desert tribesmen have strained relations with Britain by shooting a party of surveyors.

—The Ancient Air Line Co. has won the nation's highest safety award for 3 million air miles without an accident. The company president was flying to Washington to receive recognition, however. . . .

—Down through history, dogs have saved small children from fires, rescued drowning men, provided companionship with unwavering loyalty. A dog has always been man's best friend. Except for Grover, who Tuesday attacked. . . .

—Millions of Americans are owners of color television sets. A government study shows there is no danger of radioactivity from more than 99 percent sold. Helping to make up the remaining 1 percent is Herman K., who was admitted to the hospital for radiation burns. . . .

—Stanley G. is one of nine brothers in his family. Three of his brothers are ministers, two are in government foreign service, one is a doctor, one is a sociologist and one is a welfare worker. Tuesday, Stanley became a murderer when he was convicted of poisoning his wife. . . .

Or, as Thomas Paine didn't say, "One morning the world woke up and there was no news." [4]

---

[4] *Scripps-Howard News,* Oct., 1968, p. 8.

Roger Tatarian, vice president and editor of United Press International, writing in the UPI *Reporter* on November 30, 1967, said:

> The suggestion that news media cause riots attracts some people simply because it is such an easy explanation. It is far easier than having to admit that a vast job of national reclamation lies ahead and that the cost will be immense. It is for the same reason that some believe in the "conspiracy" theory of riots—that a few conspirators, probably communists, are the root cause of these disorders and that if these troublemakers were rounded up, the trouble would go away. This is as realistic as blaming aircraft accidents on the law of gravity.

Terrence O'Flaherty, a radio-television columnist for the San Francisco *Chronicle,* quoted a letter from a reader and, though the complaint in this case was made about a television production, the charges made are similar to those many express about the press in general. An excerpt follows.

> I hope you will agree with me that the NBC spectacular "The Pursuit of Pleasure" requires the network to present the other and healthier side of the picture. Theirs was a one-sided, grotesquely distorted view of the lives of a small minority whose ideas of "pleasure" seem to consist exclusively of sex and drugs. If, as the experts assure us, only 25 percent of the American people have ever flown in an airplane, I believe I would be justified in assuming that a considerably smaller percentage have seen a topless show, smoked marijuana, taken LSD, belonged to a rowdy motorcycle gang, or rolled on a tiger skin with a blonde.
>
> Why not show us the vast majority of people, young and old, who find pleasure in yachting on San Francisco Bay or in golf or football or hiking or camping in the open or gardening?
>
> The real trouble with all the people shown in the NBC film is they are bored—bored with life, bored with themselves and bored with a developing history they don't understand and are too intellectually indolent to cope with.

O'Flaherty offered the following comment on the letter:

> You have hit the nail on the head. . . . Television, like the nation's press, is obsessed with the idiot fringe and neither medium can be excused for not labeling it as such.

The complaint is a common one, but the remedy it calls for is hardly adequate—the problem is not that simple. One thing is certain: immorality cannot be expunged by refusing to admit that it exists.

Newspapers would be shirking their duties if they were to sweep society's blemishes under the rug. Reporting, on the other hand, must be accurate and fair. In *Near v. Minnesota,* a case challenging a Minnesota law empowering public officials to enjoin publications considered as nuisances, Chief Justice Charles Evans Hughes said in 1931:

> . . . the administration of government has become more complex, the opportunities for malfeasance and corruption have multiplied, crime has grown to most serious proportions, and the danger of its protection by unfaithful officials and of the impairment of the fundamental security of life and property by criminal alliances and official neglect, emphasize the primary need of a vigilant and courageous press, especially in great cities.

Robert Miller, veteran UPI correspondent, commented in a talk at Fresno State College:

> Unfortunately, it seems that all the news that we reporters write today is bad news and that most of the bad news seems to come out of Asia. I don't think the world is any better or worse since man has tried to take it over and civilize it.
>
> It's just the fact that we have better communications today than we've ever had. The same things have been going on in the world for decades and decades, but we are more aware of them today because of our improved communications.
>
> It used to be that the prime ministers of various nations would get together and they'd carve and slice up the world and no one would know anything about it. Today if you have a garden party over in Monaco and Princess Grace gets snubbed by Queen Elizabeth, you not only know about it right away but we even get a picture of it to you while they're still not talking.
>
> For instance, back in the 30s the Russians and the Japanese fought a full-fledged war back on the Amur River. There were thousands of people killed. Nobody ever heard of that war. It was never covered. There was never any communications on it. . . .

It seems fair to conclude that most of the better newspapers of today attempt to present a balance of news.

On Guard against Hoaxes

A man in his early twenties walked into a newsroom some years ago and started telling the city editor about unusual experiences he had had in Yucatan. The city editor assigned a reporter to take the story. The reporter began by asking some pointed questions and the man interrupted, saying he wanted to get something from his car.

"You'll be amazed," he told the reporter.

The man never returned and the reporter dismissed the incident as a hoax attempt.

Why do some persons try to perpetrate hoaxes on newspapers?

In some cases it may be a desire for publicity. In others it is an attempt to gratify a perverse sense of humor.

A newspaper used a story about a California coed who purportedly was chosen homecoming queen by the students of a New England college. The newspaper, using the young woman as its only source of information, reported that the institution was a college for men. It also said that the coed was uncertain how she won the distinction but that she thought the nominations were made by fraternities.

The editor of another newspaper was skeptical and held the story until he could check it with officials at the college. It turned out that the college was coeducational, that it did not have homecoming queens, and that it did not have fraternities or sororities.

Some readers will remember the story from Santiago, Chile, saying that a woman had given birth to septuplets. It turned out to be a hoax.

Some hoaxers take particular delight in making false reports of engagements, marriages and deaths. To these persons it seems funny to report to newspapers that persons who may even dislike each other have become engaged or married or that certain persons enjoying good health have died. Most newspapers today have become wary and have set up verifying procedures to detect or guard against such hoaxes.

EXERCISES

I. Questions for Discussion

1. What objections, if any, do you have to M. Lyle Spencer's definition of news?
2. What refinements, if any, would you make in it?
3. Do you believe an editor should select the news he runs on the basis of what he thinks should be of public interest or on the basis, in his estimation, of what is of public interest?
4. It has been said that significance should be an important factor in determining news value. Do you agree? How would you define significance as a news factor?
5. Do you agree with Sulzberger or Wechsler on what should be the function of a newspaper?
6. What is the difference between news that offers the reader an immediate reward and that which offers him a future reward? Would you favor a preponderance of one type over the other?
7. Do you believe that the press, through undue publicity, is helping to create confrontations on college campuses, riots in the streets, and violence in general?
8. A letter published in the U.P.I. *Reporter,* May 28, 1970, urged a one-

month moratorium on news of any campus unrest. Would you favor the idea?
9. In what way may policy affect the selection of news?
10. What precautionary suggestions would you offer to prevent hoaxes?

II. Assignments

1. Prepare your own definition of news and be ready to defend it.
2. Study your local newspaper or newspapers and make a comparison of the proportionate usage of "positive" and "negative" news.
3. Select some wire service news stories from your local newspaper about occurrences in communities more than 1,000 miles away and decide what should have been added had the stories been local.
4. Study the news selections in a metropolitan and in a weekly newspaper and make some comparisons.
5. Prepare your own list of news factors.

Chapter 2

OBJECTIVITY—A CRITERION

> *One cannot speak the truth with false words.* —Goethe

The concept that fact and opinion should be separated in newspapers was not recognized until the turn of the present century. The great journalistic titans of the era of personal journalism gave little thought to divorcing news from editorial opinion. To them, objectivity—factualness—was not a criterion for a good newspaper. True, Horace Greeley is credited with creating the editorial page, but he was far from objective in the rest of his newspaper.

The principle that news should be presented without prejudice, without attempting to influence the thinking of the reader, was furthered by the press associations, which felt they could not cater to the whims of editors. One presentation had to be made for all newspapers. The result was a new standard for evaluating newspapers—fairness in the presentation of the news—factual reporting in the news columns and editorial opinion restricted to editorials.

There are those who believe that complete objectivity is impossible because news is written by human beings and because, it is argued, human beings cannot detach themselves from the events they report on.

The persons who take this view ask whether a Democrat can be entirely objective in writing a story about Republicans and vice versa, whether an ultra liberal can depict accurately the views of ultra conservatives and vice versa, and whether an atheist can be fair in presenting sectarian views and vice versa.

Frank Luther Mott took the following view:

> The term [objectivity] is doubtless unfortunate. It means, of course, reports which are written or broadcast without any bias or influence from opinions of the reporter or editor, as opposed to subjective news, which would be controlled and presumably distorted by the ideas and views of the reporter and editor.
>
> The trouble is that complete objectivity, in this sense, would never be possible even for a robot to achieve, for there must have been some mind behind the creation of the robot. News is gathered, written, edited, and distributed by human beings, all of whom have certain ideas, feelings, attitudes, opinions, and prejudices. These men very generally make a conscious effort to handle what they call "facts" with an open mind. . . .[1]

Magazines generally profess objectivity less than do newspapers. Thomas Griffith, who was once affiliated with *Time,* wrote:

> *Time* was founded by two audacious men fresh out of Yale. They were full of young men's impatience with cant; they would end the prevailing pretense between editor and reader that both knew what they did not; they would blow away the fog of pomposity which equated soundness with dullness; they scorned the mealymouthed and would not be afraid to have opinions . . . Very well, said these young men from Yale, there will be no affectation of a nonexistent objectivity; whoever selects and discards the news is exercising judgment: he is no eunuch free of bias; it will be healthier to admit that he even has opinions. And, they went on, let us be rid of this humbug that equal space to one politician's sensible remark and the other's platitude makes an impartial balance. They could see that each time the President of the United States made a speech, the news services would solicit congressional "reaction," evenhandedly balancing three condemnations from the opposition with three predictable plaudits from his own party, and always therefore finding congressional reaction "mixed." Was this a useful truth?[2]

There can be no denial that there is a place in American journalism for subjective publications, including the so-called opinion magazines, such as *The Nation, The National Review* and *The New Republic.* It must be recognized, however, that the backbone of the American press is made up of newspapers and broadcasting stations that attempt to pre-

---

[1] *The News in America* (Cambridge: Harvard University Press, 1952), p. 75.
[2] *The Waist-High Culture* (New York: Harper & Row, 1959), p. 79.

sent the news accurately, objectively and fairly. As Leo Gurko put it, "One test of an enlightened newspaper is the extent to which it assembles facts and how fairly it presents them to the reader." [3]

Areas of Judgment

There are areas of judgment in publishing the day's news, and it is in these spheres that critics often charge bias. To start with, an editor is limited in the amount of space he has for news each day. The total number of columns available for news is spoken of as the "news hole." There is not room for everything that might be of interest to some groups of readers; consequently, the editor must decide which stories he will use and which ones he will discard.

An editor could use a story about a speech made by one politician but reject a story about a speech delivered by another. He could give space to the activities of one organization but not to those of another. Readers are quick, however, to charge discrimination, and most editors take pride in the reputations of their newspapers. If anything, many editors lean over backward in their attempts to be fair.

While the editor must decide on a story's position—front page or inside, top or bottom of the page—and on the size of its headline and how long, how detailed, it should be, it is the reporter's task to write his news story objectively.

The Reporter's Responsibility

News generally is presented in condensed form and it is the reporter who is responsible for making the condensation. He is responsible for selecting the pertinent information for the story, and he decides what is unimportant, what should be omitted. He also decides what should be played up in the lead, what should come early in the story, and what should be buried.

When a reporter covers a speech, for instance, he must decide which parts of the speech merit space and which do not. And it must be remembered that, since much of what is said in a speech is opinion, attribution is necessary.

Care should be exercised in the choice of attributive words. To say that a speaker *"claimed* farmers are getting a raw deal" is different from saying he *"said* farmers are getting a raw deal." Another shade of meaning is given if the reporter writes that the speaker *"charged* farm-

[3] *Heroes, Highbrows and the Popular Mind* (Indianapolis: Bobbs-Merrill, 1953), p. 115.

ers are getting a raw deal" and still another if the story says he *"insinuated* farmers are getting a raw deal."

Slanting Stories

Stories may be slanted deliberately because the reporter is unable to take a detached position or unintentionally because he is careless in his choice of words. The results may be the same.

It is one thing to say that a public official "resigned" and another to say that he "quit under fire." Either could be true. It likewise is one thing to say that the police "failed to find any clues" and another to say that they "continued their search for clues."

"There is considerable difference between saying that legislators "voted to raise sales taxes" and saying they "voted to raise sales taxes still higher." Again, there is a difference between saying an official "criticized" his adversary and saying he "flayed" his adversary. To say that a city councilman "made a point" at a meeting is not the same as saying that he "scored a point," and even the former has a subjective tinge. Why not simply say he "asserted"?

George Gruner, managing editor of the Fresno (Calif.) *Bee,* commented:

> When I was a cub reporter, a desk man would take me over my stories asking, "What is the *sense* of this word?" He didn't want the definition, but wanted the *effect* on the reader.
>
> Definitions often overlap, but the fine shades of meaning, the picture the writer conjures up for the reader, is different in each case. I think it was the best lesson I ever learned. I jump on our young writers with the same question to this day.

The writer of the following probably did not realize he was being subjective:

> The county planning staff objects to the shopping center because it violates the Asbury Park Community Plan and because there already is an abundance of commercial zoning in the area.

The writer obviously is saying that the shopping center would violate the Asbury Park Community Plan and that there is an abundance of commercial zoning in the area. Slight changes make it objective:

> The county planning staff objects to the shopping center. It *maintains* that it would violate the Asbury Park Community Plan and it *feels* there already is an abundance of commercial zoning in the area.

The writer of the following put his own feelings into his writing:

His sudden death on a handball court was a tragedy for his family and colleagues, a severe shock for local and state political leaders, and it left the city's mayoralty campaign, which he had entered Feb. 1, in a state of confusion.

Evaluating and Particularizing Words

In description, the reporter may use evaluating adjectives, words that provide subjective appraisal, or particularizing words, terms that give details of what is seen, heard, felt, tasted or smelled. To say that a woman is beautiful is to evaluate, for a particular woman might appear beautiful to some but not to others. To describe her as a slender, five-foot blonde with blue eyes would be to make use of particularizing words.

To describe an apartment as lavish, lush or luxuriant is to evaluate, but to refer to it as a $250-a-month or a $2,000-a-month apartment is to particularize. To describe a house as large or small is to evaluate, but to refer to it as a 12-room or a three-room house is to particularize. To describe a man as a high-salaried executive is to evaluate, but to refer to him as a $50,000-a-year executive is to particularize.

Nouns as well as adjectives and adverbs can be evaluative. A few examples are banquet, beauty, charm, hero, mansion, prig and shack.

Evaluating words are used more frequently than particularizing words because the use of particularizing words is more difficult. Hundreds of additions could be made to the following list of evaluative adjectives:

Able	Careless	Husky	Murky
Absent-minded	Clear-cut	Incredible	Neat
Adept	Close-fisted	Insipid	Neighborly
Admirable	Deadpan	Long	Obdurate
Attractive	Diffident	Massive	Oppressive
Beauteous	Disheveled	Matronly	Peaceful
Big-hearted	Extravagant	Maudlin	Peaked
Bigoted	Gaunt	Morose	Poor
Blase	Grim	Mournful	Sad
Blatant	Heavy	Muddled	Scatterbrained

It is generally conceded that particularizing words are more objective than evaluating words. A good example of particularizing description was used in an Associated Press report about a civil rights leader in Alabama who was struck in the mouth by a sheriff while the former was being arrested on charges of criminal provocation and contempt of court:

> The sheriff, a powerfully built 6-footer weighing more than 200 pounds, contended that the Rev. Mr. Vivian, who weighs 165 pounds and is 5 feet 11½ inches tall, deliberately provoked the incident.

The majority of students discussing the story in a journalism class, however, felt that, even though much of the description particularizes, the paragraph is subjective. It should be noted that the words "powerfully built" are evaluative.

Although it is generally agreed that particularizing description is both more objective and more effective than evaluative description, it would be useless to attempt to manacle reportorial writers by trying to prohibit the use of the latter. It seems helpful, however, to suggest the frequent substitution of particularizing words for evaluating ones.

Evaluative terms can offend readers, whereas particularizing words, used correctly, can provide purely factual description. Many readers who have reached the age of 50 would snort at a lead that said an aged man was killed by a hit-and-run driver and then gave the victim's age as 50. The particularizing words "aged man" are not needed; giving the man's name and age would be good, clear, objective reporting.

The most questionable use of evaluative description usually occurs in stories that verge on the controversial. It undoubtedly would be better to use a particularizing description of a defendant in a criminal trial than it would be to describe him as gaunt, grim or morose. The effectiveness of the following description in a UPI dispatch on the Eichmann trial comes from the use of particularizing words:

> Hausner, a small hawk-faced bald-headed man in a black legal gown, faced the defendant with both hands on his hips. An angry flush appeared on Eichmann's ashen-grey cheeks as the prosecutor pressed his attack.
> A nerve in Eichmann's jaw twitched and he licked his lips nervously between questions. His voice rose angrily as he answered some of the more pointed questions.

Sometimes the use of evaluative description can be supplemented effectively by a particularizing statement, as in the following paragraph from a Louisville *Courier-Journal* story on the Gethsemane monk, Thomas Merton:

> He was a humble and unpretentious man, said to have been amazed by the acceptance of his writings. "The Seven Storey Mountain" has been translated into eight languages and has sold millions of copies.

It would be questionable, however, to refer to a political candidate in a news story as a "sincere and unpretentious man." It would not be to say he "maintains that sincerity is one of his basic qualifications for office."

Reporters have learned, partly because of criticism, not to use evaluative words, such as "huge," "large" and "big," in describing the numbers participating in walkouts, sit-ins, demonstrations and riots; instead, estimated figures are used.

Beware of Superlatives

Superlatives, such as "greatest," "best," "biggest," "most" and "strongest," frequently are used as subjective generalities, and often times their usage is inaccurate. It is safe to say that the United States Steel Corporation is the largest steel manufacturer in the country or that China has the largest population of any country in the world because the statements can be verified.

It is dangerous, however, to say that a particular man is the greatest chemist in the world or that an author is the best writer in the nation. It is safer to use qualification and say that a man is one of the greatest chemists or that an author is considered one of the best writers.

The author remembers well the admonition of a professor that superlatives should be shunned because too often they are lies. "You usually will find that there is someone or something else just as big, great, famous or old," he insisted.

Relevant was the remonstrance of a news service executive after a story from California said that Disneyland's 306-foot-long painting of the Grand Canyon would be "the longest painting in the world." The executive pointed out that the "Battle of Atlanta," painted in 1885 and hanging in the Cyclorama Building in Atlanta's Grant Park, is 400 feet long.

Keep It in Context

In their eagerness to seize upon a startling statement, reporters sometimes ignore the context—what precedes and follows—to such an extent that they distort meaning. The most serious out-of-context statements are found in the leads of stories, particularly when the reporter has tried too hard to find something with which to shock his readers.

If a speaker said that nuclear war is inevitable unless the great world powers start concentrating their efforts on peace, and a reporter wrote a lead saying that the speaker said nuclear war is inevitable, the reporter would be distorting meaning. And if a politician said that taxes must increase or governmental services decrease, it would be distortion simply to quote the man as saying that taxes must go up.

Exaggeration

Another type of distortion takes place when a reporter blows up what a speaker meant to be only a minor point in his talk and makes it appear to be a major point. Suppose, for example, that a college administrator in a speech gives the background and a number of factors involved in recent confrontations on his campus.

Suppose he casually remarks that some off-campus agitators took part in the confrontations. It would be a type of distortion for a reporter to place the emphasis in his story on the comment on off-campus agitators. It would not be amiss, however, for the reporter to mention the comment, giving it emphasis commensurate with that given it by the speaker.

Pertinent Facts

A tree may block the view of motorists at a crossroad when a fatal accident occurs, a fence guarding a canal may have been broken when a boy drowned, or onlookers may have slowed the approach of firemen to a blazing building.

These are pertinent facts that should be reported. The lead of a UPI story started, "With good visibility and veteran pilots at the controls," a jetliner crashed with a private plane in flight, killing 26 persons. The writer gave the readers pertinent information—neither weather nor inexperience at the controls of the jetliner was a factor in the accident.

Policy Rules

Some newspapers establish policy rules in an attempt to provide equal treatment for all in certain types of news. A newspaper may, for instance, adopt a rule that head pictures of brides-to-be should be restricted to one column. This makes it easy for a society editor to explain to a woman who wants a bigger picture in the paper why she cannot have it.

Other newspapers may run drunk driving arrests in a column with only the bare details listed. Other newspapers use obituary columns and still others use standard columns for club notices.

Small newspapers sometimes solve the problem of local "poets" seeking space for their verse by adopting a policy of running no poetry.

The importance of policy lies in equal application, since it helps to overcome pressures from those who see their situations as exceptional.

Political Campaigns
—A Time for Care

Particular care in the reporter's choice of words and phrases should be taken during political campaigns. Roger Tatarian, United Press International vice president and editor, and Sam Blackman, Associated Press general news editor, issued staff warnings prior to the 1968 general election.

Said Tatarian:

> As political sensibilities become more acute, your every word and nuance will become subject to closer partisan scrutiny.

Blackman commented:

> The haste of campaign coverage is no excuse for the careless phrase, the wrong verb or the trite adjective or adverb used in the mistaken belief that it adds impact.

Both warned against the use of attributive words with shaded variations of meaning. The UPI memorandum said that among the worst are "warned," "cautioned," "admitted" and "claimed," and the AP memorandum included "warn," "charge," "blast," "blister," "indict" and "lambast."

The AP labeled as "trite and meaningless claptrap" such expressions as "beat the drums," "took pot shots," "put on the gloves" and "locked horns." [4]

Italics indicate questionable words in the following paragraph, which is from a story about a speech made by United States Senator Alan Cranston of California:

> In an *unusually harsh* statement, Cranston *assailed* "the shabby manner in which Mr. Nixon's Department of Justice investigated Judge Carswell and concocted 'support' for this *unfortunate* nominee."

In using the three italicized words, the writer permitted his bias to show.

EXERCISES

I. Questions for Discussion

1. Do you believe it is possible for a human being to be objective? Why or why not?

[4] Lenore Brown, "Warning Signals Up For Campaign News," *Editor & Publisher*, Feb. 17, 1968, p. 26.

2. Do you agree with Griffith's statement on the pretense of objectivity by newspapers?
3. Would you favor the total exclusion of evaluative words in newspapers?
4. How can slanting be done through the use of attributive words?
5. What is meant by taking something out of context?
6. What is your attitude toward "propaganda" papers, such as those constituting the "underground" press?
7. Do you agree with the following comment of a San Francisco columnist?

> PASSING REMARKS: Maybe it's time the newspapers changed their manner of reporting deaths. The thought struck me while reading the obituary of a good friend . . . who died this week, much too young, much too tragically. The stories were coldly correct and journalistically precise: the sacred five W's of reporting, the next of kin, the time and place of the funeral—all the facts were there. It's too bad that the strictures of newspapering made it impossible for the reporter to add, "She was warm, charming, friendly, merry and intelligent, and everybody who knew her will miss her," for that is a fact, too.

8. What should have been done to make the following objective?

> Smith urged greater support for education in the state. Education pays for itself in the long run by improving the economic status of the people.

9. Is the following objective?

> The Soviet Union's attempt to condemn Israel as the aggressor in the Middle East was vigorously and eloquently rejected yesterday by Foreign Minister Abba Eban.

10. One of the following leads appeared in a San Francisco newspaper and the other in a wire service dispatch. Which is the more objective and why?

> Governor Reagan may ask the Legislature for another $180 million in new taxes.
> This would come on top of the $250 million tax boost he requested in his budget message Tuesday.
>
> SAN FRANCISCO—Gov. Ronald Reagan—already seeking about $250 million in higher taxes—now says he may ask for up to $180 million more.

II. Assignments

1. Substitute particularizing words for the following evaluative adjectives:

   a. Angry
   b. Attractive
   c. Blighted
   d. Capable
   e. Charming
   f. Deadpan

g. Disheveled   i. Husky
h. Gaunt   j. Luxurious

2. Compare the objectivity of the writing in the news magazines to that in your local newspaper.
3. Observe uses of attribution in your local newspaper on the basis of their objectivity.
4. Report on Herbert Brucker's article, "What Is Wrong with Objectivity?" in the *Saturday Review*, October 11, 1969, pp. 77–79.
5. Report on I. William Hill's article, "Subjective Jottings on Objectivity," and Derick Daniels' article, "Separating Fact/Emotion—By Edict or by Example?" in the January and February 1970 issues, respectively, of the *Bulletin* of the American Society of Newspaper Editors.

Chapter 3

SIX HONEST SERVING MEN

*I keep six honest serving-men
(They taught me all I knew);
Their names are What and Why and When
And How and Where and Who.*
— *Kipling*

Not many decades ago most reporters relied on Kipling's six honest serving men in writing leads for news stories and, to complicate matters, most of them defined the lead as the first paragraph. Thus it was not uncommon to find such cumbersome, complex leads as:

> John Jones, 45, a baker who lives at 2102 Maryland Street, was injured yesterday when the automobile he was driving was hit by a light truck driven by Henry Smith, 38, 245 Chestnut Avenue, at the corner of Lombard and Fruit Streets.

Some writers today persist in using burdensome leads, but the number is dwindling. An example follows:

> Dr. Norman E. Shumway, the Stanford University surgeon who performed the first adult heart transplant in the United States earlier this month, will speak Thursday, March 21, at the combined annual meeting of the Stanislaus and Merced Counties Branches of the Central California Heart Association.

Dull and tedious? Yes, but such leads accomplish the questionable goal of getting the answers to the six questions into an introductory sentence. Here is another example:

> Charles Brown, the president of the Oakdale Bank and Trust Company, will speak on "What's Ahead for Business" at a meeting of the Clarksburg Chamber of Commerce May 15 at noon in the Clarksburg Hotel.

Times are changing and so is news writing. The better writer of today answers only the essential questions in the first paragraph and saves the answers to the others for following paragraphs. He might write the preceding lead thus:

> Charles Brown, Oakdale Bank and Trust Company president, will tell what's ahead for business at a meeting of the Clarksburg Chamber of Commerce.

The following details would be saved for a second paragraph:

> The meeting will be held at noon May 15 in the Clarksburg Hotel.

Other writers would further shorten the opening paragraph:

> An Oakdale banker will tell the Clarksburg Chamber of Commerce what's ahead for business.
> The banker, Charles Brown, will address the group May 15 at noon in the Clarksburg Hotel.

There are newsmen who object to the preceding presentation because it necessitates some repetition or otherwise added words. In this case, the words "the banker" were necessary in the second paragraph. If the repetition is slight, however, the increased readability seems to warrant it.

Keep It Short

The first prerequisite in writing a readable, interesting lead is to keep it short. Journalistic writing would benefit if the term "lead" were broadened to include more than just the first paragraph. Thirty words, give or take a couple, should be enough for most first paragraphs. Forty are too many and 50 excessive.

The veteran news executive Basil L. (Stuffy) Walters was known as a stickler for short sentences. The Feb. 14, 1962, issue of *Time* told the story of how, when he was the news editor of the Chicago *News,* he insisted upon short introductory paragraphs and would toss back any running more than 14 words. A reporter handed him a story on economic conditions with a first paragraph of eight words: "Will there be a boom or a bust?"

The reporter got the story back with instructions to cut the number of words. With some frustration, after several trials, he came up with:

>Boom?
>Bust?
>That is the question.

Walters was pleased.

This may seem to be carrying matters to extremes, but more first paragraphs suffer from lack of brevity than from any other fault. The following is an interesting example of conciseness:

>Abandon ship . . .
>That will be the order today aboard the freighter Chickasaw, hopelessly grounded on remote Santa Rosa Island. (Los Angeles *Times*)

Would it have been better to combine the two paragraphs into a single sentence?

>The order to abandon ship will be given today aboard the freighter Chickasaw, hopelessly grounded on remote Santa Rosa Island.

The combination is questionable, but if it were used the lead still would be only 20 words.

The following is an interesting and concise opening paragraph:

>SAN DIEGO (AP)—Home wash days may be regulated as an emergency measure in San Diego.

The story went on to tell that the measure was being considered as a means of easing the load on sewer mains until a new sewer system could be completed. Slightly longer but still sharp is:

>MIDLAND PARK, N.J. (UPI)—A housewife said Tuesday she had growing support in her fight to persuade one of the nation's largest food stores not to distribute trading stamps.

The idea of boiling the first sentence down to bare essentials is well illustrated in the following:

>A countywide building code seems to be a sure thing today.
>The Fresno County Board of Supervisors, meeting as a committee on public works, unanimously reaffirmed its stand favoring the adoption of building standards for the entire county. (Fresno *Bee*)

The idea is to select the most important fact for the first paragraph, to express this fact as simply as possible in the first paragraph, and then to put complementary details in the second and third paragraphs. Details that can wait for the second or third paragraph should not be put in the first paragraph. Notice the following:

> The city planning department estimates 605,420 persons will be living in the city at the beginning of next year, an increase of 32,196 since the start of the year.

This lead, according to the suggestions made, could have been written:

> The city planning department estimates 605,420 persons will be living in the city at the beginning of next year.
> This will be an increase of 32,196 since the start of this year.

Even a better revision might have been:

> An estimated 605,420 persons will be living in the city by the first of the year.
> This would be an increase of 32,196 over the start of this year.
> The estimate comes from the city planning department.

The following introductory paragraph, though more succinct than many leads, still is more detailed than need be:

> The County Historical Society today offered the Board of Supervisors a plan to begin operating the old Smith Mansion as a public museum.

A rewrite offers simplification and greater readability:

> A plan to operate the old Smith Mansion as a public museum is in the hands of the Board of Supervisors.
> It was submitted to the board today by the County Historical Society.

Although it is essential that expressions of opinion be attributed to the persons whose views are stated, it should be understood that the attribution does not necessarily have to come in the first paragraph. In the following example, the attribution is not given until the start of the third paragraph:

> The Republicans will try to capitalize on many Johnson policies and programs, including the Great Society.
> But Viet Nam will not be one of them, unless it is the charge that the administration has not taken strong enough action in Asia.
> This was made clear by. . . .

This method has been used to simplify the presentation of the first two paragraphs. If in writing an introductory paragraph for an interview or speech story the writer can pick out the most salient remarks for the first paragraph, he can handily put the attribution at the start of the second paragraph:

> Law enforcement officials today are making use of scientific methods unthought of a decade ago.
> This view was expressed by. . . .

The attribution, however, should not be recklessly delayed to the confusion of the reader. Usually it should come by the start of the second or third paragraph.

Some Common Faults

Five common faults, easily corrected when identified, plague the leads of today's news stories. They are:
1. Succumbing to the temptation of trying to squeeze too many facts into the lead
2. Separating the subject of the sentence from the main verb by using a long subjective complement
3. Using needlessly long identifications
4. Injecting too many names into the lead
5. Using long introductory phrases and clauses.

Let us turn to examples of these faults and ways of correcting them.

Too Many Facts

Prior comment in this chapter should make it simple for the writer to detect what is wrong with the following:

> A jury convicted five persons Wednesday night of vote frauds during the last general election at the polling place of the 5th Division of the 37th Ward, Ninth Street and Boston Avenue.

A period should have been placed after "frauds" and the remaining facts put into a second paragraph. Grammatical surgery may seem a bit more difficult for the following:

> HANOVER, N.H.—Club-swinging state troopers waded into a crowd of several hundred howling and jeering students Wednesday night at Dartmouth College after they stopped, rocked and beat in the roof of a car containing former Alabama Gov. George C. Wallace. He was visibly shaken but uninjured.

In this case, it is not so much a matter of encumbering the lead paragraph by trying to answer the six questions as it is a matter of trying to provide too much of an answer to the question of *what*. The writer could also have simplified the lead and made it more interesting through better use of chronology:

> HANOVER, N.H.—Several hundred howling and jeering Dartmouth College students stopped, rocked and beat

in the top of a car in which former Alabama Gov. George C. Wallace was riding.

State troopers, swinging their clubs, waded into the crowd to disperse it.

Wallace was visibly shaken but uninjured.

Typical of overcramming in the lead is:

TRENTON—A five-pound dog from Ohio was named tops over the field of 3,455 purebreds which vied Sunday at Trenton KC's 38th annual record-breaking show on the Trenton artillery grounds after a day of rain and high winds.

Much more readable would have been the following:

TRENTON—A five-pound dog from Ohio topped 3,455 purebreds competing Sunday at Trenton KC's 38th annual show.

The event took place on the Trenton artillery grounds after a day of rain and high winds.

Not only have too many facts been crammed into the following but doubt also exists whether the significant facts come first:

The County Rural Health and Education Committee will conduct a dinner meeting at 6:30 p.m. Feb. 27 in the Garden Grove School to review its progress over the last seven years and discuss plans for the future.

A better introduction to the story would have been:

The County Rural Health and Education Committee will review its progress for the last seven years and discuss the future at a dinner meeting Feb. 27.

The session will be in the Garden Grove School at 6:30 p.m.

The following illustrates how complex situations can be simplified in an introductory paragraph:

The fear of a firebug was renewed in Fresno last night by two unrelated events, a hotel fire and a telephone call. (Fresno *Bee*)

Too Far Between

If after noting the subject of a sentence the reader is required to pass through a lengthy subjective complement to get to the verb, he is likely to lose the relationship. Note the following.

The youthful host *at a suspected dope party in a Nob Hill home last week* was sent to the state prison yesterday.

The sentence has only 22 words but of that number 12 words (indicated by italics) separate the subject, which is "host," from the verb phrase "was sent."

The following is difficult to read because of the long separation between the subject and the verb:

> A 14-man finance committee *to raise and disburse a $111,600 operating fund for the first-year activities of the 100-man committee to promote the industrial advance of the city* was named today.

The long separation between the subject and predicate is confusing. A simple change brings some improvement:

> A 14-man finance committee was named today to raise and disburse a $111,600 operating fund for the first-year activities of the 100-man committee to promote the industrial advance of the city.

Even after the change, however, the sentence is cumbersome. It would have been better if simplified to:

> A finance committee was named today to raise $111,600 to help promote the city's industrial advance.

The other facts could have been saved for succeeding paragraphs. The writer of the following lead strained too hard in his attempt to provide an adequate background:

> John Doe, 47, of 3132 Needles Ave., *a would-be safe cracker who might have been killed had his efforts not been interrupted by the police,* was convicted last night by a superior court jury.

The following is an improvement.

> A superior court jury last night convicted John Doe, 47, 3132 Needles Ave., a would-be safe cracker who might have been killed if the police had not halted his efforts.

A still better job could have been done:

> A superior court jury last night convicted John Doe, 47, 3132 Needles Ave., a would-be safe cracker.
>
> Doe might not be alive if the police had not halted his crude efforts in the use of dynamite.

Burdensome Identifications

The identification of persons in the news is necessary. The questions are how much identification is needed in the first paragraph of the story and how can that identification be simplified. The problem of overextended identification is obvious in the following:

> Tinus (Marty) Nordahl, 76, a veteran bandleader whose orchestra became a favorite of senior citizen groups during the past decade, died Monday.

The identification comprises 16 words of a 21-word lead. The result is similar to that considered in a previous section dealing with a long separation between subject and verb. The effect of trying to cram too much identification into an opening paragraph is illustrated in the following:

> SANTA BARBARA—Leroy Jackson, the University of California at Santa Barbara's starting basketball center and leading scorer with a 20.3 average, has been lost for the season and with what doctors have described as an ulcer condition, Coach Barkey announced Thursday.

Not only should some of the identification have been saved for a later paragraph, but also the shirttail attribution could have been delayed. Some of the identification details in the following lead likewise should have been withheld for a later paragraph:

> John Jones, Pond area rancher and long active in Delano Harvest Holidays Junior Livestock shows, Thursday night was elected president of the festival board.

Another example of burdensome identification is:

> James R. Smith, former representative, industrialist and military man who had played an important role in Pennsylvania Republican politics, died Tuesday. He was 83.

Sometimes a slight change in sentence construction will solve the problem. Observe the following:

> William Jones, who has served the Salt Lake Area United Fund as executive director since January of last year, resigned today.

Note the improvement a change in sentence construction brings:

William Jones today resigned as the Salt Lake Area United Fund executive director, a post he has held since January of last year.

The following identification is pertinent and does not monopolize the lead:

> WASHINGTON—Sen. Carl Hayden (D-Ariz.), a member of Congress since Arizona became a state in 1912, is not expected to run in November for an eighth term in the Senate. (Don Irwin, Los Angeles *Times*)

An interesting but brief identification is used in the following:

> LONDON (AP)—Mary Quant, the lioness of British fashion, has leaped to the defense of the miniskirt. (Nadine Walker)

Names, Names, Names

Bogging down leads with names is a fault more prevalent in small newspapers than in large ones. Some weeklies commit the sin with frequency, and school newspapers commonly indulge in name orgies in their leads. Everyone may know everyone else in the small community and names may make news, but there is little excuse for the following lead:

> Members of the Mt. Gordon Women's Club at a meeting last night in the clubhouse elected the following: Mrs. Edgar Botts, president; Mrs. Cyrus Williams, vice president; Mrs. John Doss, secretary; Mrs. Albert Smith, treasurer; Mrs. Edward Mooney, historian; Mrs. Carl Reed, publicity chairman; and Mrs. Richard Mahoney, keeper of the seal.

Here is an equally bad lead found in a weekly:

> Hilga Wetzel, Janice Wood, Alma McCoy, Sandy Rethwisch, Audrey Rose, Elizabeth Davis, Jerry Hansen, Nancy Keller, Carol Miller, Nita Ressler, were initiated into the Atwater Women's Club last Thursday evening at a regular meeting. New members unable to attend were Delores Wack and Margarette Kappe.

More of the same follows:

> Three Redwater High School seniors, Carol Nelson, Mary Andrews and Jane Gregg, are vying for the title of Basketball Homecoming Queen.

How simply the lead could have been improved:

> Three Redwater High School seniors are vying for the title of Basketball Homecoming Queen.
> They are Carol Nelson, Mary Andrews and Jane Gregg.

The fault is recognizable in the following though not as strongly pronounced:

> Harry Dodd was elected vice president of Nash DeCamp Co. and Bud Erickson was elevated to executive vice president at the annual meeting of the board of directors.

Grammatical surgery would make two sentences out of it. Names make the following lead loose and soggy:

> President Ernest A. Bedrosian and General Manager Del L. Liddle of the Raisin Bargaining Association visited Congressman B. F. Sisk Friday and asked the congressman's assistance in amending the Agricultural Marketing Agreement Act of 1937 to include raisins under Section 6.08.

The lead is far too long and loosely worded and suffers from the inclusion of too many names. The first paragraph could have been amended thus:

> Two officials of the Raisin Bargaining Association are seeking the help of Congressman B. F. Sisk in amending the Agricultural Marketing Agreement Act to include raisins.

It is not difficult to correct the fault in the following:

> Gordon Jones will be the new president of the Prairieland Farm Bureau, succeeding Walter Smith, and John Greene will be the new vice president, succeeding Carl Jasper.

A period should have been placed after "Smith" and the rest put into a second paragraph.

A trend, advanced by radio, has been to withhold the name of an obscure person who makes news until a second paragraph and to use only an identifying phrase in the first paragraph, as in:

> HOUSTON—The 19-year-old son of a prominent Dallas civic leader was shot and killed Monday night.
>
> Houston police said the youth, John Doe, was shot in an incident near one of Houston's hippie hangouts. Police said the youth's father was Richard Doe, well-known Houston civic leader and real estate magnate.

Out of the Past

In years past, it was not uncommon for journalism professors and texts, striving for variety in the writing of leads, to stress the use of so-called rhetorical devices. Using the periodic sentence as a tool, the professors and texts suggested the use of infinitive phrases and causal clauses to emphasize cause, participial phrases to emphasize the *how*, and conditional clauses to stress probable results.

It was a time when many self-styled critics deplored the use of an article to start a lead. It was not uncommon to see one of these critics scan a front page and circle all the leads beginning with "a," "an" or "the." If many such leads were found, the page was pronounced dull. "Lack of variety," the critic would say profoundly.

The following examples illustrate the method of using rhetorical devices:

To raise funds for new scenery and sets, the Community Theater will stage three one-act plays in the Memorial Auditorium Sept. 29 and 30. (*Infinitive phrase stressing purpose.*)

Because a driver backed his car in front of the west entrance to the State University campus, traffic was held up for more than an hour yesterday. (*Causal clause stressing cause.*)

Faced with a need to give more effective occupational counseling to students, the State University faculty senate yesterday recommended a campus-wide survey to get information on students' vocational interests. (*Participial phrase stressing the reason.*)

When Prof. John Doe came to State University 35 years ago, only four of the buildings now standing had been constructed and the ground on which the men's gymnasium now stands was used as an athletic field. (*Temporal clause stressing time.*)

Staring at a picture of herself taken when she was a flashing eyed star, silent screen actress Olive Borden died yesterday in a skid row mission five miles from the glittering Hollywood which forgot her long ago. (*Participial phrase stressing* how.)

Struck by a plank hurled from a saw in the South Cedar Mill, Joe Bloke, a sawyer living at 3307 Columbus Ave., suffered a broken shoulder yesterday. (*Participial phrase stressing cause.*)

Braced by a champagne send-off and well stocked with California made duds, a party of San Francisco models and dress designers is en route to Paris by air today to show the world style capital what local talent can produce. (*Participial phrase stressing* how.)

If all the initiatives and referendum measures that have been titled by Attorney General John Jones should qualify for the November election, voters will receive sample ballots large enough to use for table cloths and possibly bedspreads. (*Conditional clause stressing probable results.*)

By train, bus and the familiar "thumb hike" method, two score women college graduates filed into the state capital today as representatives of the "white collar" march to demand greater equality for women. (*Prepositional phrase stressing the answer to* how.)

The reader should not infer that the writers of the foregoing leads deliberately selected a rhetorical device, but professors did make use of the periodic sentence as an instructional aid. Many editors today believe that the simplest and most natural way to write a lead is to start with the subject and move directly to the predicate instead of using inversion.

The suggestion made here is that the writer should do what comes naturally, provided that what comes naturally will be easy to read and understand. It is the long introductory phrase or clause that should be shunned. An example should suffice:

> SACRAMENTO—Confronted with the warning this may be the last chance for state action to save the beauty of Lake Tahoe, the Assembly passed a bill to create a regional agency representing both California and Nevada to control the future planning and development of the Tahoe region.

An introductory participial phrase serves the purpose well in the following:

> Using an inner tube of an automobile tire, Harold Jones, a 22-year-old college student, saved two boys from drowning in Lake Oneida today.

An introductory phrase is used effectively here:

> JERUSALEM—For the first time in nearly 20 years Jerusalem is a single city. (New York *Times*)

A temporal clause, likewise, is used effectively to start the following:

> When their graduation ceremonies end tomorrow night, Fresno's high school seniors will shuck their caps and gowns and begin partying. (Fresno *Bee*)

What must be remembered is that it is not the first word of the lead that counts, be it an article, a preposition or a participle, but the first combination of words.

Simplicity Is the Key

The safest advice to offer the beginning journalist is that he should give the gist of the story in the simplest, most concise manner possible in the opening sentence. Many examples can be found in today's newspapers. Here is one:

> LOS ANGELES (AP)—An 18-year-old girl says she killed her father with a shotgun after her mother told her to.

Here is another:

> SAN FRANCISCO (UPI)—Even a computer can't cope with the Christmas rush.
>
> This was an assessment of a failure in the computerized postal data center at San Mateo, which didn't process the first paychecks of some 500 Christmas season workers of the San Francisco Post Office.

The idea is to capsulize what the story purports to say:

> BERKELEY (UPI)—The radicals at the University of California at Berkeley have a new issue—high rents.

How simply the writer of the following started his story:

> Utah has lost one-fourth of its estimated $11 million fruit crop to sub-freezing temperatures during April and early May. (Salt Lake City *Deseret News*)

The following lead, simply written, uses the second person or direct address to appeal to the reader:

> If you see a 96-ton railroad locomotive on the freeway in Merced Wednesday, don't call your psychiatrist.
>
> It really will be a locomotive—the old fashioned kind that spouts steam and belches smoke from its stack. (Merced, Calif. *Sun-Star*)

Sparkling Leads

Sometimes a story, by its very nature, invites an interesting and original twist in its telling. Notice the use of paradox in the following:

> Gov. John J. McKeithen sent eight state troopers swooping down on a plush Laplace gambling casino Friday night to no avail. Gambling, it seemed, had taken a holiday. (New Orleans *Times Picayune*)

Contrast is used in the following:

> SACRAMENTO (AP)—California is getting an attractive woman to work on the not so pretty problem of juvenile delinquency.

Here is an interesting summation of a meeting:

> The leaders of the garbage world convened here yesterday and agreed that the biggest problem in garbage today is people.
>
> The public and politicians, they said, must be taught to face the realities of trash. (Mike Mahoney, San Francisco *Chronicle*)

Another interesting summation is this one:

> A nobel laureate chemist took a broad look at the future last night and spied a dazzling galaxy of alleged improvements for man. (San Francisco *Examiner*)

More and more there has been a tendency to use feature-type leads for news stories. A writer used the following lead for a story telling that a convention of bill collectors was coming to town:

> Head for the hills. The bill collectors are coming to town. (Fresno *Bee*)

The following makes use of a clever play of words:

> TANGA—The United Women of Tanzania, a mass organization dedicated to improving the lot of womenfolk, is up in arms about legs. (San Francisco *Chronicle* Foreign News Service)

Question Leads

"Tell 'em, don't ask 'em."

That is the curt advice given by many brusk city editors to cub reporters who try to use questions to construct their leads. Correctly written, though, the question lead does have a place in modern journalism: when a question best poses the problem dealt with in the story. But the reporter should never put the question in such a way that the reader assumes he is supposed to answer it. When a question lead is used, the reporter should always come up with either the answer or the significance of the question immediately following it. For example:

> LONDON (UPI)—Would you marry the same person again?
> The Daily Sketch put the question to its readers, and the answer came as a shock to many complacent British husbands and their wives.

Here is another example:

> DETROIT—Will Walter Reuther pull his giant United Auto Workers Union out of the AFL-CIO?
> "Absolutely," say some, expert and non-expert alike.
> "Not a chance," say others. (Dick Meister, San Francisco *Chronicle*)

Once Upon a Time

Almost every adult can remember four words that used to capture his attention as a child. The words were "Once upon a time. . . ." Modern journalists are moving more and more toward the use of narrative leads, particularly in feature stories.

This lead was used by Associated Press sports writer Bob Green to introduce a story about golfer Sam Snead:

> The old man sat there and waited, his brightly banded straw hat on the bench beside him.
> He just sat and waited, one trademark beside him and another behind him.
> Then the word came. The cutoff was 146. And Sam Snead, the possessor of all the world's great golfing titles—except one—had missed. For the second straight year he failed to qualify for the U.S. Open, the only major title that has eluded him.

The method likewise was used by UPI's Rodney Guilfoil in writing a feature about the Florence Crittendon home in San Francisco:

> Peggy is an extraordinarily pretty girl. She's poised and she's smart. She could be your daughter, your niece, your sister or the girl next door.
> And she's like 325,000 other young women in the United States this year. Peggy is pregnant out of wedlock.
> "When I first started feeling my baby move," she says, "I used to cry myself to sleep. I used to say 'it's not going to be mine.'"
> Peggy is one of nearly 50 girls living in the Florence Crittendon Home of San Francisco to await the birth of their babies. All are at least seven months pregnant.

The author singled out one girl to introduce his story, but he definitely tried to identify her with the reader: "She could be your daughter, your niece, your sister or the girl next door."

A hypothetical situation is contrived in the following opening:

> Joe Bloke sat in the reception ward for the mentally ill in Harrisburg.
> His hands trembled nervously and his lower lip quivered.
> He saw an iron door with bars and knew that when he went through that door it would be a long time before he would be free to move about again in the world he was being forced to leave.
> Joe is like thousands of other Americans who need help and know that they need it, but who are afraid of what's going to happen to them when they face admission to a mental institution.

Notice the attempt in the fourth paragraph to identify Joe with many other Americans.

Updating the Lead

There was a time when many dailies insisted that time be specified in the lead paragraph. News events, to be admitted to the papers, had to have happened not longer ago than yesterday, and for some afternoon newspapers yesterday was not recent enough. Thus, using "today" or "yesterday" was mandatory. Problems often arose when editors marked their edition matter—stories held from one edition for later editions. The time had to be changed in stories run in late editions and marked for use in early editions the following day.

The wire services took the lead in using the name of the day instead of "today," "last night" or "yesterday." Few dailies, however, would want to have a news event tagged as happening Wednesday appear in a Friday edition. The practice of expressing time in the lead is dwindling and reporters have found ways of updating time in a story.

Suppose a correspondent's story of a Wednesday meeting arrives Friday:

> DELANO—A special committee was named to campaign against litter in the city by the Delano Chamber of Commerce at a meeting Wednesday.

This lead could easily have been updated:

> DELANO—A special committee has begun tackling one of the city's major problems—litter.
> The committee was appointed at a meeting of the Delano Chamber of Commerce Wednesday.

Some newspapers would even delete "Wednesday" from the second paragraph, and others would say "at a recent meeting."

Past-Tense Leads

Some newcomers to journalism practically rewrite an advance lead with a change in tense. Suppose a newspaper carries the following introduction to a story:

> George Jones, a Philadelphia industrialist, will talk on the economic crisis in the United States Tuesday.
> He will speak at a meeting of the Hampton Chamber of Commerce in Skidoo's Restaurant at noon.

The temptation of the novice, as he writes the follow-up story, is to say the same thing with the exception of changing the tense:

George Jones, a Philadelphia industrialist, discussed the economic crisis in the United States at a meeting of the Hampton Chamber of Commerce yesterday.

The follow-up lead needs some specifics about what the man said. A similar weakness appears in the following:

Mayor John Smith answered critics of his administration at a City Council meeting today.

Something more specific about his answers is needed in the lead.

Dangling Leads

A news writer should never abandon the subject of his lead. The weakness of the dangling lead is illustrated by the following:

> The City Council today approved the appointment of a new city engineer.
> The Council members disagreed on the location of a new city park.
> Two of the members favor the acquisition of land in the southeastern part of the city.
> Three believe such a site would create transportation problems for most of the persons who would want to use the park.
> Four other members favor the appointment of a committee to study the matter. The four were accused of delaying tactics. . .

Obviously, the writer should have given a few more details on the appointment of the new city engineer before changing the subject.

EXERCISES

I. Discuss the Following Leads

1. Failing to get out of the path of an oncoming truck despite warning shouts from his companions, Robert Jones, 48, of 916 East Washington Street was crushed to death Saturday night between the machine and the stalled truck he was assisting in pushing on the Syracuse–Watertown highway at Hastings, a few miles north of Central Square.
2. NEWPORT BEACH—John Doe, 54, described by sheriff's detectives as a "brooder," today faced charges of attempted murder for allegedly attacking the pilot of a chartered plane with a hammer 10,000 feet above the Pacific Ocean.
3. CHICAGO—More users are "shooting" amphetamines instead of "popping" pep pills for a better, deadlier high which is deadlier to themselves and to others near them as they become increasingly paranoid and disorganized, it was reported in the current journal of the American Medical Association.
4. MIAMI—John Wesley "Boog" Powell is awesome evidence the Baltimore Orioles can win something besides the World Series.
  The baseball world was beginning to wonder.

Earl Weaver was edged by the Yankees' Ralph Houk for manager of the year. Minnesota Twins pitcher Jim Perry captured the Cy Young Award over the mound triumvirate of Dave McNally, Mike Cuellar and Jim Palmer.

Then came Boog.

Powell, a blond behemoth at first base, Tuesday was named Most Valuable Player in the American League. . . .

5. An 82-year-old retired nurse who is credited with assisting in the births of 4,008 children, many without a physician, was given a party here by 250 of her alumni.
6. Three more candidates—Charles Jones, a real estate broker; George Rose, a lawyer; and George Smith, an insurance man—have thrown their hats into the ring in the mayoralty race.
7. John Adam Blaine, world traveler and author, spoke on newly developing countries in Africa at a meeting of the Montclair Women's League last night.
8. Edward Rose, 98, who came to Mill Valley 60 years ago and has been in business ever since until he retired 20 years ago, died last night after a short illness.
9. A fire believed to have been started by a lightning flash in the severe storm which hit Cedar City last night destroyed the home of Edgar Ralston at 2490 East Lane Ave.
10. City Parks Director Gene Ross defended his proposal to charge a small admission fee at all the city's parks at a meeting of the city council last night.

II. Write Leads for the Following

1. Charles Jordan, the president of the American Society for the Benefit of the Aged, will speak at a meeting of the Health Improvement Society Wednesday at 8 p.m. in the Roosevelt High School Auditorium. His topic will be "Hope for the Aged." All persons interested in gerontology are welcome.
2. Roger Johnson got the surprise of his life yesterday. He opened the door of his refrigerator to get a platter of cut pheasant to broil. He found his year-old cat lying beside a platter of bones. The cat was numb from the cold but thawed out soon. Johnson lives at 1909 Lake St.
3. Frederick Olson, 417 McKinley Ave., was watching television last night. He heard a noise on his front porch and, on investigating, he found an MG automobile driven by Carl Smith, 19, had missed a curve at Echo and McKinley and ended on his porch. He said he doesn't mind company but he likes to see it come to his door on foot.
4. Harry Jones, a husky 25-year-old burglary suspect, attempted to get all the prisoners in the County Jail to join him in a jail break last night. The other prisoners listened to Jones' pitch as a leader but refused to follow him. Jones escaped alone but was captured three hours later in Pinedale.

5. A burglar took jewelry valued at $6,200 from the apartment of Mrs. Sara Smith, 2206 West Seventh St., last night while she was away. The burglar evidently was in such a hurry that he left other jewelry of an equal value spread on the bed.
6. Mrs. John Roe refused to pay a $1 parking fine two weeks ago. By the time she reappeared in court yesterday, the fine and court costs had risen to $35. She said she wouldn't pay the fine because she had put a dime in the parking meter and it wasn't her fault that the meter only registered pennies and nickels. Judge Donald Jones ordered her to pay the fine, go to jail for a week, or appeal the case. She went to jail, saying she wouldn't pay a fine she didn't owe and the appellate court had more important things to consider.
7. The Westmore Park will be dedicated tomorrow at ceremonies starting at 10 a.m. Rain has been forecast but Parks and Recreation Director Kenneth Adams said the dedication will take place rain or shine. If it rains, Adams said, the ceremonies will be held under one of the large covered picnic areas.
8. John Harvey died last night of pneumonia at the age of 62 in an inexpensive hotel room. He held a $45-a-week night watchman job in the Westlake Building until he became ill a week ago. He was found dead by another tenant. Harvey, once a millionaire stockbroker, gave the city the land for Hillside Park. It is estimated the land today, if it were not being used for a park, would be worth $300,000.
9. Three windows were broken and a hole six feet in diameter was torn into the front lawn of the home of Frank Black, 3475 Gettysburg Ave., by a dynamite blast last night. Black, who was asleep at the time, was not injured. His wife was in Lawrence at the time. The police saw no connection between this blast and two others which occurred at business institutions last week. Black is a truck driver.
10. Dr. Louis H. Evans will be the guest minister of the First Presbyterian Church "Spiritual Enrichment Week," which will begin tonight. He will speak at a 7:30 p.m. youth rally in the church today and will give the 11 a.m. sermon tomorrow. He also will participate in the church's evening sermon series held Sunday through Thursday at 7:30 p.m. Dr. Evans is a former pastor to President Dwight D. Eisenhower.

Chapter 4

SAYING IT BEST

*Though old the thought and oft exprest,
'Tis his at last who says it best.*
  —*James Russell Lowell*

If it is fair to expect a plumber to know his tools, a football player to know his signals, a painter to know his brushes, and a musician to know his notes, is it not equally fair to expect a journalist to know his parts of speech? But alas! This is not always the case.

No attempt will be made here to provide a handbook of English. Many good ones have been written, including a grammar for journalists. All that will be done here is to point out some of the most common writing faults of journalists.

Sentences like the following one do not endear newspapers to literate readers:

> Jones' reports said the episode began with a fight between two boys in the schoolyard, which was broken up by the assistant principal and another teacher.

The author was startled by the following lead until he reckoned that it was the rock and not Surveyor 3 that was gone:

> One minute Surveyor 3 had a tiny lunar rock in its teeth, the next minute it was gone.

One news item told of a girl who related her sad story "between tears." Another said, "Jordan said it lost one officer killed and nine soldiers wounded." Still another reported some political suspects "were sentenced and executed in the space of two and one half hours." A lead told of a conservation-minded group that sought legislation to "discourage litter created by bottles and cans."

Please Page Rudolf Flesch

Probably the best way to avoid the "mile-long," complicated, confusing sentence is to substitute two or three sentences for it. No news writer should inflict a sentence such as the following on his readers:

> The palace, which belonged to Saud's brother, King Faisal, until Nasser seized it and other Saudi Arabian properties earlier this year in retaliation for seizure of two Egyptian bank branches in Saudi Arabia, is being modernized and redecorated under the personal supervision of Saud's last remaining wife.

Even worse is this:

> Goncharoff, who broke with his Communist background and schooling when he had his first chance as a Russian soldier held captive by the Germans and freed by liberating American armies in World War II, returned recently from a four-month, 50,000 mile tour of the Middle East and Africa as a staff member for the international committee of the Young Men's Christian Association, sponsors of the local forum.

Observe the following:

> The three brought suit charging the statute creating the commission was unconstitutional because its power overlapped the executive and legislative branches of government and violated the concept of separation of powers.

Then notice what a slight revision will do:

The three brought suit, charging the statute creating the commission was unconstitutional.
They argued that the commission's power overlapped that of the executive and legislative branches of government and violated the concept of separation of powers.

Rudolf Flesch originated a readability formula that based reading ease or difficulty on the average number of words in sentences and the average number of syllables in the words used. If the average number of words in the sentences of an article ran high and the words used, on the average, contained many syllables, the readability was judged difficult.

The formula, which had both critics and believers, would seem to have significance if used generally as a guide rather than if rigidly followed.

Flesch later added a human interest factor. In so doing, he listed certain classes of words as having human interest, and the number of such words used indicated the human interest appeal.

Theodore Bernstein, in the April 14, 1954, New York *Times* staff publication *Winners & Sinners,* started a "one idea-one sentence" campaign. Said he, "Now don't go and take this as a rule or a formula, but generally it speeds reading if there is only one idea to a sentence."

Some grammarians might say that the "one idea-one sentence" suggestion was implicit in the definition of a sentence. A common definition is that a sentence is a group of words, with a subject and a predicate, expressing a complete thought. Bernstein's suggestion, nevertheless, is explicit and should be heeded by the writer who is tempted to burden his sentences with complexities.

No Space for Drones

Words either enhance or hinder the readability of a passage. They are never used passively. All of which means that a writer should only use words that perform a service. Superfluous words do not. Conciseness is a discipline all journalists should strive for. Only the lazy writer indiscriminately indulges in redundancy.

The author, recently scanning a number of newspapers, found such verbose expressions as "a 9-month-old baby girl," "was greeted by a peaceful band of about 15 pickets," "no other alternative," "the scene was repeated several more times," "after winning his first PBA title ever," and "pool tables were covered over for a buffet."

Two words used redundantly almost as often as they are effectively used are "up" and "down." Does "he sat down" provide more meaning than "he sat," and does "he stood up" say more than "he stood"? It would make sense to say "he sat up" or "he stood down," but it seems unnecessary to say "he jumped up from his chair" or "the kite rose up in the air." Similarly, it seems unnecessary to say "he backed up into the car" or "he climbed up the ladder." There is justification for saying "he climbed down the ladder."

A redundancy used even by better speakers and writers is "at the present time." "At present" says just as much and "now" often suffices.

Some writers use a prepositional phrase when an infinitive would be stronger and more concise, as in "The group met for the purpose of honoring Jones" instead of "The group met to honor Jones."

How often do we run into the expression that a group "held a meeting" instead of that a group "met," and how often are we told that some actors "held a rehearsal" rather than that they "rehearsed."

The expression "whether or not" is often redundant. Many times the "or not" is unnecessary.

To say that a building is situated "at the corner of Chestnut and Madden Avenues" is little more explicit than to say it is situated "at Chestnut and Madden Avenues." Likewise, to say that a man walked "in back of" or "in the rear of" bodyguards says no more than that he walked "behind" bodyguards. The expression "at that time" says no more than "then," and "in the near future" says no more than "soon."

Reporters often write, "Asked to comment on such and such, Jones said . . ." The "Asked to comment on such and such" can readily be omitted. Just let the man say it and the reader assume that he probably was asked to comment on it.

Many times an appositional phrase can be used instead of an adjectival clause. It is better to write, "Smith, a graduate of the University of Kentucky, is a candidate," than to write, "Smith, who is a graduate of the University of Kentucky, is a candidate."

The words "which is" or "which are" often are superfluous, as "The C. W. Chester home, which is situated three miles north of the city, will be the meeting place." Many times the word "that" can be implied rather than expressed, as in "He said he will attend the meeting" instead of "He said that he will attend the meeting."

The following list of redundancies and wordy phrases (italicized) is far from complete:

>*Actual* facts
>All *of* the signatures
>Appeared *to be* true
>Arrived *on* Monday
>*Back* in 1948
>*Beginning* novice
>Both *of them* declared
>*Completely* destroyed
>Confessed *to* the crime
>Consensus *of opinion*
>Depreciated *in value*
>*Distance of* 50 feet
>During *the course of* the evening
>During *the month of* August

Early pioneer
Fatal drowning
Filed suit for divorce *from her husband*
Five *different* stores
Future *ahead of him*
Half *a* dollar
He *first* began his work
In order to
Limited *only* to
Long Distance call from Philadelphia to New York
Moved *over* from second base
New beginner
Old adage
Old veteran
One *additional* seat was added
Only one man was there
Past experience
Period of two years
Present incumbent
Ran *headlong* into
Recovered from *an attack of* pneumonia
Shifted *over* to
Skyrocketed *upward*
Small tot
Still persists
Throughout the *entire* state
Tiny baby
Totally destroyed
Trees were torn up *by their roots*
True facts
Two *separate* accidents
Was present at the meeting and spoke
Widow of *the late*
Widow *woman*
Will *give a* talk on
Will *go to* help
Will talk on *the subject of*
With anxiety *of mind*
Witnessed by *a man by the name of*
Young child

Word Preferences

Many literate readers and most editors have their preferences in word usage. Joe Bloke may say to his crony, "I ain't going." His companion understands him and expects him to talk that way. But if Joe were to talk that way to some better educated persons, he might be considered crude in his use of English.

Language is not static, however, and what is considered a corruption today may be accepted as standard tomorrow. The point is that journalists are writing for today's readers, not tomorrow's, and newspaper readers have a right to expect reasonably good standards in the writing they read.

An editor has a right, by virtue of his position, to inflict his word preferences on his staff. The editor has a greater responsibility than the reporter and, though a reporter may disagree, he must, if he hopes to succeed in his job, follow the dictates of his superior.

The author remembers a managing editor who, when he found the word "contact" used in the sense of "communicate with," would blue pencil the story and send it to the city desk with a reprimand. When that managing editor retired, his successor did not object to the usage. Another managing editor, when he found the expression that a witness "took the stand," would say sarcastically, "Where did he take it?"

The adoption of the AP or UPI stylebook by many subscribing newspapers undoubtedly will reduce the number of independently published stylebooks. This is too bad in some respects, for it is always interesting, if not refreshing, to read the comments on word usage in stylebooks. It is true that there was a lot of nit-picking and some of the views were highly puristic but, on the other hand, some of the suggestions had much merit. Inconsistencies could be found. An astute cub reporter might well wonder why most stylebooks insisted that the word "widow" be used for a surviving wife, but "widower" was never suggested for a surviving husband. And one New York City newspaper said to use the word *wife* in preference to "widow."

Many stylebooks point out that colleges and universities "graduate" students but that the students "are graduated." Common usage, however, has induced the dictionaries to approve students "graduated." Some stylebooks point out that a man "marries" a woman and that a woman "is married" to a man. The man, supposedly, does the proposing and his surname is taken by the woman. The stylebooks also state that a man may "suffer" a broken leg or that a man's leg "may be" broken, but that sadism would be indicated if he "had" his leg broken. There are many who would say that this reflects a puristic attitude on the part of editors.

The following list of faulty expressions is not original but is worth noting:

Accidents occur but they do not "take place." Weddings take place because they are planned.

Addresses and speeches are made, not given.

Affect is a verb, not a noun.

Aggravate means to make worse or to add to a burden, not to annoy or irritate.

All-round is a better expression than "all-around."

Alternative originally meant a choice between two possibilities. There was not more than one alternative. Today the term is used more loosely as a choice among several possibilities. The looser usage provides for several alternatives.

Audience involves hearing. Operas have audiences, but football games have spectators.

Bag is not a good substitute for "capture."

Brought should not be confused with "took." Someone may bring something to my home but he takes it to a neighbor's home.

Claimed as a synonym for "asserted" is objected to by many.

Couple is not a synonym for "two" and *trio* is objected to by many as a substitute for "three." Trio is a musical term.

Divorces are granted but not won.

Drowned should not be used in such verb phrases as the boy "was drowned." The boy "drowned" is a better way of saying it.

Endorse sometimes is used when "approve" would be better.

Enjoyed is used rather ridiculously in such expressions as dancing "was enjoyed." Not many participate in amusements they dislike.

Enthused should not be used in place of "enthusiastic."

Experiments are made, not tried.

Following should not be used as a preposition to mean "after."

Ill with, not *of*, is the better idiomatic usage. Persons die "of" a disease.

Flags fly at "half staff" on land and at "half mast" at sea.

Gun should not be used in place of "pistol," "revolver" or "automatic."

Hanged applies to executions by hanging, but objects are "hung."

Home often is a house but not all houses are homes. A vacant house is not a home.

Injury is suffered, not sustained.

Knot is a nautical mile an hour. A ship may travel 20 knots but not 20 knots an hour.

Lady is the feminine counterpart of gentleman. We don't write that five gentlemen were hurt in an accident. Why five ladies? "Woman" is the feminine counterpart of "man."

None is a contraction of "no one." It is better used in the singular than the plural.

Procession too often becomes a "cortege."

Proposition often is used when "proposal" would be better.

Protagonist is a principal or leading figure and often the leading actor in a play. He is not a "proponent" or an "opponent."

Resolution is adopted, not passed.

Riot should not be used to designate a fight involving five persons.

Robbery involves force or intimidation. It is not a synonym for "burglary."

Shambles originally designated carnage. Today it is used to signify great disorder but it should not be used in place of "messiness."

Time is passed, not spent.

Transpire means to leak out or to become known gradually. It does not mean "occur" or "take place."

Unique means the only one of its kind. It does not mean unusual.

Unknown should not be used in place of "unidentified." A dead person probably was known by someone though he may be unidentified.

Words Often Confused

Careless writers fail to make a distinction in the meanings of some very common words. "Anticipate" and "expect" are examples. You may expect a crowd and even worry about it, but if you anticipate a crowd, you usually do something about it, such as provide more chairs. A good dictionary, though a stranger to poor writers, should be the journalist's best friend.

Here are some words commonly confused:

Affect-effect—You may affect someone's views when you influence them, but if you effect something you bring about a result, as you may effect a change in the plans of your business.

Amateur-novice—An amateur is a nonprofessional whereas a novice is a beginner in a field or activity.

Between-among—Two burglars may divide loot between them but more than two would divide it among them.

Boat-ship—A boat is a smaller vessel than a ship.

Compliment-complement—A compliment is an expression of praise but a complement completes something.

Continual-continuous—Sporadic rain may be continual but rain that is continuous has no pause or interruption.

Dock-pier—A dock is the water between piers or beside a pier.

Farther-further—Farther denotes distance. Further should be reserved for abstract usages (degree, quantity, extent), such as "He studied the subject further."

Healthy-healthful—A man may be healthy, particularly when the environment he lives in is healthful.

Hustle-hasten—A person may hustle to catch a plane, but he hastens progress and results.

Less-fewer—Less refers to general quantities or the abstract, as less wheat in a sack or less faith, but fewer should be used in numbers that can be counted, such as "Fewer persons attended the concert."

Lay-lie—Lay is a transitive verb and must have an object, whereas lie is intransitive. Confusion arises because lay is the past tense of lie. A person lay on a couch yesterday, but he laid a book on the table.

More than-over—Most editors prefer "more than a thousand persons" to "over a thousand persons."

Part-portion—Some editors feel that portion should be used to designate parts that are allocated.

People-persons—It is correct to say the people of a country but better to say 5,000 persons attended an event.

Proof-evidence—Evidence is data used to establish proof.

Raise-rear—Crops are raised, but children are reared.

Rise-raise—Rise is an intransitive verb and does not take an object, but raise is a transitive verb and must have an object. Wages rise but a person raises a ladder.

Sewage-sewerage—Sewage is the waste handled by a sewerage system.

Sit-set—Sit is an intransitive verb, but set is transitive and must have an object. A man sits but he sets an object on a table. An exception would be "the sun sets."

General-universal—General should be used when prevalent or widespread is meant. Universal means worldwide.

Make It Simple

The intended readers are usually a determining factor in a writer's choice of words. A man writing a paper to be read by college presidents would hardly use the same words that a man would in writing a paper for grocery clerks. Newspapers are written for the masses. The language, therefore, should be simple. Observe the differences:

Affixed his signature—signed	Conflagration—fire
Aggregate—total	Contemplate—think
Apprehend—arrest	Corpse—body
Approximately—about	Deceased—dead man
Assist—help	Defeat—beat
Attempt—try	Donation—gift
Banquet—dinner	Dwell—live
Beverage—drink	Emerge—come out of
Commence—begin	Endeavor—try
Complete—finish	Endorse—approve
Conceal—hide	Establish—start

Forecast—predict
Inaugurate—begin
Initiate—start
Lacerations—cuts
Mobile—moveable
Mobilize—assemble
Obsequies—services
Observe—see
Obtain—get
Odor—smell
Partake—share or take part
Passed away—died
Peruse—read
Progress—advance

Proportion—part
Purchase—buy
Remainder—rest
Remains—body
Rendition—performance
Reply—answer
Repudiate—reject
Request—ask
Research—study
Reside—live
Seek—try
Sufficient—enough
Terminate—end
Transmit—send

Utilize—use

Keep It Fresh

One of man's perpetual problems is to make his thoughts and feelings known to others. Some do a far better job than others, and it is natural for those who find difficulty in putting words together effectively to borrow the phrases of the more articulate. Hundreds of persons today, for example, repeat the phrase "brown as a berry," penned by Chaucer.

The problem is that once a poignant or witty expression is given to the world in prose, poetry or song it is repeated so frequently that it becomes stereotyped and the user subjects himself to the vituperation of the cliché hater.

Few persons, if any, could qualify as being original all the time, and there are those who could profess to being original rarely. Some persons are honest in their sensitivity to clichés; others probably are more critical than sensitive.

Some clichés are more objectionable than others. Some should be abolished, but others may be used effectively. Communication would suffer greatly if all clichés were to be abandoned. One question the writer should ask himself is whether he can substitute an original expression that would be equally clear and brief. In other words, does the hackneyed expression serve a useful purpose?

The ornate cliché particularly annoys the more literate reader: "the lone sentinel," "grim reaper," "death rode the gales" and "cold, gray dawn" are among the worst. The author, for one, certainly does not object to such clichés as an "empty handed" burglar left a store or a socialite "kept an eye on" her husband at a party. Neither does the author see any objection to the cliché used in the following feature lead:

> It was "tit for tat" in Municipal Judge George Anderson's courtroom yesterday.

It would seem better, however, to say simply that the police searched the city for a suspect than to say they "combed the city," and it would seem more appropriate to say "The mayor disproved the myth that voters can demand more services without paying higher taxes" than to say he "exploded the myth." There is the question, too, of whether "myth" is the proper word. "Belief" probably would be better.

The following words and phrases usually add nothing but staleness to a news story:

At pistol point	In the wake of
Beefed up their forces	Jam packed
Blizzard whipped	Kickoff dinner
Blunt instrument	Limped into port
Cautious (guarded) optimism	Long hours of the night
Dampened the enthusiasm	No immediate comment
Deafening roar	Oil-rich nation
Death and destruction	Racially troubled
Detectives rushed to the scene	Riot torn
Erupted	Rushed to the hospital
Escaped with minor injuries	Snow blanketed
Featured	Sparked
Fire broke out	Stocks soared
Firemen responded to the alarm	Strife torn
Flatly denied	Tinder dry woodlands
Floods rampaged	Triggered
Fog rolled in	Turkey and all the trimmings
Grinding crash	Usually reliable sources
Ground to a halt	Violence flared
Gutted by fire	Voters marched
Hailed into court	Weather permitting
Hopes sank	Whisked

Sportswriters also use their share of hackneyed expressions:

Dazzling runs	Scorekeeper hard pressed
Pay dirt	Vaunted running attack

The following expressions would seem to provide some usefulness in communication when used appropriately:

Break the ice	In hot water
Buy a pig in a poke	Jump the gun
By the skin of one's teeth	Lame duck
Call a spade a spade	Left holding the bag
Eat crow	Pass the buck
Feather one's nest	Play second fiddle
Get cold feet	Pull strings
Get on the bandwagon	Swap horses in midstream
Go against the grain	Turn the tables
Have an axe to grind	Upset the apple cart

It should be remembered that the only justifications for using a trite expression are word economy and clarity. It would be difficult for a writer to come up with a concise substitute for "brain trust," and many expressions in modern usage, some of them difficult to replace, have become trite. Two that are coming under criticism are "backlash" and "confrontation." Others that seem to bother readers less are:

Bamboo curtain	Left
Cold war	Peaceful coexistence
Desegregation	Right
Integration	Underprivileged
Iron curtain	

Nearly all fields of specialization have their jargon. The words "bull" and "bear" will continue to be used in finance. And sociologists are not likely to quit using "ghetto."

The journalist should nevertheless avoid such journalese as "brought under control," "held at bay," "end unrest," "missed by a hair," "paid tribute" and "scot free."

Elegantisms

Newspapers have forgotten much of the squeamishness so prevalent not too many years ago. Words such as "syphilis" and "gonorrhea" no longer are considered taboo by most editors, and such euphemisms as "social disease" for venereal disease and "street walker" for prostitute are rarely found. "Intimacy," likewise, is less frequently used as a substitute for adultery.

Society in general has liberalized its views of what is poor taste, and newspapers have followed. By far the majority of readers consider certain four-letter vulgarisms distasteful and, until there is a significant change in attitude, these words will not creep into the news columns, albeit they may be used in some campus and underground newspapers.

Less frequently is "passed away" used for died and "united in matrimony" for married. Rarely would a lead such as one used years ago in a Michigan weekly be found today:

> Again the Angel of Death has entered the ranks of the copper country pioneers, and again there is mourning in one of the oldest families in the district.

A few euphemisms persist, such as "deceased" for dead person and "interred" for buried.

Part of today's problem is the effort of persons in government and other professions to adopt elegantisms for public relations reasons. A government official uses the term "lower income bracket" instead of saying someone is poor, a teacher uses the term "exceptional children" for mentally retarded children, a businessman refers to "company net income" instead of profits, and social workers prefer "planned parenthood" to birth control.

Figures of Speech

Figurative language can be both interesting and effective but, on the other hand, it can be ineffectual and abortive. One writer compared figures of speech to firearms and said both should be used with care.

Two of the commonest faults with figurative usage are mixing figures and resorting to triteness. A radio announcer commenting on French opposition to Britain's entering the Common Market said the French were "trying to rock the boat but finding the digging tough."

The following causes one to ponder the relationship between "fever" and "benefits," since the latter is not expected to result from the former:

> ALBUQUERQUE, N.M.—Ski fever has hit New Mexico and the metropolis of Albuquerque is reaping the benefits.

The figure of speech is sustained, as it should be, in a lead written by James Doussard, Louisville *Courier-Journal* television critic:

> NBC and CBS have laid their fall programming cards on the table, but ABC's chief decision maker continues to play poker.

The figure of speech is sustained also in a lead by Don Ridings of the same newspaper:

> FRANKFORT, Ky.—A governmental stepchild wanting to become a full-fledged member of the family of state agencies is expected to start waving its arms for some attention from the General Assembly this week.
> A bill giving legislative sanction to the Kentucky Program Development Office. . . .

The figure of speech is also sustained in this Chicago *Tribune* lead from a story on horse racing:

> The mercury tumbled to 10 below last night at Balmoral Park, but Farlen warmed the hearts of his backers among the 1,647 fans with an impressive win in the $1,200 Champagne purse. (Reprinted by permission of the Chicago *Tribune*)

"Warmed the hearts" may be a bit shopworn but it does sustain the figure of speech.

A sports writer spoke of six innings of a baseball game being played "under a gray sky that wept a little toward the end." This is nearly as bad as the trite expression that "rain failed to dampen the spirits of the crowd." The same writer spoke of two "deafening homeruns" and, in describing a hart-hit ball, said "the fateful blow sailed through the mist of the darkening day."

More interesting writing is exemplified in a lead by Hugh A. Mulligan:

> LONDON (AP) Once again in world-famous Piccadilly Circus the city fathers have tried to wash those hippies right out of their square.

Subordination

It is not difficult to teach students that the conjunctions "and," "but" and "for" should be used only to connect grammatical equivalents, but it is sometimes difficult to teach them that these words likewise should be used only to connect equivalent ideas. An example follows:

Jones is the chairman of the committee and he did not vote.

Just as bad is this:

Jones is the chairman of the committee. He did not vote.

The fact that he is the chairman of the committee should not receive the same emphasis as the fact that he did not vote. It should be written this way:

Jones, the committee chairman, did not vote.

Here is another example:

Barnes said Smiley (a dog) *looks like their former pet and will make his daughter, Patricia, 8, very happy.*

It is better written this way:

Barnes said Smiley, who looks like their former pet, will make his daughter, Patricia, 8, very happy.

The following sentence does not offer easy reading:

One apartment house collapsed and it was near there that a falling hotel wall killed Cabrera.

Subordination brings an improvement:

One apartment house collapsed near the place where a falling hotel wall killed Cabrera.

The decision not to subordinate is wise when complexity will result:

> *The First Lady spent the past week in Texas working on a script for the tape recording. It will cover the highlights of her husband's early life at the two homesteads he has restored and refurbished.*

It would be cumbersome if written:

> *The First Lady spent the past week in Texas working on a script for the tape recording, which will cover the highlights of her husband's early life at the two homesteads he has restored and refurbished.*

Be Careful with Plurals

Although persons in conversation frequently use the wrong number with certain pronouns, the writer should be more careful. It should not be "Everyone got their ballots." It should be "Everyone got his ballot." The word "his" is common gender in this case. It is not necessary to say "Everyone got his or her ballot."

The following pronouns and words referring to them are singular:

Anybody	Everybody	One
Anyone	Everyone	Somebody
Each	Neither	Someone
Either	Nobody	

The use of an anglicized instead of a foreign plural probably is better for those words for which we have anglicized plurals:

Apparatus	Apparatuses
Appendix	Appendixes
Canto	Cantos
Cherub	Cherubs
Criterion	Criterions
Fungus	Funguses
Index	Indexes
Medium	Mediums
Memorandum	Memorandums

It is rare today, for example, to find "campi" used as the plural of campus." We do not, however, have anglicized plurals for some words:

Alumna	Alumnae
Alumnus	Alumni
Bacterium	Bacteria
Datum	Data
Insigne	Insignia

Ignorance is shown when a person writes "the data is" or "he is an alumni."

Some words do not change to form the plural. Examples are "deer," "gallows," "series," "sheep," "swine" and "vermin."

Gender

The feminine forms of some words are no longer used. Examples are "authoress" and "poetess." Distinction still should be made with many words, such as:

Buck	Doe
Drake	Duck
Duke	Duchess
Earl	Countess
Executor	Executrix
Gander	Goose
Hart	Hind
Marquis	Marchioness
Peacock	Peahen
Ram	Ewe
Stag	Hind
Steer	Heifer
Testator	Testatrix

Grammar

Inattentiveness to simple rules of grammar results in sloppy writing. It is not difficult to see what is wrong with the following:

> Yesterday the Conservation District voted to restrict cloud-seeding *operations* to areas where *it* will produce snow.

The writer should have noted that the following sentence is confusing:

> Proxmire criticized the Air Force's dismissal of Fitzgerald on grounds of economy.

Were "grounds of economy" used by Proxmire or the Air Force? The following should not even have been written on the reporter's worst day:

> He said if it means political suicide to vote a certain way on this issue, he would be glad to have his career end with such an epitaph.

The lack of parallel construction is obvious in the following:

> These recommendations call *for* the consolidation of obstetrical facilities within the community, and *to* utilize the existing areas to meet the critical needs for additional medical-surgical patients.

If a writer uses two subordinate clauses joined by the conjunction "and," he should not imply the subordinate conjunction "that" with the first clause and express it with the second:

> But supporters of the legislation have amassed a lot of information showing the dates of most holidays have been set arbitrarily and that the calendar itself has been changed.

Dangling phrases can be easily detected:

> Pouring water from firehoses on the crowd, it was quickly dispersed.

The participial phrase should be followed by who poured the water. Neither is faulty reference difficult to detect:

> He found a pistol in the hallway which had been fired twice.

"Which" should modify pistol, not hallway. It should be:

> He found a pistol, which had been fired twice, in the hallway.

Or it could be written:

> In the hallway, he found a pistol which had been fired twice.

Punctuation

There is a growing tendency for news writers to ignore punctuation. Sentences punctuated like the following are becoming common:

> Mrs. Brown was taken to the Nassau County Jail where she was searched, briefly handcuffed and fingerprinted.

The writer has failed to note that the subordinate clause beginning with "where" is nonrestrictive and should be preceded by a comma. The clause does not designate the jail but serves the purpose of providing added descriptive details. Another example follows:

> Rayyan left Jordan 16 years ago and lived in South America until 1963 when he came to the United States.

A comma is needed before "when." Observe the following:

> Sandra wants to go back to school but is unlikely to reenter the Piet Retief School where schoolmates taunted her about her appearance.

What the writer implies is that there is more than one Piet Retief School but that Sandra is not likely to reenter the one where she was taunted. If there is only one Piet Retief School, the subordinate clause beginning with "where" does not designate or point out the school but provides added information. A comma should precede "where."

Punctuation faults like the following are too prevalent in newspapers today:

> Binder succeeds Dr. Paul S. Smith who retired last June.

The meaning of the main clause is not restricted by the adjectival clause. If there were more than one Dr. Paul S. Smith, the writer should have said:

> Binder succeeds the Dr. Paul S. Smith who retired last June.

The dash is probably the most misused punctuation mark. The trend is to use it in place of other marks, particularly the comma:

> A search for the bodies of two men—presumed drowned early yesterday when a car plunged into the Madera Canal—was to continue today with the Madera County Sheriff's department in charge.

Why dashes instead of commas? Here is another example:

> The pair—John Doe, 37, and George Blow, 23—had been held under $200,000 bond each since they were arrested July 24 outside a police precinct station.

And still another example follows:

> Swinging down Omar Mikhtar Street was a shapely bundle of trouble—a young Israeli blonde in an eye-opening yellow miniskirt eight inches above her knees.

Dashes are used correctly in the following:

> Beautiful women are nothing new in Gaza—legend has it that Delilah, Samson's jealous mate, once lived there—but a blonde in a mini-mini was something else.

The interruption in thought is too great for commas.

It should be obvious that the following sentence would have been easier to read if the writer had used a comma before "including":

> The All-Stars are loaded with talented receivers including the likes of Jack Clancy of Michigan, Rod Sherman of

Southern California, Gene Washington of Michigan State and Dave Williams of Washington who caught a couple of bombs in last week's 23–22 scrimmage loss to the Chicago Bears.

And, overlooking the fact that the adjectival clause beginning with "who" makes the sentence a bit cumbersome, the reader has the right to expect a comma before the clause.

EXERCISES

I. What is wrong, if anything, with the following sentences?
1. He fell a distance of 50 feet.
2. The first constitutional amendment was cited by the committee, which provides certain safeguards for the freedom of the press.
3. The meeting of the commission got under way, and they elected Jones chairman.
4. Walking to the rear of the room, a long pause took place before Smith spoke.
5. John Jones, together with his partner, are being held.
6. Everyone started turning their heads.
7. The official reached for a report on his desk which described the plan.
8. His arms flying, the police subdued the frightened man.
9. The police are hunting for a man who was seen leaving the scene shortly after the accident.
10. The reward was divided between the three men.
11. Two women on the committee are alumni of State University.
12. All of the passengers had left the bus.
13. He is 45 years old, married, and has eight children.
14. He was asked to describe the affect the ruling had on the employees.
15. Black was fined $300 for killing a female deer.
16. Asked what he thought about raising the sales tax, Brown said he was opposed.
17. Roberts came to Carmel Valley with his father when he was 2 years old.
18. Police said it appeared he had been beaten, suffering facial lacerations and abrasions.
19. Johnson said he was not very enthused when his wife took the job but that she felt she was needed.
20. The Packers have been installed two-touchdown favorites.
21. He just completed five weeks of training in Cochabamba and Oruro, Bolivia, following 10 weeks of preliminary language, community development, cultural and technical training at the University of Washington in Seattle.

22. Firebombing and rock-throwing incidents occurred in Chicago, Peoria, Ill., Hartford, Conn., and in Wyandanch, N.Y., a Long Island suburb of New York City.
23. Rawlins said the data is not convincing.
24. The program is unique in that the students, instead of learning the rules first and then making their experiments, make their experiments first and then, by deduction, draw a set of rules.
25. Ralston compared the one man with the other, noting their similarities.

II. Discuss the figurative usage of language in the following

1. PHILADELPHIA—Willowy Jim Bunning, who loses to the Giants about as often as people buy flags with 48 stars, did them in again last night, 8–0, as Philadelphia ran its recent reign of terror to seven wins in a row.
2. Sanford, struggling like a fish out of water, finally, getting his wind, turned and ran with the speed of an antelope.
3. The mayor said he had finally lit a fire under some of the councilmen and now expects them to listen to cold facts.
4. High Sierra travelers today are warned that many of the back-country passes still wear a mantle of snow, and a few still are closed to those who travel on horseback.
5. OLYMPIA—The Washington Environmental Council and House Transportation Committee skirmished yesterday in the committee room, a place as calm as an Arab-Israeli border.

III. Questions for Discussion

1. What are the meanings of "confrontation," "demonstration," "disorder," "disturbance" and "riot"?
2. To what extent should profanity be used in quoting persons?
3. What standards would you set up to determine whether a cliché should be used?
4. What is meant by a "mixed figure of speech"?
5. What is the difference between a restrictive and nonrestrictive clause or phrase?

IV. Which of the following clichés do you object to and why?

1. Brown urged his listeners to get on the bandwagon.
2. Jones accused his opponent of having an axe to grind.
3. Two burglars were left holding the bag today.
4. Mayor John Alden had to eat crow today.
5. A blizzard whipped three Arizona counties today.
6. Jordan's dazzling run came 19 seconds before the sound of the gun.
7. Jeffry was greeted by a deafening roar.
8. A would-be burglar got cold feet today.
9. Violence flared at State University today.
10. Death rode the gales today.

Chapter 5

IDENTIFICATION, BACKGROUND, ATTRIBUTION AND EXPLANATION

Literature flourishes best when it is half a trade and half an art. —W. R. Inge

Since a substantial portion of the day's news comes from what persons say as well as what they do—be those persons great, notorious, powerful in their own spheres, or ordinary men and women who by chance become subjects of public interest—identification, personal background and attribution become requisites in reporting the news.

In looking for news, the reporter frequently uses human beings as his sources. Newsmen learn early in their careers that much of the information they write is only as accurate as the sources they get it from, and they weigh the integrity and the motives of their informants. More than that, journalists usually cite their sources.

Who Is He?

If John Jones, a plumber, says the world is moving swiftly to chaos, it means little to the multitudes, but if the president of the United States says it, many persons may feel concern. Joe Bloke, a perennially unsuccessful candidate for the city council, may stand on a soapbox in a downtown street and shout that the community's governing officials are crooked, but only a few curious persons may bother to stop and listen. Let the mayor resort to the same tactics and it becomes news.

A man's name may not be familiar to large numbers, but his title or position may lend import to what he says. Only the better informed citizens in the United States may know the name of the president of the University of Michigan, but many others are familiar with the name of the institution and would esteem what the head of that university might have to say on such a subject as the crisis in higher education in America.

Persons who acquire stature in the professions, the arts and varied fields become "experts" and their views on their particular specialties may be of interest to segments of the public. Much depends on their views and how well they are expressed.

Means of Identification

Names are rarely used in news stories without some identification, although that identification may be simple. Some of the commoner ways of identifying persons are by title, occupation, age, street address if the story is local, accomplishments and reference to prior involvement in the news.

In quoting an eyewitness to an airplane crash in a local newspaper, it would be ample to say, "John Jones, 2142 Cedar St., who saw the plane hit the ground and explode, said. . . ."

In local stories of arrests, injuries and deaths it is common practice to give the age, address and occupation, such as: "Carl Bloke, 39, a plumber living at 614 Cypress St., was arrested on a charge of. . . ." The reason is to avoid erroneous identification. If there is another Carl Bloke living in the community, the reporter, to avoid the danger of faulty identification, may even write: "This is not the Carl Bloke, a tailor, who lives at. . . ."

Many times the title preceding the name is adequate identification, as in the following:

Pres. Richard M. Nixon
Defense Secretary Melvin R. Laird
California Gov. Ronald Reagan
New York City Mayor John V. Lindsay

It is better, to avoid cumbersomeness, to put long titles after the name instead of before it, such as: "J. Bryan Sullivan, Jr., commissioner of the State Economic Development Agency. . . ."

Occupation is the most appropriate means of identification in some cases:

Actress Elizabeth Taylor

Industrialist Roger Keenan

What a person stands for may be the best means of identifying him:

Black power leader H. Rap Brown. . . .

Charles Jones, an advocate of nationalized building code regulations. . . .

John Smith, who for 15 years has advocated legalized abortions. . . .

Accomplishments or prior involvement in the news is frequently an effective means of identification:

John Jones, the first person to shoot the Penequin Rapids. . . .

Mary Smith, who led a fight six months ago for equal employment of women in city government. . . .

World War I hero Gen. Hanford MacNider. . . .

More novel or unusual means of identification are sometimes resorted to. The author well remembers the identification, used years ago by a United Press writer, for Madame Sylvia:

> Madame Sylvia, dynamic masseuse who claims to have "slapped enough flesh off Hollywood stars to make another King Kong," was irked today. . . .

Here are some other examples:

> WASHINGTON (AP)—Bobby Baker, the erstwhile Senate whiz kid, is on the go and doesn't expect a jail sentence to trip him up.
>
> DALLAS (UPI)—Funeral services were held today for Joe Reichman, musician and band leader known as the "Pagliacci of the piano" during the early days of radio.
>
> Joseph Jones, who has married 11 women, three of them still living. . . .

Relationship to a prominent figure may serve as a means of identification:

Svetlana Alliluyeva, daughter of Josef Stalin. . . .

Mrs. David Packard, wife of the deputy secretary of defense. . . .

The identification may be implied by the facts in the lead:

> ROCHESTER, N.Y. (AP)—Nelson A. Rockefeller embarked on his quest for a fourth term as governor today with a supporting cast of two veteran campaigners. . . .
>
> STOCKHOLM, Sweden (AP)—Dr. Jerome H. Holland arrived here today to take up his post as U.S. ambassador amid anti-American demonstrations.

Although some identification is usually given in the lead of a story involving a person, there are times when a reporter delays it until a second paragraph:

> PARIS (AP)—H. Ross Perot tried unsuccessfully today to give the North Vietnamese and Viet Cong lists of prisoners held in South Vietnamese camps, and concluded that "they have no concern" for their own captives.
> The Texas computer magnate arrived. . . .

More often, identification comprises the *who* in the lead and the name will be delayed until the second paragraph:

> A 21-year-old grocery deliveryman was arrested and charged with first-degree murder yesterday in the strangulation of a severely crippled Silver Spring woman whose body was found Sunday.
> The suspect, John Doe. . . .

Personal Background

Oftentimes identification of a person in a lead is sufficient, and no personal background is necessary. When the president of the United States makes a speech, simple identification by title is adequate. The same would be true when a county health officer announces plans for a clampdown on lax sanitary practices in restaurants, or when the president of a university reveals plans for campus expansion.

If, however, a president of the country dies, a university president resigns, or a county health officer is fired, some personal background is appropriate. In situations in which speakers who are not widely familiar to the public are scheduled to make talks in a community, some background is usually given. Background is also used in death stories and in announcements of political candidacy, of honors to be bestowed, and of appointments to public office.

Two paragraphs in a death story might say:

> Smith was a graduate of the Kingston High School in 1965. He entered the navy and was discharged from active duty in March, after having served seven months in Vietnam. Returning to Kingston, Smith was employed by an optical firm as a stock clerk.
> He was born in Denver, Colo., and came to Kingston in 1957.

If a university professor not generally known to be an expert on Africa is scheduled to make a talk in a community on "Africa After a Decade," the advance story on his speech might read:

Brown was a member in 1956–59 of the U.S. National Commission for the United Nations Economic, Social and Cultural Organization and its subcommittee on underdeveloped areas, which organized conferences on Africa, Asia and Latin America. He recently returned from a trip to Africa.

If Wilson Riles, California's state superintendent of public instruction, announces staff changes in his department or disagrees with the curriculum commission on the selection of textbooks, a simple identification of the official in the lead is sufficient. When the former superintendent, Max Rafferty, sought the Republican nomination for the U.S. Senate against the incumbent, Thomas Kuchel, however, a McClatchy Newspapers Service writer gave the following background in a story:

> Rafferty was elected to the officially nonpartisan post of state superintendent of public instruction in 1962. He won reelection in 1966.
>
> Although he was elected to a nonpartisan post, he quickly became known for his strongly conservative views, which are not limited to educational issues. He has denounced Kuchel as not being representative of Republican thinking because of his moderate views.
>
> Rafferty also has described the senator as being as popular among Republican rank and file activists as "a skunk at a picnic."

When the Rev. Thomas D. Terry was named president of Santa Clara University, UPI released this story:

> SANTA CLARA—The Rev. Thomas D. Terry, S.J., will become the 25th president of Santa Clara University Mar. 12.
>
> Terry, 46, was named to the post Friday at a board of trustees meeting on the campus. He will succeed the Very Rev. Patrick A. Donohoe, S.J., who was appointed California provincial of the Society of Jesus two weeks ago.
>
> Terry, academic vice president at Loyola University of Los Angeles since 1966, was a former dean at Santa Clara.

The third paragraph was essential if readers were to learn the Rev. Terry's qualifications for the position.

Identification by Synonym

One of the most common devices used to avoid repetition is what journalists call identification by synonym, but some critics speak of it as the art of elegant variation. It is the use of synonyms to avoid the repetition of names. The practice, not new by any means, is widespread in all forms of literature. It is prevalent in the sports and society stories of newspapers as well as in news stories.

After using the name Pres. Richard M. Nixon in the lead of a story it becomes simple in a later reference to say "the chief executive" or "the president." Similarly, after using the name of evangelist Billy Graham in a lead, the writer might later refer to him as "the evangelist." Instead of repeating the name of a football player, a sports writer might say "the all American." A woman's page writer, instead of repeating the name of a woman who has announced her engagement, might say "the bride-to-be."

Identification by synonym is used not only to avoid repetition but also to insert background piecemeal. William Saroyan, for example, can be referred to as "the author of 'The Time of Your Life' and 'The Human Comedy.'" David Rockefeller can be referred to as "the president of the Chase-Manhattan Bank and major investor in the $150 million Embarcadero Center."

Lengthy identification by synonym becomes clumsy. Most editors agree that it is better to lump personal background in one or more paragraphs rather than to introduce it piecemeal.

Here are a few examples of identification by synonym, both effective and ineffective, found in newspapers:

The hot-shooting Louisiana State star, the nation's No. 1 scorer
The hijacker
The Senate's Republican leader
The new commissioner
The newsman
The two amateurs
The golfers
The pacifists
The doctor
The Minnesota senator
The mediator
The newcomer
The IOC executive
The Pennsylvania State University professor
The former vice president
The defense chief
The Assembly minority leader
The bald-headed puncher
The trim, red-headed Bakersfield divorcée
The statuesque brunette
The 42-year-old Cape Town physician
The heavy set, short man

It should not be difficult to appraise the preceding examples according to their effectiveness.

Sir Arthur Quiller-Couch, in a book published in 1916,[1] commented:

> Let us turn to another trick of jargon; the trick of elegant variation, so rampant in the sporting press that there, the undergraduate detects it for laughter:
>
> "Hayward and C. B. Fray now faced the bowling, which apparently had no terrors for the Surrey crack. The old Oxonian, however, took some time in settling to work. . . ."
>
> Yes, you all recognise it and laugh at it. But why do you practise it in your essays? An undergraduate brings me an essay on Byron. In an essay on Byron, Byron is (or ought to be) mentioned many times. I expect, nay exact, that Byron should be mentioned again and again. But my undergraduate has a blushing sense that to call Byron Byron twice on one page is indelicate. So Byron, after starting bravely as Byron, in the second sentence turns into "that great but unequal poet" and thenceforward I have as much trouble with Byron as ever Telemachus with Proteus to hold and pin him back to his proper self. Halfway down the page he becomes "the gloomy master of Newstead"; overleaf he is reincarnated into "the meteoric darling of society"; and so proceeds through successive avatars—"this archrebel," "the author of Childe Harold," "the apostle of scorn," "the ex-Harrovian, proud, but abnormally sensitive of his club foot," "the martyr of Missolonghi," "the pageant-monger of a bleeding heart." Now this again is jargon. It does not, as most jargon does, come of laziness; but it comes of timidity, which is worse. In literature as in life he makes himself felt who not only calls a spade a spade but has the pluck to double spades and redouble.

Identification by synonym, nevertheless, is effective when used skillfully and with restraint.

Off the Record

One of the ethics ingrained in the newsman is never to violate a confidence. A minor official may observe irregular practices in a governmental agency but feel that he would jeopardize his position by revealing what he knows, particularly if his superiors were to know that he was the informant.

He may, in confidence, pass the information to a reporter. The kind of confidence he imposes on the reporter is significant. He may insist that the reporter accept the information for his own background purposes only. This would mean that the reporter would not, in any story, relate the information given to him. The person, on the other hand, might agree that the information, if revealed in a story, may be used with no attribution of any kind. The reporter, under these circum-

---

[1] *On the Art of Writing* (New York: G. P. Putnam's Sons, 1916), pp. 112–114.

stances, could give the details in a story as if they were first hand—it would be the newsman saying it without listing any source.

If the department in which the informant works is a large one, he might permit the use of general attribution, feeling that under those circumstances his anonymity would be secure. In that case, the reporter would cite an "official in the department who does not want his identity disclosed." It would, of course, be better if the informant were courageous enough to agree to specific attribution.

Even though a news source insists that information be used for background only, a resourceful reporter may be able to utilize that information in uncovering facts he can use in a story.

Some newsmen refuse to accept anything in confidence—they resist shackling of any kind.

It is not uncommon for a speaker at a meeting to tab part of what he says as off the record. The validity of the speaker's request depends upon the type of meeting—nothing should be off the record at a public meeting. If the meeting is private and the reporter attends on guest status, the speaker should have off-the-record privileges. Any meeting, however, which is open to the public, regardless of whether or not an admission price is required, should be on the record.

The Pittsburgh *Press,* for example, refused to accede to the stipulation of Henry Cabot Lodge, when he was United States ambassador at large, that remarks he made at a luncheon sponsored by the Pittsburgh World Affairs Council in 1967 were to be off the record. The *Press* maintained it was a public meeting that anyone could attend by purchasing a ticket.[2]

Fact or Opinion

Newspapers do run newsworthy opinions of persons but only with the proper attribution. Verifiable statements of fact usually do not require attribution, but when statements are made as factual and are not readily verifiable it is better to cite the source.

Here is an example in which attribution was used but not needed:

> Plans for a new clubhouse will be discussed at a meeting of the Bates Women's Club Friday, according to Mrs. Mary Jones, the president.

The attribution used in the following is needed:

> GALVESTON, Tex. (UPI)—The "shrinkage" of domestic oil reserves has reached a critical state, the president of Petroleum Equipment Suppliers said.

[2] *Editor & Publisher,* Oct. 7, 1967, p. 48.

The opinions of persons may be run in direct or indirect quotations. An example of indirect quotation follows:

Jones said the school district is not subject to payment of local drainage fees.

An introductory sentence may introduce direct quotation:

Dr. Barth explained the task of the church as he understood it:

"The whole question is whether the task of the church is to cultivate religion or whether it is to announce the good word of God. Even the word 'religion' should disappear in this discussion.

"Religion means man going around and around with higher aspirations, but that's not what counts. What counts is the encounter between God and man. And that's another thing."

It should be noted that, when more than one paragraph of direct quotation is used consecutively, all the paragraphs should have a beginning quotation mark but only the last one should have an end quotation mark.

In direct quotations, the most suitable spot for the attribution is at the end of the first sentence:

"I told them the money was in the safe and I didn't know the combination," Jones related to the police. "Then the tall man said you'd better think of it in a hurry or you'll get a bullet through your head."

When several consecutive paragraphs of direct quotation are used, attribution need be given in only the first:

"But I believe integration is fundamental to the health of American society and that benefits would flow to all Americans from a sound policy of integration," the senator said.

"Beyond that, I believe stable, integrated schools are succeeding in many parts of this country, including the South. I hope in the work of our committee we can demonstrate that.

"When I say integration is working well in many places, I mean children are doing better and learning more. This is particularly true of the black children, but the white children in these schools are not doing any worse."

Indirect quotations, however, do not have quotation marks and therefore require an adept use of attribution to make certain that the reader understands who is saying what. Here is an example of inadequate attribution:

Identification, Background, Attribution and Explanation 71

> Mott said that, with Jeeps and trail bikes, persons are able to go places to which they could not go before. They are covering every square inch of California.

It is written better this way:

> Mott said that, with Jeeps and trail bikes, persons are able to get to places they could not reach before. He added that they are covering every square inch of California.

Or it could have been written:

> With Jeeps and trail bikes, persons are able to get to places they could not reach before, Mott said, adding that they are covering every square inch of California.

One criticism of stories containing many paragraphs of indirect quotation is the excessive repetition of such attributive expressions as "he said." Roy H. Copperud, in his Sept. 11, 1954, column in *Editor & Publisher,* pointed out that many words can stand duty for "said," when appropriate, including: admitted, admonished, affirmed, agreed, avowed, barked, begged, bellowed, called, chided, contended, cried, croaked, declaimed, demanded, disclosed, drawled, emphasized, entreated, exclaimed, hinted, implored, insisted, maintained, mumbled, murmured, muttered, pleaded, proclaimed, proposed, rejoined, retorted, roared, scolded, shouted, shrieked, yelled, wailed.

He explained properly, though, that care should be taken in selecting substitutes. Some touchy words, he pointed out, are these: insinuated, grumbled, whined, whimpered, prated, spouted, ranted, stammered. But he noted that even for the timid there are many innocuous substitutes: added, announced, answered, asserted, commented, continued, declared, remarked, replied, reported, responded, returned, stated.

These are some of the many additions that could be made to Copperud's list:

Acknowledged	Droned	Recounted
Argued	Ejaculated	Reminded
Blurted	Groaned	Reminisced
Boasted	Interjected	Reprimanded
Cautioned	Interrupted	Suggested
Chanted	Lamented	Swore
Commanded	Opined	Threatened
Complained	Offered	Urged
Conceded	Ordered	Uttered
Concluded	Pointed out	Vouched
Confessed	Reasoned	Vowed
Confirmed	Recalled	Warned

Admittedly, these variations offer more opportunity for the fiction writer than they do for the reporter, since many of them are not exact synonyms for "said." It would hardly be appropriate to say, "Coach Jones stated that his team will put up a good fight" or "The Rev. Smith declared that the picnic will be held in Roeding Park this year." Still, many substitutes for the word "said" can on occasions be used appropriately and objectively.

"Said" is the simplest and most neutral of the attributive verbs in the opinion of many.[3] "Uttered," though less common, is equally neutral. Other objective attributive words are "commented" and "remarked." Equally neutral but with more limited applicability than "said" are "added," "concluded" and "recalled." "Answered" and "replied" are objective but limited to expressions of response.

Many of the attributive verbs have connotations that go beyond signifying mere expression, among them: admitted, argued, boasted, confessed, demanded, reasoned, refuted, vouched, warned.

Attributive variants are usually used to avoid the dull repetition of "he said." Variety can be obtained in handling indirect quotations through the use of such indirect attributives as "believes," "thinks," "advocates," "repudiates" and "warns":

> He believes property taxes will be extinct in 20 years.
>
> ———
>
> He thinks the major powers could do far more than they are to restore peace in the Far East.
>
> ———
>
> He advocates a pay-as-you-go plan of financing state buildings.
>
> ———
>
> He repudiates the idea that more employees will increase the efficiency of the department.
>
> ———
>
> He warns against the resurgence of right-wing radicalism in West Germany but thinks German democracy is strong enough to deal with extremism of any sort.

Usually, the present tense is preferred in the use of indirect attributives.

Another type of indirect, passive voice attribution offers opportunity for variety:

> It was pointed out that no pay increases had been granted in three years.
>
> ———
>
> An inadequate staff was held to be the most serious of the problems facing the bureau.
>
> ———

---

[3] See Robert C. McGiffert, "Whisper, Whimper, Wheedle: The Art of Attribution," *Montana Journalism Review,* Nov. 12, 1969.

Identification, Background, Attribution and Explanation 73

> The man was described as being about 30 years of age, 5 foot tall, stocky, and quick of foot.

> The proposal is not considered likely to pass.

In usages of this kind, it is assumed that direct attribution has preceded in the story.

Repetition can often be avoided through the use of an introductory statement of attribution which serves for a number of paragraphs to follow:

> Jones described the robbery this way to the police:
> Two men approached the bus after he had closed the door and prepared to move. One of the men rapped on the door and motioned for Jones to open it.
> He did and the two men entered. They appeared to be reaching in their pockets for change when one of them pulled out a revolver and aimed it at Jones' head.
> The other man then pulled out a pistol and aimed it at the passengers. He told them not to move or he would shoot them.
> Then the first man told Jones to hand over the money.

The same method can be used in speech and interview stories:

> Robertson expressed the following views on the federal government's role in taxation:
> It is the task of the federal government to redistribute the wealth and this can be done only through a much higher graduation of taxes for the higher income brackets.
> A percentage of the federal income tax revenue should be redistributed to the states with no strings attached.
> Welfare should be nationalized with the federal government paying the full cost.

Other devices, such as the rhetorical question, can be used for variation:

> Will the Stanford team try another transplant?
> The surgeon answered with a provisional yes, "depending entirely on a post-mortem examination of Mr. Kasperak."

Explanation and General Background

The reader should not be left with questions in his mind after he reads a story. It is the responsibility of the writer to anticipate the thinking of his reader and to provide adequate explanation and background. When that is not done, a city editor frequently asks the reporter to go back to his typewriter and "plug the holes in the story."

The Associated Press' managing editors launched a campaign years ago for explanatory writing and the AP issued a series of reports on that campaign in 1949. Says one of the reports:

> There should be no attempt to disguise explanatory writing or background material. Don't try to sprinkle it throughout the story in an effort to make it look like fresh material. Put it boldly right where it belongs in the story. . . .

Dr. Rudolf Flesch, who was engaged by the AP to analyze copy and come up with suggestions for improvement, listed five rules of thumb for the attainment of reader clarity. These were the five rules listed in the first of the reports:

1. Explain pertinent geographical facts for readers who live at a distance
2. Explain all words and terms not generally used in everyday conversation
3. Answer all questions an average reader would raise, but don't try to do more
4. Don't make your explanation unreadable
5. If you can help it, don't use words that need explanation.

A later report in the series answered the question of how the editors wanted the explanatory matter:

> Right in the body of the story, and well up in it. They don't like parenthetical matter . . . And of course they would much prefer that we get the explanation quick enough to include in the original story—not send it later as an insert.

There has been a growing awareness by editors of the need for explanation when it can improve clarity or the readers' understanding of the story. Note the third paragraph, for example, in this dispatch:

> COTONOU, Dahomey (AP)—A military junta seized power in a burst of gunfire today and was reported to have arrested Pres. Emile Derlin Zinsou.
> A group of military men, believed headed by Lt. Col. Maurice Kouandete, took over the presidential palace.
> A former French colony on the underside of the West African bulge, Dahomey has about 3 million people and has had a half-dozen coups since gaining independence in 1960. . . .

A San Francisco *Chronicle* story from San Jose, Calif., reported that an ombudsman had been appointed at San Jose State College to search out and remedy racial discrimination. The fourth paragraph of the story said:

The title "ombudsman" is in imitation of the Scandinavian official who takes up citizens' complaints.

A Newark *Star-Ledger* story describing an annual Crispus Attucks parade said in the fourth paragraph:

> During the pre-parade ceremony held in front of city hall, William Booth, chairman of New York City's Human Rights Commission, said that Attucks, who was killed during the Boston Massacre in 1770, had gone unnoticed for a long time.

Note the explanation used in a story about Winston Churchill:

> LONDON (AP)—Doctors disclosed today Sir Winston Churchill is suffering from a blood clot in his broken left thigh.
> A medical bulletin issued from the hospital where he is under treatment says:
> "There has been no extension of the thrombosis and the left leg is less swollen."
> Until now, the circulatory condition in the 87-year-old former prime minister's leg had been described as phlebitis —inflammation of a vein. This was said to have developed last Saturday.
> A thrombosis, however, is a blood clot in a vein or artery. . . .

A UPI story telling of Israeli army efforts to get the story of Passover to front line troops used a paragraph to explain the festival:

> The Passover festival—one of the three principal Jewish holidays—lasts eight days, commemorating the end of 210 years of Jewish slavery in ancient Egypt and the emergence of the Jewish nation under the prophet Moses.

A Chicago *Daily News* story on sonic booms contained this paragraph of explanation:

> A so-called sonic boom is a shock wave of air. It builds up in front of a plane flying fast enough to exceed the speed of sound (mach 1). When the shock wave reaches the ground, it may sound like a loud explosion, and can—depending on its strength—cause damage to buildings and windows.
> (Reprinted with permission from the Chicago *Daily News*)

A Fresno (Calif.) *Bee* story dealing with citizens' proposals to end de facto segregation in schools used the following explanatory paragraph following the lead:

> De facto segregation denotes the situation in which neighborhood schools have a preponderance of minority

group students because the housing patterns of a community have resulted in concentrations of minority group families in those residential areas.

Theodore Bernstein, in the June 21, 1962, New York *Times* newsroom publication *Winners & Sinners,* commented:

> This department has previously suggested as a newspaper slogan, "Keep two readers in mind: the high school sophomore and the man who has been marooned on a desert island for three months." If the story mentions "most-favored-nation" treatment . . . don't keep that sophomore waiting for three paragraphs to find out what that means and then hide the explanation in an oblique reference. Tell him plainly and at once: ". . . 'most-favored-nation' treatment, which grants the lowest tariffs extended to any trading partner of the United States." If the story refers to the Soviet Union's 30 per cent increase in the price of meat and 25 per cent increase in the price of butter . . . the reader is justified in wanting to know what are the approximate prices in American terms. . . .
>
> (© 1962 by The New York Times Company. Reprinted by permission)

It may be that background instead of explanation is needed to make a story clear. An AP story telling of the disappearance of the French submarine, Eurydice, used this paragraph of background:

> The missing Daphne-class attack submarine was the second of her kind in a little more than two years to disappear on a Mediterranean practice dive.

A city editor, commenting on a story run in his newspaper, said the addition of one sentence would have given the reader a much clearer picture. The story was an account of a legislator's criticism of the state director of education. The city editor's comment was that many readers might wonder why the legislator would make the attack, since it was not based on anything particularly timely.

The explanation the city editor felt was missing was that the legislator and the state director of education had been feuding for years.

EXERCISES

I. Questions for Discussion

1. When is it effective to use identification to answer the question of *who* in the first paragraph and not give the name until the second?
2. When are age and street address not needed for identification?

Identification, Background, Attribution and Explanation 77

   3. What kind of statements need attribution? What kinds do not?
   4. Do you think that identification by synonym is an effective means of avoiding a paragraph or two of solid background?
   5. When several paragraphs of direct quotation are used, where should the quotation marks go?

II. Under what circumstances do you believe the following attributive words would be appropriate?

   1. Boasted
   2. Claimed
   3. Droned
   4. Ranted
   5. Refuted

III. How would you identify each of the following in a news story?

   1. Mrs. Charles (Shirley Temple) Black
   2. William Buckley
   3. Charles A. Lindbergh
   4. Greta Garbo
   5. Ted Williams

IV. Comment on the following usages of identification by synonym

   1. The tall, lank second baseman who led his team in batting last season. . . .
   2. The quiet, unassuming teacher for more than 30 years. . . .
   3. The 42-year-old educator, author and administrator. . . .
   4. The author of more than a dozen books. . . .
   5. The longtime opponent of man's encroachment on nature's beauty spots. . . .
   6. The former husband of one of Mt. Vernon's most prominent socialites. . . .
   7. The crafty business leader. . . .
   8. The twice defeated candidate for the state legislature. . . .
   9. The slender, blond mother of three children. . . .
   10. The coarse featured, heavy jowled foreman. . . .

V. Comment on the following background used in a story about a dairy organization

> The international group has, in the past four years, conducted surveys in 12 countries, launched long-range educational programs to increase milk consumption in six countries—Colombia and Brazil in South America, Thailand, India, Pakistan and Burma in the Far East—and demonstrated the recombining of milk and the manufacture of ice cream at 12 great international trade fairs.
> It has provided the first taste of ice cream and the first taste of pure, safe milk to countless potential customers,

and through its sampling program has introduced safe milk products to more than 2½ million people throughout the milk-short nations.

VI. Which of the following terms, when used in a story, should be explained?

1. Barbiturate
2. Cloture
3. Common market
4. Curia
5. Depletion
6. Filibuster
7. Lie detector
8. Lockout
9. Methedrine
10. Prime rate

VII. Comment on the following two paragraphs of explanation used in a story on drag strips

> Proponents of drag strips argue they provide an outlet for a commendable urge to compete and give mechanically minded youngsters an opportunity to use their talents.
>
> Opponents contend the drag strips are only an incentive to rowdyism, where exuberant drivers practice their skills for later use on public streets and thoroughfares where lives and property are endangered.

VIII. How would you react to the following situations?

1. A speaker at a Lions Club meeting in your community makes some asides about a governmental official and then says the remarks are off the record.
2. You overhear inadvertently that a staff shake-up is going to take place in the county health department. You ask an acquaintance in that department about it and he agrees to tell you about if if you will use the information for background purposes only.
3. A rumor has spread among teachers in your community that the school superintendent is going to resign at the end of the current school year to accept a position with another school system. You ask the superintendent if the rumor is true and he says he will answer the question if you agree to keep his comment confidential until after the next school board meeting.
4. A local conservation club has opposed a proposal to establish a commercial resort at a nearby lake. The club has called a meeting. You attend and notice that no one is checking at the door to see that only members are admitted. The club president recognizes you and, before opening the meeting, states that all discussion will be off the record.
5. A minor city official calls on you and tells you that a big scandal is "going to break" at city hall. He agrees to tell you about it if you will keep it in "strict confidence."

IX. Comment on the action of the newsmen referred to in the lead of the following Associated Press story

> WASHINGTON—More than half a dozen reporters walked out on a meeting today with Jerris Leonard, assistant U.S. attorney general for civil rights, when they were told his remarks would be "off the record."

Chapter 6

IS THERE AN INTERESTING ANGLE?

Stung by the splendor of a sudden thought.
  —*Browning*

Two reporters could run into the same set of circumstances and one of them see nothing interesting but the other observe an unusual angle for a story.

What is an angle?

Call it an unusual twist or slant, though the latter word has a negative connotation in much journalistic usage. One way of defining an angle is to say that it is the describing of phenomena from a novel or unusual perspective, as in:

> Joe Blow turned the tables in divorce court today.
> Married six times, Blow was divorced by five of his former wives on grounds of mental cruelty.
> Judge James Brown granted Blow a divorce from his sixth wife, Mary, on grounds of mental cruelty.

The following story would be little more than a brevity if it were not for the angle:

Is There an Interesting Angle? 81

> Police Judge John Jones believes wholeheartedly in the Gilbert and Sullivan axiom, "let the punishment fit the crime."
> He was hearing the case of Mrs. Mary Doe, 65, of 9579 17th St., accused of shooting her son-in-law, Henry Bloke, 35, of 2402 H St. in the leg because he shot and killed her dog.
> Bloke was accused of a crime against public decency, a misdemeanor.
> His mother-in-law was charged with disturbing the peace. Both had pleaded guilty.
> Judge Jones sentenced Bloke to 60 days in jail.
> As he was about to sentence Mrs. Doe, her attorney, Samuel Smith, gave an impassioned plea for a light sentence.
> "Mr. Smith," the judge interrupted, "I just gave this woman's son-in-law 60 days for shooting a dog.
> "You don't think I am going to give the woman any less for shooting a human being, do you?"
> Attorney Smith was speechless.
> Judge Jones sentenced Mrs. Doe to 90 days in jail.

An unusual angle may be used as a wedge to move into a story or it may be used as the underlying idea for an entire story, long or short.

Using the Angle as a Wedge

Two would-be burglars entered the home of a chief of police and landed in jail. The writer used this as his lead:

> Whatever the two men were doing, they were in the wrong house—that of Police Chief Harold R. Brown.

The rest of the story described the incidents of the arrest of the two men.

Here is another example of an angle being used as a wedge:

> SAN FRANCISCO (AP)—The first woman ever chosen to lead the medical association of a large state is a bouncy, grey-eyed charmer who stands 5 foot 2 in her stocking feet.
> "They like women," laughed Dr. Roberta F. Fenlon when the California Medical Association—with 24,000 doctors, the second largest in the nation—chose her president elect yesterday at its annual meeting.

The remainder of the story gave details of the meeting and background on the new president elect.

The writer of the following Fresno (Calif.) *Bee* article used an interesting angle to move into the story:

Police Sgt. William H. Roberts was not too concerned about what his neighbors thought of his running around in his pajamas early today.

Duty called at 1:30 a.m. and he did not turn his back on it.

Before the incident was over Roberts fired three shots from a .45 caliber revolver and took a burglary suspect into custody.

Roberts, who lives at 2009 East Fountain Way, reported his wife woke him and told him there was a prowler next door. The officer grabbed his revolver and went outside, where he flagged down Patrolman Phillip L. Oliver.

About that time they saw a shadow of a man moving across the street. Oliver went one way and Roberts another to corner the suspect.

Roberts got to him first but the man attempted to jump a fence. The officer said he fired a shot in the air to stop him. That did not do the trick, so Roberts said he tackled the man and his revolver went off again. In the struggle Roberts hit the man on the head with the weapon and it discharged again. By then the prowler was subdued.

The man was identified as John Doe, 20, of 2905 Cobblestone Road.

The police said Doe and four others are suspects in a burglary at the Triangle Store in the Manchester Shopping Center. Investigators said the burglars apparently were frightened off and dropped nine suits near the store and fled on foot.

The other suspects are being sought.

After all the commotion, Roberts managed to get a couple more hours sleep before he reported for work this morning.

(Reprinted from the Fresno *Bee*)

When the Angle Makes the Story

Unusual angles provide the substance for many bright features, short but amusing. A computer mix-up provided the grist for this story:

PHOENIX, Ariz. (AP)—John Jones, 37, entered a local hospital recently for treatment of pneumonia but, according to his bill, suffered complications.

Jones said that, in addition to charges for treatment of the chest ailment, he was also billed for the use of a delivery room and the nursery.

The bill said the father of six children had given birth to a girl.

The hospital blamed a computer for the error. An unusual incident in a college bookstore prompted this story:

> PORTLAND, Ore. (UPI)—The student disciplinary board at Reed College is looking into a raw matter.
>
> The college bookstore recently put out a new rule which required shoppers to leave their book bags and coats near the front of the store.
>
> The idea was to cut down on shoplifting.
>
> Eight students went a little further. In addition to coats, they disrobed entirely in front of the store, then bought a few books.
>
> Store operator Dick Edlebe said other students paid little attention "because they have got used to everyone doing his or her own thing."
>
> But he said some of the other shoppers got a "bit fidgety."

The following story has a timely angle:

> RENO (AP)—A high school group has asked Gov. Paul Laxalt to order antipollution measures for Nevada's state seal.
>
> "The Nevada seal, among other representations, also contains a smokestack emitting black smoke," said a letter received from Students to Oppose Pollution at Earl Wooster High School.
>
> The students suggested the smoke be removed from future copies of the seal.
>
> The seal depicts sun shining over mountains onto a scene which includes a factory and a railroad locomotive, both belching smoke.

An amusing twist in this story should bring a smile from readers:

> SAN CLEMENTE (UPI)—Brink's Inc. sent a harried request to authorities here to stop one of its trucks.
>
> There was no robbery or kidnaping, a Brink's spokesman at their Los Angeles headquarters told the police dispatcher.
>
> The armored truck company just wanted police to deliver the message: "You forgot the money."

Not only short features but also many longer articles are based on interesting angles. The social problems created by prostitution, for instance, have been treated in more than a few stories. Clampdowns by law enforcement agencies, the flagrancy with which prostitutes operate in some places, and arguments by some sociologists that prostitution should be legalized and regulated are only a few of the treatments of the subject in newspapers.

A Canadian sociologist's research, however, provided an entirely different angle for the subject:

> WINNIPEG, Man. (AP)—A sociology professor says many of Winnipeg's better class prostitutes are happy sub-

urban housewives who help out with the family budget. Some husbands don't mind at all, he adds.

Prof. William Morrison, head of the University of Winnipeg sociology department, is conducting research into sex-for-hire with the aid of a $2,500 grant that he uses to cover office expenses and pay the prostitutes for interviews. The grant is from Canada Council, a government body.

He reported that more than 50 prostitutes he interviewed said they were happily married, and many had families. Some said their husbands know what their wives are doing, he added, and don't mind because "it brings in more money to support the family."

His study has centered on call girls who usually accept appointments only on recommendations of a previous client, unlike the less-selective streetwalker.

"These girls honestly believe they are doing a service to society . . . and their clients are usually happily married upper-middle-class types who think they cannot get sexual satisfaction with their wives," he said.

Business usually is conducted from the home during the day, although some is transacted in hotel or motel rooms selected by the clients, Prof. Morrison said.

He said he sees no reason why prostitution should not be made legal in Canada, particularly since restrictions have been removed on homosexual relations between consenting adults.

Prof. Morrison is married and has two school-age children. He plans to write a book that will give the prostitute "a better name than she has been labeled with in the past."

An Idea Sprouts

A pending meeting between Pres. Richard M. Nixon and former Pres. Harry S Truman is newsworthy. One is a Republican and the other a Democrat. What will the two talk about? What is the political significance, if any? What kind of an exchange of ideas will take place?

A reporter thought of an interesting angle and put it to work:

> WASHINGTON (AP)—Will Richard M. Nixon apologize for once having called his host a traitor, a lemon picker, a little man, one of the poorest presidents the United States ever had?
>
> Will Harry S Truman, 84, "start a fight" or "punch someone" when Nixon comes to call?
>
> Or, as is more likely, will the nasty political hatchet get a quiet, decent burial when the past and present presidents get together today in Independence, Mo.?
>
> The presidency has sometimes had a way of blurring old

quarrels as incumbents reach out to their predecessors—the only human beings who can knowledgeably commiserate over the burdens of the office.

Nixon, who will drop in on Truman on the way to a West Coast weekend, is leading with a hefty peace offering: the piano Truman used to relax with in the White House. He once called Truman a "piano-playing letter-writer." It will go to the Truman Library.

And Truman? "He has the greatest respect for the job of president," his former military aide, retired Maj. Gen. Harry H. Vaughan, said yesterday. "He would be courteous and respectful to anyone who occupied that office."

But Vaughan was quick to concede that "there has never been a very warm rapport there. The President (Truman) was mad as the devil after Mr. Nixon made a very unfortunate statement about '20 years of treason' in the 1952 campaign."

The 1952 campaign was often savage. Nixon, then a 39-year-old California senator, was running for vice president and making the really tough political speeches shunned by the leader of the Republican ticket, Dwight D. Eisenhower.

Communism was the big issue. And in Texarkana, Tex., one October night, Nixon, who had a reputation as a Red-hunter, said this:

"The Truman-Acheson-Stevenson Democrats have forfeited their rights to the support of millions of good, rank-and-file-members of the Democratic Party. They are traitors to the high principles in which many of the nation's Democrats believe. Real Democrats are outraged by the Truman-Acheson-Stevenson gang's toleration and defense of communism in high places."

Dean Acheson, of course, was Truman's secretary of state; Adlai Stevenson was the Democratic candidate to succeed Truman.

"We need a big man as president," Nixon said in Sheridan, Wyo., "because we have had a little man for the last seven years."

In choosing the men around him, Nixon said in Indianapolis, Truman was "the champion lemon-picker of all time."

And Truman, Nixon told a crowd in Joplin, Mo., "probably will go down in history as one of the poorest presidents the United States ever had."

Two years after Truman was out of office, Nixon, then vice president, resumed the attack in the 1954 congressional campaigns, contending that the Eisenhower administration had cleaned out thousands of Communists and other security risks accumulated during Democratic years.

Truman was furious. In November, 1955, the Los Angeles Times said Truman replied as follows when asked by a reporter what he thought about Nixon as a possible 1956 presidential candidate:

"I don't like the son of a b——and I don't care who

knows it. I don't even want to discuss that son of a b———. Don't even mention his name to me."

Truman later denied having used profanity.

He was taking one of his morning walks in New York City a few months later. Chatting with reporters, he said:

"I wouldn't meet Nixon again. It would just start a fight.

"That's the awfulest thing a man can be called—a traitor. When I get started on that, I don't want to swear, I want to punch someone. It's hard to take—being called a traitor after 30 years of service to your country."

In Rio de Janeiro that day, Nixon declined comment on Truman's remarks.

"I never comment on what he says," Nixon said. "It wouldn't do any good anyway."

It's not likely old times will be discussed at Independence.

Timely Occasions Offer Opportunities

"Harry, write a feature for Valentine's Day," said the city editor to one of his reporters. And Harry scratched his head as he sought an inspiration for a story.

City editors may make similar demands of reporters on numerous other timely occasions—World Religion Day, Washington's Birthday, Ash Wednesday, Rosh Hashanah, Memorial Day, Columbus Day, United Nations Day and Thanksgiving, to list a few.

Sometimes a city editor may be satisfied with a routine story listing the celebrations to take place locally. At other times he may want a feature. It is at such times that a novel angle will help, such as AP staffer Frank Carey's science feature pointing out that if a person has a valentine-shaped heart he is suffering from mitral stenosis.

Another AP writer, J. Michael Rouse, cashed in on an interesting angle for a story on Andrew Jackson's birthday:

> Today is the birthday of Andrew Jackson, soldier, statesman and seventh president of the United States. He was born March 15, 1767. . . .
>
> Well, we don't exactly know where.
>
> Most reference books say it was in the Waxhaw settlement in Lancaster County, South Carolina. North Carolina says it isn't so—that Jackson was born just across the border in Union County, North Carolina.
>
> The Tar Heel state has employed a young historian, Max Harris, to find the facts. If he succeeds in settling the 195 year old argument, one of the states will have to tear down a monument.
>
> "Here was born, March 15, 1767, Andrew Jackson, sev-

enth president of the United States," reads the legend on a monument in a wooded area of Union County, N.C.

A half mile away, just across the state line in South Carolina, is another monument to Jackson's birth. It stands on the edge of South Carolina's Andrew Jackson State Park.

The story begins in 1765 when Andrew Jackson, Sr., an Irishman, settled with his family in the Waxhaw Indian lands spanning the border of the Carolinas, just inside North Carolina.

He died two years later, leaving two small sons, Robert and Hugh, and a pregnant wife.

Mrs. Jackson decided to move, before the child was born, to the plantation home of a sister and brother in law, Mr. and Mrs. James Crawford, just inside South Carolina.

Enter the controversy.

The South Carolinians say Mrs. Jackson and her sons arrived at the Crawfords before Andy was born.

Not so, say the North Carolinians. Labor pains, they claim, set in midway in the journey, and she stopped at the home of another sister and brother in law, Mr. and Mrs. George McKemie (or McKamie), and gave birth to the child, moving on to the Crawfords when he was 6 weeks old.

The site of the McKemie cabin, of course, is on the North Carolina side of the boundary—by a distance of 407 yards.

Jackson was the only president in U.S. history with the advantage of having two "home states" to back him up on election day. And, apparently relishing the situation, he never directly disputed the claim of either state.

The students in a sophomore reporting class discussed possible angles for a story on Seward's Day, celebrated in Alaska, March 30, the anniversary date of the acquisition of that state as a territory from Russia. The most obvious angle was the criticism by many Americans of what, in 1867, was called Seward's icebox. One student, however, came up with another angle:

> Alaskans are celebrating an event today that might never have happened had a would-be assassin's aim been more accurate more than 100 years ago.
>
> The event is Seward's Day, commemorating the signing of the treaty through which Russia sold Alaska to the United States more than 100 years ago.
>
> The man considered responsible for the purchase was William H. Seward, the secretary of state under Pres. Abraham Lincoln and his successor, Pres. Andrew Johnson.
>
> When John Wilkes Booth assassinated Lincoln, an accomplice broke into Seward's home and shot him. Seward slowly recovered from his wound and lived to negotiate the Alaska purchase the following year.

Critics called the purchase "Seward's Folly" and referred to the territory as "Seward's Icebox" and "Seward's Frog Pond."

The American Flag did not formally rise over Alaska until March 30, 1867, for it took Seward time to persuade congress to approve the $7.2 million transaction.

The land once described as "590,000 square miles of icebergs and polar bears" today produces $54 million in minerals, $47 million in timber and millions from fisheries and furs.

Alaska became the 49th state of the Union in 1959.

Angles Spark News Presentation

A "different" angle can increase reader interest in what is basically a news story. An example is this Miami *Herald* story written by James Malone (names have been changed):

The Greek immigrant father of a young Miamian sought for two years on murder charges publicly pleaded Friday with his son to surrender so he can attend his mother's funeral.

The mother, Mrs. Sophia Kouras, 48, died early Friday of a pulmonary ailment.

The father said he believes it was the result of lung injuries she suffered when she was tortured during the Greek civil war in 1946.

Mrs. Kouras was eight months pregnant when she was captured and tortured. She gave premature birth to her now-fugitive son shortly afterwards.

Members of the Kouras family said they do not believe the missing son knew that his mother was ill.

The fugitive is Peter Kouras, Jr., now 24 years old, sought by police across the country for the last two years on charges stemming from the killing of Ike Macy, a Coral Gables tennis pro and socialite.

A gunfight broke out when two bandits broke into Macy's home Jan. 7, 1968. The robbers were later identified as Kouras and Fred R. Yoka. Yoka is serving a life term in Raiford.

All three men were wounded, Macy fatally. The bandits fled the state after they were secretly treated by a North Miami Beach doctor.

The FBI spotted the men in Los Angeles in September, 1968. Yoka was captured and later sentenced to Raiford for life. Kouras escaped the dragnet.

Mrs. Kouras' two younger sons, George and Paul, returned home Friday. They joined their father in the public plea that their brother give himself up.

"We want him to come in on his own voluntarily for his

mother's funeral," George said. "No one knows where he is, but we suspect he reads local papers every day. He will have to give himself up to the police to come to the funeral."

Because Kouras may be afraid local police would refuse to accept a peaceful surrender, George said he had asked the FBI to take over if his brother returns.

The elder Kouras, who lives at 5550 55th Ter., said his wife suffered lung afflictions when she was captured by Communist forces during the Greek civil war.

She was eight months pregnant when her captors beat her to force her to reveal her freedom-fighter husband's hiding place, he said. When she refused, they forced her to stand in a neck-deep pool of water for "several days" while the torturers threatened to deepen the pool and drown her.

Still, she refused to inform on the guerrilla soldiers, he said.

Because he still doesn't speak English clearly, the father spoke through his son, George.

"My mother never learned English," George added. "She used to say, 'My duty is in my home. I have no need to learn another language.'

"She never became a U.S. citizen."

Remembering the troubled years before the sons left home, George said, "She used to sit by the door when we went out at night. No matter how late we came home, she was always there.

"She was afraid of what would happen to her sons in this country.

"So she always waited for us, and when we were all home, she locked the doors and turned off the lights. Then she could sleep in peace."

(Reprinted from the Miami *Herald*)

The preceding story is strengthened by liberal doses of human interest—the angle used to introduce the story has emotional appeal. The following story has a human interest angle:

FOWLERVILLE, Mich. (UPI)—A mechanically minded 14-year-old who remembered a televised warning about explosives dismantled a live bomb "big enough to blow up everything for two acres."

"If I knew then what I know now, I wouldn't have touched anything," Melvin Roddenberg said. "I would never do that again. I'm still pretty shaky."

Police were still puzzled yesterday why the bomb—four 8-by-2-inch bombs screwed together—failed to go off.

Roddenberg, of Westland, Mich., and his cousin, Larry, 9, found the bomb with an explosive power of seven dynamite sticks Sunday in an abandoned farmhouse near here.

Roddenberg ordered his cousin out of the house, then proceeded to separate the bomb's wires. He said he had seen a public service commercial on explosives and watched his father dynamite tree stumps.

"I wouldn't have touched those wires myself," Livingston County Detective Sgt. David Teggerdine said. "I would have cleared the area and exploded the bomb at a safe distance, using a rifle. All he had to do was wiggle one of those wires the wrong way and adios."

Police said the bomb was among 35 stolen from a truck last August, apparently by schoolboys, and planted in the old farmhouse because they wanted to see the old house blow up. Nineteen of the explosives, used in oil exploration, are still missing.

The angle in the following court-action story is threaded through the article:

SAN FRANCISCO (UPI)—A jury Wednesday awarded $50,000 damages to Mary Doe, the 29-year-old former Sunday school teacher whose attorney claimed a runaway cable car gave her a runaway sex life.

The eight women and four male jurors deliberated for eight hours, during which two held out for a $300,000 award in the lawsuit against the city and its transit system.

John Roe, Miss Doe's attorney, said he might appeal the award—one tenth of the $500,000 he was asking.

But he hailed the verdict as a "legal breakthrough" which established the principle of "psychic damages."

Miss Doe was on a Hyde St. cable car . . . when it broke loose, plunged down a hill and smashed into a power pole.

As a result, Lewis contended in the trial, she suffered from uncontrollable sex drives which drove her into the arms of more than 100 men.

Miss Doe, who testified for two and a half days during the trial, said she was a former Sunday school teacher and choir singer whose college friends used to kid her about being "the world's only 21-year-old virgin."

Although the award was considerably higher than the city had expected, Dep. City Atty. William Taylor said he was "not unhappy."

Taylor had conceded Miss Doe suffered some injury as a result of the accident and that city negligence was involved, but said the mishap had nothing to do with her sexual activity.

Roe said the principle involved in the judgment was that a neurosis induced by an accident could not be considered more serious than "the loss of a leg."

"If we can break through and prove that psychic injuries are injuries, we are making progress," he said.

He said that the case was difficult to try because of its "humorous element."

"It was hard to get the jurors to think seriously about it," he said. "Everybody who talks to them feels it is a joke."

There is no limitation, as far as types of stories go, to the possibility of using interesting angles, as is illustrated by an obituary story on the death of a noted culinary artist:

> REDONDO BEACH (AP)—Chef Henri Carpentier, who made a mistake in fixing breakfast for a future king and gave the world crepes suzette, is dead at 81.
>
> Carpentier, one of the last of the world's great culinary artists, died yesterday of a heart attack in his modest Cafe-Home, a Mecca for gourmets the world over.
>
> Henri, as an apprentice of 10, caught the favor of Queen Victoria while she vacationed on the French Riviera. With that royal nod, his future was assured.
>
> At 16, he was maitre d' at the Cafe de Paris in Monte Carlo when the prince of Wales, later Edward VII, was its most distinguished guest.
>
> "I can remember that morning as if it were yesterday," Henri once recalled. "Among the diners at the prince's table was a beautiful French girl named Suzette.
>
> "His highness ordered crepes—the French pancakes. I mixed a special sauce and a special blend of brandies. I wanted everything to be perfect but the head of the chafing dish accidentally set the simmering cordials afire.
>
> "I was embarrassed but I did not show it. Ah, monsieur, I had confidence of youth. I poured the fiery sauce on the crepes as if the flames were set on purpose.
>
> "The prince tasted; then he smiled and said:
>
> " 'Henri, what have you done with these crepes? They are superb.'
>
> "I was thrilled and offered to name them crepes Prinz de Gaulle in his honor. He declined.
>
> " 'Henri,' he said, 'we must always remember the ladies come first. We will call this glorious thing crepes suzette.'
>
> "That was the day, monsieur. People had been eating pancakes from the time of the Romans but never before that day crepes suzette."
>
> Born in Nice, Henri was a cousin and protege of the great Escoffier.
>
> "Escoffier took me to Paris. There he advised that I should work one month in each of the great kitchens—or until I learned the specialty of the house. I worked in every restaurant in Paris."
>
> He followed Escoffier to the Savoy in London, later becoming its chef, cooking for the dandies of the Edwardian age. In 1905, the famed Delmonico's in New York lured him. There he became a favorite chef of Diamond Jim Brady, Lillian Russell, Teddy Roosevelt and John D. Rockefeller, Sr.
>
> From Delmonico's, Carpentier went into business for himself. He said he made millions.
>
> Then came the motor age. Henri's era of elegance was gone and, before long, so was his fortune.
>
> With only $10 to his name, Henri came to this suburban

Los Angeles city and started one of the world's unusual restaurants.

From the outside, it looked little better than a hamburger stand. Inside was served a meal, family style, which would make a sultan's mouth water.

He served one dinner a day—never to less than 12, no more than 16. The meal took all day to prepare, four hours to consume. The cost—a modest $8.

Because so few could be served at one time, it sometimes took four years to get a reservation.

Wives, awed by his Victorian hand kissing and gallantry, invariably nagged their husbands on the way home: "Why can't you act like Henri?"

But the husbands had the final word, for once: "Why can't you cook like him?"

Production Increases

By learning to spot different angles, a reporter can increase his production. While others wait for news to come to them, the reporter with a resourceful mind develops a stockpile of ideas to follow up.

Here is one example of many stories based on interesting angles:

Summertime may mean vacation time for most persons but it simply means time to catch up on unfinished business for the principals of Lake City's three high schools.

The principals are George A. White of the Roosevelt High School, Melvin C. Stuart of the West Side High School, and Donald Holder of the Young High School.

Despite the fact that most teachers get three months of vacation, the principals are planning no vacations with the exception of free hours during weekends.

Just a few of the items which will occupy their attention during the summer are:

Taking the wrinkles out of course schedules for next fall, rewriting school bulletins, preparing student body projects, supervising the cleaning and repairing of school buildings, ordering supplies, seeing that textbooks are repaired, and revising office forms.

"Administering a high school is a 12-month-a-year job," the three insist. They added:

"Buildings must be put in shape, floors must be maintained, classrooms repainted and lockers checked."

Then, they point out, "We have to answer all the numerous letters which come during the summer requesting transcripts of graduates, as well as varied other types of communication."

"Anyone wanting much playtime shouldn't become a high school principal," quipped one.

"You have to get your enjoyment from your work," said another.

Take away the angle in the preceding example and you have no story, for it is the angle that makes the story.

EXERCISES

I. Compare the angles in the following two excerpts with each other and then with the student-written story on Alaska quoted in the chapter

FAIRBANKS, Alaska (AP)—One hundred years ago Russia sold the whole 586,000 square miles of Alaska to the United States for $7.2 million, two cents an acre.

In Congress there were anguished outcries. The deal was dubbed "Seward's folly," after Secretary of State William H. Seward, who engineered it.

One member of the House, opposing the appropriation to pay the Russians, asserted that Alaska was something "we did not need, that nobody wanted and, as far as it is known, is utterly worthless."

So much for that clouded crystal ball.

The Alaska Purchase Centennial opened Mar. 30, a century from the day the treaty was signed, and the official exposition, Alaska 67, begins here on a 45-acre tract May 27.

In Fairbanks alone, tourists are expected to spend. . . .

BY ELDON BARRETT

FAIRBANKS, Alaska (UPI)—One of the greatest horse trades in history occurred 100 years ago Mar. 30, when the United States purchased Alaska from Russia for $7.2 million.

At the time, most Americans figured Russia had slickered Uncle Sam. But the fact is the purchase price was just about the smallest item connected with Alaska.

And by the end of this summer thousands of folks from the "lower 48" are going to be aware of the fact for Alaskans are preparing to throw a multi-million dollar party called the Alaska 67 Centennial Exposition that will last from May 27 through Sept. 30 to show off "the great land."

The exhibition site is a 41-acre area on the banks. . . .

II. How important are the angles used in the following stories?

The old time "hookey cop," the dread of the young truant who preferred a circus or fishing trip to attending school, is nearly a relic of the past.

His modern counterpart, a school attendance officer, is a different breed, according to J. E. Korne, the director of the city schools attendance department.

Korne took over as the director of the attendance department 21 years ago, when the city schools enrollment was about 12,000. He had one assistant.

Today the enrollment is more than 60,000 and Korne has four assistants.

The old time "hookey cop" used fear as a first resort to enforce school attendance, whereas, Korne says, an attendance officer today tries to take a positive approach and uses fear only as a last resort.

Korne and his staff hold thousands of conferences with pupils, parents and school officials during the course of a school year.

"We try to make the youngster and his parents realize the importance of education," Korne said.

When poverty is responsible for absence, Korne's office contacts welfare and civic agencies, and tries to make arrangements for food and clothing.

The attendance officer today has to have a special credential, know all the laws pertaining to juveniles, and cooperate with the welfare department, the juvenile court, the probation department and the district attorney's office.

"Frequently, problems in the home are the basic factors in truancy," Korne said.

"Parents sometimes keep children out of school to take care of them while they are ill, to shop for them, to run errands, or even to drive a mother to a doctor's office.

"In other cases parents lose all control of their children."

Korne said his office gets immediate reports from police and sheriff's headquarters of all detainments and his office notifies the schools involved. He gets reports from school nurses when cases of minor illness result in prolonged absence.

Last year his staff held 3,189 consultations with pupils or parents.

JOLIET, Ill. (AP)—"Life—it's a great trip. Try it before it's too late," an 18-year-old youth wrote in a letter before he died during the weekend.

Coroner Willard Blood of Will County said the youth, Percy Patrick Pilon of Joliet, died of a self-inflicted gunshot wound.

In a letter released by Blood at the request of Pilon's family, the youth urged others to "say no" if offered drugs.

"Drugs played a big part in ruining the last year of my life," the letter said. The dead youth said he had used many drugs, including LSD and amphetamines. The letter condemned drug pushers.

"Please, if you need help, get it," Pilon's note urged other drug users.

If you hear your child uttering strange sounds in secluded parts of your home during the next few weeks, don't try to squelch it—encourage it.

Your child may be getting in tune for Oral Reading Month, which the city's junior high schools are sponsoring for February.

The move for a revival of oral reading is originating in the city's schools.

Spearheading the drive is the junior high school speech arts curriculum committee, headed by Mrs. Mabel Green, a speech consultant for the schools.

Mrs. Green asserts that what students learn to read aloud they will remember.

"Much writing, including all poetry, was written to be read aloud," she said. "The beauty of rhythm—the joy of communicating—is lost in silent reading."

III. Do some research on the following and come up with story angles

1. Easter
2. Halloween
3. Mother's Day
4. Thanksgiving Day
5. Valentine's Day

IV. Seek story angles by consulting authorities on the following

1. The changing emphasis put on literary classics in English classes.
2. Coeds who major in agriculture.
3. Football players' wives.
4. The importance of memorizing dates in history classes.
5. Television's effects on language usage.

V. A survey of the 1,478 birth certificates filed last month in the county recorder's office revealed the following names, among others. Write a story.

GIRLS

Alfreda, Alphonsine, Antoinette, Augusta, April, Baby, Bobby, Charity, Claudia, Christiana, Cora, Eddie, Edie, Ernestine, Evangeline, Eve, Faith, Freddy, Frederica, Gabriella, Georgia, Georgie, Guinevere, Henrietta, Hope, Infant, Jo, Joe, June, Justina, Kathy, Leonora, May, Octavia, Paula, Pauline, Pomona, Prudence, Rachel, Rebecca, Regina, Ruth, Sabina, Sue, Suzy, Urania, Victoria, Virginia, Zenobia. (The names Baby and Infant appeared once.)

Spelling Variations

    Aileen, Eileen, Ayleen
    Annabel, Annabelle, Anna Belle
    Catharine, Catherine, Katherine, Kathrine, Kathryn
    Eleanor, Elinor, Eleanora, Ellinor
    Gladis, Gladys
    Grace, Grayce
    Harriet, Harriett, Harriette
    Margaret, Margarette
    Marguerite, Marguerita
    Valerie, Valery

BOYS

Aaron, Abel, Abraham, Adam, Al, Albert, Art, Arthur, Ben, Benjamin, Bert, Berton, Bill, Bob, Bud, Burton, Carl, Charles, Carlos, Carlton, Dan, Daniel, Dave, David, Dennis, Denny, Eddie, Edward, Everett, Ezekiel, Francis, Frank, Harry, Henry, Jacob, James, Jim, Jimmy, Job, Jonah, Joshua, Karl, Karlis, Lanny, Lloyd, Myron, Oscar, Otto, Paul, Peder, Pedro, Peter, Richard, Rickey, Rickie, Robert, Ronald, Ronnie, Sam, Samuel, Tom, Thomas, Victor, Ward, Walter, Wilfred, William.

Chapter 7

THE ORGANIZATION OF THE NEWS STORY

*The path which good order prescribes
is the direct one, even though it has
windings.   —Schiller*

The veteran reporter has a quick answer to the question: How should a news story be organized?

Present the facts, he will say, in the order of their importance—the more significant ones first, of course.

Not a few textbooks illustrate this rule of organization through the use of an inverted triangle—the widest space at the top signifying the breadth of importance and the gradually dwindling space in descent indicating diminishing importance.

This explanation of the organization of a news story is fundamental and is helpful as far as it goes, but it is far from adequate for the complex news story.

Simple Organization

The facts in a simpler type of news story are usually presented in the order of their relative importance, as in this sample:

> John Doe, 56, of 4998 Lansing Ave., was sentenced today by Municipal Judge Carl Freeman to serve 40 days in the County Industrial Road Camp for drunk driving.
>
> Doe, who was placed on three years probation, was cited Oct. 24 at Cherry and East Avenues.
>
> Richard Roe, 30, of 2660 Placer Ave., Easton, pleaded guilty to a drunk driving charge. He will be sentenced Jan. 20. He was arrested Nov. 13 at Maple and Lombard Avenues.
>
> James Blow, 28, of 7643 Pine Ave., was fined $300 and placed on 90 days probation for failing to heed a stop sign at Main and O Streets Sept. 30. The charge was a reduction from a drunk driving charge.
>
> Mary Dokes, 47, of 6909 Alexander Ave., was fined $200 and placed on 90 days probation for reckless driving. The charge was a reduction from a drunk driving charge resulting when her car hit a parked automobile at Oakdale and R Streets Aug. 20.

For the lead, the writer selected the person receiving the most severe sentence. Had the four been sentenced for drunk driving, a comprehensive lead, followed by explanatory details, would have been appropriate:

> Four drunk drivers were sentenced today by Municipal Judge Carl Freeman.
>
> John Doe, 56, of 4998 Lansing Ave., and Richard Roe, 30, of 2660 Placer Ave., Easton, were sentenced to 40 days in the County Industrial Road Camp and placed on three years probation. Both had prior convictions.
>
> James Blow, 28, of 7643 Pine Ave., and Mary Dokes, 47, of 6909 Alexander Ave., were sentenced to five days in the County Jail and each fined $150. They were placed on one year probation.
>
> Doe was cited Oct. 24 at Cherry and East Avenues and Roe Nov. 13 at Maple and Lombard Avenues.
>
> Blow was arrested when he failed to heed a stop sign at Main and O Streets Sept. 30. Mrs. Dokes was cited when her car hit a parked automobile at Oakdale and R Streets Aug. 20.

Had all four received the same sentence, the organization would be changed to read:

> Four drunk drivers were sentenced to 90 days in the County Jail today by Municipal Judge Carl Freeman.
>
> All were placed on one year probation.
>
> They are. . . .

The same simple organization is often used in more complicated stories, as is illustrated by a Miami *Herald* story:

> A 51-year-old Latin, despondent over a marital separation, shot and killed his wife and then committed suicide

Friday as they sat in an auto 75 feet off busy Biscayne Boulevard.

The double shooting came shortly after 11 a.m. in the front seat of a Volkswagon sedan parked alongside the partially finished MacArthur terminus of the East-West Expressway near NE 13th Street and the Boulevard.

Miami homicide detectives identified the woman as Mrs. Andrea Nila Rodriquez, 35, of 1000 SW 14th Ave., and her husband as Carlos Rodriguez.

Detectives Tony Fontana and E. F. McDermott said three suicide notes found within the auto, one attached to a safety deposit box key, indicated Rodriguez was "terribly upset" over his wife's refusal to rejoin him.

While the contents of the notes were not revealed, it was learned that Rodriguez mentioned a desire to "die quickly rather than die slowly."

No witnesses heard the shots and the deaths weren't discovered until moments later when nearby workers saw the woman's body as it lay spilled from the auto in view of passing motorists.

A cigaret Mrs. Rodriguez had been smoking when struck by the single shot from her husband's revolver still smoldered between her fingers after she fell face down in the gravel.

It appeared, police said, that Mrs. Rodriguez had been sitting in the car with the door ajar and had been knocked sideways and out of the auto when the bullet struck her in the left breast and passed through her body.

Rodriguez was found slumped behind the steering wheel, an apparently new snub-nosed .38 caliber revolver beside his hip. He had been struck once in the head and died an hour later at a hospital.

An employee of . . . , Rodriquez is believed to have called his wife and asked for the meeting at the off-street site, driving there alone.

(Reprinted from the Miami *Herald*)

Using the simple organization of listing details in the order of their relative significance, the news writer selects for the first part of his story the most important of a series of facts and details it. After that he briefly lists the other facts in order of importance. This method is illustrated in a Seattle *Post-Intelligencer* courthouse story:

One of two men charged with breaking into the Seattle Police Department's processing room and stealing an automobile in the pre-dawn hours of May 21 was found guilty yesterday in Superior Court.

Judge Theodore Turner found John Doe, 25, guilty of second-degree burglary and taking and riding a motor vehicle without the owner's permission.

The second man charged in the case, Richard Roe, 21,

failed to appear for arraignment and a $5,000 bench warrant was issued several months ago.

Deputy Prosecutor David C. Hotchkin charged the two men stole the car from the police station because police were examining it to determine if the engine was stolen property. . . .

In the Superior Court trial two material witnesses, acquaintances of the defendant, repeatedly took the Fifth Amendment against self-incrimination.

Hotchkin then called Justice Court Judge Bill Lewis, a detective, and a former deputy prosecutor to the stand and they recalled the testimony of the two witnesses given in the justice court hearing on the case.

(Reprinted from the Seattle *Post-Intelligencer*)

(*There followed, in order, five court items not related to the preceding case and introduced by the phrase "Other courthouse news"*)

Complicated Stories

The organization of a complicated story is less direct: it does more than merely list details in order of occurrence. Suppose a reporter is faced with the task of combining the remarks of more than one speaker in a single, convention-type story. He is hardly likely to give the remarks of Speaker No. 1 first and those of Speaker No. 2 second, and then end the story with the remarks of Speaker No. 3.

Better reporting would mean that he would devote some paragraphs to the remarks of the one he feels made the most newsworthy speech, but before writing all he intends to use on the best speaker he turns to some of the more poignant comments of the next most important speaker, then moves on to the third speaker. To finish his news story, the reporter then cuts back to the remaining remarks of the three speakers, dealing with them in the same order.

Sometimes, instead of concentrating in the lead on the comments of one speaker, a reporter uses a combination lead, moving on to the speakers in order of importance, and then makes use of cutbacks. A combination lead and cutbacks were used in this San Francisco *Chronicle* story:

> The future role of the proliferating automobile in California brought sharply divergent opinions from recognized authorities in traffic and planning here yesterday.
>
> Addressing an "Engineering for People" Conference arranged at the Hilton Hotel by the American Society of Civil Engineers, Edwin S. Moore, president of the American Automobile Association Foundation for Traffic Safety, hotly defended the increasing use of private automobiles—and more freeways to serve them.

And John E. Burchard, dean of the College of Environmental Design at the University of California, Berkeley, defended with equal insistence the concept that many modes of travel will be needed—from footpath to airplane—with each to be used only where it is reasonably effective.

"This does, among other things, suggest serious limitations on the privately driven automobile tomorrow," Dean Burchard said.

And in addition to this, he noted, is "the more interesting problem of really integrating the various modes of travel so that the movement of the individual from doorstep to destination is always pleasurable as well as efficient."

Cutback

Moore, however, described the automobile as the answer to man's centuries-old dream of moving swiftly, easily and comfortably as his desires or needs dictate.

"Why is it, then, that the automobile, which stands so high on the list of things people want or must have, should also be subjected to blind and bitter attack from some quarters?" he asked.

Some critics of the increasing use of autos, he said, "have services or equipment to sell for a competing form of transportation."

Such critics, Moore added, "would personally profit if their campaign to eliminate or severely restrict the use of motor vehicles were to succeed. Their motives can be easily understood."

Others, he said, simply "long for the good old days and would like to turn back the pages of time," or else have the feeling that California will one day become "one vast concrete pad" of streets, highways, freeways and parking lots.

"While this is a frightening picture," he said, "it is no more accurate than Chicken Little's prediction that the sky was about to fall."

California's 12,500-mile expressway and freeway program, to handle traffic needs of 1980, is now 30 per cent complete, he reported—and although its completed freeways are less than 2 per cent of the total road and street mileage in California, they carry 26 per cent of the traffic.

He also said there's no reason why a highway project cannot be beautiful—and if people want to turn back the clock, he said sharply, they could walk or ride horseback instead of building modern highways.

Cutback

Dean Burchard argued in his morning speech to the conference, however, that in the future "megalopolis" form of urbanized living, "each mode of travel will need to be used only in situations where it is reasonably effective."

He conceded the difficulties of keeping the increasing flood of auto traffic in check but noted "a lot can be done by enforcing laws and declining to try to build ever more freeways and urban parking lots for vehicles whose active use is one or two hours a day."

To design the needed integrated system of various modes of travel, he said, will take "as much political and social ingenuity as it does engineering."
(Reprinted from the San Francisco *Chronicle*)

The use of the cutback is by no means limited to stories of conventions and of meetings where several persons speak. An Atlanta *Constitution* story written by Gene Stephens illustrates the usage in another type of news story:

Two news elements introduced	Gov. Lester Maddox Friday signed into law a bill to increase the motor vehicle inspection fee from $1.25 to $3 and vetoed a proposal to allow cities and counties to levy a 10 per cent tax on mixed drinks.
Another element introduced	Maddox also signed into law a controversial bill which will relieve the Democratic and Republican Parties of the cost of primaries and place the financial burden on the counties and state.
Another element introduced	Among other bills the governor approved Friday was one which, for the first time, will make police training mandatory in Georgia and set up basic standards a person must meet to become a policeman.
Cutback	Under the new motor vehicle inspection Georgians should get a better car checkup each year but they'll have to pay a bigger price when the measure takes effect next Jan. 1.
	With the rate increase comes additional checks of brakes, windshield wipers and exhaust systems.
	The increase in fee was demanded by many of Georgia's more than 1,000 private inspection stations—mostly garages and service stations—which claimed to be losing money at the $1.25 fee.
	But sponsors said they hoped the increased items to inspect and the $3 fee would change the program from "slapping a sticker on the car" to a "true safety check."
	In signing the measure the governor quipped about "making the authors happy." He only smiled when asked why the bill's sponsors weren't present for the signing, as is the case on many measures.
	The bill was sponsored by Reps. Ben Brown, Julian Bond and Gerald Horton of Atlanta, Bobby Hill of Savannah, and Leon Farmer of Athens.
Another cutback	The bill making requirements more stringent for law enforcement officers provides for a mandatory 114-hour training course for all new law enforcement officers hired after July 1. To obtain a job they must have at least a high school education.
	"If a man doesn't know his duties and responsibilities then he is not actually a law enforcement officer," Maddox said.

On hand for the signing was State Safety Director Col. William Burson, who commented during the fight in the legislature for the measure, "This giving a man a badge and calling him a policeman is for the birds." Burson's department will develop and administer the training program.

Another cutback

The primary bill, one of the most controversial of the legislative session, moves the financial burden of financing elections from the political parties to the county and state governments.

It levies a qualification fee on candidates of 5 per cent of the annual salary of the office sought except in legislative races where the fee is a flat $400. Counties get 75 per cent of the fees to help pay the cost of primaries. The rest of the fees go to the parties and if primaries face any additional cost, they are defrayed by taxpayers.

Many Democrats opposed the measure because they felt it would force the majority party to underwrite in part the expenses of primaries for the minority party.

But faced with increasing primary costs themselves and a chance qualifying fees will be ruled unconstitutional, most Democrats voted for the measure.

Another cutback

The mixed drink tax would have meant about $3.5 million to Atlanta if imposed, more than enough money to solve the current money crisis occasioned by the strike of city employees for higher pay.

But Maddox, calling the tax "discriminatory against hotels and motels and restaurants," vetoed the measure, saying the only fair tax to help cities and counties was his proposed statewide sales tax under which $40 million would have gone back to local government—$16 million to Fulton County and Atlanta.

Another news element introduced

The governor, meanwhile, had dire predictions for the cities and counties saying the labor difficulties Atlanta now faces could "snowball" across the state and nation, bringing conditions "worse than the riots of 1966."

"We have to get into real trouble before we do anything," Maddox said. "We don't ever work ahead. This (labor) situation should have been handled 10 years ago."

Another element introduced

Maddox also signed into law a bill to allow local authorities to use speed timing devices in traffic enforcement. He did so only after checking to see that the law requires the devices to be visible from 500 feet away.

"That's the only way you can stop speed traps in some of these cities and counties," Maddox explained.

(Reprinted from the Atlanta *Constitution*)

The principle behind the use of cutbacks is that the detailing of the first news element should continue only to the point at which further details are not as significant as the introduction of the second news element. Minor additional news elements may be introduced after the cutbacks.

The idea is well illustrated in a Fresno (Calif.) *Bee* story written at the time the wreckage of a small plane carrying three persons was found in the Sierra. The plane had been missing 19 days before the wreckage was discovered. Meanwhile, a search plane carrying two men was lost. The story follows.

The bodies of three Fresnans missing since their light plane went down 19 days ago were found today in the wreckage of the plane 10 miles northeast of Edison Lake in the rugged Sierra.

It is assumed all aboard—Fresno State College Prof. Charles H. Cehrs, 47, of 3035 E. Buckingham Way; his wife, Betty, 44, and a family friend, Mrs. Joanne Graves, 42, of 1306 E. Loftus Lane—were killed instantly in the crash.

The plane, whose wreckage was spotted from the air yesterday afternoon on a snow-covered granite ledge near Red and White Mountain, crashed while on its way back to Fresno from the Mammoth Mountain ski resort.

Undersheriff James D. Long said Lt. H. E. Hallam in a plane flying over the area radioed shortly after 11 a.m. today that the bodies were found in the main fuselage of the aircraft by a four-man team flown to the scene this morning in two helicopters.

The recovery team included Chief Deputy Coroner Lt. Walter A. Cook and a Navy medical corpsman. Long said the bodies would probably be returned to Fresno this afternoon.

Second news element introduced

Meanwhile, the search for a second plane missing since Sunday continues. A Thorpe 180, piloted by Russell E. Basye of 4957 E. Nevada Dr., was last heard from about noon Saturday. Basye and Al Kraiss of 4504 E. Olive Ave., also a pilot, were searching for the Cehrs plane.

Reverts to discovery of plane wreckage

Hogan Steele of Fresno, the pilot who spotted the wrecked Cehrs craft, said he "came around Red and White Mountain and was about to turn east" when he saw a reflection in a relatively open area below.

What he saw, he said, was a wing from the silver and cream colored plane, partially buried in snow and about 50 feet from the fuselage. Its numbers were visible.

Although the plane was "in the open" at about the 11,000 foot level, Steele said it was still "very hard" to get a fix on it. He said he was scanning a section just below the intended search area when he noticed the reflection.

"Just looking at the fuselage, it looked like a big black rock."

Asked if that meant the light plane had caught fire, Steele said no.

Steele piloted a Helio Courier, a short takeoff and landing craft which can "hover" at about 55 miles an hour.

He said he was able to fly about 15 feet above the wreck

and noted parkas still in the plane. "There are no trees in the area, just scrub brush," said the pilot. Animal tracks led to and away from the plane.

Steele described the crash site as a "somewhat flat" ledge surrounded by mountains except for a creek bed which runs nearby. He theorized Cehrs' single-engine four-place plane probably climbed above the mountain but encountered severe icing and was forced down. He estimated the plane hit the ground at about a 45-degree angle.

Searchers said the plane was probably covered by two to three feet of snow just three days after it was reported missing April 18, when the trio left the ski resort on a return trip to Fresno.

Searchers said the site, just a mile and a half south of Red and White Mountain, near the Fresno-Mono County line, had been well covered by search planes, "just as much as any other area," but the wreckage apparently was hidden by snow.

The last radio contact was reportedly made over Crowley Lake. The Mariposa Airport heard Cehrs calling but could not reach him. Cehrs had 600 hours of flying time and was known as a cautious pilot.

Reverts to second news element, introduced in sixth paragraph

Basye and Kraiss were searching the Sierra west of Crowley Lake when the pilot radioed an Air Force C97, which was circling overhead to provide communications with Fresno, of its position. Basye reported he had about two and one-half hours of fuel left.

The other missing craft is white with no other markings and is believed down in the same general area as the Cehrs plane. The still-missing plane was home built and constructed for racing, searchers said.

Cuts back to discovery of first plane missing

Aboard the search plane piloted by Steele, an instructor for the Fred Mazzei Flying Service, were. . . .

(Reprinted from the Fresno *Bee*)

Chronology

Chronology, though not generally used as an organizational method for the entire news story, is often resorted to in arranging parts of news stories. In the following Los Angeles *Times* obituary, the spot or timely news is given in the first two paragraphs, the background of the dead priest follows in chronological order in the next four paragraphs, and the article concludes with the survivors.

Requiem Mass for the Rev. Hugh T. Lavery, 75, a Maryknoll missionary who worked among Japanese-Americans in Los Angeles, will be held today at Maryknoll Chapel, Maryknoll, N.Y.

Father Lavery died last Tuesday after a long illness at Fairfield, Conn. Interment will be at Maryknoll cemetery.

He began his work among Japanese-Americans at Seattle in 1932 and came to Los Angeles three years later.

During World War II, when Japanese-Americans were interned at various relocation camps, Father Lavery worked to see that they obtained fair prices for property that had to be sold and stored their personal effects at his mission school.

He was transferred to New Orleans in 1957 and retired in 1961.

In 1966, the Japanese government awarded Father Lavery the Order of the Sacred Treasure, fifth class, for his aid to persons of Japanese descent.

A Washington *Post* story, written by Alfred E. Lewis, on the robbery of the Commerce Department's credit union gives spot news details in the first four paragraphs, follows with a transitional paragraph, and then lists the details in chronological order in the next 12 paragraphs. The story ends with background.

Spot news

Three gunmen robbed the Commerce Department's federal credit union of $128,600 in cash yesterday after using a secret hand signal to gain entry to the office.

Capt. Ralph L. Stines, head of the metropolitan police department's robbery squad, said that sum is the largest cash amount ever taken in a holdup at a Washington financial institution.

The robbery occurred at 8:15 a.m. on the second floor of the block-square Commerce Building, 45 minutes before the credit union was scheduled to open and 15 minutes before most employees arrived for work. The Commerce Building is between 14th, 15th and E Streets, NW, and Constitution Avenue.

The credit union cashes the paychecks of Commerce employees every Thursday.

Transitional paragraph

Police gave the following account of the holdup.

Chronological order starts

Maximino Crespo, 29, an employee, arrived early yesterday and was working in the main office when there was a knock at one of the two glass front doors.

When Crespo went to answer the knock, a man was standing in the corridor with his palm pressed against the translucent glass—a signal that Crespo recognized as a secret means of credit union employees to identify one another.

Crespo opened the locked door slightly and asked the man what he wanted. He replied: "A loan application."

Crespo locked the door, went back to the main office, picked up an application, and returned. But as soon as he opened the door, a second man, holding a sawed-off shotgun, was standing beside the "loan applicant," who had drawn a pistol.

Both pushed past Crespo, and a third man, also armed with a pistol, followed moments later. The man with the shotgun locked the door and asked Crespo to point out the money.

Crespo replied that it was in the safe, that he didn't know the combination, but that the man who did would arrive at any moment.

The three men then forced Crespo to lie face down on the floor behind a counter. They squatted alongside him to wait.

About five minutes later, using a key, credit union manager Clyde M. Cook, 47, arrived with his daughter, Donna Lee, 18, who also works in the office.

The three men jumped up from behind the counter, forced Cook to open the safe, then forced Cook and his daughter to lie on the floor beside Crespo while they emptied the cash into a black attaché case.

As soon as the safe was empty, the Cooks and Crespo were herded into Cook's office, where they were loosely tied to three chairs with a necktie and two belts.

The three men asked whether there was money in any of the drawers, but abandoned that venture when they could not find a key.

They were last seen running down a corridor that leads to any one of a number of exits on 14th or 15th Streets. Minutes later, the Cooks and Crespo freed themselves and called police.

Background begins — Yesterday's robbery was the first of a financial institution in the city this year. There were. . . .

(Reprinted with permission from the Washington *Post*)

There are critics who believe the use of more chronology would improve the introductions to some news stories, as in this sample:

> John Doe, 38, 4420 Spruce Ave., shot his wife to death early this morning after a quarrel which awakened their neighbors.
>
> The neighbors, Mr. and Mrs. Richard Roe, said they were awakened by the raised voices coming from the Does' bedroom at 1:30 a.m. but hesitated to intervene. . . .

The question is whether the opening would have been improved if written:

> Neighbors hesitated to intervene when they were awakened early this morning by a quarrel between Mr. and Mrs. John Doe, 4420 Spruce St.
>
> Five minutes later they heard the shot that killed Mrs. Doe.

The "One, Two, Three" Order

The "One, Two, Three" method of organization is one of the oldest, and few who have engaged in expository writing have not used it at some time or other. It is the method of listing the main points of discourse in first, second and third order. The term "One, Two, Three" is purely arbitrary—the number of main points may vary.

Suppose the mayor of a city suggests a three-point program to eliminate slums. The simplest method of organizing the story would be:

> Mayor Robert Smith today suggested a three-point program to erase the city's slums.

Three subsequent paragraphs would list the points in one, two, three order. The remainder of the story could elaborate each of the points or give supplementary information. An example follows.

> NEW YORK (AP)—Cyrus R. Vance, former U.S. negotiator at the Paris peace talks, has proposed a three-step plan for effecting a peace in Vietnam.
>
> "If it works it would stop the fighting now," Vance told New York University law students at the Loeb Student Center Tuesday.
>
> The first step would be to terminate all search-and-destroy missions and "very substantially" reduce the number of B52 raids.
>
> Second, the United States should call for an immediate "military standstill cease-fire," he said. Both sides would stop fighting and neither would be allowed to take political or military advantage, he said.
>
> Third, Vance said, the United States would announce a timetable for withdrawal of all its troops within "say 12 months" after the cease-fire.
>
> He proposed that a reactivated International Control Commission supervise elections following the withdrawal. The Viet Cong, the Saigon government and the "broad middle spectrum" would participate in the elections, he said.
>
> Vance criticized President Nixon's program of Vietnamization, saying it made a settlement of the war too dependent on what the enemy does. . . .

It is not necessary to use figures or the words "first," "second" and "third" to designate the main points. Dots, dashes and small arrows are often used as substitutes. The method is further illustrated by this Seattle *Post-Intelligencer* story written by Maribeth Morris:

> Washington State nurses—500 strong—voted overwhelmingly yesterday for a series of resolutions on social issues which included:

· Support of sex education programs in the schools;

· Endorsement of an abortion reform referendum on the November ballot;

· Establishment of and participation in family planning services to help check the population growth.

Delegates to the 62nd convention of the State Nurses Association meeting here at Seattle Center also remembered to elect a new president.

She is Mrs. Barbara I. Curtis of Spokane. She said:

"This has got to be the most exciting convention this association has ever held.

"The time has come for nurses to stand up and be counted on issues, no matter how controversial, affecting the health and welfare of society.

"This, the nurses have done. And I'm proud of them."

Of the abortion reform referendum, Mrs. Curtis said:

"As to the moral aspect of abortion, I'm personally against it.

"But I spoke for the referendum because we know that criminal abortion is going on and as long as there are abortions they should be done by doctors."

Convention delegates decried the lack of planned parenthood services and the "high incidence of unwanted pregnancies."

The convention, which for the first time in the association's history has addressed itself to social problems of the day, voted their support to "programs designated to cope with implications of an unchecked population growth."

The resolution, passed by 503 delegates, declares:

"All individuals have the right to plan and space their children in ways consistent with their own creed and mores."

The abortion reform resolution sailed through the House by a two-third majority. One delegate said:

"I couldn't believe it. Even nurses against abortion on religious grounds voted for it."

The nurses pledged both their support of the abortion reform referendum and personal involvement toward its passage in November.

· A resolution supporting sex education in the schools from kindergarten through senior high passed easily.

A fourth resolution, which caught the convention by surprise, called for a smoking ban during all sessions of the House of Delegates.

Some chain smokers shouted:

"What about our civil rights?"

But the weed was booted out, anyway, "in the interest of positive health education."

(Reprinted from the Seattle *Post-Intelligencer*)

The simplicity of the "One, Two, Three" type of organization is exemplified by this Louisville *Courier-Journal* story:

> Jefferson County Judge Todd Hollenbach thought he was going to a closed meeting of the Hospital Council of Metropolitan Louisville yesterday to learn something about the hospital situation in the Louisville area.
>
> When Hollenbach got to the meeting at St. Joseph Infirmary about 15 minutes late, he found about 40 persons, including television and newspaper reporters, waiting for their guest speaker—him.
>
> After apologies for the mixup, the judge volunteered to try to answer some questions "because I am totally unprepared for a speech."
>
> So, through questioning, Hollenbach threw out some ideas he had gathered since he has been in office. These included:
>
> · Louisville General Hospital should be a university almost unequaled in the nation. With greater involvement by the U of L School of Medicine, it should become a health center for a larger area of Kentucky and Southern Indiana.
>
> · The problems of alcoholism and drug abuse will receive a lot of attention by Hollenbach's office "because it's one of our major health problems."
>
> · Yes, Hollenbach would like to see several more neighborhood health centers established in Louisville for persons whose health needs can't be met by overcrowded hospitals.
>
> · No, the judge had no comment on the phasing out of Hazelwood TB Hospital next year unless Gov. Louis B. Nunn vetoes a section of the budget. He said he also hadn't heard a recent proposal that the hospital be divided so that both tuberculosis and mental patients could be treated on a long-term basis.
>
> At the end of the session, Hollenbach promised to "be back next time with statistics and some proposals for health care in this area."
>
> The hospital council is made up of administrators and other hospital officials in this area.
>
> (Reprinted from the Louisville *Courier-Journal*)

Multiple-Story Coverage

The actions taken by city, county and school boards usually cover more than one subject. Many papers lump all the actions into a single story. Other papers use more than one story to detail what took place. One newspaper, for example, ran five stories on a city council meeting. Briefly, the contents of the stories were:

1. The council postponed action on a proposal to liberalize a provision that all city employees must live within the city limits.

2. The group endorsed a requirement that persons using municipal buses must have the exact change.

3. The council discussed a recommendation by the city manager that an executive committee be set up to interview candidates for the job of personnel director.

4. After voting to rescind a policy that members of city boards and commissions must resign those posts before filing papers for candidacy for elective office, the board was told by legal counsel that the action was meaningless, since an ordinance already had been passed on the matter. The council was told another ordinance, not a resolution, was needed.

5. The council rejected a parking recommendation offered by the city engineer. A transitional paragraph was then used to introduce varied minor actions.

Another newspaper used five wire stories in one issue to detail the actions taken at a session of the United States Supreme Court. The leads will give an idea of the content of the stories:

> WASHINGTON (AP)—The Supreme Court agreed yesterday to decide whether welfare workers need a search warrant to conduct house-to-house investigations. . . .

> WASHINGTON (AP)—The Supreme Court has agreed to review a case in which an accused Kentucky moonshiner won a reversal of his conviction on a plea that a warrant issued for a search of his premises was based on insufficient information. . . .

> WASHINGTON (AP)—The Supreme Court yesterday declined to become involved in a case involving liability of the American Tobacco Co. in the death of a cigarette smoker of lung cancer. . . .

> WASHINGTON (AP)—The Supreme Court rejected yesterday appeals by eight Roman Catholic activists convicted of burning Selective Service files in an antiwar protest in Cantonsville, Md., in 1968. . . .

> New York Times News Service
> WASHINGTON—The Supreme Court took the following actions yesterday:
> Let stand a ruling. . . .

One of the stories contained three paragraphs and two others were relatively short. The last one covered minor actions.

One of the advantages of multiple-story coverage is that it eliminates the need for the reader to wade through a lot of gray type. Another is that, by separating items, each can be given the relative play it deserves.

It should be noted that news story organization is affected by the philosophy and size of the newspaper. Some editors prefer to use relatively short stories but more of them. Others must hold down the length of stories because of space limitations. The organization can be influenced accordingly.

Transitional Words

Nothing is more annoying to a reader than to become confused about where he is at any point in a story. It is up to a writer to so direct his reader that he does not get lost but knows where he is going. Adequate transition should be used with cutbacks.

There are ample transitional words and phrases to help the reporter to maintain continuity. Here are some of the most common:

Above	Finally	Otherwise
Accordingly	Further	Similarly
After	Furthermore	Since
Afterward(s)	Hence	Soon
Again	Henceforth	Still
Albeit	However	Subsequently
Also	Later	Then
And	Lest	Therefore
Another	Likewise	Thus
Before	Meanwhile	Too
Behind	Moreover	Underneath
Besides	Nearby	Until
But	Nevertheless	Wherefore
Concerning	Next	Whereupon
Consequently	Notwithstanding	Within
Correspondingly		

Transitional phrases, too, can be put to work effectively at times when a single word is inadequate:

Adjacent to
Along the way
Aside from
As a consequence (*Consequently* is shorter)
At the same time (*Meanwhile* is shorter)
Beyond this (that)
In accordance with (*Accordingly* is shorter)
In addition
In as much as
In so far as

In like manner (*Similarly* is shorter)
In the meantime (*Meanwhile* is shorter)
For example
For instance
For this (that) reason
For want of
On the one hand
On the other hand
The result was
Turning to

At times a transitional sentence may be needed to make clear to the reader where he is going:

The attorney then turned to the jury.

Jones switched his remarks from the tax bill to attack his opponents.

Transitional devices should never be used when they are not needed. Used superfluously, they add only verbosity to a story.

EXERCISES

I. Questions for Discussion
1. What are the advantages and limitations of the simple news story organization?
2. What precautions should be taken when cutbacks are used?
3. Do you agree with the critics who say not enough chronology is used in organizing news stories?
4. What are the advantages of multiple-story coverage of some types of meetings over single-story coverage?
5. Does the number of facts in or the length of a news story affect the organization?

II. Comment on the organizations of the following stories

FORT MYERS—Lee County Bank President Joe Ansley yesterday confirmed that $100,000 his bank sent through the mail last January is missing.

The money reportedly was in a bag which has turned up in Atlanta, Ga.

The shipment was meant for the Federal Reserve Bank in Jacksonville. The money was replaced by an insurer last month, Ansley said.

Postal inspectors have been quietly investigating.

Meanwhile, in Tampa, postal authorities refused any comment to questions about the money. In Atlanta a postal spokesman said a statement about the loss will be made later.

The shipment, made Jan. 23, was taken by security guards to the Fort Myers post office. But the money never arrived in Jacksonville, Ansley said.

Law enforcement and postal authorities were notified immediately, he said.

Ansley said shipment through the mail is "normal procedure" used in shipping to the Federal Reserve when there is "too much cash" on hand and to turn in mutilated, or worn, money. He said he did not know the nature of the Jan. 23 shipment. (Tampa *Tribune*)

BY SUSAN MILLER

Dade banker Shepard Broad will finance construction of 200 units of low-rent housing for Miami Beach if the city will promise to appoint a "nonpolitical" board to administer the project, Beach Councilman Norman Ciment said Wednesday.

Ciment told the council that Broad, head of the American Savings and Loan Association of Miami Beach and Mayor of Bay Harbor Island, had pledged a bank loan to cover the construction costs.

The housing would be build above two city-owned South Beach parking lots. In November, voters authorized the city to lease the air rights over the lots for the specific purpose of erecting low-cost rental units.

Broad's only stipulation would be that the council appoint a five-member nonpolitical board of top civic and religious leaders "to ensure a harmonious administration" of the project, Ciment added.

The banker also requested that the project be rented on a strictly nonprofit basis and only to the extremely needy, the councilman continued.

At Ciment's request, full council discussion of Broad's offer is set for the April 15 meeting.

In other business, the council:

· Rescheduled a public hearing on the city's April 23 legalized casino gambling referendum for 10 a.m. April 9 in the Cypress Room of the Beach Convention Hall.

· Authorized City Manager Clifford W. O'Key to get cost estimates for a new appraisal of all the artworks in the Bass Museum and for city insurance on the collection.

· Denied an application from property owners on the west side of Trouville Esplanade from 71st Street to the Normandy Canal to rezone their nine lots from single-family to multiple-family use. (Miami *Herald*)

BY TIM HOLLAND

Walter R. Greene began working in government while he was a student at Eastern High School.

"I worked with my dad, who was a constable for the Common Pleas Court," Greene said. "It was the only office a black man could get elected to in the 1930s."

Ten days ago, Mayor-elect Roman S. Gribbs asked Greene to serve in the top job on the new mayor's staff.

"I said 'yes.' It was just that simple," said the new special assistant to the mayor.

In a press conference Wednesday to announce Greene's appointment, Gribbs told reporters, "He'll do everything I have to do but don't have time to do personally.

"Like most young fellows, I'm sure. . . ."

As a constable, Walter R. Greene Sr. was responsible for serving process papers on parties to law suits and enforcing writs of the court.

"I was his chauffeur and I did a lot of his paperwork," Greene said.

In 1936, his father got him a $150-a-month job as deputy clerk in the Circuit Court commissioners' office. "I've been with nothing but government since then," he said. . . .

During President Kennedy's administration, Greene was one of the first nine persons to join the contract compliance division of the Defense Department.

From his Detroit headquarters, Greene reviewed defense contracts. . . .

Shortly after, Greene joined Gov. George Romney's administration. As deputy director of the Civil Rights Commission, Greene brought his employment opportunity views to bear on firms doing business with the state of Michigan. . . . (Detroit *Free Press*)

BY DAN L. THRAPP
TIMES RELIGIOUS EDITOR

The environmental crisis has given theologians "a great new opportunity and a heavy responsibility," the dean of a Washington, D.C., seminary told a Theology of Survival convention Wednesday at Claremont.

Dr. L. Harold DeWolf, of Wesley Theological Seminary, said the new theology would require "hard metaphysical, as well as ethical and scientific work."

More than 200 attended the daylong session at the First Methodist Church.

Theologians around the world are running a crash program for formulating a "theology," or at least a fresh ethical base, to correct an impression of man and nature that had its origin in the Old Testament. By affirming that God gave man "dominion" over the earth and its creatures, the Bible has been widely interpreted as giving him the right to plunder and destroy nature.

This has reached the point, speakers pointed out, where it may mean the quick demise of the human species itself, if not corrected.

Dr. John B. Cobb Jr., Ingraham professor of theology at Claremont, was the guiding force of the conference and delivered a keynote address.

"Churches have the responsibility of arousing public support for needed action, even when it goes deeply against the grain established by habit and custom," he said.

Dr. Cobb noted that the type of change needed for this crisis differs from that necessary to meet civil rights and other demands, for the latter are directly in the mainstream of Christian concerns, while the environmental crisis implies that the ideals themselves of the faith have been at fault. . . .

Dr. Robert T. Voelkel, professor of religion at Pomona College, brought a word of dissent, however.

"If it comes to a question of beauty or survival, most would opt for survival," he said.

"Man will care for the subhuman world sufficiently to heal it," said Dr. Cobb, "and to adjust himself to its needs only if he views it as having some claim upon him, some intrinsic right to exist and to prosper."

He said the proper course for the future was not to attempt to reverse history toward a simpler life. . . .

Dr. DeWolf noted that a federal task force about a decade ago decided that if man continued to use up his environment as he has, the human species would become extinct in about 200 years, but if it surmounts the growing crisis, the species might "continue development almost indefinitely, perhaps for periods on the order of hundreds of millions of years. . . ." (Los Angeles *Times*)

III. Assignments

1. Find examples in your local newspaper of cutbacks used in news stories.
2. Find examples in your local newspaper of stories you think could have been improved by the use of more chronology. Rewrite one of the stories to prove your point.
3. Cover a meeting on your campus at which several persons speak.

IV. Write a story based on the following facts

The county board of supervisors, at a meeting last night, granted the following zoning change requests:

R-6 apartment to R-7 for the area bordered by Seventh and Ninth Streets and Maple and Cortney Avenues.

R-7 apartment to C-2 commercial for a tract on the south side of Blaine Avenue between 14th and 16th Streets.

R-6 apartment to C-1 commercial for four lots at Cornelius and Maurine Avenues.

R-6 apartment to R-8 apartment for a tract at West and Curtis Avenues.

It denied a request to change from R-5 residential to C-1 commercial a tract at Porter and Bowe Avenues. Supervisor John Ralston, in whose ward the tract is located, fought this particular change. "The people out there don't want it," he exclaimed.

All five requests were opposed by the county planning commission.

Chapter 8

TYPES OF JOURNALISTIC LITERATURE

Of all those arts in which the wise excel,
Nature's chief masterpiece is writing well.
　　　　　　　　　　　—John Sheffield

The most common types of articles found in newspapers are news stories, features, interpretative pieces, human interest stories, editorials and columns. It is essential that the beginning journalist learn to distinguish among them.

Journalism professors often get editorials from their students instead of news stories, and columns instead of feature articles. Nor is it uncommon for a student to attempt to make a feature story out of what should be a news story.

The News Story

The distinguishing characteristics of the news story are immediacy, factuality and objectivity. The primary purpose of this type of story is to provide timely information of interest and significance to the reader. Usually the news story tells what happened or took place.

Note the emphasis on facts in the following example:

118   Reportorial Writing

BURBANK (UPI)—A $2 million flash fire Sunday destroyed the main building and control tower at Lockheed Air Terminal, longtime headquarters for the Flying Tigers line and other airlines.

Firemen battled for more than two hours to quell the fire, which broke out in the kitchen of a second-floor restaurant, the Sky Room. Authorities indicated hot grease caused the blaze.

About 150 persons, including Federal Aviation Agency personnel controlling takeoffs and landings from the tower, were evacuated. No injuries were reported.

Smoke and flames from the fire were visible for miles in the San Fernando Valley and attracted about 1,000 sightseers.

Some planes landed while firemen fought the flames, but departures were canceled.

Some flights were diverted to nearby Van Nuys Airport or to Los Angeles International Airport. Air traffic was controlled from a ground mobile unit after the tower was consumed by flames.

Additional electronic gear was rushed to the site so normal operations could be resumed today, spokesmen said.

About one-third of the $2 million loss involved elaborate electronic gear in the control tower, according to Louis W. Wulfekuhler, terminal president.

Airlines using the facility, which opened in 1930, included Pacific Southwest Air Lines and Pacific Air Lines, Inc.

At one time, the terminal handled as many as 1.3 million passengers a year as the center of Southern California's air traffic. But in 1946, four major airlines switched to the then new Los Angeles International Airport.

The Burbank facility, which has only a 6,900-foot runway, today serves only smaller jet planes and propeller-driven aircraft.

But private and commercial planes using the terminal have made it one of the nation's busiest airports. It served some 400,000 persons last year.

The largest privately owned airport in the country, Lockheed Air terminal is a subsidiary of the Lockheed Aircraft Corp.

The story tells what happened, relates some of the effects, and gives the history of the airport. In no way does it express the opinion of the reporter.

Feature Articles

The news story deals with bare facts. The feature article, too, deals with facts but makes use of a different organization and presentation. The feature article has more of a tendency to elaborate on the news.

There are various types of feature stories, but the treatment at this point will be general.

If the following Louisville *Courier-Journal* feature article by Joe Ward had been written as a news story it would have merited but two or three paragraphs.

> Roy Fleischman is a "reactionary" where automobile bumpers are concerned.
>
> He contends today's bumpers are puny and weak, and he yearns for a return to the pre-World War II days he considers the golden age of bumpers.
>
> Fleischman has reason for concern. As manager of a fleet of 75 B-Line taxicabs in Louisville, he has a lot of bumpers to worry about.
>
> As a matter of fact, it's not only the bumpers but the entire design of today's cars that gets Fleischman's goat. He's been complaining for a number of years that Detroit no longer "makes cars for people."
>
> But it was bumpers—gone too much to "chrome and gingerbread"—that pushed him beyond the toleration point two years ago and caused him to put his money where his mouth is.
>
> He called all 75 cabs back into the Louisville shop and equipped them with special rubber impact bumpers filled with water. He says it cost him about $140 a cab—that comes to a total of about $11,200—but he's been "very happy" with the results.
>
> The new bumpers project six inches out from the cab—he says Detroit bumpers are too close to flush. If a cab hits something, 15 pressure caps pop off, releasing the water and absorbing the impact. (In cold weather, the bumpers contain anti-freeze.)
>
> Fleischman says the bumpers have almost eliminated damage on minor collisions and have cut costs down considerably on major ones.
>
> But Fleischman is still mad at Detroit. The bumpers produced just after the war could be used with only minor reinforcement, he reminisces, and the "pre-war stuff" required no shoring up at all.
>
> Fleischman once offered the Chrysler Corp. "today's price" for a fleet of "brand-new 1935 cars" for use as cabs. But they didn't take him up on it.
>
> "I'm just an old conservative reactionary," Fleischman says.
>
> (Reprinted from the Louisville *Courier-Journal*)

The writer of the foregoing story elaborated on the facts—he went into detail about Fleischman's reactions to newer cars and their bumpers and about the cab company manager's attitude toward Detroit's car manufacturers.

The feature may be light and breezy or it may deal seriously with a significant subject.

Radio and television have had their impact on printed journalism. The days of the scoop and the extra are gone. Although spot news is still important to newspapers, more and more attention and space are devoted to following up the news with feature stories dealing with broad social problems—health, education, slums, poverty, crime, narcotics and racial oppression.

Words and pictures on television are momentary, but the printed page permits a person to read at his own speed—to study difficult subjects as he chooses.

Neither radio nor television has the time to present news with the thoroughness that newspapers do. It is true that television has made effective use of documentaries—films concentrating on social conditions —but even these do not go into the detail that newspaper articles do. The following Chicago *Sun-Times* article by Joel Havemann, for example, does not rely upon the overt but takes the reader behind the news scenes.

> The Detroit public school system is so broke that it has stopped repairing many of its school buildings.
>
> In Philadelphia, all school administrators down to assistant principal took pay cuts last month.
>
> Chicago is not the only big city that is fighting a losing battle to get enough money to run its schools. All over the country, urban educators are struggling to get more help from rebelling taxpayers, conservative state legislatures and the federal government.
>
> A novel idea has been suggested to assist Detroit schools —a proposal that the state assume full responsibility to raise money to run the schools. But the proposal has little chance of acceptance, and it probably would not provide enough funds anyway.
>
> It is Detroit that seems to have the most unmanageable money problems. Although the school board adopted a budget with a $16 million deficit last month, it still had to put off about $25 million in spending this school year.
>
> The board is spending only $4 million for permanent building repairs, instead of the $12 million it needs.
>
> "This is going to catch up with us all at once," says one school observer. "When it does, the schools are just going to fall apart."
>
> Among other economies, the board did not hire new teachers to fill the positions of about 200 teachers who left the system last summer.
>
> Philadelphia's recent $4 million budget cut was the third in the last 18 months, increasing the total reductions to $12 million. The board faces another cut on July 1.
>
> The salaries of the top 20 administrators were cut by 5

per cent, and all other administrators took a 2½-per cent reduction. In addition, the board reduced its after-school program, eliminated 22 school bus routes and cut back on purchases of classroom supplies.

"These cuts have opened a vein from which will ooze the life blood of our system," declared one board member.

Philadelphia faces another problem that has plagued Chicago. The board has been unable to sell construction bonds within the 7 per cent interest limit imposed by the state legislature.

In New York, the problem is not a conservative downstate legislature, but a conservative upstate legislature. New York Mayor John V. Lindsay is constantly condemning the legislature and Gov. Nelson A. Rockefeller for failing to support the city's schools.

New York spends the most on education of all the big cities—$971 a pupil in 1968–69, compared to $809 in Chicago. New York teachers soon will be the best paid among big city school systems, with beginning teachers getting $9,400 a year in 1971, compared to $8,400 in Chicago now.

New York schools rely on the city government for their money, because there is no local property tax for the schools. Last summer Mayor Lindsay announced that the schools would get $86 million less than they needed to continue all programs through 1969–70.

What happened then was a replay of the annual crisis in Chicago.

Pleading for more funds, the school board announced that 4,400 teaching positions would have to be cut and class size would go up by two pupils a room. The board threatened to move full steam ahead until the money ran out and then close the schools a month early.

The board was bailed out by a combination of increased state aid, reforms in the administrative offices and revised calculations of federal aid and certain expenses.

Now the board is preparing to go through the same old crisis again. It needs $281 million more next year just to meet all mandatory expenses and avoid cutbacks.

If big-city schools need more funds each year just to stay even, they need a lot more money to get better. Innovation is expensive, and nobody ever said the schools are good enough as they are.

Morgan Community School in Washington, D.C.—a successful experiment in community control and permissive classroom organization—spends about 60 per cent more than an average elementary school. Most of the extra money pays for two teacher aides in most classrooms.

Philadelphia's Mantua Mini-School, a similar kind of experiment, spends about $1,100 a pupil, compared to the citywide average of $700 for junior high schools. Mantua has 11 teachers so its 130 pupils can get individual instruction.

The Intensive Learning Center, another Philadelphia experiment in individualized instruction, costs about $1,500 a pupil. The Career Development Center, where trade unionists teach vocational students, spends about $1,300 a year on each student.

New York's compensatory education programs—more teachers, more classroom materials, more field trips—are costly. The College-Bound program, which prepares high-risk, poverty-area students for college, costs about $2,000 a student—twice as much as the ordinary high school.

Decentralization also costs money. New York plans to spend $25,000 for the headquarters of each of its 30 decentralized school districts next year, for a total of $750,000 annually.

Only Detroit, where the school board sued the State of Michigan two years ago for more aid to education, has taken any unusual steps to try to solve its financial problems.

The Detroit suit notes that the city spends less money per pupil than many suburban school districts. It argues that the city, with large numbers of disadvantaged children, actually needs more money per pupil to provide an equal education.

The suit is still in Circuit Court.

Meanwhile, Michigan Gov. William G. Milliken proposed last year that a state property tax replace the local property tax as the primary source of revenue for the state's public schools. In distributing school aid, the state could make sure that Detroit got its fair share.

The Milliken plan also calls for state aid to private schools. The controversial package got nowhere in the 1969 state legislature.

Observers give the state property tax no chance in the legislature if it is tied to private school aid, and little chance if it stands by itself.

Even if the statewide property tax and school aid distribution become law, Detroit probably would not get enough extra money to solve its problems.

"The federal government will finally have to step in and provide more than half of all school aid," says Detroit Schools Supt. Norman Drachler. "Otherwise we're going to have a revolution in this land."

(Reprinted with permission from the Chicago *Sun-Times*)

The fact that the preceding article was part of a series on big-city school problems gives some idea of the depth into which the newspaper went in treating one of today's difficult situations, school finance. The article, though timely, is not based on spot news—immediacy—but the news story usually is. News stories would have been written at the time the Detroit board brought suit against the state and at the time Gov. Milliken's proposal was made.

The following Miami *Herald* article written by Carolyn Jay Wright further exemplifies the detail with which some subjects are treated.

The two old beige barrack buildings stand side by side. Isolated in a corner of the Opa-locka Airport, they squat in front of an ancient red-and-white water tower.

They are military remnants of World War II, and they are beginning to show signs of aging. Paint is peeling from the top. A few screens are gone. A vacant lot is just next door.

But the anonymous square structures are surprisingly deceptive.

Inside the chain link fence that surrounds the buildings all sorts of revolutionary activities are going on and 207 young lives are being dramatically altered.

Formally known as the Junior High Opportunity Center, the barracks actually are classrooms for Dade County's most disruptive junior high school students.

The 12- to 16-year-old boys in the all-male student body are there because their neighborhood schools and teachers gave up on them.

Guilty of offenses that range from fighting and truancy to antagonistic classroom behavior, the boys were recommended to the center by their principals or guidance counselors.

Recommendation, however, does not mean mandatory attendance. Each student must want and volunteer to transfer to the center.

"I tell each one of them that I don't want them here unless they want to be here," said Donald Wilson, the center's principal. "If it were a mandatory thing they would enter with a negative attitude and we couldn't do anything with them anyway."

Most of the boys are anxious to attend the center. They may not fully comprehend that they are guinea pigs in an exeriment in local education but they do know that they will be part of something different.

Many of them are like Mike. A tall, long-haired, blond boy, he was constantly getting "ripped off" by the teachers at Carol City Junior High.

He transferred to Norland Junior High School, but before the school year was complete his parents were divorced, he was put into the custody of his mother and he was faced with returning to the alma mater where he had so much trouble.

But he had heard about the center from David, a friend of his and a pupil at the institution. Monday, Mike and his mother were in Wilson's office, seeking a transfer.

"David told me it was good," said the gangly, growing young boy as he puffed on a cigaret.

"David told me you were allowed to smoke before and after school and at lunch. I was always getting ripped off about that at Carol City."

Towering over his mother, a thin, red-haired, sincere woman, nervous and obviously worried about her son, Mike suddenly turned serious and said, "I came because I'm tired of trouble. I want to stay out of trouble and I want to learn a trade."

"Get on the bus tomorrow with David," Wilson said. "We'll talk later."

Mike, like so many other students before him, probably will find that for the first time in his life he will look forward to going to school.

The reason for the change in attitude is a system and philosophy of education called behavior modification.

Simply explained, behavior modification is based on teacher understanding and positive reinforcement of desirable social behavior. Instead of punishing a student for doing something wrong, the faculty and administration make a particular point to encourage good behavior.

A system, established and observed by the teachers, gives each student points for doing what he is supposed to—preparing his lessons, remaining quiet and attentive in class and showing behavior "above and beyond the call" of classroom duty.

With these points, the students buy free time to pursue their own vocational pleasures or amass credits toward special outings, such as the one they took Tuesday to Haulover Beach.

Included in the students' daily schedule is a study hall hour that is purposely kept dull and uninteresting. Called "negative reinforcement" by Wilson, this time is so meaningless that the child immediately seeks to escape it.

But the only way he may be excused from the class is to "buy out" of it with the good behavior points he has earned in his academic classes. Thus good behavior is encouraged by making bad behavior an empty vacuum.

Concurrently, the study hall is used to punish misbehavior. Wilson, who will use the paddle but does so infrequently, prefers to sentence a student to two or three hours of study hall per day as punishment.

Also helping to encourage good behavior and foster the point system is a variety of vocational and physical educational activities.

The buildings may be just barracks and other facilities often improvised, but the school has the good fortune to be just across a baseball field from a North Dade County park, which is equipped with tennis and basketball courts, swimming pool and, of course, the baseball field.

An agreement between park personnel and school officials permits the 207 young boys, many of whom are underprivileged, to splash about in the blue green waters of the old, and formerly exclusive, officers' swimming pool on the wartime base.

Surrounded by lush green grass and tall thick shrubs, the pool area is just next door to a high-rising mound of earth upon which sits the crumbling structure that once was the enlisted men's pool.

The site had been boarded up and long since abandoned until the students decided they would renovate the old building to serve as a combination band area and rehearsal hall for their "Salt and Pepper Blues Band."

The band, which took its name from its integrated make-up, is a highlight of the school. Beating out soul, rhythm and blues and astonishingly good renditions of popular tunes, it has two lead singers. . . .

It also has a personable young band instructor, Clyde Preston, who quietly and with a mild manner puts the boys through their paces and inspires them on to bigger and better things—like the professionalism that rates them $75 for each local performance.

Preston and the point system have paid off for one band student.

A husky and hip young black boy, he was recommended to the center because he preferred hanging around poolhalls in the Central Negro District to going to school.

But once at the center, he developed an interest in music, soon became hooked on "grooving" with the band and now rarely misses school or a practice session.

The only thing he probably does miss is girls. While Wilson and the teachers thank their lucky stars the center isn't coeducational (they feel their problems would be magnified), several of the boys expressed the same sentiment as Larry. . . .

"I don't like it. There ain't no girls. If there were girls I'd like it here. Everything else is OK."

The center, along with its educational experiment, encourages community participation in everything it does. There is not a formal Parent Teacher Association because the boys are drawn from widely different sociological and geographical areas in the three closest school districts—North Central, Northwest and South Central.

But there still is community "involvement," Wilson said.

The North Dade area carpenter, plumber and electrical unions volunteered the labor needed to renovate the bandroom, a woman volunteer donated an expensive partition used to divide the science class from the art class, lumber companies donate the wood used in the shop, a north Miami music store donated band instruments and several service clubs donated the darkroom's photography equipment.

This activity is in spite of the fact that Wilson has purposely tried to keep his center under wraps since its opening in December, 1968. He feared that too much publicity and public awareness might harm rather than help his program in its initial stages.

Referring to the donations he also said that the school was not "poormouthing" and could probably get all it needed from the School Board by just asking but that it simply was the philosophy of the center to do everything it could itself.

Like the curriculum and the discipline, the spirit of volunteerism is both uncommon and successful.

According to Wilson and the school psychologist, Michael Stokels, only "about five to 10" of the more than 200 boys fail to rehabilitate themselves.

(Reprinted from the Miami *Herald*)

The feature article is more dramatic than the average news story—it makes more use of incidents, examples, anecdotes, particulars and details.

Interpretation

The news story tells what occurs, the feature story expands on what is told in news stories, and both add to the reader's store of knowledge, but the interpretative article explains the news and thus adds to the reader's understanding of it. News and feature stories tell what is taking place, but interpretative articles tell why something has taken place and what the outcome may be.

The purpose of the following *Christian Science Monitor* article by David R. Francis, for example, is to explain a situation.

WASHINGTON—The administration has reversed its economic gears.

The emphasis has changed from slowing down the economy in order to dampen inflation to one of stimulating business in order to prevent further deterioration of economic activity into a serious recession.

"Gradualism" was a favorite description last winter for the antiinflationary policy. Though the word has lost its popularity, it could be applied to the new modestly expansionary policy. The administration does not want to overdo its stimulus to such a degree that the inflationary fires burn brighter again.

Prime reliance for the shift in direction is being placed on monetary policy. The Federal Reserve System's open market committee decided at its meeting Feb. 10 to ease money a little.

Dr. Arthur F. Burns, chairman of the Federal Reserve Board, all but admitted that change in testimony before a congressional committee Wednesday. The 12-man group was divided in February. But at its meeting this month, the open market committee was unanimous in deciding to continue its easier money policy.

On the fiscal side, the administration made what amounts to a gesture of ease by releasing $1.5 billion in construction funds that were frozen last year. But the government does not regard full-scale pump-priming action as necessary.

For one thing, the administration is afraid that Congress might get out of hand and start spending too liberally. President Nixon is still aiming for a budget that is at least nearly in balance.

During earlier recessions the government has usually poured fuel into the economy from both the fiscal and monetary sides.

Administration economists have more faith in the potency of monetary policy than economic advisers to previous presidents had.

The economy has been slowing somewhat more rapidly than administration economists expected.

In January, when the Council of Economic Advisers made its economic report, it predicted that gross national product—the value of all goods and services produced in the nation—would be in the $980 to $990 billion range this year. Currently administration economists are thinking the figure will more likely lie at the bottom of that range.

This means that unemployment may run higher than the administration has anticipated.

Dr. Paul W. McCracken, President Nixon's top economic adviser, had earlier told Congress that unemployment this year would average 4.3 percent. At a press conference this week he modified that by referring to the "4.3 percent zone."

With an election coming up, the political implications of high unemployment are obvious.

Thus the administration was keenly pushing this week for implementation of its more liberal unemployment insurance scheme immediately. It was disappointed Thursday when the Senate Finance Committee decided to follow the House and make the new rules effective in January, 1972. The administration will seek to reverse the vote on the floor of the Senate.

With a more generous unemployment scheme, the burden of the unemployed would be reduced.

Administration economists have been speaking of an upturn in the economy in the second half, implying around July. Now some of them speak of the upturn coming in the fall. That might still be in time for the election.

As unemployment rises, it can be expected that the Democrats will attempt to pin the blame on the Republican administration. It will be a curious effort because most "Democrat" economists were as bullish, if not more bullish, than Dr. McCracken in their economic forecasts. Indeed, Dr. Walter W. Heller, chairman of the Council of Economic Advisers under President Kennedy, counseled retention of the income-tax surcharge, though primarily for revenue purposes.

Some prominent Democratic economists urged the Federal Reserve Board to ease its tight-money policy as far back as December. Dr. James Tobin of Yale University and Dr. Paul A. Samuelson of Massachusetts Institute of Technology were two prominent economists to do so.

However, the administration also began urging the independent central bank to gently reverse gears as early as January. When Dr. Burns was sworn into office, President Nixon broadly hinted that he wanted money more available.

(Reprinted with permission from the *Christian Science Monitor*)

Interpretative articles seek to analyze the news—to put into perspective the bare facts related in news stories. They do not supplement the facts, as feature stories do, but instead explain and thereby give more meaning to those facts.

The New York *Times* regularly runs an interpretative article on politics. Each article is designated as news analysis and is written by a different newsman each day.

Here is an example written by Max Frankel:

WASHINGTON—It is said here of the Cabinet job that President Nixon has now transferred from Robert H. Finch to Elliott L. Richardson that whoever holds it for any length of time is bound to grow in education and to diminish in both health and welfare.

The title itself is formidable: Secretary of Health, Education and Welfare. The Department's acronym around Washington is hardly edifying: HEW. It takes up more space in the phone book than any department except Defense and its three major divisions probably have less to do with each other even than the Army, Navy and Air Force at the Pentagon.

Though only 17 years old, HEW employs 110,000 people and spends more than $50-billion. It houses—and tries to run—the Office of Education, the Environmental Control Administration, the Food and Drug Administration, the National Air Pollution Control Administration, the Health Services and Health Administration, the National Institutes of Health, the Public Health Service, the Social and Rehabilitation Service, the Children's Bureau, the Social Security Administration and much, much more.

Besides administering nearly 300 major Federal programs of services in these fields, the department must design and win support for national strategies to aid and desegregate education, deliver health services and provide financial assistance to the old, the infirm and the poor. Accordingly it must wage perpetual political and budget battles both inside the executive branch and with Congress.

Secretary Finch never pretended to like the job and openly yearned to follow one of his unhappy predecessors, Abraham A. Ribicoff of Connecticut, to the Senate. But George Murphy insisted on running for re-election in California and Mr. Finch, shut out, refused to challenge him directly.

He did not like the administrative burdens at HEW. He did not like the constant tension between loyalty to the demanding bureaucracy below and to the Presidency above. He did not like waging visible battles for the great domestic programs against other arms of the Government and often against the White House itself.

And as an old associate and confidant of Mr. Nixon he cannot have enjoyed the conspicuous loss of so many of those battles—from the early effort to hire Dr. John H. Knowles to manage the health programs to the recent effort to save Leon E. Panetta in his civil rights office.

A personable and sensible kind of political operator, Mr. Finch did not enjoy his reputation as the "house liberal" in the Nixon Administration. But he was responsible for liberal programs and accountable to liberal subordinates, clients, constituencies and Congressmen, and he felt obliged to press their claims.

How much he was consumed became physically apparent a month ago after the Cambodia invasion and the shootings at Kent and Jackson and the internal struggle over Mr. Agnew's inflammatory rhetoric. On the very day that several thousand of Mr. Finch's employes wanted him to lead their cause against his own President and to account for Administration policy to them, he drew up with a puzzling numbness in his arm, forcing a brief hospitalization and an extended rest.

So it was probably not too difficult to persuade him to "come home," as Mr. Finch put it, to Mr. Nixon's personal staff of counselors and to his own circle of friendships, forged in the many Nixon campaigns.

Less clear in this first Nixon Cabinet shift, however, are the motives of the President and the other friends of Mr. Finch who arranged it. It may be that they wanted simply to accommodate their ailing associate, to relieve him of distasteful pressures and simultaneously to give new zest to their most troubled department of government.

But the shift may also reflect the feeling by the President that he has neglected the moderate and compassionate elements of his party and that he hopes, after the turmoil of the last month, to obtain a new perspective on many of his policies, foreign as well as domestic. Time alone will tell whether Mr. Nixon wants to feel a new influence and how Mr. Finch might exert it.

Only time will show, also, how Mr. Richardson intends to tame the HEW monster. He is a man of extraordinarily tidy thought, which he expresses with slow deliberation, usually while doodling complicated but clear and neatly balanced forms in the tradition of modern op art.

As Undersecretary of State over the last 16 months, Mr. Richardson amazed much of Washington with his swift mastery of nuclear technology and the issues of arms control, the diplomatic history of the Vietnam negotiations and dozens of other previously unfamiliar subjects. In the process he demonstrated a rare combination of intellectual subtlety and bureaucratic agility. (©1970 by The New York Times Company. Reprinted by permission)

The news of the switch of Robert H. Finch from the HEW post to the president's advisory staff was published ahead of the preceding article. The purpose of the article was not to announce the shifts in positions but to explain them.

The interpretative story, as has been said, should help the reader to understand what has taken place—it puts the news in context—but it should never attempt to influence opinion. It may diagnose a news occurrence, but it should avoid editorializing.

Human Interest Stories

The human interest story, as the name indicates, appeals to the emotions. A dog saves the life of its 9-year-old master, a former film star now makes a living scrubbing floors, an army veteran offers to sell one of his eyes to raise the money to bring his foreign bride-to-be to the United States, a small girl dies after running into a burning house to rescue a doll—these are incidents that stir human emotions.

Here is an old but still appropriate example:

> WILLOUGHBY, Ohio (AP)—Willoughby's lonely "girl in blue" will be remembered by a cemetery visit this Christmas Eve just as she has been for 20 years.
> On Dec. 24, 1933, the girl, who never was identified, threw herself in front of an express train. This year, as they have every year since, townspeople will spread flowers on her grave.
> Wearing a dark blue topcoat, a navy blue skirt, a light blue sweater and a dark blue turban, the girl got off a bus from Cleveland that depression year and took a room in the home of Mrs. Mary Judd.
> Later, she went to the door and wished Mrs. Judd a "merry Christmas." Those were the last words anybody reported hearing her say. Then she walked to the tracks, along sidewalks partially illuminated by Christmas tree lights, and jumped in front of the train.
> Residents, failing to learn her identity despite widespread reports of the tragedy, buried her and marked the grave with a three-foot granite headstone. It read:
> "In memory of the girl in blue, killed by train, unknown but not forgotten, Dec. 24, 1933."

If a human interest story brings a tear to a reader's eye it has been successful. Its purpose is to grip the emotions. The following story offers another example.

> PITTSBURGH (UPI)—"Yes, Linda, a plastic heart does have love in it."
>
> Dr. Michael DeBakey, renowned heart specialist from Houston, Tex., gave this assurance to 7-year-old Linda Griggs of Pittsburgh.
>
> The second grader wrote to DeBakey last week when coal miner Marcel Deruker, in whom a partial plastic heart had been inserted, died suddenly seven days after the operation.
>
> She said, "We are sorry that the man died and hope the next person will live longer." Then she asked, "Does a plastic heart have love in it?"
>
> "A plastic heart does have love in it, a very great deal of love," DeBakey wrote back. "It isn't the kind of love you're thinking of.
>
> "It isn't Mr. Deruker's love. His own heart had that kind of love in it. Your heart and my heart have that kind of love in them.
>
> "The love in the plastic heart is the love of many people who love other people and don't want them to die just because their hearts are not strong enough to keep beating.
>
> "So these people worked all day and often all night to build a heart that will help people live longer. They work hard and they worry.
>
> "If you can think of how much love there would be in hundreds of hearts, then that is how much love there is in a plastic heart."
>
> DeBakey concluded: "When you grow up you will understand how very much love that is."

Pathos is often the strength of a human interest story, but bathos has no place in it.

The Column

Columns, in a sense, defy definition because of the multiplicity of types and purposes. There are columns written for businessmen, for sports fans, for women and for persons interested in travel.

Columns are written on international affairs, on politics, on finance, on health, on fashions, on cooking and on dozens of other subjects. Supposedly, because of background or profession, the columnist is an expert or specialist in the subject or field he writes about.

Columns stressing politics and national affairs began in the 1920s with such writers as Mark Sullivan of the New York *Herald-Tribune* and David Lawrence of the *United States News*. The number has grown through the years and syndicates have given wide distribution to many of them.

Columns dealing with politics, national affairs and world relations often reflect the views of the writers, some of whom have won widespread followings. Among the columnists concentrating on Washington is James Reston of the New York *Times*. One of his columns follows as an example of the political column.

> WASHINGTON—Ever since President Thomas Jefferson announced that Aaron Burr was guilty of treason in the Gen. James Wilkinson conspiracy case (he was later acquitted) presidents of the United States have been in trouble over careless or ill-considered public remarks.
>
> Accordingly, there is nothing particularly new about President Richard Nixon's recent statement that Charles Manson, the gypsy cultist now on trial in California, "was guilty, directly or indirectly, of eight murders without reason."
>
> Like former Atty. Gen. Herbert Brownell, who got in trouble during the Eisenhower administration for passing judgment in the Harry Dexter White case, Nixon merely talked before thinking, and is entitled to a presumption of innocence, which he later granted to Manson.
>
> The incident raises, however, the old question of how to protect the President of the United States in these days of instant news from unintended and potentially damaging blunders during extemporaneous news conferences.
>
> Every president since Herbert Hoover has become increasingly casual or bold about talking to reporters. Hoover insisted on written questions at his news conferences; Franklin Roosevelt banned them at his first press conference, but insisted that his answers be reported in the third person. With the advent of television, news conferences were first taped in advance for release later, but Nixon has insisted on addressing the reporters "live" on TV and without notes.
>
> He is a master of the art and the political advantages are obvious. He conveys the impression of controlling a wide range of complicated subjects and of facing his critics manfully under difficult and often dangerous conditions.
>
> But presidents, like baseball pitchers, don't always hit the mark. Unlike Jefferson, who assured the Congress in writing that Aaron Burr's "guilt is placed beyond question," Nixon merely stumbled into the guilty charge against Manson and then hesitated about setting the record straight.
>
> It is odd that a president, trained in the law, should have violated the elemental presumption of innocence, particularly during a lecture on the majesty of the legal process, but what is even more surprising is why his staff did not protect him in time to keep the blunder from going out on the national television.

Atty. Gen. Mitchell was at his side. He and other members of the President's official family realized what had happened, but either they hesitated to make it clear to the President in time or the President's instructions were not carried out accurately by Ronald L. Ziegler, the White House press secretary.

Accordingly, the correction was not made until four hours later when the presidential plane got to Washington, and even then the big jet was circling Andrew Air Force Base to get the correction in order.

The interesting thing here is that the President's original charge of guilt was not going out on live network television. It was being taped for release later. Thus, the blunder could easily have been corrected before the damage was done. The question, therefore, is whether the staff was alert and confident enough to tell the President what had happened, and if so, why Ziegler came back with a mystifying "clarification."

The relations between a President and his staff are private, and nobody can be quite sure whether Nixon's staff is timid or intimidated. It is certainly intelligent, but in this case something obviously slipped.

Beyond this, it is not quite clear why these presidential news conferences cannot always be taped and checked for bloopers before they are released. After all, even the football games have instant replay, and even congressmen have the right to revise and extend their remarks in the Congressional Record.

The trouble is in catching up with charges after they are made, even when corrected. . . .

(© 1970 by The New York Times Company. Reprinted by permission)

Many columns that deal with national affairs, such as the preceding example, offer explanations of what has been reported in the news, and in this respect they are interpretative. But most of them provide commentary that is far more subjective than would be expected in the typical interpretative article.

Many newspapers have local columnists. The successful ones, depending on how much their columns transcend local news, are inclined to seek syndication.

The Editorial—the Voice of the Newspaper

The editorial differs from the column in that it expresses the views of the newspaper rather than those of the columnist. The views may be those of the publisher or owner, though not a few newspapers make use of consultative procedures.

Many large newspapers and some of the smaller ones have set up editorial councils that meet to determine the policy to be taken on controversial issues and the political candidates to be endorsed. Besides the editorial writers or the chief editorial writer, others who may sit on the council are the publisher, the managing editor, the political reporter and the business manager.

The editorial writer is not confined by the requirements of objectivity —opinion has a valid place in the editorial. One of the patterns of writing an editorial—there are many—is to refer to an item of current news, express opinions, and give reasons for those opinions.

There was a time when argument was the dominant form of discourse used in editorials. This form of discourse can still be found in many editorials, but along with espousing causes numerous newspapers use editorials as a means of explaining and interpreting the news.

The following Atlanta *Constitution* editorial exemplifies this type of journalistic literature:

> The governor of Massachusetts signed a remarkable piece of legislation this week, one already approved by the Massachusetts legislature.
>
> The measure provides that servicemen from Massachusetts may refuse combat duty unless there has been a declaration of war by the U.S. Congress—so, in effect, it means refusing combat duty in Vietnam.
>
> The purpose of the legislation is to force a test, ultimately in the U.S. Supreme Court, of the constitutionality of such a measure.
>
> The real issue is whether the President of the United States can involve this nation in a war—like Vietnam— without a formal declaration of war by the Congress.
>
> Yet, the significance of the proposal goes beyond even this significant issue. Passage of such legislation is simply another indication of the deep unhappiness in this country about our continued involvement in Vietnam. Our involvement has seemed to drift along without purpose . . . without any real achievement to justify the thousands of dead . . . without any indication that the conflict will end soon.
>
> President Nixon has without question tried to wind down the war. He has moved adroitly, in a political sense, to mute criticism of our Vietnam policy. But the Massachusetts legislation should be a clear sign to Mr. Nixon that the deep American discontent about Vietnam is still very much with us. (From the Atlanta *Constitution*)

No attempt was made in the preceding example to be objective—the policy of the newspaper is clearly expressed. It should be noted that the writer referred to a current news event early in the editorial. That event is often referred to as a news peg.

Some Comparisons

The Hartford *Courant* ran two feature articles on the plight of the aged poor in Hartford. The articles were followed by an editorial. The time was during the Christmas season. Here is the second of the two feature articles, written by Kenneth Hooker:

> The plight of the aged in Hartford housing projects takes many forms: An old woman recently complained, "If you have something like a piece of candy they will grab it and run away laughing."
>
> The reference to "they" is often heard as the aged relate their problems with unbridled youth and with the agencies that seem to control the lives of the old.
>
> Of 21 elderly persons interviewed in Hartford, every one expressed fear for personal safety.
>
> "This could be a little paradise for us if we weren't afraid of them," said an old woman at Charter Oak Terrace.
>
> Councilman George Athanson recently said that the "subjective reality of fear" must be dealt with even where circumstances do not wholly justify the fear of the aged.
>
> At Mary Mahoney Village in the North End, the fear of the residents is real. And in other parts of the city where the aged are congregated there is, indeed, a state of justified fear.
>
> The situation at Charter Oak Terrace is indicative of the plight of many of Hartford's aged. Each elderly resident interviewed there had a story of an actual assault upon himself or his neighbor to tell.
>
> "There isn't a week goes by that one of us isn't hurt," said a spokesman for the aged at Charter Oak Terrace. "We're on the edge of the city and deserted. Almost anything goes."
>
> Most of them feel there is little hope. "Once you come here you stay 'till you die," said one of them.
>
> Charter Oak Terrace was built as wartime housing in 1941, and has since come under Hartford Housing Authority control with 265 of its 1,000 units allocated for elderly residents.
>
> Armand Panazza, manager of the project, says that the aged are his best and most peaceful tenants, but nonetheless it is necessary to board the windows of their Golden Age Clubhouse with unpainted sheets of plywood. In the rooms where they meet to play cards and attend art or cooking classes, no sun enters.
>
> An elderly resident standing before the boarded door pointed across the playground to a mammoth pile of rubbish. "They set fire to it the other night just for the deviltry of it," he said.
>
> Panazza says his 15-man maintenance crew never quite catches up.

The overall aspect of Charter Oak Terrace is discouraging: the project is littered with waste and rubble. Just lately, 33 derelict cars were scattered through the lots.

A vigorous old lady said that one of them was hers. She said she used to transport friends about town for relaxation and recreation, but now they're without transportation. "They" destroyed it, bit by bit. "I'll never get it fixed," she said. "I could never afford it."

"It's vicious," said Panazza.

The fear of the aged is fed again and again at Charter Oak. Elderly residents tell of the rape and robbery of a 72-year-old woman, and of the death of a Hartford policeman on the street their apartments overlook.

"Check Day," when they receive their social security payments, brings as much apprehension as relief. "Crime is especially bad since they know our checks come in now. So we're all extra frightened for the next few days," said one aged resident.

Though the aged have been repeatedly warned not to carry cash or pocketbooks, they sometimes find compliance neither possible nor effective. Old women at Charter Oak told of a friend there whose pocket was cut from her coat to get a handful of change one Sunday morning as she was walking to the bakery. Then her young assailant knocked her down and ran away laughing, her friends said. When an elderly person is assaulted, the youths usually threaten worse attacks if the victim calls the police.

Racism is mentioned as one of the causes of the trouble for the elderly residents at Charter Oak. "It's desegregation in reverse," said one man. "When I came here five years ago it was three whites to one black; now it's 75 per cent black and Spanish-speaking. And almost none of them are elderly. So the elderly become the scapegoats of the children," he said.

"We've got black power, they tell us," related an old woman. "They'll push us off the sidewalk right in front of our homes, saying, 'we've got black power.'"

Another said: "All they'll usually do is shout vile language at you. You can learn to live with that."

Elderly persons elsewhere in the city face similar problems. Four residents of Dutch Point Colony interviewed were angry with the management there. On the first day of snow in Hartford when they were interviewed, their apartments were without heat. It is a chronic situation, they said.

A woman there whose immaculate apartment contains only ancient and rickety furniture described how a maintenance man, when asked not to put soiled plumbing fixtures on a cherished rug, replied: "If you weren't such an old lady I'd whop you one." Her concern was wasted. A few days later a pipe in an adjacent apartment broke, and her ancient oriental rug was saturated.

In a private apartment building in Hartford primarily

occupied by the aged, the residents have agreed never to answer the buzzer unless a caller is expected.

"Sure we're scared. Everybody's scared," they said.

A family in another private building said that a broken soil pipe that made their bathroom practically unbearable had gone unrepaired for years because they could not pay a rent increase. The apartment has not been repainted in the 15 years they have lived there, but the landlord still wants to raise the rent. They are applying for a place in a housing project, but the lists are long, they said.

Others of Hartford aged, perhaps as many as 800, according to services performed with the aging director Robert Casstevens, live in downtown hotels and rooming houses, paying up to $100 a month from their small incomes for small, dark rooms.

(Reprinted from the Hartford *Courant*)

No exhortation for change in the situation is explicitly made in the preceding article—the story simply states the plight of the aged—but the following *Courant* editorial urges that changes be effected.

Yes, yes, "Tis the season to be jolly," and doubtless many of us are. But there are people in this city who haven't been jolly for a long time, who certainly aren't now, and who probably won't muster the courage even to smile for quite a while.

They are the elderly poor living in some of Hartford's housing projects. Their plight has been described in two articles printed in The Courant. To the reader, "heartbreaking" is one word that sums up the stories. To the aged inhabitants of Mary Mahoney Village in the North End, and in Charter Oak Terrace, which is southerly, "terrified" is the word that fills the bill in recounting their condition. Let's not split hairs over whether they are subjected to terrorism or simple harassment. On the receiving end it's all the same—the . . . taste of fear is in their mouth day to day.

What frightens them are the uncontrolled youths in their area. Youngsters who snatch a piece of candy from an elderly woman one day, and return the next when Social Security checks are handed out, to rob an old man. Youths who make it necessary for the windows of the Golden Age Clubhouse to be boarded up so old people can play a hand of cards in safety. Youths who trample a few flowers and assault someone week in and out, or set fires or take cars apart piece by piece.

This is the story inhabitant after inhabitant has to tell, and it is told without hope. "Once you come here, you stay until you die."

Can't there be some way to rescue persons from such a pitiful plight? Old age and being poor are burdens enough without fear, harassment, terrorism, or you name it. Naturally, the first thought that comes to mind is more police protection—if, of course, the City can afford, provide and find the manpower. This certainly seems the most urgent, immediate step to be taken. The housing projects have always had some sort of policing, even if only by the management staff. But now this obviously is not sufficient.

However, this probably is not the whole answer. The harassment in local housing projects is part of the urban violence afflicting the whole country. Racism plays into it, as does the gap between young and elderly people. Bad social conditions are certainly at the root of it. Permissiveness on the part of parents is a factor. The problems of violence and crime in the streets, as everyone says, must be attacked on many sides. Except for what more police protection can do, they will go uncured for a long time. So, for a start, more protection has to be found for the elderly poor here. It won't be easy, but it is imperative, and the City must bend its efforts to the task.

(Reprinted from the Hartford *Courant*)

Observe the distinctions among some of the different types of journalistic literature in the following excerpts from a news story, a feature article and an editorial, all of which were run on the same day in the Louisville *Courier-Journal*. All were based on a Kentucky teachers' strike. The first excerpt is from a news story written by Mike McKinney.

The statewide strike by Kentucky schoolteachers moved a step closer to the courts yesterday as some 25,000 teachers remained off the job.

These were the developments:

—In Jefferson County—the state's largest school district—the Board of Education directed Supt. Richard VanHoose to "take whatever action" necessary if teachers refuse to return to work by tomorrow.

The teachers were given until 4 p.m. today to reply to the board's request, but they are expected to continue striking. VanHoose declined to comment on what action he might take. He has said previously, however, that he would seek an injunction if the strike is prolonged.

—In Paducah and McCracken County, where school boards have filed suits seeking temporary injunctions to end the strike by tomorrow, a court hearing is set for 2 p.m. today to consider the Paducah case.

—The president of the Kentucky Education Association said in an interview that the strike would not extend beyond March 20, the day the current state legislative session ends.

—In Frankfort, hundreds of parents and teachers took part in an all-out lobbying effort, urging legislators to take action on such measures as additional revenue for higher teacher salaries and passage of a professional negotiations bill. The legislators told the teachers and their supporters to plead their cases in their hometowns. . . .

—Gov. Louie B. Nunn, ending a period of silence on the current teacher crisis, issued a statement that advised the striking teachers that only the General Assembly can solve their problems.

The governor called the work stoppage a tragedy and said his office is evaluating the situation daily.

The teachers strike began Monday.

Yesterday, the Kentucky Education Association estimated that 118 of the state's 193 school systems, employing more than 25,000 of Kentucky's 33,000 teachers, had canceled classes.

Classes remained open in. . . .

KEA officials last night said they expect the teachers of at least four more school districts to join the strike today. One of those districts was certain. Bullitt County schools, with 279 teachers, will close today as a result of a strike vote Monday. . . .

If the strike were to last until March 20, it would consume four weeks of classes, making it the longest statewide teachers' strike in the nation's history. Florida teachers staged a three-week walkout in early 1968. . . .

Aside from the Bullitt school's closing today, the status of all other schools in the Louisville area is expected to remain unchanged.

The KEA originally asked for an immediate pay increase of at least $1,000 annually for teachers. This was later scaled down to $600 over the biennium when Gov. Nunn included no money in his executive budget proposal for teacher salary increases. . . .

(Reprinted from the Louisville *Courier-Journal*)

The way in which a feature story supplements the news is well illustrated by this article, written by Kathleen Arnold, which accompanied the news story just cited:

The average Kentucky public school teacher earns $7,125.

But one statistic seldom describes everyone. There are 193 school districts in the state, each with its own salary scale. General comparisons are difficult because, even within one district, salaries vary with the individual teacher.

The statistics—as compiled by the state Department of Finance—do show a few broad conclusions:

—The Kentucky teacher with a college degree can earn anywhere from $5,000 to $11,172—depending on his education, his experience and the school district.

—Kentucky ranks 40th among the 50 states in its average teacher salary, $7,125, and well below the national average of $8,551.

—Kentucky pays its teachers less than most of its neighboring states that touch Kentucky; only two, West Virginia and Tennessee, pay a lower average.

While an increase in teachers' pay is only one of four demands being made by the Kentucky Education Association, it's considered to be the key issue in the statewide teachers' strike that began Monday.

The figures in this . . . story reflect current pay scales. New rates enacted by the legislature would start to take effect the next fiscal year, which begins July 1. These new rates are a $200 increase for. . . .

Basically, the salaries for Kentucky's 32,000 public schoolteachers are set by the state's Minimum Foundation Program, the mechanism which distributes school money to guarantee that even poor school districts can provide a certain level of instruction and facilities.

The Minimum Foundation guarantees every public schoolteacher a minimum salary, according to his education and experience. Local school districts may choose to pay their teachers more—so the statewide salary picture is a crazy quilt of different scales in Kentucky's 193 public-school districts.

It's impossible to point to an individual district as being "best" in terms of teacher pay. For the B.A. (Bachelor of Arts) teacher with no experience, the best salary in the state comes in the Beechwood Independent School District in Owen County—$7,200, which is $1,000 more than Jefferson County pays for an equivalent instructor.

But a teacher with his M.A. (Master of Arts) degree and 10 years of experience would be more than $1,000 better off in Jefferson County, where he could earn $9,428, in contrast to Beechwood's $8,400.

The highest possible salary in the state, $11,172, would go to a teacher with a doctor's degree and more than 19 years of experience—paid by both the Owensboro and Daviess County schools.

While there are exceptions, the highest salaries generally are paid in Kentucky's larger cities and the counties around urban areas. It's also generally true that teachers are better paid in the north central part of the state.

For example, 13 county districts start B.A. teachers with no experience at $5,700 or more.

If they were colored in on a map, 10 of the 13 would make up one unbroken area around Louisville and stretching up the Ohio River—Jefferson, Bullitt, Nelson, Spencer, Shelby, Oldham, Trimble, Carroll, Gallatin and Boone.

Only Woodford, Union and Daviess Counties would be isolated on such a map.

In general, teachers tend to be paid a little better if they work for independent school districts instead of county districts, particularly in the upper education ranks and as they accumulate more experience.

Top scale averages $7,900 in independent districts; $7,650 in county districts.

It's a bit easier to point the finger at the "worst" school districts. They're the ones whose salary scales are pegged right at, or just a few dollars above, the Minimum Foundation's requirements, no matter what the teacher's individual qualifications.

Here are parts of the salary scales for some representative school districts in the state. . . .

(Reprinted from the Louisville *Courier-Journal*)

The difference between the news story and the feature presentation should be obvious. The news story deals with the immediacy of events in the teachers' strike. These facts are supplemented by the feature article, which is based on research. The information presented in the feature story is not new, but it is timely.

The rounded out efforts of the newspaper staff come in an editorial. Here is the one from the *Courier-Journal:*

> Kentucky's dramatic teacher strike is effective in terms of the percentage of teachers participating—around 75 per cent—and the number of schools closed. At this point there is no telling how long it will last. Much depends on the response of the legislature. A completely negative response might give legislators some personal satisfaction, but it wouldn't help matters.
>
> The responsible course of action is for the legislative leadership to try to work out, along with the Kentucky Education Association, a realistic compromise.
>
> There are several KEA demands the legislature could meet without appropriating additional state money. Had it shown more interest in these features of the KEA program earlier, the showdown we now have on our hands might have been averted.
>
> The legislature can and should authorize professional negotiations between teachers and school boards over curriculum and working conditions. This is a prime goal of the KEA, and it could prove to be the most significant element in the KEA program.
>
> The legislature can and should lift the ceiling it imposed on local property taxes in 1965. The decision on whether to raise these taxes for the benefit of the schools would then be a home-rule decision. Legislators who are complaining about the pressure being put on them now on the tax issue for schools should be reminded that it was the legislature that intervened to impose the property tax ceiling. In so doing, it guaranteed that the schools would have to turn time and again to the legislature to provide state money for them, when more, not less, support should be coming at the local level.
>
> The legislature also should approve at least some of the fringe benefits being asked by the KEA. Why not authorize local school districts to work out plans for group health and life insurance for school employees? This is strictly permissive legislation.

Considering the cold shoulder the public schools got first from the Governor, who did not include a cent for teacher salary increases in his budget, and the failure of the legislature to act on KEA proposals that did not even involve more state money, it is not surprising that Kentucky is only the second state to have had a statewide teacher strike.

Now it is the task of responsible leadership to take the initiative for a reasonable accommodation.

(Reprinted from the Louisville *Courier-Journal*)

The editorial makes use of exhortation and in so doing provides reasoning for the position taken. The feature story should stick to the facts and background. True, the presentation of figures on teachers' salaries may imply a need for some changes, but the story does not argue for or against any cause.

EXERCISES

I. Questions for Discussion

1. What are some of the fundamental differences between the news story and the feature story, between the feature story and the interpretative article, and between the interpretative article and the editorial?
2. What justification exists for newspapers to devote space to human interest stories?
3. How does a human interest story differ from a general feature story? What is the purpose of each?
4. What is the relative importance of timeliness in the types of journalistic literature?
5. What effect, if any, is television having on newspaper emphases?

II. The following are examples of opening paragraphs of varied types of journalistic literature. Identify each and state the basis for your identification.

BY BILL PURVIS

Lt. Gov. Ray Osborne, who happened to be in the area yesterday, had filed in federal court in Tampa a $250 million damage suit stemming from the Tampa Bay oil spill of a month ago. (Tampa *Tribune*)

Lt. Gov. Ray Osborne's $250 million damage suit over the Tampa Bay oil spill appears to be another case of trying harder to make political capital out of pollution than to prevent it. (Tampa *Tribune*)

BY JIM FULLER AND DENNIS CASSANO

The annual stockholders meeting of Honeywell, Inc., was adjourned after 14 minutes Tuesday as antiwar stock and proxy holders protested loudly against the way the meeting was run and the way it ended.
(Reprinted by permission of the Minneapolis *Tribune*)

ELIZABETHTOWN, Tenn. (AP)—The heartbreak of the Vietnam war has come to a Tennessee mother once again. But unlike 15 months ago, this time it appears her grief will not be lifted.

BY BOB COOPER

RICHMOND, Ky. (AP)—Race and religion don't mean much around the Richmond Federal Credit Union. Just ask the bank examiner who visited here a few months ago.

So far, the floor argument for confirmation of Judge G. Harrold Carswell to the Supreme Court has been about as uplifting to the spirit as the appointment itself. (*Arkansas Gazette*)

BY DAVID PERLMAN

LA JOLLA, Calif.—Scientists held a requiem for the world's ocean environment here yesterday. (San Francisco *Chronicle*)

BY NORMAN C. MILLER

WASHINGTON—For Democratic politicians, happiness is higher unemployment, shrinking overtime pay, rising prices, lofty interest rates and tight money.
(Reprinted with permission of the *Wall Street Journal*)

BY ROD BEAUDRY

A move to ban all lead in gasoline—a major contributor to air pollution—is gaining momentum with bipartisan support coming from the State Legislature and the governor. (Sacramento *Union*)

BY JOSEPH REILLY

An air-pollution alert plan that would curb all nonemergency vehicles during heavy contamination periods is being considered by the city, it was announced Thursday.
(Reprinted with permission from the Chicago *Sun-Times*)

BY CATHERINE WATSON

Striking Minneapolis teachers approved by an 85-percent margin a settlement with the school board Tuesday night and officially ended the strike that has closed schools for 14 class days.
(Reprinted by permission of the Minneapolis *Tribune*)

The settlement of the Minneapolis teachers' strike and the reopening of the schools after a 14-day "vacation" seem like a bright sunny day after weeks of stormy weather. The settlement probably was no less welcome to teachers and restless students than to parents and the general public.

(Reprinted by permission of the Minneapolis *Tribune*)

III. Assignments

1. Select a news story and a feature article from your local newspaper and note contrasts in their structures.
2. Select an interpretative article and draw contrasts between it and the feature article selected for assignment No. 1.
3. Select a political column and compare the writing in it with that in a feature article.
4. Find a human interest story in your local newspaper and describe how the writer structured it.
5. Study the editorials in one issue of your local newspaper and report on the exhortation and reasoning used by the writers.

Chapter 9

COVERAGE

Nothing great was ever achieved without enthusiasm. —Emerson

News does not come to a newspaper by magic and rarely does it come by accident. For the most part it comes through careful organization and systematization.

In a sense, a newspaper is a processor that through carefully established "machinery" turns out news and feature material. It is on the basis of this machinery that the courts have recognized a property value in news.

Admittedly, facts cannot be copyrighted. It is the organization and presentation—that which is original—that is entitled to the protection of copyright. In earlier newspapering days, it was common practice for an afternoon newspaper's rewrite man to rewrite some of the stories, usually relatively unimportant ones, run by a morning competitor. This is done far less today. Instead, newspapers make their own inquiry, though they may find competitors' stories helpful as tips.

Several court actions have been brought by newspapers against radio stations that picked up early editions and, with little or no change in wording, put the newspapers' stories on the air with the implication that the news was gathered and written by the radio staff. The courts, in enjoining those radio stations from airing the news for a period of time, usually 24 hours, have held that the newspaper goes to the expense of setting up an organization to gather and write the news, that the sale of advertising depends upon that news, and that the newspaper thereby has a property right in the news it collects and publishes.

Such news pilfering by radio stations has also been held to be an unfair business practice.

Organization

A newspaper's size is a determining factor in establishing a news organization. On a small weekly, one person may bear most of the responsibility for gathering and writing the news, writing the headlines, writing the editorials, and making up the pages.

Even then, that person functions well only if he establishes some system of operation. He prepares a list of established agencies, organizations and other news sources and keeps in touch with them by telephone and by personal visits.

A metropolitan newspaper, on the other hand, must have a large staff and a much more complex systematization.

Let us first consider a medium-sized newspaper that has a circulation of more than 100,000; the Fresno (Calif.) *Bee* is a good example.

That newspaper has 110 employees, including clerical staff and copy boys, in its editorial department. Ninety-two of these work full time and the other 18 work part time. In addition, the newspaper employs 125 stringers. A stringer is a part-time correspondent who is paid by the column inch.

Of the 110 regular employees, 25 are full-time city reporters and 10 are engaged in collecting San Joaquin Valley news. Some of these employees man the valley desk and others are full-time correspondents in county seats in the valley. The sports department has eight full-time and six part-time staffers. Covering women's activities requires six full-time and two part-time persons. The paper has seven full-time photographers who take black-and-white pictures and one photographer who devotes all his time to color pictures. Thirteen full-time persons work at the copydesk, where copy is corrected, headlines are written, and instructions are given on the handling of all the stories by the composing room.

Change the scene to a larger city such as San Francisco, Los Angeles, Minneapolis, Cleveland, Kansas City, Chicago, Philadelphia or New York, and the staff size of the metropolitan newspaper is expanded considerably. In addition to beat and general assignment reporters, specialists cover politics, science, education, finance, music, art, the theater and many other subjects.

The top position on most newspapers is that of publisher or editor and publisher. This person may be the owner, a major stockholder or a hired executive. He is familiar with both the news and the business operations of a newspaper. His job is usually to coordinate the major divisions of the newspaper: the editorial department; the business division, which includes accounting, advertising and circulation; and the mechanical division, which includes the composing room, engraving, stereotyping and the pressroom.

The top boss in a newsroom is usually called the managing editor, although he may have other titles, such as editor or news editor. Under him is a city editor, who is responsible for the news coverage of the city and environs. He is the boss of the reporters who cover the community, and he may also supervise women's activities and sports, although these two departments are frequently responsible directly to the managing editor.

A telegraph editor handles news coming in on the wire, and on newspapers that maintain foreign correspondents a cable editor is part of the staff. Depending on size and the circulation area, a newspaper may have a county editor or a state editor, although the state editor on most medium-sized newspapers has charge of rural area news coverage. The copydesk, with a copy chief or slot man in charge, is the place where stories are corrected and headlines written.

The foregoing is only a general sketch of newspaper organization. Large newspapers may have executive editors, assistant managing editors, day and night city editors and assistants, news editors and various other news executives whose functions necessarily depend upon the peculiarities of the paper's news coverage and processing problems.

Closely related but not always directly connected with the newsroom is the editorial writing staff. Large newspapers may have an editor in chief, a chief editorial writer or an editorial page editor who is in charge of a battery of editorial writers, usually called associate editors.

A somewhat smaller newspaper may have one editorial writer, probably called an associate editor. He may be responsible to the managing editor. On some small newspapers an editor may write the editorials and supervise the newsroom. Often, in such cases, the editor passes on to an assistant, who perhaps has the title of news editor, much of the responsibility for managing the newsroom.

There is no one method of news organization. The functions of newsmen, along with their titles, vary from one newspaper to another.

Systematization

The newspaper sets up a system of beats as a methodical means of assuring that principal news sources will be covered. A beat is a designated source or list of sources assigned to a reporter for regular and systematic coverage.

The number and types of beats vary according to the size of the community in which a newspaper operates. Governmental offices, business organizations, civic leaders, undertakers, hospitals and labor unions are some of the news sources usually included in beats. It makes a difference if a city is a county seat and thereby the center for many county offices. It makes a difference, too, if a city is large enough to have state and federal buildings.

Some beats may be important enough to require full-time reporters; the police department, the city hall and the county building typically require one reporter each. It is likely that, as a city grows very large, the offices in the city hall and in the county building will be divided into more than one beat and will require the full time of more than one reporter. A large city has many police precincts and they may need more than one reporter for coverage.

Of the many news sources included in beats, some provide only sporadic news, so a number of such sources may be clustered into a single beat. Most reporters with beats are likely to devote some time to general assignments, and in many cases the coverage of general assignments is primary and the beat coverage secondary. The reporter is still responsible to see that his beat is covered with regularity.

Just a few of the sources of news which may constitute complete beats or may be clustered into beats are:

Agricultural commissioner	Labor unions
Chamber of commerce	Library
Churches	Local office of state department of motor vehicles
City hall	
City schools	Local office of state highway patrol
Civil defense	Municipal transit
Clubs	Planning commission
Convention center	Police department
Coroner	Sheriff's office
County building and courthouse	Undertakers
County schools	Veterans' service
District hospital	Welfare department
Federal offices	
Fire department	

To supplement his beat, a reporter develops his own news sources. He becomes acquainted with persons who, by virtue of their activities or proclivities, are in positions to know what is going on in certain areas of the community or at certain levels of community life.

Systematization goes beyond all that. Each day someone on the city desk clips what are called futures from the newspaper and files them. The city editor keeps an all-round future book and each reporter should keep his own book in which he records coming events.

A commission has begun a three-months study of the city's waste disposal problems, a scientist will speak at a meeting, a labor union sets a strike date if contract negotiations are not completed, a court sets a trial date for a man accused of manslaughter, groundbreaking ceremonies are announced for a new $1 million building, an antipollution league announces plans for a convention—stories about these and numerous other coming events are clipped.

A simple system of filing these clips is to insert them in the appropriate pages of the future book. As a page is turned each day, the corresponding clips can be put into the boxes or typewriters of the reporters who are to cover the stories.

This system is all right for a small newspaper, but it is hardly adequate for a large one. A filing system may be more suitable for the larger newspaper. One good filing system is composed of a current month's file broken into days, a yearly file broken into months and a five- or 10-year file broken into years.

At the beginning of each year, the current year's file is broken into 12 monthly files, and at the start of each month the current monthly file is broken into days.

What would go into a five- or 10-year file?

The construction of a new freeway is scheduled to begin in four years, or a piece of highway is to be completed in five years. A two-year study of certain city problems begins, or a five-year urban development plan is approved.

Large newspapers post a daily assignment sheet or log, which helps the city desk keep track of reporters.

Volunteers

Much news comes to a newspaper from volunteers, some of whom may have a personal interest in seeing that certain occurrences are published.

A relative calls the city desk to say that a nephew has been awarded some honor, a man informs a newspaper that a neighbor has a rare gem collection, a businessman wants a newspaper to know that his firm is opening a new branch, a service club president will be quick to inform a newspaper that his group is sponsoring a new charity drive—these are only a few of the many bits of volunteered information that come to a newspaper.

The mail each morning is likely to bring tips from readers. Some of them may be in the form of complaints, a number of which revile the service provided by public agencies. Some will be insignificant, such as one that barking dogs are disturbing a family's sleep. The complainer, of course, should be advised to go to the proper officials.

Over half of the complaints may be of no news value or inaccurate. But even the inaccurate ones may provide a germ for a story.

Publicists

The publicist, by occupation, is a pusher of news that is favorable to his client and a buffer for unfavorable news.

Yet a good publicist performs a service for the press by providing at least some information that meets news standards. No matter how adequate a news staff may seem, a city editor will be chary about assigning reporters to cover what on the surface appears to be marginal news. Yet on lean days what might ordinarily be submarginal may rate space in a newspaper.

A good publicist knows what news values are and that what he turns in to a newspaper must compete with the news of the day. He searches for information that, in addition to being favorable to his client, has public interest.

Reporters always have an opportunity to interrogate the publicist to try to bring forth any hidden information that is of news value.

The morning's mail usually brings an abundance of handouts (publicity stories). Many go straight to the wastebasket, but some are worth following up.

Interchange

Newsmen should be on the alert for news tips even if the tips apply to beats other than their own. If a reporter gets a tip about something newsworthy relating to another reporter's beat, he should inform that reporter or write a memorandum to the city desk.

The interchange helps to maintain the news gathering efficiency of a newspaper. The cub should never, for self-aggrandizement, try to garner stories from another reporter's beat. It is assumed that each reporter is best qualified to handle the stories on his own beat.

Timidity

Nothing said in the previous section should give the idea that the beginner should be timid. He should not be afraid to ask questions in the newsroom or on his rounds. He should approach his news sources positively. He should never, in approaching a news source, say:

"Is there any news today?"

Nor should he start by saying:

"I'm from the Gazette, and I've been assigned to get a story on . . ." and then wait for the source to start talking.

A better way is to say:

"I'm from the Gazette and we're interested in your new plans for expansion. Just how far have you gotten with them?"

When he gets evasive replies, he should not hesitate to bore in with sharp, specific questions.

The Qualities of a Good Reporter

A good reporter is alert at all times. He is not only ready with appropriate questions but also observant of the actions, reactions, grimaces, hesitations and mannerisms of the person he talks to.

He gains the trust of his news sources by being meticulously accurate and by keeping confidences.

He is courteous and tactful, but he is never subservient or suppliant.

As he talks to different persons, he constantly adds to his storehouse of knowledge. When he makes a blunder, he remembers it and is more careful in the future.

When he must write stories that are unfavorable to certain persons, he learns to avoid personal animosity. The next time he meets those persons, he acts normal and polite—not apologetic or haughty.

He is aggressive and resourceful but never obnoxious. He converses with persons at their level. He strives constantly to overcome any ignorance he may have, but he never tries to hide his ignorance by professing to know what he does not know.

He keeps trying to develop techniques to improve his news gathering ability and the quality of his writing. He often resorts to a dictionary or a handbook of English.

He does not confine his reading to his own newspaper but also reads current magazines, books and a competitive newspaper, if there is one.

Fresh from College

The journalism school graduate, in getting his first reportorial job, should be eager to learn the routine of the newspaper he works for if he wishes to succeed. He should carefully observe the procedures followed by that newspaper in gathering and handling the news.

Nothing raises the blood pressure of a veteran newspaperman or editor more than the cub fresh from college who knows it all or is brash enough to tell the editor how the staff should be reorganized. A good reporter should always be a good listener, and the beginner, particularly, should be responsive to advice.

If the city in which the newspaper operates is new to a reporter, the first thing he should do is study a city map and learn to refer to it. Well-edited newspapers object to Richmond Avenue being referred to as Richmond Street, or Channing Way being called Channing Boulevard.

The newsman should read his own newspaper carefully each day and in so doing should make note of changes the copydesk makes in his stories. One of the most severe criticisms a city editor can make of a reporter is, "He not only doesn't read the paper, but he doesn't even bother to read his own stories."

The beginner should learn the idiosyncrasies of his newspaper. Some newspapers are fussy about the use of first names and do not like nicknames to be used as substitutes. The naming of children has changed, however, and it is not uncommon for parents to name a boy Bill or a girl Pat. It is up to the reporter to find out what the real name is.

Even newspapers that are less fussy about the use of names are likely to eschew such nicknames as Butch, Spud, Spike and Shorty. But when a person is better identified by a nickname than by his real name, many papers put the nickname after the real name in parentheses or quotation marks, as in Charles (Bud) Brown.

Sports writers commonly use nicknames instead of real names.

The reporter who fails to study his paper's stylebook will earn the ire of the copydesk. The trend today is for newspapers to standardize their styles by making use of the joint stylebook of the Associated Press and United Press International. Whatever style is used, the reporter should adhere to it.

The beginner should learn his beat and should also build his own list of news sources. At first his production will no doubt be limited to covering assignments and gathering news from his beat. After a short time, however, by developing news sources and using a future book, he should produce many stories independently.

Copy Preparation

Newspapers use an inexpensive type of woodpulp paper called copy paper.

In preparing his copy, the reporter should put his last name in the upper left-hand corner and the slug directly beneath it. The slug is the name given to a story: "City Council," "Fire," "Burglary," "Investigation," "Chamber" (for chamber of commerce), or whatever.

Some newspapers use a guideline system. In such cases, stories are not slugged until they reach the copydesk and heads are written. The first two words of the headline become the slug. This system is more likely to be used on small newspapers than large ones, but there is no hard-and-fast policy.

The reporter should leave two to three inches of space before starting the first paragraph of his story. This space is for use by the city desk or copydesk in writing the headline and giving instructions to the composing room.

Full one-inch margins should be allowed on both left- and right-hand sides of the page.

If the story does not go beyond a page, the writer designates completion by inserting a double cross or two number marks (##) after the last paragraph (the symbol "30" is rarely seen anymore). If the story runs more than a page, the reporter does one of two things, depending on the practice used in his newsroom. If the newspaper prefers that all multi-page stories be pasted together, he should do so and put a double cross at the end.

If the pages are not to be pasted together, he should encircle the word "more" at the bottom of each page except for the last one and be sure each page ends on a paragraph. A double cross should be placed at the end of the story. In the upper left-hand corner of each subsequent page he should write the slug and page number, such as "Chamber—2" or "Chamber—3."

The Telephone

The telephone is one of the reporter's handiest tools. It saves miles of travel and hours of time.

Some news can be gathered as handily by phone as by personal visit, but the reporter should not yield to the temptation never to leave the office to talk personally with his news sources. Personal contacts help to make subsequent telephone calls more personal and possibly more fruitful.

If a reporter wishes to call someone who does not have a listing in the telephone directory, he can resort to the city directory and find a neighbor, call him and, after identifying himself, politely request the neighbor to ask the person to call the reporter.

The back pages of city directories classify residents by street address and usually provide a symbol for those who have telephones.

Deadlines

Editors are persistent in seeing that a newspaper is on time each day. If the paper is late in coming from the press, the entire system of distribution is thrown off schedule. Contract dealers are annoyed. Carriers are delayed. Subscribers grumble.

Deadlines are therefore established and adhered to. The city desk has a final deadline for each edition. Shortly after that comes the copydesk deadline, then the composing room deadline and finally the pressroom deadline.

These deadlines apply only to last-minute news, not to just any story. If the city desk gets many stories shortly before deadline, some of them cannot be set by the composing room in time to get into the paper.

The reporter's deadline is the moment he can get the story to the city desk—not later. A city editor has reason for irritation if a reporter turns in a story an hour or two later than he could have turned it in, even if the story reaches the desk before the deadline.

A reporter should spend the hours before deadline working on timely copy. After the deadline for the final edition, he should devote his time to any stories he has for the next day and then to features.

EXERCISES

I. Questions for Discussion
   1. What is a future book and how is it used?
   2. In what ways may a publicist be of help to the press?
   3. Why is it important for a reporter starting work in a city unfamiliar to him to study a city map?
   4. What do you think a newspaper's policy should be regarding the use of nicknames?
   5. What is wrong with approaching a news source and saying, "I came to get a story on your new invention"?

II. Discuss the following comment made by a managing editor

Journalism schools are graduating students who don't know how to handle quotations. Most of them don't know how to write concisely. Many of them don't know how to spell. Some can't even type accurately, speedily or neatly. We have to pass them by or teach them ourselves. They use nicknames instead of bothering to look up the real names or to check back with news sources. They not only use Ray, Al, Bill, Ed, etc., but Butch, Dutch, Chick, etc., seem okay to many.

III. Assignments

1. Visit your local newspaper and prepare a report on the staff organization of the editorial department.
2. Report on the system of beats used by your local newspaper.
3. Study the news stories in your local newspaper and try to determine the news source for each.
4. Go through an issue of your local newspaper and clip the futures. How would you file them?
5. Obtain a copy of the stylebook used by your local newspaper and report on it.

Chapter 10

THE ART OF INTERVIEWING

> *"You can tell your paper," the great*
>   *man said,*
> *"I refused an interview.*
> *I have nothing to say on the question, sir;*
> *Nothing to say to you."*
> *And then he talked till the sun went down*
> *And the chickens went to roost.*
>   —*O. Henry*

Asking questions is a big part of a reporter's job, for much of the information a newspaper supplies comes from human sources. A reporter may question the survivors of a plane crash, a mayor who has fired his assistant, a fire marshal about the cause of a hotel blaze, a politician about a government scandal, a power official about a blackout—it's all part of the day's work.

The concern of this chapter, however, is the type of interview which serves as the principal basis for an article, usually called an interview story. Interview stories generally are of two types; one exploits the opinions of the interviewee and one other captures an interesting personality.

If an associate justice of the United States Supreme Court, an assistant secretary of defense, the president of the National Manufacturer's Association, the lieutenant governor of the state or the president of the United Auto Workers visits town, it is likely that the city editor will assign a reporter to get an interview story for the purpose of learning the person's opinion.

If, on the other hand, an actor, a noted mountain climber, a lion tamer or a jungle explorer comes to town, the city editor, in assigning a reporter to get an interview, may expect a story that will portray the personality and adventures of the interviewee. The editor is after a feature story.

Preparing for the Interview

Because of the time factor, it is sometimes necessary for a reporter to interview someone cold, but whenever possible the newsman should make preliminary preparations. It is essential that he know something about the background of the person to be interviewed—his experience, accomplishments, education and stature in his field. Has he previously been in the news? Have writings of his been published? Has he won any distinction? Has he been involved in controversies?

One of the first things to do is to find out whether there are any clips on the person in the newspaper library. It may be that he is listed in *Who's Who in America* or in one of the other biographical volumes, such as *Who's Who in American Art, Who's Who in Commerce and Industry* or *Who's Who in Engineering*.

If the person is an educator, some local school officials may know something about him; if he is a businessman, some local persons involved in commerce may know about him; if he is a musician, some local musicians may be able to provide information on his accomplishments.

The reporter, within reason, should also give consideration to the subject matter to be discussed. If the person to be interviewed, for example, is a scientist who has specialized in cosmic ray research, the reporter might at least read what an encyclopedia offers on cosmic rays.

The beginning reporter, particularly, should prepare a list of questions in advance. According to the way the interview goes, he may not use all of them, but just having them for emergency use is good insurance against embarrassing falters.

The person to be interviewed does not have to come from out of town. A local man may be appointed to a government commission, a college professor may return from the Middle East, a local woman may become a leader in the crusade for feminine independence, or a sociologist may have made a study of local ghettos.

There is always a reason for an interview assignment and it is up to the reporter to be aware of what that reason is and to word his questions accordingly. A reporter would not ordinarily ask a musician for his views on the Middle East or a businessman what he thinks of pop art.

Interviewees React Differently

There is no average person when it comes to interviewees. Some are used to newsmen, and others are not. Some are brash in answering questions, whereas others are cautious. Some crave publicity, but others shun it. Some are impatient with the reporter's ignorance on a subject, whereas others patiently try to be of help. Some are witty and vibrant, but others are dull.

The reporter must quickly size up the person he interviews and act accordingly. It is best if the newsman can put himself on a level with the interviewee, whether he is of high position or otherwise. Advance preparation should be of great help, but it is not always adequate. Some reporters are frank and readily confess little knowledge of a subject, but by all means the interviewer must have confidence and should never be unduly apologetic or subservient.

Depending on the interviewee, the reporter may start softly with sociable comments, or he may move quickly into the interview. The low-key approach may bring rapport with someone who seems apprehensive or uneasy, but it may be a waste of time to a person who is busy and who must budget his minutes carefully. Some persons fear reporters, and to be successful the interviewer must find means of getting them to lower their guards. A few sociable words, even comments on the weather, may help perform the trick.

The reporter should carefully measure the time to reach for pencil and paper. To the wary or timid this action could bring increased uneasiness, for it will remind him that what he says will go into print. The interviewer can help the situation, while reaching for pencil and paper, by making some casual comment such as: "I want to make sure I get your name spelled correctly."

Dominating the Interview

It is the reporter's task to dominate the interview in an unobtrusive manner. Questions are the tool he uses to do this. When the interviewee starts wandering away from the subject, the reporter should use an appropriate question to steer him back on course. This does not mean that the reporter should interrupt the interviewee in the middle of a sentence; he should skillfully and politely inject a question.

When the interviewee drifts into long generalizations in response to a question, it is necessary for the reporter to regain control. A specific question is his means of doing so.

> Reporter: What are your views on the recent campus disorders?
> College administrator: Disturbing, very disturbing. Somewhere, somehow, we must resort to greater creativity in seeking solutions. We

must create a climate of trust, of mutual concern. We must recognize that our problem is a joint one requiring cooperation from everyone. We must be ready to listen as well as talk. We must find a common meeting ground—

Reporter: What I mean more specifically is do you feel that the demands being made by the students are justified and what steps will the college take if the disorders are resumed?

There is no place for timidity on the part of a reporter in an interview. He has a job to do and he should make every effort to see that he does it thoroughly and effectively.

The Art of Questioning

The interviewer is constantly faced with the temptation to slump into dull, routine questioning. It is the easy thing to do. Interviewing is an art that requires alert, poignant questioning—a constant interrogative interweaving to get spontaneous response. One reporter referred to it as moving on mental tiptoe.

One of the problems the reporter faces is that some interviewees say what they think they should say rather than what they really believe. A veteran reporter, after interviewing a successful "queen" candidate chosen in national competition, commented: "I've been interviewing the ones chosen over a period of years and the problem is that they all say the same thing."

The best job usually is done when the reporter can reduce the interview to a guided conversation—guided, of course, by the newsman's questions. Formality invites formality in return. Interviewees are more likely to respond naturally when informality prevails.

> Reporter: I'll bet you were afraid when night came and no one came to your rescue.
> Woman: You bet I was.
> Reporter: I've often wondered what kind of thoughts come to a person's mind in a situation like yours—trapped in a well and no one around to help you.
> Woman: You just try not to think and do a lot of praying.
> Reporter: I'll bet you did pray.
> Woman: You can say that again.

General questions usually get general answers. The interviewer will get more information by breaking the general question into several specific ones. Note the vague information received in response to a general question:

> Reporter: Do you feel that the national outlook for the coming year is any brighter?

Senator: Yes, I feel that there are some reasons for optimism. We've faced many problems at home and abroad, but I think we're headed in the right direction in our attempt to solve them.

The chief value of a general question is to direct the course of the interview. Specific questions should follow in rapid succession:

Do you think inflation can be curbed without wage and price controls?
Hasn't reliance on money controls to curb inflation proved futile?
Is an increase in unemployment necessary in an attempt to halt inflation?

When he sits to write his story, the reporter may have cause to regret it if he did not jockey in the interview for something to use for a lead —something with headline value. On the other hand, he certainly should not pick out some striking comment that was made as an aside.

The interviewer, furthermore, must be constantly on the alert for comments well suited for use as direct quotations. A school superintendent, interviewed about a new teacher-parent conference program, might say:

We welcome the opportunity the program provides to discuss mutual problems with parents.

A rare superintendent would have said:

We wish the parents would stay away and let us concentrate on our work.

The reporter can use thoughtful questions to encourage quotable statements:

Reporter: Will the conferences simply lapse into discussions in which the teachers tell the parents what already is being told in report cards?
Superintendent: By no means. There will be discussion of the students' emotional problems, study habits, attitudes, relations with the teachers and other students, interests—many things impossible to put in report cards.
Reporter: Will the conferences be geared mainly for the parents of problem children? What about the students who don't have problems, who have good study habits, who like school and like the teachers?
Superintendent: Even the best students usually have some problems. We'd be making an awful mistake just to concentrate on the so-called problem children. The conferences should bring closer cooperation between the school and the home.
Reporter: In other words, the responsibility of the parents when the students are not in school?
Superintendent: No, not entirely. The parent who feels that his responsibility for a son or daughter ends during school hours is shirking part of his responsibility.

Reporter: Do you find many parents who do not feel that the schools are fully responsible for their children during school hours?

Superintendent: The sad part of it is that many parents feel that the school is fully responsible during school hours until a son or daughter starts flunking classes or in other ways gets into difficulties. These are things we hope to avert through our conferences. Prevention is better than cure.

One of the surest ways for a reporter to avoid an inaccurate portrayal of a person's views, particularly in interviews that deal with technical subjects, is to paraphrase what he understands the interviewee to have said. If the interviewed person affirms the paraphrase, the reporter knows he is accurate in his interpretation. If his paraphrase is not accurate, the person has an opportunity for correction:

Reporter: As I understand it, you feel that abortion is morally justified, and that there is need for making it legal.

Respondent: Not exactly. It depends upon the situation in different cases. I feel that it may be justified when there is danger of mental or physical health impairment for the mother or physical deformity for the child. I favor a liberalization of abortion laws but I'd hesitate to endorse abandonment of all legal restrictions.

Effective interviewing is hard work. The degree of difficulty, of course, depends partly upon the interviewee and the subject, but mental laziness on the part of the reporter rarely achieves a good story.

Personality Touches

The interview story can often be made more vibrant, particularly the feature interview, by having some personality touches injected into it:

> Has the legislature made any substantial progress in fighting pollution?
>
> The question brought a grim smile to Smith's bearded face. He dropped the pencil he was playing with, leaned back in his swivel chair, put his hands behind his head, and replied:
>
> "It would be a gross exaggeration if I were to say that the legislature has moved at anything faster than a snail's pace."

Studied observation of the interviewee is important. Did his voice rise at times? Did he slap the desk with a hand? Did some questions bring a sparkle to his eyes or a smile to his lips? Did his hands make any gestures? Did he answer questions spontaneously or hesitate frequently?

What does the person look like—tall, slender, muscular, pale faced, energetic? What did he wear—a freshly pressed gray suit or a yellow, short-sleeved shirt, open at the neck, and brown slacks? If a woman, is she blond, brunette or red haired? What are the color of her eyes? Does she smile easily?

Was anything about the surroundings worth noting? If the interview took place in an office, what kind of desk was there? Was it cluttered? Were there numerous pictures on the wall?

The reporter obviously should not clutter his story with insignificant details. Bits of color, however, may make the story more interesting. Description that will embarrass an interviewee is rarely used—the essential thing is to make the person more real to the reader. The reporter is not likely to write, "As he smiled, he displayed an uneven row of dark brown teeth," or "The shoulders of his dark blue coat were sprinkled with dandruff."

Staying in the Background

The reporter need not impress upon the reader the role he took in the interview. Space is wasted with such remarks as, "Jones, asked by a Times reporter what he thinks of . . . replied. . . ." It is simpler to write, "Jones thinks. . . ."

Neither is it necessary to say, "Jones, asked what he feels about . . . said. . . ." It is simpler to write, "Jones said that. . . ."

The reporter does not have to inform his reader that remarks were made in an interview, as in, "Jones, in an interview last night, said. . . ." Only when such clarification is needed should it be used. It might be significant to say that the President of the United States last night said "in an interview," since that official frequently issues statements to the press and the clarification would be helpful.

The rhetorical question can be used effectively in writing interview stories:

> Who's responsible for the delay?
> "The committee, of course," Smith said. "It hasn't met for more than a month and, to my knowledge, no definite meeting date has been set."

This type of rhetorical device offers variation if it is not overused.

Tape Recorders

Newsmen have mingled feelings about tape recorders; nevertheless, they are coming into increased use. One of the objections raised is that they make the interviewee uneasy. But they offer assurance against misquotation.

The time angle, too, is important, since more time would be consumed in writing a story from a recording than from notes. To offset this, the reporter, even though he uses a recorder, should still take notes. Some experienced reporters take few notes in feature interviews, but the beginner is advised to take ample ones.

The Opinion Interview Story

The basic organization of the opinion interview story usually involves an interweaving of direct and indirect quotations with an interspersing of background information.

The lead may be based on the general impression the interviewee left with the reporter.

The pattern is illustrated by a Minneapolis *Tribune* story that leans heavily on background:

Indirect quotation presents central idea	Women's liberationists who picket and demand equal rights don't use the right tactic, said a woman who has crusaded in the Minnesota Legislature for equal pay and equal work.
Direct quotation	"I'm all for the girl who wants to work. But I don't think screaming and demanding will get her a job," said Rosemary McVay, a part-time lawyer and mother of five.
Background	Mrs. McVay was the first woman to serve on the Minneapolis Fair Employment Practices Commission, has been president of the American Association of University Women (AAUW) and has been active in the League of Women Voters. While active in the AAUW she worked for women's equality through the law-making body.
Direct quotation	"I can honestly say I don't think I've ever been discriminated against because I'm a woman," Mrs. McVay said.
Indirect quotation	When a woman gets a job, initially she may have to produce more than a man, she said. But, if the woman performs well, she will be accepted equally.
Background	Mrs. McVay, a native of Minneapolis, is a graduate of the University of Minnesota Law School. She was in private practice for four years and was with Cargill, Inc., for seven years. She has continued her law practice on a limited basis.
Direct quotation	"When I left Cargill and was expecting our first baby, an old client asked me to do some work for him. My desk hasn't been clean since," she said.
Indirect quotation	For example, the AAUW study on penal reform several years ago resulted in the formation of the Prisoner's Aid Society. This became the Minnesota Correctional Service

Background	from which the council on crime and delinquency grew, she said. Appointed to the state junior college board in December, she is presently serving on a special committee to select a new president for one of the colleges. Mrs. McVay, who lives at 2711 Dean Blvd., is also a member of the Minnesota Citizens' Council on Crime and Delinquency, and she is a member of the board of the Children's Health Center and the Women's Association of the Minneapolis Symphony Orchestra. (Reprinted by permission of the Minneapolis *Tribune*)

The liberal use of background in the preceding story is appropriate because it shows that a critic of women's liberation tactics has, herself, been active in struggling for social progress. It also indicates professional activity.

A simple way for a reporter to organize an opinion interview story is for him to select the main points stressed by the interviewee. The strongest of the main points can be used as the basis for the lead. The other points, each supplemented by specifics, follow in order. The main points usually take the form of indirect quotation and the specifics usually take the form of direct quotation.

In other words, the organization moves from the general to the specific, back to the general and again to the specific until all the major points have been covered.

This organization is illustrated by an *Arkansas Gazette* story:

First major point	If Miss Betty Buford of Plainview, Tex., a teacher for 21 years, were made czar of all education tomorrow, the first thing she would do would be to "throw out all the tradition and routine of Carnegie units."
Explanation	This is the system under which a student must have four units of mathematics, four of English and so on, for a total, usually, of 16, in order to be eligible to graduate from high school.
Background tied in	That reaction carries more weight by virtue of the fact that Miss Buford has been serving since July, 1969, as president of the Association of Classroom Teachers of the National Education Association, and has been traversing the nation since her election, appearing before local classroom teacher groups and observing education at first hand as it is conducted across the country.
Supplementary specifics	"I would throw out the whole system and erase from the minds of people the kinds of educational programs we've had in the past," Miss Buford said. "We wouldn't fit the students into the system but would fit the system to the students."
Second major point,	She also would abolish the grading system, although she concedes there "must be some method of evaluation."

with specifics omitted	Grades she thinks are a very poor way of measuring progress.
Third major point, followed by specifics	Miss Buford feels there is a great deal of community apathy toward education and she considers that tragic. "We haven't decided what goals the public schools should have; they can't be all things to all people. If we mean a goal is to teach every child to be a comprehensive reader, then this probably could be done. But if we're just teaching a body of facts, we are out-dated and irrelevant."
More specifics	What then would she consider a proper goal? "I can see it only in terms of the individual," she said, "to develop each to be a contributing member of society...." Would it not also require putting education on a one-to-one basis, one teacher for every child? "Good teachers have been putting it on a one-to-one basis for years," she said.
Fourth major point, followed by specifics	Miss Buford believes that educational improvement, if it comes, must come from the teachers, with help from the community and all others with a vested interest in it. "Our job is to communicate the need for improvement, for adequate funding, for legislation. If we're going to get these, we must become politically active."
Rhetorical question introduces major point	Should this political activity extend to strikes? "Without passing judgment on whether it is morally right or morally wrong to walk off the job," Miss Buford said, "it gets results. And as long as it gets results when nothing else will, we will see more and more of it occurring unless more constructive ways are found to solve the problems of education."
Specifics	She personally would be "reluctant" to strike but there are, she said, "much worse things" and one of them is to permit the continuance of mediocre or poor education....

It should be remembered that the word "specifics" as it is being used includes supplementation. Though many reporters sometimes put direct and indirect quotations into the same paragraph, it usually improves readability to use them in separate paragraphs.

The reporter should keep in mind that an interview story should be punctuated with direct quotations. The following story by George Sibera is made up of an effective balance of general paragraphs and supplementary, specific paragraphs.

Summary lead	VENCE, France (UPI)—Gen. Henri Navarre has seen it all before—the Communists' stalling at the peace table, their diversionary actions in Cambodia and Laos, their demands for withdrawal from Indochina of the "imperialist aggressors."
Background	Gen. Navarre, now 71, but still ramrod straight, commanded the French armed forces during their illfated war

against the Communist Viet Minh, which ended in disaster at Dien Bien Phu just 16 years ago last Friday.

General

He still is not reconciled to that defeat.

Specifics

"The Americans could have saved Dien Bien Phu," Navarre said . . . "If the American Air Force had intervened at Dien Bien Phu, this would not have allowed the French to win the war but it would have won them an honorable way out. And the Americans, I believe, would have saved themselves 15 years of war in Vietnam.

"Thanks to their overwhelming material superiority the Americans will not suffer a Dien Bien Phu," the military leader said, contemplating Pres. Richard Nixon's effort to extricate the United States from the war.

"The Americans will get an honorable exit. But the fact remains that they risk losing the war."

General

Navarre has no advice to offer Washington. He shrugged his broad shoulders when asked what he would do if he were back there in embattled Vietnam in the shoes of his American successors.

Specifics

"There are distinct parallels between the two situations," he said, sitting comfortably in the living room of his villa, La Bastide Malvan, high in the sparkling air of this Riviera resort.

"First, American parliamentary and public opinion is getting tired of the war. The Vietnamese Communists know it, just as they knew France was getting weary of the war when I was in command."

General

The silver haired French general said the Viet Minh—as he keeps calling the Communist enemy in Indochina, making no distinction between Hanoi and the Viet Cong—are trying out the tactics tested successfully against the French years back.

They are playing for time at the Paris peace talks while trying to speed up the American disengagement by stirring trouble in Laos and Cambodia, Navarre said.

Specifics

"In 1952, six years after the start of the war, the Viet Minh were confining their military operations to Vietnam," he recalled. "Then, on Feb. 18, 1954, when France agreed to go to Geneva to negotiate peace, they expanded the war to Laos and Cambodia.

"To speed up the process of prospective French departure, they decided to make a decisive, final effort at Dien Bien Phu to win new cards for Geneva."

Background

At Dien Bien Phu the exhausted remnants of 11 elite French battalions, altogether 16,000 men, were overrun after an epic 56-day siege.

General

Navarre is distinctly skeptical about the chances of Nixon's Vietnamization program.

Specifics

"Vietnamization is an old idea," he said. "It was the basis of my own plans when I was sent to Indochina in

1952. In my days the South Vietnamese did not fight well. Now the situation seems to have changed. The South Vietnamese regime seems to have a more solid base.

"The key question is whether they will be able to hold on once the Americans pull out. The question would be different if the Americans merely withdrew to bases. But announcing in advance evacuation withdrawals—" Navarre shook his head.

General

Navarre believes North Vietnamese Defense Minister and Chief Commander Vo Nguyen Giap and his Hanoi colleagues have the same aim today they had in the 1950s —to dominate all of Vietnam and the neighboring countries—and that they are using the same effective political and military strategy.

Specifics

"In Paris, they let negotiations drag on in the hope of wearing the Americans down," Navarre opined. "Mind you, each resultless session makes the Americans a little more impatient, losing a little more heart. So far all the concessions have come from the American side—halt of the U.S. bombing raids over North Vietnam in 1968, followed by the announcement of the U.S. pullout."

General

Navarre has strong doubts about the chances of insuring peace in Vietnam through a new Geneva conference.

Specifics

"The North Vietnamese will always seek to dominate the south," he said.

In the preceding story, the paragraphs marked "general" stress major points made by the interviewee and the paragraphs marked "specifics" provide supporting detail.

The Feature Interview Story

The primary difference between the opinion interview story and the feature interview story is that the former deals more basically with the opinions of the interviewee, whereas the latter, though it may present some opinions, deals more with the personality of the interviewee or with his exploits or both.

In the feature type, paragraphs of direct quotation are alternated with paragraphs devoted to incidents, background, interests, habits, activities, views and bits of color and personality. Unconventional leads are used to lure the reader on. The writing style is usually light and breezy.

The following *Christian Science Monitor* article by Kimmis Hendrick exemplifies the feature interview type.

Lead invites reader to read on

LOS ANGELES—Maggie Smith talks about film acting almost as though she were a tyro instead of one of the five women just nominated for the "best actress" award of the Academy of Motion Picture Arts and Sciences.

Supplementation	"It's a technique I don't really understand," she says. "I haven't done enough work in films to understand how you save yourself and where you use yourself. "You see," Miss Smith goes on to explain, "until I did 'The Prime of Miss Jean Brodie,' I had never done a long film. The films I had done had involved me at the most three weeks. I would be just drifting in and drifting out—I didn't have much connection with the thing as a whole."
Personality	If there's one thing Miss Smith conveys by the serious, unpretentious way she talks about her work, it's that as an actress she's always searching to find its wholeness. It's like a quest for meaning. Although making films obviously interests her, it's also plain that it's to the stage she is fundamentally and irrevocably committed. Maybe the Oxford Playhouse School of Drama was instituted so she could find this out. She laughs at the notion and refers to the circumstance delightfully as "pure fluke."
Background	It lasted just three years. But those were the years when, turned 16, Maggie Smith wanted to study acting. She lived in Oxford. Her parents—"for obvious reasons," as their daughter puts it—didn't want her to be going all by herself to London.
Supplementation	"I'd always wanted to act but I'd never had the opportunity," she recalls. "I'd never been in school productions. I did have one teacher, an English teacher, who influenced me a great deal, and it was just something I wanted to do. "And that," Miss Smith sums up tersely in a way that seems to suit her, "was all there was to it."
Background and interests	Acting became her whole life—a life and career she has been sharing with her actor-husband, Robert Stephens, since they were married in 1967. For the two of them, says Mrs. Stephens, nothing could seem more wonderful, more advantageous to both of their careers, than being able to work together as professionals. They did so in "Brodie," as she calls the movie for which she may receive an Oscar. They did it here in the two plays the National Theatre Company of Great Britain brought to Los Angeles for its first visit in America: Farquhar's Restoration comedy, "The Beaux' Stratagem," and Chekhov's "Three Sisters."
Supplementation	"I suppose two people in the same profession will talk shop all the time," Miss Smith observes. "So for Robert and me to be in the same production is always very stimulating to both of us. We can go home and talk about it. We can discuss what we're doing or decide that something else is a good idea." She smiles and says, "I suppose an actress couldn't do this if she were married to a dentist. Maybe that would be good—I don't know. But it just so happens that we love the theater and the whole profession that we're in, and therefore we don't find it a drag to talk about it and live with it 24 hours a day."

The Art of Interviewing 169

Interests	What about other interests? Should one have them? "Well I think that's possibly so," responds Miss Smith thoughtfully. "But neither Robert nor I seem to have time. Our interests are within the theater, and they're endless."
Habits and personality	If one works in a repertory system, she points out, all extra time goes into rehearsing. She says the nearest she gets to relaxation is reading. Miss Smith says the word "reading" so beautifully that it conjures up another world.
Interests and habits	Mr. and Mrs. Stephens do have two other interests, actually—their two sons. Christopher, 2½, flew from London to Los Angeles with his parents; Toby, just 8 months, stayed home. Like their mother, they are both redheads. There's always time for them, she comments, except when she's working in a movie. Then the "lunatic hours" of moviemaking don't coincide with their day at all.
Question raised	Considering competition from film and television, does Miss Smith think theater can survive?
Supplementary answer	"I think it definitely will," she answers, her voice rising to "definitely" in a way that makes it mean "inevitably" or "irresistibly" or both. Her voice is a rich instrument. It can sound conclusive, even matter-of-fact, and at the same time range marvelously with color. "I think it will always be fascinating," says the Maggie Smith who makes it so herself, "to see a real, live, breathing person on the stage." (Reprinted with permission from the *Christian Science Monitor*)

The attempt to capture a personality and portray it for the reader is illustrated in this Atlanta *Constitution* story by Israel Shenker:

"Come on and read" type of lead	COLLEGE PARK, Md.—Katherine Anne Porter has reached that peak in a writer's life when occasional writings are collected and enduring wisdom cherished.
Background and activities	She will be 80 in May, and her latest book—"The Collected Essays and Occasional Writings of Katherine Anne Porter" (Seymour Lawrence-Delacorte Press)—has just come out. Miss Porter topped her publication week by selling the movie rights to an earlier book, "Pale Horse, Pale Rider," to Keir Dullea, the actor. She now lives alone in a modest two-story house here, but in many ways the last few years have been the softest. Until the million dollars earned by "Ship of Fools"—in 1962—as she said . . . here:
Supplementation	"I lived a life of the most incredible discipline and privation. "I'm getting to sound like something out of the ark," she said. "I've had three husbands, and that isn't so bad. But I never had a man who could understand what I needed for my work. They were ready to give me all the time I needed, except when I needed it."

Views	Miss Porter said it was mad for a woman to try to combine career and home and family.
Supplementation	"You get older and tired and your faculties begin to draw in," she said. "I got frightened and realized I had to make a choice. I had to be an artist—which means you work at a trade, whether it's writing or sitting on a bench making shoes.
"Each time, without any quarrel, without any row," she continued, "we just got divorced and stayed on being friendly. I had nothing against them and they had nothing against me. I said to my third husband, 'There must be something wrong with me.' 'No,' he said, 'you've just got a standing engagement with another power, and no man can put up with it.'
"Anybody who wants can have my rights. I want my privileges. I want to be able to say to a husband or to anybody else: 'I can't do the cleaning now, I can't do the shopping or the cooking. I have to write a short story.' "
Views	But she does not believe in every emancipation. "These Women's Liberation Movement women feel inferior," she maintained. "I don't and I never did.
Supplementation	"I don't know what women want now that they haven't got. What they should work for is to make the relations better between men and women. Men are full of doubts and suspicions and don't trust women.
"Eventually, women will learn there's no such thing as freedom. Their husbands are just as fastened to the deck as they are. Men get onto a treadmill and never get off until they destroy themselves: the percentage who die of heart trouble is way ahead of women."
As for youth: "You have only one time the great gift of balanced strength and health, and it's a great shame to waste it on drugs and drink and sexual hoodlumism. You're wasting your life and it's not going to be given back to you. Use what you have more gracefully and gratefully. What is there about life that's so terrible that you have to throw it away?"
Personality	When she went for a physical checkup, not long ago after long illness, a young man sat down and questioned her. Miss Porter was furious when she later learned he was a psychiatrist. "I've never talked to a psychiatrist and I didn't want to," she protested.
When she saw the psychiatrist's report that she was an old woman frightened of age, she was doubly furious. "I was never afraid of growing old," she insisted, "and in fact I didn't think I was going to.
Supplementation	"People speak of old age as if you were all over a bad case of hardening of the arteries. I was afraid my mind would clatter, and I'm a little bit more careful now to try to control my thoughts a bit more. At this point of life you do think—as President Roosevelt said—that things are

very iffy. But I'm not afraid of life and I'm not afraid of death: dying's the bore."
(Reprinted from the Atlanta *Constitution*)

Although certain parts of the preceding example are marked as portraying personality, several other paragraphs with different designations actually help to portray personality, such as those denoting habits and direct quotations that are listed as supplementation.

The tense used with attributive verbs, such as "say" and "assert," varies. One is likely to find the past tense used most in opinion interview stories and the present tense used most in feature interview stories, but there is little consistency among writers. It is preferable, nonetheless, to use the present tense with such attributive verbs as "believe," "feel" and "think."

Multiple Interview Stories

The occasion arises when a reporter is assigned to get the views of a number of persons on a timely topic. A plan to raze an historic building, for instance, might prompt an assignment to get various views on the subject.

The reporter should be honest and make known the extent of his survey. A campus reporter, for example, should not imply a wide reflection of student opinion in a story based on interviews with five or 10 students. The extent to which opinions were sought is revealed in the following Minneapolis *Tribune* story by Greg Pinney:

> A young mother on Wheelock Parkway in St. Paul said, "To tell you the truth, my husband and I don't know if we want to vote for either one of them."
> She was talking about Robert D. North and Charles P. McCarty, Jr., the two candidates for mayor in Tuesday's election, and her remark was typical of the disenchantment and detachment expressed by people in many neighborhoods of the city.
> "We just haven't heard much about any of the candidates," she said.
> A reporter's conversations with prospective voters across the city, *in what was, of course, an unscientific survey,* indicated that the whole local election process may be remote from the very people who are expected to participate in it.
> A television repairman in the Como Park area said, "I really haven't made up my mind yet. I'm still reading the papers to see how it's going to go.
> "It's probably my own ignorance that's making me answer this way. Like a lot of voters, we don't make an educated vote and then we cry about it afterward."

A retired plasterer's helper who was waiting for a bus on North Dale Street said he has voted for 50 years and will vote this time. But he did not know who was running and saw no reason to know.

"I'd just as soon put one man in there as another," he said.

A foundryman, sitting in a bar on Arcade Street, said, "You just go in there and pull the levers down and you leave, that's all."

"I'm going to vote for the younger man—what's his name . . . ?" said a man sitting in a lawn chair on Grotto Street. "I think he'll get along with the younger generation."

A woman who answered the door in the north-central part of town said, "One is so young and the other one I'd rather not comment on. It certainly is a shame in a city of this size that you can't have better candidates."

"You can throw them both in the same basket," said a liquor store clerk on West 7th Street. "I really haven't made up my mind."

(Reprinted by permission of the Minneapolis *Tribune*)

The author of the preceding story frankly commented that it was an unscientific survey and described the persons interviewed.

The Press Conference

When officials, public or otherwise, hold a press conference, the subject is supposedly of public significance and the event itself, since it is not restricted to a few publications, eliminates partiality and provides the opportunity for a wide dissemination of information. Even though he must compete with others clamoring to ask questions, the reporter must overcome any timidity. He has the advantage of hearing answers to questions asked by others as well as by himself.

The following article, written by James K. Batten of the Detroit *Free Press'* Washington staff, is an example of a story based on a press conference.

WASHINGTON—The Negro Republican who heads the Equal Employment Opportunity Commission (EEOC) has complained bitterly that he inherited an agency riddled with politics and incompetence.

"In sum," declared William H. Brown III, "on May 6, 1969, I became chairman of an institution which was no more prepared to perform the task set out for it by Congress than it was at its inception."

Background   The EEOC was created by Congress under the 1964 Civil Rights Act to enforce the new law's provisions against discrimination in employment.

Brown, a normally softspoken, 41-year-old Philadelphia lawyer, delivered his charges at a press conference called to rebut published suggestions that the EEOC was doing virtually nothing under his chairmanship.

Brown's principal target was his predecessor as EEOC chairman, Clifford L. Alexander, Jr., a 30-year-old Negro lawyer who was squeezed out last spring by the White House.

Background

Brown, whose quiet manner contrasts sharply with Alexander's flamboyance and flair for publicity, has been stung repeatedly in recent weeks by charges that he was not aggressively enforcing the law against job discrimination.

Liberals in Congress and civil-rights groups have viewed Brown with mistrust, suspecting that he was an agent of the Nixon administration's allegedly soft approach to civil-rights enforcement.

Brown apparently decided over the weekend that Alexander, now with the Washington law firm of Arnold and Porter, had helped inspire an article in the Washington newspaper which said EEOC was dragging its feet.

Without naming Alexander, Brown lashed out at the former chairman on several counts.

Before he arrived, Brown said, the EEOC had tended to "adjust agency structure and activities to accommodate the needs of personal and political associates"—meaning to provide jobs for Alexander's friends.

Brown denied reports that he intended no further public hearings on discrimination in certain industries. *Hearings were a favorite weapon of Alexander's.*

Background (italicized)

In an obvious reference to Alexander, he remarked, "I do not regard public hearings as mere publicity stunts to be forgotten once the television cameras are turned off."

Brown also complained—in another obvious thrust at Alexander—that EEOC's mounting case backlog in years past "demoralized those staff members who cared more for civil rights than rhetoric."

Alexander replied that Brown's charges "are well off the mark."

"The real question," said Alexander, "is whether this administration as presently directed has any concern for the aspirations of minorities."

Alexander later issued a formal, one-sentence statement:

"This administration and its spokesmen should spend less time issuing press releases and more time protecting the lawful rights of minorities and women."

(Reprinted from the Detroit *Free Press*)

A reporter will be lost at a press conference if he has no knowledge of the subject being discussed. The preceding story would suffer considerably were it not for the background paragraphs. It is important, too, that a person criticized be given an opportunity to present his side of the story.

Speech Stories—A Similar Type

The speech story is very similar in presentation to the interview story, particularly the opinion interview type. The most marked difference is that there is an occasion for a speech story—a program of some kind, often with a sponsoring group.

There is also a difference in the way information is obtained. A speech is set. Questions do not determine what the speaker says, although his talk may be followed by a question-and-answer period or by random questions from reporters as he leaves. In any case, a newsman should tell his readers under what circumstances the comments used in his story were obtained.

Some speakers prepare advance copies of their talks. Others do not. An advance copy should be helpful to a reporter in writing his story, but it does not relieve the reporter from his job of hearing the speech, for some speakers depart from their prepared talks and others inject off-the-cuff remarks. If a newsman does rely on an advance copy, he should make certain that the talk was made and that the speaker followed his prepared speech. Carelessness has been responsible for some newspapers, relying on advance copies, running stories about speeches never delivered because of last minute changes or emergencies.

There are editors who prefer interview stories to speech stories and who assign reporters to arrange for advance interviews. The feeling is that the interview, by permitting questions, provides more significant information than that given in speeches. Interview stories in such cases mention that the information was obtained in an interview so that the reader who attended the speech will not be confused. Reference should also be made in such stories to the fact that the interviewees were in the community for the occasion of making speeches.

The following example of a speech story written by Donovan Bess of the San Francisco *Chronicle* illustrates the similarity of the speech story to the interview type.

Indirect quotation	Senator Frank Moss said here yesterday that radical reforms in the Federal Government are needed to keep the affluent society from smothering in its own wastes.
Moves into direct quotation	Unless all of the environmental cleanup problems are brought into one cabinet-level department, the Utah Democrat asserted, "we are spinning our wheels—duplicating, overlapping, wasting effort—and failing year after year to deal with man's total environment as a whole."
Occasion	Moss spoke in the Fairmont Hotel to open a three-day national conference attended by more than 1,000 persons, mostly engineers and officials charged with fighting pollution of the land, the water and the air.

The Art of Interviewing 175

Moves from indirect to direct quotation	He praised college and high school students for their lively campaign to protect the environment. The movement, he declared, "has equated the word 'ecology' almost with the word 'motherhood' " as a sacrosanct matter.
Direct quotation	The senator said that when he first tried to get Congress to establish a Department of Natural Resources, five years ago, "the bureaucrats all indicated they would rather fight than switch."
Indirect quotation	Currently, Moss said, he proposes that the Department of the Interior be abolished and various agencies transferred into the new department.
Direct quotation	"After some communities remove all of the water in their waste treatment process, they burn the sludge, befouling the air," he declared. "Who is to referee that one?"
Indirect quotation with direct quotation	The senator said the Army Corps of Engineers should be put under the Secretary of Natural Resources. For example, he said, the corps building of a canal on the edge of the Florida Everglades preserve has "imperiled and destroyed" wildlife which "The National Park Service has preserved and guarded."
	Spokesmen for industry at the conference. . . .

The interweaving of direct and indirect quotations should be noted. This method is further illustrated in a Chicago *Sun-Times* speech story:

"Come on and read" type of lead	All he has ever sung is "We Shall Overcome" (off key, by his own admission), but former CORE director James Farmer addressed a music conference here Monday.
Supplement to lead	Farmer talked about James Brown; Aretha Franklin; Ray Charles. Soul. Rock. He also discussed Bach and Beethoven and Brahms.
	Farmer, now assistant secretary in the Health, Education and Welfare Department, wasn't giving a music lecture—he was talking about culture.
Direct quotation	"Forget the melting pot cliche," Farmer urged the Music Educators National Conference at the Conrad Hilton Hotel.
	"We're not a melting pot; we're pluralistic in culture. . . . If we recognize and honor ethnic contributions, we strengthen the fabric of the whole society," he said.
	"A few years ago, a man who was called black would consider it an insult. Now he says it with pride," said Farmer. "We have a culture to reclaim; we are trying to find ourselves in art and music."
Indirect quotation	That's where singers Brown and Miss Franklin come in. Blacks have been so busy in past years getting "bleached," they rejected their own music, Farmer said. Now it's time to realize it all belongs in the American culture.
Supplementation	"Music education can give an appreciation of self, then mankind—a sharing of soul," said Farmer.

General	Farmer advised educators to get out in the ghettos and try to understand the lives of the children they teach.
Supplementation, though only partial quotation is used	A music teacher "must have walked the streets" and heard the cacophony of sounds that include bad plumbing, family fights, and rats being chased with a broom, if he wants to reach the child who lives there, Farmer said. (Reprinted with permission from the Chicago *Sun-Times*)

The organization of the speech story usually follows the pattern of moving from the general to the specific, back to the general and again to the specific, and so on. The organization is much like that of the interview story.

EXERCISES

I. Comment on the following statement made by a newspaper executive

In assigning a reporter to an interview, a factor considered is the type you are after. If the subject is expected to be antagonistic, a "bulldogger" gets the assignment—someone who will not just be a recording device for the speaker, but one who will pin the subject down on specifics, inaccuracies, wild statements, etc. The trend today, particularly on the part of TV newsmen, is to conduct the "sweetheart" interview—regardless of individual involved. They make no attempt at comeback, but just voice an introductory question to set the guy off and then hold the mike to his face. Press conferences frequently devolve to this state and for that reason newspapermen (specifically my newspaper) kiss off press conferences in favor of exclusive interviews when subjects can be examined in detail without loss of continuity—or opportunity for the subject to evade sharp questioning.

II. Comment on the following excerpts from the Aug. 6, 1970, issue of the UPI Reporter

Sen. J. William Fulbright must have touched more than one journalistic nerve this week with his remark that when reporters appear on television with the President of the United States, they act like "suppliants at Nero's court."

Sen. Fulbright was talking about T.V. interviews rather than presidential news conferences. But his unflattering characterization could apply just as well to presidential conferences that are carried live on television. For it is a fact of life that the White House conference is simply not what it used to be.

This has nothing to do with the political affiliation of the occupant of the White House. It was as apparent in Lyndon B. Johnson's day as it is today that with the TV cameras there, there is less give and take than there used to be and that the initiative is more overwhelmingly the President's than ever before. . . .

A major factor in these changes, of course, is television. Good reporters are not necessarily good performers; thus, the fact that several million people are watching can only have an inhibiting effect. . . .

To remind the President, when only your colleagues are listening, that his answer, however admirable, does not respond to the question, is one thing. But to do it with millions watching and listening is another matter. Will the audience appreciate that the reporter is really seeking vital information, or will they suspect him of trying to harass the President or hog the spotlight? These thoughts do arise, with obvious effects. . . .

III. Discuss the Following Leads

BY DAVID KUHN

NORTHFIELD, Minn.—It's not an original question, but it's hard to avoid asking a new college president why he'd want such a job in this era of campus tensions. (Reprinted by permission of the Minneapolis *Tribune*)

Lt. Gov. Thomas P. Gill last night called for resisting "fast-buck artists who would create the slums of tomorrow, sear the mountainsides, and pave everything in sight." (Honolulu *Star-Bulletin*)

BY MAGGIE SAVOY

He tops 6 feet by half a foot, this gangly 29-year-old British lord, and though he was born in a London apartment during the blitz, he played in the halls of a palace so big the roofline covers more than 7 acres. (Los Angeles *Times*)

BY BOB THRELKELD

In a powerful speech which left the audience in a cathartic clamor, nationally noted black leader, Dr. George Wiley, challenged the some 1,000 delegates to the Colorado Conference of Social Welfare Thursday to join welfare recipients in a grass-roots movement to obtain dignity, justice and an adequate income. (Denver *Rocky Mountain News*)

Millions around the world may be shaking in their boots, sandals or plain size 12s over the possibility that Russia plans to blow the world into Kingdom Come.

But Sir John Slessor . . . is not one of them. (San Francisco *Examiner*)

IV. Comment on the effectiveness of the following excerpts from interview and speech stories

He is an education expert with a fondness for words like "thrust" and "input," but managed to convey his true feelings—he far prefers activists to parents sunk in apathy, he doesn't see what all the fuss about busing is over, he wants to work in harmony with all the community, black and white. (Maitland Zane, San Francisco *Chronicle*)

As she sits relaxed and casual in corduroy slacks and a blouse, music from the jukebox weaves through Alison's conversation. (Sherry Petchul, *Christian Science Monitor*)

Dressed in a pale blue minidress and white boots, her dark hair at shoulder length and flashing a mischievous smile, Miss Devlin seemed rested and healthy. (UPI)

The broad grin still recalls the playboy prince of yesteryear, but today Hussein's eyes are darkly shadowed, his face lined and his thinning hair touched with gray. (Eddie Adams, AP)

He wears faded blue bell-bottom denims, beads around his neck and cowboy boots. . . .

His golden locks are starting to creep over his collar and down to the bridge of his nose. (Bill Peterson, Louisville *Courier-Journal*)

V. *When Professor Melvin Mencher of the Graduate School of Journalism, Columbia University, was a reporter in California, he interviewed Dr. Serge Korff, a professor of physics at New York University. Excerpts from that interview follow (Q represents the reporter and A the interviewee).*

Q. I understand that you were the president of the Explorers' Club. Is that right? What do you have to do to earn that kind of title?
A. Yes. Oh, I've been about a good many parts of the world.
Q. Where have you been?
A. Well, I have been all through South America—
Q. Exploring?
A. Yes, and through Africa.
Q. Did you ever go to Ecuador?
A. Yes, indeed, I've been to Ecuador. Many times.
Q. A good friend of mind went there hunting for gold a few weeks ago.
A. Did he find any?
Q. No, but he had a good time.
A. Well, that's the important thing.
Q. He wanted to find the hidden gold of the Incas.
A. Oh, that? Yes, I know. Everybody does. People have been looking for that for 300 years. . . .
Q. What I wanted to talk about is this: there have been many estimates as to where the safety factor is in radiation. I think it's Mueller who says that a generation can absorb 80 roentgens without genetic difficulty, and some say as low as three. If you would not mind, I'd like to pursue that.

A. Well, the problem, however, is that that's a biological problem and I'm not a biologist. I can't give you any quantitative numbers, because I just don't know them. And when my friends, the geneticists, differ among themselves and one says 80 and one says three, I, who am not a geneticist—how would I know?
Q. No, I don't want you to set any specific limits at all. I'm just sketching out the general problem. As I get it, man will absorb something like five or six or seven roentgens of cosmic radiation alone.
A. I don't remember the number, but there is a certain definite cosmic ray background that he does get.
Q. You're talking about cosmic rays?
A. Yes.
Q. This is what you call natural radiation?
A. Yes.
Q. That is very dangerous, and we're also getting it?
A. We're getting it; we certainly are. We've been getting it for thousands of years.
Q. Now, of course, we're getting more of it?
A. No, cosmic rays are the same. They haven't changed.
Q. Do they vary from place to place?
A. Yes, they do.
Q. Where? Is there a standard place of variation?
A. No, there's no standard place. They vary from actually almost anywhere in the United States. At sea level they have the same value. If you go down to South America you will get just a trifle less at sea level. But, of course, you'll get a good deal more if you go up to high elevations.
Q. This is cosmic radiation. As I understand it, it does produce a certain number of mutations.
A. Actually, nobody knows. We just go on assumptions, but we do not know whether that assumption is correct. . . .
Q. Well, then, this idea that it does produce mutations, I think, stems from—I forget whether it's Mueller or whose theory it is—but any radiation will create mutations at a certain point.
A. It has been probably known for 50 years that mutations occur and then they try to figure out why. Now, they don't yet know why, but some of them happened that they call spontaneous. Whether they really are spontaneous or not, we don't know. Spontaneous may be just a way of saying we don't know.
Q. To pursue this, and if you're reluctant to pursue it—
A. No, I'm not at all reluctant to pursue it.
Q. Because everybody is concerned with it, and—
A. I know, and I'm not at all sure that they know why.
Q. Well, I think the fact that it was raised as a political issue, and then everybody thinks it—well now, if you don't mind, let's talk about the role of the scientist in society. You people have a special knowledge of this thing that bothers a lot of us, and I notice that you were assigned to the advisers to the U.N.

A. Yes, I was.
Q. What did you do, incidentally, when you were assigned to the advisers?
A. Most of what we did was to prepare the International Bibliography on atomic energy. We went through all the journals in which anything was written in any and all languages and all countries, and we made a total compendium of 25,000 titles on atomic energy, and then, as the years went on, we had to issue supplements to this so that the total issue now is a perfectly tremendous thing. It must be four inches thick, just only listing the titles. So from that, then, you can look up any subject that you want in the whole field of atomic energy.
Q. When did you do this work?
A. Well, let's see—my term expired about 12 years ago and it was in the previous three years that we did the bibliography.
Q. Well, now, when you were working on this project, to get back to the role of the scientist in society, did you—among your fellow scientists was there a great feeling of responsibility to the public?
A. No.
Q. Not at all?
A. I wouldn't say not at all. But the point really is that the basic decisions are not made by us, they're made by the politicians.
Q. Do you feel there should be more scientists in politics?
A. No, we have no expert knowledge of politics.
Q. Yet some of the political decisions have a scientific basis.
A. That's correct, and therefore what we should do is to serve as consultants and to enlighten them on the scientific points when they ask for it. But I don't think that scientists as such should get into politics, because this is a realm where they are not experts. . . .
Q. But there's a role you think they should perform.
A. Well, it's for every man to decide for himself.
Q. I still get from what you said that a scientist has no business in politics.
A. I didn't say that. I said that I feel that I should not go into a domain in which I am not an expert and pretend to be an expert.
Q. Well, what about the scientific argument—the ban on nuclear testing?
A. Yes, but you see the point is that there isn't a scientific argument. It's a political argument. Should we or should we not conduct the tests? This is a political argument, not a scientific one.
Q. Well, I thought the basis was, we are reaching a point in atmospheric saturation that is dangerous, and the National Academy of Scientists has said, "No," and the Federation of Atomic Scientists said, "Maybe," and there was, it seemed to me, a scientific line.
A. Well, no, I think that such an argument did take place, but it involved problems of genetics. And I have seen no data and I don't know where there are any data that will support any such statement.
Q. Support which statement?
A. That there is any danger or that this thing is an issue. I don't know—

maybe it is. I don't know where the data are. I should think the National Academy would have available any data that it wants. . . .
Q. Do you think a wide large-scale approach to the whole subject is worthwhile—what is the danger point?
A. Yes, I think it might be worthwhile. But such a study would have to be made by geneticists rather than by physicists, if you're talking about genetic damage.
Q. Has there been any experimentation, do you know (again, I'm sorry that this is about genetics) in areas where there is more cosmic radiation? Do you know if there's been any study of whether there has been corresponding increases in mutations?
A. I don't know—I wouldn't think so, because after all there are great areas of the world up at high elevations. If you want to go up to La Paz, Bolivia, you'll find a nice city with 150,000 people in it and whether the death rate there is greater or not, whether the mutation rate is greater or not, I wouldn't know, but people live there very happily.
Q. I understand they have made some surveys in parts of Scotland where certain families have been subjected to a higher radioactive degree. And they have made an interesting study of it. Hemophilia and other—
A. Well, again, I haven't seen the data on that. That's out of my field and I've never studied the genetic effects of radiation.
Q. Let me ask you—being in such close contact with the U.N. as you are in New York, and having served with the U.N. atomic energy commission, do you have any feelings one way or the other about the point which we have reached in the nuclear ban and the ban on nuclear weapons?
A. This is a completely political problem. It is outside my field of expert knowledge.
Q. Dr. Korff, I'm not asking you about your expert knowledge. I simply say you were close to the discussions.
A. Yes, I knew a lot of them and heard them argue these points.
Q. Do you think we're any closer to a general viewpoint?
A. Oh, I don't know—that's a hard question to answer.
Q. I'm not quite sure I know what you mean.
A. Well, our machines, which we are very pleased with ourselves when we can generate particles, the energy of which is just barely equal to the minimum in cosmic rays, and the cosmic ray energies just start from there and go way up and if you want to make any studies of what a 10-billion-volt gamma ray does, the only way you can find out is to measure it in cosmic rays.
Q. Why should we be interested in knowing what a 10-billion-volt gamma ray does?
A. Well, you just asked me about the genetic effects of radiation. There's your answer.
Q. In other words, you people are gathering basic data.
A. That's right, and genetics is one area in which basic data may apply.

There are many others. The earth is being bombarded by this radiation. What does it do? We would like to know. We're trying to find out. . . .

Q. What have you learned in the last few years that is radical in the sense of upsetting previous theories?

A. Well, we have a pretty good mechanism now for the origin of radiation and this is specifically the thing I'm going to talk about today. That is certainly in the sense of upsetting previous theories. It supersedes all of them.

Q. That's what I wanted you to get into, in your own words, so that it will make it fairly clear.

A. We know that radiation is generated in the galaxy by the magnetic fields of the galaxy. By really using the galaxy itself as a sort of enormous betatron.

Q. What is a betatron?

A. A betatron is one of the high energy accelerating machines which accelerates particles to high energy by making use of the varying magnetic fields. It's one of the big atom-smashing machines.

Q. They've got this huge betatron accelerating the particles and bombarding the earth. Now, specifically what kinds of information have you found, again getting back to the biologist or the botanist. Have you found—can you relate your findings to something practical?

A. The old problem of pure research is to find out the basic facts and then, later on, other people will make some practical use of them. Each new fact will have practical applications in some very surprising and quite different places. For instance, if you wanted to help a surgeon to find a better way to set bones, it would probably not occur to you to start experimenting with electrical discharges in a rather poor vacuum. And yet that is the way that X rays were discovered. So you have many applications which come about in very surprising places and quite far from where you think they're going to come about. And what we are doing in our business is finding new facts. Where they will be applied, no man knows yet.

Q. Well, that's what I wondered about. Is this fact-gathering process, in which you're engaged, at a fairly early level as far as application is concerned?

A. Well, it is at no level at all, as far as application is concerned.

Q. It doesn't exist then?

A. Oh, yes, it exists. Certainly applications exist, but I don't do them—somebody else does.

Q. I was just wondering if you knew specifically—

A. Yes, it is a tool of high energy investigation. This is the principal use of cosmic radiation.

Q. Can you tell me what particular—

A. If you wish to know what the effect of cosmic rays and what the effects are which they can produce—we have no source of high energy radiation above a certain limit which we can generate today in our machines, other than cosmic rays. All applications and all knowledge of what these things do will ultimately come from these cosmic rays.

Q. I don't think I'm making myself too clear. What I'm trying to get at is that, while I realize you're developing studies which will later be applied, I'm just wondering if you can tell me what studies you have made that have already been applied specifically to something understandable to the average reader.

A. Well, for example, I don't know whether the average reader is familiar with magnetic storms. Magnetic storms are sudden variations in the earth's magnetic field. These magnetic storms sometimes can be quite large. They can result in very important effects, such as the compass pointing very far away from its normal direction, normal magnetic north. The compass may be many degrees out for a given period. If you are a ship's captain at sea and you are steering a magnetic course, and there is a magnetic storm going on, you have no way of knowing it, and yet, all of a sudden, your compass may be in error by many degrees. The study of magnetic storms is very much tied up with cosmic ray studies and our knowledge of them and the mechanism which produces them is tied up with this study, and we have learned something about their nature by cosmic ray studies.

Q. What about the relationship of cosmic rays to radio carbon dating?

A. That is another very good application. Cosmic ray neutrons in the upper atmosphere make radio carbon—carbon 14—and carbon 14 in the atmosphere becomes part of the carbon structure of all living matter, plants and animals, and as soon as the plant or the animal dies it stops building carbon into its structure, so that from then on, the radio carbon simply slowly decays. All you need to do is to find a piece of wood, for example. Measure the amount of radio carbon left in it, compare that with a piece cut today to give you the current production, and then you can tell how long ago that piece was cut.

Q. Tell me, you spoke about carbon 14—everybody's talking about this strontium 90. Is that a product of—

A. No, that is not. That's a man-made affair completely. . . .

Q. That Explorers' Club is quite a club.

A. Oh, yes, we've had a lot of very distinguished people in it. Actually, we have in it practically all of the important scientific explorers of the present day. It's a scientific club, you see. Most of the people in it are scientists. . . . The majority of the scientific explorers of the world are members of it.

Q. Well, when you were in Africa and South America, was that a scientific journey?

A. Oh, yes, certainly. I was studying cosmic rays and arranging for cosmic ray observations with the people down there.

Q. Isn't there an observatory in Africa?

A. There are several very good ones. . . .

Q. Why do you go to South America and to Africa to arrange the cosmic ray—

A. Well, you see, because of the deflection of the cosmic ray particles in the earth's magnetic field, the intensities in the southern hemisphere or in the equatorial zone are a little different from what they are up here in the temperate zone. We study cosmic rays everywhere, all over the earth: here, in the south, and also up north in the polar regions.

Q. I take it . . . that the research in cosmic radiation . . . has accelerated tremendously in the last few years.

A. Oh, yes, it's gone along very fast in the last few years.

Q. And probably will gain momentum, and as we move on increasingly —I wouldn't use the word valid, but I suppose that's as good a word as any—the theory that they use one year becomes superseded the next.

A. Oh, yes, we learn more. That's just what we're trying to do, you see, is to learn what's going on. . . .

Q. Are you disturbed at all by . . . the apparent decrease in the high school requirements in such fields as mathematics?

A. Well, I think that's very unfortunate because the result is that the students come to the universities badly prepared. I think—you see, for instance, in England the high school students get calculus in high school.

Q. Oh, they do?

A. Yes, they do. . . .

Q. Do you think that there's a great reservoir of ability that some educators are not tapping?

A. I do—yes, I think there is.

Q. Is there a softening up of the curriculum?

A. I think so.

Q. Why are they doing this?

A. I don't know, but, you see, we are not doing it in the colleges. We are, on the contrary, fighting against it. We observe the students coming to us from high schools and some of them are really not very well trained, and they seem to have, when we ask them, had to take many courses that just seem to have had not much to do with anything and really contain subject matter which maybe they should have learned at home or something.

Q. That's a very interesting observation, because in speaking to educators that I've interviewed in various parts of the country, the school seems to be taking on the role of the home. For example, in the old days the parents used to teach the children to drive—now it's a part of the curriculum.

A. Yes.

Q. Something has to go and maybe it's your advanced algebra or solid geometry that is sacrificed.

A. Well, I don't see why the parents can't teach their children to drive. I know my parents taught me and I don't see anything wrong with that. It seems to me perfectly simple and elementary. . . .

Q. Well, with that I'm going to let you go, because I've detained you long enough.

1. Comment on the questions asked after reading the biographical sketch of Dr. Korff in *Who's Who in America*.
2. Write a story based on the interview.
3. Atomic testing has gone underground since the preceding interview was made. The reporter was a reader, among other things, of the *Bulletin of Atomic Scientists,* which had expressed a concern about atomic testing. Is the reporter's concern indicated by his questioning?
4. After you write the story, turn to Appendix C.

VI. Critical Questions

1. In the second paragraph of the Minneapolis *Tribune* story on Rosemary McVay, notice the handling of attribution. Would it have been better if handled:

"I'm all for the girl who wants to work," said Rosemary McVay, a part-time lawyer and mother of five. "But I don't think screaming and demanding will get her a job."

2. In the second paragraph of the *Arkansas Gazette* interview with Miss Betty Buford, do the words "in order to" say more than would the simple word "to"?
3. Would the sixth paragraph of the same story have been improved if the indirect and direct quotations had been put in separate paragraphs?
4. In the second paragraph of the Detroit *Free Press* story on William H. Brown, III, was it better not to wait until the end of the quotation to bring in the attribution?
5. Was the attribution needed at the end of the fifth paragraph of the Chicago *Sun-Times* story about James Farmer's speech?

Chapter 11

INTERESTING THE READERS

> *Gentle words, quiet words, are, after all,*
> *the most powerful words. They are*
> *more convincing, more compelling,*
> *more prevailing.* —*Washington Gladden*

People's interests vary. Some people have wide interests, others have narrow ones. Some like opera, others prefer jazz. Some like to read, others prefer to watch television. Some enjoy the mountains, others like the seashore. Some like golf and fishing, others want more sedentary pastimes. What subjects appeal to people? The reader's age, sex, education, occupation, experience, income and wealth all affect his tastes.

When it comes to journalism, one thing is certain: the reporter who does not take an interest in writing a story is not going to make it interesting to his reader. Writing done as routine must depend entirely on content to interest readers. Writing done with enthusiasm is more likely to kindle a spark of interest.

Sensory Appeals

Human beings communicate with each other only through the five senses. The person who suffers the loss of one or more of the senses finds an accompanying loss in his ability to communicate, though he may compensate to a certain extent by learning to make fuller use of the senses he still has.

The skilled writer learns that, though his basic communicative method—the use of print—is a visual one, he can make varying appeals to the imagination of his reader. Depending on the type of writing he is doing, he may be able to make the reader, in his imagination, see it, hear it, feel it, taste it and smell it.

An example of how this can be done is illustrated in the opening paragraphs of a *Christian Science Monitor* story by John Allan May:

> LONDON—The drills clatter, the hammers thud, the mixers grumble, trucks rev and rattle, traffic rumbles, an airliner growls overhead. The lights are on in myriad office windows in a dozen rectangular blocks nearby.
> They shine in the puddles of the building site, accentuating the grayness. The sky is gray. The mud is gray. The 43-story towers being constructed are gray. The eight-story quadrangles are gray.
> On the site of the as-yet-uncompleted "Barbican," grayness is all.
> And the scale is massive. Huge gray concrete pillars. Vast concrete walls. Thick concrete balustrades. Towers rising 400 feet, concrete floor on massive gray concrete floor. . . .

The reader can almost hear the noise in the first paragraph, see the grayness in the second, feel the massiveness in the fourth. Repetition can be used effectively, as in the description of grayness.

A hushed feeling is the effect created by this Fresno (Calif.) *Bee* story by Wanda Coyle:

> The first thing you noticed was the hush.
> The Convention Center Theater was nearly filled on the main floor, and a few scattered onlookers were in the balcony. But there was no anticipatory buzz of conversation, no laughter.
> For these Fresnans—young and old, poor and rich, black, brown and white—had come not for entertainment, but to do homage to the memory of Robert Francis Kennedy, U.S. senator from the state of New York, aspirant to the nation's highest office, brother of martyred Pres. John F. Kennedy and himself an assassin's victim.
> Last night's community memorial service for Kennedy continued in that same peculiar quiet. An organ prelude only heightened and pointed up the silence of the audience, broken only by an occasional fretful cry from a child or a giggle from the lobby, where some of the fidgeting children had been sent to play.
> The speakers from the stage spoke into the hush in voices sometimes strong, sometimes strained but always filled with sadness. . . .

The opening of a Sacramento *Union* story by Robert Taylor gives the reader a vivid picture of an old bus:

> It groaned up to the curb, rocking and creaking and showing off the rust and dust of 34 years of use—a wayward bus from another era.

A Long Island *Newsday* excerpt exemplifies a writer's attempt to draw an imaginary picture for his readers:

> The Commune's quarters, at 37 Union Square West in New York City, are in a long, narrow corridor with cubicles serving as offices. The floors are covered with murky-colored linoleum. There is not a thread of carpet in the place. Posters of Che Guevara, Huey Newton and President Nixon parading as a Ku Klux Klansman are plastered on walls. The doors to each office are painted psychedelic yellow and green. A bright orange water fountain stands next to a tattered couch. A draft-age young man is stretched out fast asleep on the couch, waiting for an appointment.

The idea of appealing to the imagination is indicated in a professor's comment about a sign, in front of a restaurant, depicting a cup of coffee: "There's no steam coming from it. Who wants a cold cup of coffee?"

Putting Words to Work

Words are symbols used by human beings as a means of communication. In themselves, they are neither dull nor bright and neither concrete nor abstract. They may symbolize brightness or dullness and the concrete or abstract. A writer may use them, depending upon his wit, humor, mood, imagination and talent, to communicate ideas to a reader.

To be effective, a writer learns to play with words, to shuffle them into interesting combinations, to get the maximum performance from the ones he uses. The following is dull and depends entirely upon the interest the reader has in its content if it is to be read:

> Fair today, tonight, tomorrow and over the weekend. Continued warm. High today 85 to 95, tomorrow 90–100. Low tonight 60 to 70.

Some appeal to the imagination is portrayed, however, in the following:

> Close down the furnace, Dad, and get out the plastic swimming pool, Mom, the hot weather will be with us for a while.
> (Turlock, Calif., *Journal*)

Another interesting lead for a weather story is:

> A soggy San Diego County will get a chance to dry out over the next few days. . . .
> (G. L. Schultz, San Diego *Tribune*)

An opening paragraph can be inviting or uninviting to a reader, but of all parts of a story which should be interesting the lead is one of the most important. More and more the use of unconventional leads is being resorted to. A sports story example is:

> NEW YORK (AP)—If a football tie is like kissing your sister, a majority of the coaches in this year's major bowls would rather have something more romantic—like sudden death.

Another sports example is:

> SANTA BARBARA (UPI)—The Taft College basketball coach Saturday night made a 260-mile, six-hour mistake.

An inviting lead is:

> A toothy bird that has long been a familiar sight in the Sacramento community is flying off this week to greater fame—and a final resting place in a national cemetery.
> She is "China American Girl"—a beaten and battered old F51 Mustang fighter plane. . . .
> (Paul Merz, Sacramento *Union*)

Antithesis—the contrast of ideas—can be used to achieve interest:

> BY FRANK MAZZA
> The subway rebellion rolled on yesterday and some trains didn't. Increased numbers of straphangers held impromptu sit-ins and showed their displeasure with the subways and the 30-cent fare in various ways.
> (Courtesy of the New York *News*)

Climax was used to make the following lead interesting:

> HOUSTON (UPI)—Vice President Spiro T. Agnew said Friday night President Nixon had not "muzzled" him. Then he proved it.
> Agnew verbally blasted the news media. . . .
> (Kyle Thompson)

Figurative words can be used to enhance interest:

> SAN FRANCISCO—Republican leaders in California are trying to remold their party's image from anti-youth and anti-black. But they may be using the wrong political chisel.
> (Curtis J. Sitomer, *Christian Science Monitor*)

Figurative language, a sense of humor and simple words were used to make the following opening paragraphs of a story interesting:

> Fearing that their pocketbooks might be pinched if a stretch of Trevilan Way is rebuilt, more than 75 residents of the area yelled ouch last night.
>
> And amid loud applause and more than one guffaw, they told the Louisville Board of Aldermen in no uncertain terms that they wanted Trevilan Way left just the way it is —chuckholes and all.
>
> (Bill Peterson, Louisville *Courier-Journal*)

An application of burlesque makes this lead interesting:

> WASHINGTON—The big bad bear in the bond market has been booted aside. A bull, timid as Ferdinand, is tiptoeing timorously onto the moneymarket scene.
>
> (David R. Francis, *Christian Science Monitor*)

The writer's efforts to achieve interest should not end with the opening paragraph, though unfortunately many stories with interesting leads lapse into mediocrity as the paragraphs continue. Note how a lead, reporting that a disturbed Soviet ship captain dismissed a visiting group of Jewish leaders from his cabin, is followed by interesting paragraphs (italics added):

> Captain D. R. Ryabchenko received the four Bay Area leaders in a friendly fashion when they boarded the Ostrogozhsk at Pier 9 and shook hands all around.
>
> But when the silver-haired skipper, whose command of English is limited, realized the deputation wanted him to carry a message of protest back to his government, *the wind started blowing from a different quarter.*
>
> "I refuse to discuss political questions," the uniformed captain said sternly. "This is a merchant ship. Go to the embassy in Washington. . . ."
>
> (Keith Power, San Francisco *Chronicle*)

Writing a story based on an interview with Howard J. Samuels when he was a candidate for the governorship of New York, a reporter followed up the introductory paragraph with:

> Samuels, who made it big early in business (one associate estimates his current wealth at $20,000,000), has been in politics for only seven years. And while there may be some argument *over what makes Samuels run, there is no doubt that he is running hard.*
>
> (Bernie Bookbinder, Long Island *Newsday*)

An opening paragraph of a story by B. Drummond Ayers based on an interview in Crazy Horse, S. Dak., with Korczak Ziolkowski, mountain sculptor, was followed by:

> He stands more than 6 feet and tops 230 pounds.
>
> His shaggy salt-and-pepper beard *tumbles* down a full eight inches onto his barrel chest, which periodically sends forth *foghorn* hoots and laughs.
>
> He has 10 children, five boys and five girls, for whom he has singlehandedly fashioned a home of 57 rooms and 161 doors that zigzag *like a broken field runner* through 100 shady yards of Ponderosa Pine.
>
> (©1970 by The New York Times Company. Reprinted by permission.)

Words that are symbols of abstract ideas are less likely to create exact images in a reader's mind than are words that stand for concrete objects:

> The demonstrators threw *missiles* at the Guardsmen.

This is much more exact:

> The demonstrators hurled *stones, bricks* and *empty bottles* at the Guardsmen.

Concrete words (such as "bricks," "redwood," "cement blocks") specify particular members of a class, whereas abstract words, such as "building materials," refer to general classifications. The word "tool" signifies something general, but "hammer" refers to something specific.

The word "colorful" is a symbol of an abstraction, but the words "orange" and "green" are symbols of more specific, more concrete, ideas. A noun that names a quality, such as "good," provides an abstract meaning. When abstractions are expressed, the writer should offer explanation, examples or incidents in order to provide more reality for the reader, as in:

> People in Greensboro always had considered him a good man.
>
> He went to church every Sunday, he umpired boys' league baseball games, he always contributed generously to charitable organizations, he never smoked or drank alcoholic beverages, and he was always friendly with persons he was associated with.

An imaginative writer can find many ways of putting meaning into a word:

> Ice—enough to chill all the champagne in New York—proved a bigger holiday headache than the traditional New Year's hangover after a freezing rain glazed city streets yesterday morning. (Joseph Modzelewski, New York *Daily News*)

Eliminate the words between the two dashes and notice the loss.

Impressionistic Writing

When the importance of a story does not warrant the space needed for elaborate detail, the writer may resort, very effectively, to impressionistic writing—portraying the general impression produced. The following San Francisco *Chronicle* story makes effective use of impressionism (italicized words):

> A haggard crew of policemen returned to Richmond Police Station with a burglar following a *chase over rooftops and through backyards.*
>
> They brought back an *assortment of bruises, ripped uniforms, sprained ankles* and John Doe, a 30-year-old ex-convict.
>
> Behind them they *left three fallen backyard fences, many trampled gardens, and a number of frightened householders.*
>
> The backyard chase began shortly after Mary Doakes was awakened at 3:30 a.m. by someone pounding noisily in the delicatessen below her flat at 666 Clement St.
>
> Mrs. Doakes tiptoed downstairs and saw a burglar at work on the safe. She ran upstairs and called the police.
>
> The thief slipped away into a neighboring backyard as police arrived. Every officer in the Richmond District, except Sgt. John Jones, who stayed behind to mind the station, began a backyard search.
>
> The eight officers *scrambled over fences* (*three collapsed*), *dashed through shrubbery* (*two torn uniforms*), *climbed to rooftops* (*one lost policeman's star*) and *stumbled through flower beds* (*one sprained ankle*).
>
> Finally the ragged pursuers surrounded their equally exhausted quarry upon a rooftop at 375 Ninth Ave. and Officer James Smith snapped on the handcuffs.
>
> Doe, a gas station attendant who lives at . . . , was charged with burglary. He told the officers the last time he was pursued was 12 years ago after he held up a bank in Louisiana.
>
> "I thought this would be easier," he explained.
>
> (Reprinted from the San Francisco *Chronicle*)

Impressionism was used to start the following:

> Rats, junk cars, foul odors, roving dogs, rotting leaves, dilapidated houses, damaged curbs, parking restrictions, and litter.
>
> These were typical problems brought to Louisville Mayor Frank W. Burke yesterday at his first beef session in City Hall. . . . (Vincent Crowdus, Louisville *Courier-Journal*)

Impressionistic writing covers a lot in a short space.

Parallelism

Parallelism makes use of a number of usually consecutive similar grammatical forms. These parallel forms can be put into a sentence or a series of relatively short sentences.

Two examples follow from a UPI story on flower children by Robert Strand:

> Here the hippies now sit *blowing their flutes, dropping their acid, strumming their guitars* and *letting their children run.*

> Their words resembled those of other youthful musical groups around the country—*opposing the war, condemning the draft, complaining of man's isolation from his fellows* and sometimes *praising dope.*

An excerpt from an AP story illustrates the use of parallelism in alternating sentences:

> *They served* him oysters pickled in poison alcohol. He ate them with relish and lived. *They served* him food loaded with ground tin. He never even knew it. *They gave* him tainted sardines. He would not die.

A series of consecutive parallel sentences was used in this UPI story by Richard H. Growald on corruption in Saigon:

> The corruption takes many of the forms of sin.
> *There is* the black market, chicken feed really, but the most noticeable to the American walking the streets of Saigon, Da Nang or Pleiku.
> *There is* the disappearance of cement, steel and other materials used in the billion-dollar American construction program in Vietnam.
> *There are* the American penicillin and other drugs that turn up in Viet Cong aid stations.
> *There is* the bribery, embezzlement and thievery that rouses Ky's anger. . . .

Parallelism is exemplified in a line attributed by Plutarch to Julius Caesar: "I came, I saw, I conquered." The construction is an example of asyndeton, in which conjunctions are omitted where they normally would be used. The marked parallelism of the three short clauses requires no "and" before the last clause.

Rhetorical Questions

The rhetorical question is interrogative only in form. The speaker and the writer who use it do not expect an answer from listeners or readers. It is used for effect. The answer is usually supplied by the speaker or writer. In journalism, it is often supplied by the reporter, who also cites his news source.

This device is exemplified in an excerpt from an Associated Press story on weather:

> Why does the high humidity bother you? Your perspiration doesn't dry, explains Schmidt, and instead of being cooled by the evaporation, you have a hot, sticky feeling.

Reporters sometimes use a modification of the rhetorical question by inserting the name of the news source:

> Who does Jones think should be responsible to get the project started?
> He believes. . . .

The rhetorical question provides an interesting means of putting variety into writing.

Litotes

Litotes is a figurative usage in which an affirmative is expressed by the negation of its opposite, as in:

> Jones, though a man of small physical stature, proved himself to be a man of *no small courage*.

> Smith refused to reveal the cost but said it was *no huge sum*.

Like all other rhetorical devices, litotes should be used occasionally, not excessively, to attain variety in expression.

Kaleidoscopic Writing

A series of fragmentary sentences can be used to represent opinions about a particular topic. An excerpt from a Copley News Service article illustrates this rhetorical device:

> Push "The Philippines" button in the minds of most Americans and a cliche card pops up:
> — Gen. Douglas MacArthur wading ashore to fulfill his "I shall return" pledge; natives cheering.

> — One of the few democracies in Asia.
> — Devoted ally; friendly people.
> — Lush vegetation; plenty for everyone to eat.

Kaleidoscopic writing can be hypothetical, as in the previous example, or it can be based on actual comments, as in the following excerpt from a UPI story:

> There is very little in the way of public entertainment in White, which has a population of 439, and is unincorporated, so George drew big crowds.
> "Lookit old George," they said in awe.
> "Hey George, go ahead and shoot."
> "Hey George, you got your Bible with you?"

This rhetorical device can be effectively used in certain situations in which the writer wishes to express conglomerate views or attitudes.

Reader Identification

A reader who identifies himself in some way with the content of a story is more likely to become interested in it than one who does not. Reader identification means some kind of personal association.

A number of writing devices help to create reader identification. One is the second person pronoun "you," when used in what grammarians refer to as direct address. Here are some examples:

> If you are looking for a good spring tonic, don't give up if sulphur and molasses won't turn the trick—just try your hand at a little poetry.
> This is the advice of . . . who will give a late-afternoon class in verse writing this spring on the Fresno State College campus. (Fresno *Bee*)
>
> TUDOR—You're driving north on Highway 99 and somewhere beyond Nicolaus in Sutter County you pass the Dingville Cafe.
> After a few miles of plowed fields and peach orchards, you see a road sign which reads, "Slow to 40 MPH."
> You are about to enter a little modern-day Twilight Zone—a village that God forgot.
> You are returning to 1924, and a dead man's dream—the town of Tudor. And you somehow suspect the entire scene has been lifted from an Erskine Caldwell novel.
> If you don't slow to 40, you may miss the village entirely. It is two blocks long, give or take a few yards, and its weed-choked picket fences and weather-beaten storefronts blend into the roadside scenery.
> If you like you can buy the whole town. . . . (Paul Merz, Sacramento *Union*)

> BY MONTY HOYT
> CAMBRIDGE—Trash—you could burn it, bury it, shred it, pulverize it, grind it, compost it—and now, at last, an American company will compact it for you. (*Christian Science Monitor*)

H. D. Quigg, a UPI correspondent, used a variation on direct address in writing a story about the slaying of 13 persons by a sniper shooting from the bell-clock tower at the University of Texas:

> If you are a tower receptionist named Edna Elizabeth Townsley, it is your day off. But you are there by a twist of fate—a co-worker is on vacation and you are filling in. And you are lying, barely breathing, behind a couch near your observation-deck desk, dying—your head bashed in by a madman's gun butt and then pierced by a bullet.
>
> If you are sweethearts at age 18 named Paul Sonntag and Claudia Rutt, you are walking hand-in-hand toward death—and you are here on the west mall by fate's tug: the swimming pool where he was a lifeguard, and where she always joined him, was closed for the day.
>
> If you are 17-year-old Alec Hernandez, you are working as a vacation replacement for the delivery boy who bicycles newspapers to the university area—and you are pedaling northward toward a bullet in the hip because your newspaper came out 10 minutes early on Monday. . . .

Direct address can also be used to attract readers to a story about any one of numerous topics common to all people. Almost any homeowner would be interested in this subject:

> WASHINGTON—You think you have termite problems? Whatever they are they can't compare with those the United States Navy faces. (Neal Stanford, *Christian Science Monitor*)

And many readers are concerned about problems that are not necessarily individual:

> John Jones knew he had problems—mental ones—and he feared what might happen to him and his family if he didn't find some way of getting help.
>
> *But, like thousands of other Americans, he refused to go to a psychiatrist—he felt it would be a disgrace.*

The italicized paragraph helps to broaden the appeal of the story. Many Americans have relatives or friends in the same situation.

Supplementation

Supplementation can be achieved by using examples, incidents, particulars and details, and quotations, all of which help to dramatize a story, to fill it with specific meaning and reality. The following story exemplifies the use of some of these devices.

> LONDON (AP)—Britain's gallant huntsmen, whizzing over the countryside with flashing colors, are having a sorry season—and only their disgust is running "at full cry."
>
> The foxes are getting too foxy. That's the trouble.
>
> "We have only run three foxes to earth this season," said Sir Peter Farquhar, joint master with Lord Rosebery of the famed Whaddon Chase hunt. And he added gloomily:
>
> "I believe that is the record for any country."
>
> Sir Peter complained that the hounds had failed to pick up a single scent for a whole fortnight, which, he said, left the hunting parties with nothing to do but dash around looking at the scenery.
>
> Not only are the elusive reynards scarce, however, but even when sighted they are getting a more and more annoying habit of seeking refuge in buildings—a climax which leaves the huntsmen chafing outside while the master of the hounds goes inside and puts the finishing touches on the unsporting reynard.
>
> "It's getting to be a parlor game—an indoor sport," grumbled a Whaddon huntsman darkly.
>
> Two recent instances saw a finale of that dismal caliber.
>
> Once the fleeing reynard, hotly pursued by the pack at his heels, leaped flying through the French windows of a country house, near historic Sherwood Forest, and the hounds killed it behind a bookcase.
>
> Again, the quarry scuttled into the kitchen of another home and was finally subdued amid a fanfare of flying pots and pans. The cook, incidentally, fainted.

Without the quotations and incidents, the preceding story would lack much of its interest.

An excerpt from a *Wall Street Journal* story written by Barbara Isenberg in Beverly Hills, Calif., illustrates how example can be used to gain interest:

> But the company's legion of critics contend that AIP (American International Pictures, Inc.) is not so much appealing to youth as pandering to it with simpleminded pap or films drenched in gore, violence and depravity.
>
> "Bloody Mama," for example, a tale of murderess Kate (Ma) Barker and her sons that owes much to "Bonnie and Clyde," has a Negro lynching in the first reel, homosexual sado-masochism in the second, a dope addict dying in

agony toward the end, occasional incest, multiple shoot-outs and buckets of blood. . . .
(Reprinted with permission of the *Wall Street Journal*)

An excerpt from a Sacramento *Union* story by Helen Vollmar shows how an example not only adds interest but also lends meaning to a general statement preceding it:

Raising wild creatures in captivity offers a variety of reactions and a host of problems, according to the curator, who notes the rising cost of live animals makes it important for the zoo to breed its own.

Take Tuffy [a leopard], for example. His mother killed her two previous litters. . . .

A Chicago *Tribune* Press Service story from Alaska written by Eugene Griffin further illustrates the use of example to stimulate interest:

From the schools where they were sent at the expense of the federal bureau of Indian affairs, the Eskimo teen-agers take the daily plane to Barrow at the Fairbanks airport with school sweaters, class yearbooks, autograph books, stuffed animals and other souvenirs.

One Barrow youth carried a Mexican watermelon, purchased in a Fairbanks supermarket for 33 cents a pound. . . . (Reprinted by permission of the Chicago *Tribune*)

A UPI story on hurricane Camille written by David Smothers makes effective use of incidents:

A book could be filled with stories of death and escape in Pass Christian alone. These would be some of the chapters:

— The Rev. Durrie Hardin, pastor of the 20-year-old Episcopal Church, tried to wait it out with his wife in the second floor of their rectory. He survived. She was swept away and drowned.

— Two teen-age brothers clung for their lives for four hours in the fork of a tree until Mississippi National Guardsmen pulled them to safety. They were two of scores saved by the guardsmen, who were in position before the hurricane hit and braved it in amphibious vehicles while Camille still howled about them.

— Mrs. Kenneth King sat on the front porch of a neighbor's topsy-turvy house, cleaning mud-caked silver and chatting: "Mrs. Edith Devries, did you ever hear about her? Everybody thought she was dead. She climbed out on the roof of her house with her daughter and was blown over into the water. But they found her alive behind the L & N tracks about a half mile away."

There was grief to spare along the Gulf Coast.

On Wednesday a man drove up, got out and stood beside the block-square flattened rubble that remained of the Richelieu Apartments. A woman followed him from the car, distraught. "No, no, you must be wrong," she said. "It must be farther down. This can't be it."

Besides examples and incidents, particulars and details can be used to fortify general statements. How details can be employed to create interest is illustrated in a *Christian Science Monitor* story by Elizabeth Pond. She describes a market scene in Saigon:

> The sidewalk is lined with apathetic rabbits and chickens, sometimes sharing the same woven cages.
> Plumbing faucets, Samsonite luggage, canned Chinese delicacies, new Sony radios, and shaving lotion vie for buyers' attention, as does a bewildering proliferation of nozzles, muzzles, mothballs, mops, rope, hose, stoves, soap, corks, books, film, drills, saws, chains, jeans, watches, wallets, wrenches, glasses, sandals, brushes, blankets, wads of shoelaces, Japanese underwear, toy tanks, shiny tempura pans, and spoons made out of napalm casings.
> A few vendors look bored, but there is a community of shared gossip and hot sun. There is the smell of ripe meat grease and garlic. There are sounds of sizzling fat, hammering, cap pistols, fire and ordnance disposal sirens, shouts, off-key notes from plastic pipes of Pan, and the clang of the large scissors of the sweets man as he wheels his bicycle along. Visible everywhere is the hanging blue exhaust punctuated by viscous puffs that follow every surge of traffic. . . .
> (Reprinted with permission from the *Christian Science Monitor*)

Here is a good example of how particulars can be used to supplement a lead:

> SAN FRANCISCO (UPI)—Campus crime has increased sharply at major Northern California colleges in the past year.
> Security police have little trouble with felonies but are harassed by minor thefts, stolen autos, drug usage and exhibitionism.
> Stanford University thefts skyrocketed 200 per cent during the school year. Seven rapes occurred, compared to a usual one or two. Weapons—for the first time—were reported in 10 incidents.
> At the sprawling University of California campus at Berkeley, police statistics showed 940 offenses from January through June, ranging from larceny to auto thefts, including a substantial increase in drug usage.
> San Francisco State, a commuter college which opened new dormitories this year, had "more than an average number of thefts" with stolen motorcycles, bicycles, and cars ranking high.
> Approximately 4,000 of Stanford's 11,500 students live on campus and are primary targets for the theft of wallets,

purses, hi-fi equipment, tape recorders and similar items. . . .

The following excerpt from a San Francisco *Chronicle* story by Julie Smith on a meeting of the Columbia Broadcasting System's shareholders illustrates how quotations can be used to sharpen interest.

> Nine women members (Women's Liberation Front) had filtered into the meeting in groups of twos and threes, taken seats and settled down to wait for the right moment. It came when board chairman William S. Paley said, "If there are no objections, we will dispense with the reading of the minutes."
> "I object!" shouted one of the infiltrators. Similar cries went round the room, and the women marched to the front.
> "CBS abuses women!" shouted a woman. . . .

Pungent quotations can provide a powerful spice for a story that is in need of some seasoning.

The Staccato Effect

A series of short sentences can create a staccato effect—abrupt, sharp emphasis. This style of writing is well illustrated in a wire story by Wilson Morris:

> WASHINGTON (UPI)—The day of Christmas Eve at Arlington National Cemetery.
> Rows of white headstones stretch up the sloping hills. There is the whisper of snow, the keening of a winter wind. The Flag flies at half staff. A mockingbird takes haven in a cedar tree. A squirrel huddles atop a grave marker.
> The headstones gleam in the winter sun. There are Christmas wreaths beside them, small Christmas trees by some.
>
> IN MEMORY OF
> ARNOLD JONES
> PVT. INFANTRY
>
> A man places a wreath on a grave, his wife beside him. He steps back, bends forward and adjusts the wreath, steps back again.
> He picks up a leaf, then a twig from the grave and tosses them aside.
> A woman stands alone at another grave crying. She makes the sign of the cross.
> Six soldiers carry a flag-draped coffin to a grave site. They hold the Flag above the casket as a chaplain reads the service.

> Three volleys are fired. Taps sound. The Flag is folded and presented to the "next of kin."
> At the Tomb of the Unknowns, hands slap rifles and heels click. The guard is changed. A soldier marches back and forth before the tomb.
> "Here Rests in Honored Glory an American Soldier Known But to God."
> The three unknowns—brought from the fields of World War I, World War II and Korea. . . .

The staccato effect can be achieved by using sentences comprised of fragments, each separated by an elipsis (three spaced dots) to denote a pause. UPI writer H. D. Quigg used such a sentence to describe the fatal climb of a victim to the bell-clock tower of the University of Texas, unaware that a mad sniper awaited him at the top:

> Twelve steps . . . landing . . . 11 steps . . . landing . . . turn . . . two more steps . . . turn . . . 10 steps. . . . Mark was at stair-head in the reception room, where there is a sign advising, "You are standing 231 feet from the ground."

Sentence fragments are rarely handled well by the ignorant or inexperienced writer. Used purposely for effect, though, fragments can quicken the reader's pace and provide transition and a welcome change in sentence pattern. Here is a good example:

> DONORA, Pa. (AP)—At first it was just another autumn fog that folled in off the Monongahela River. *A little colder. A little denser, perhaps.* There was no indication of the choking menace that would blot out the sun for five days and bring this western Pennsylvania mill town to its knees. . . .

Staccato style can be used effectively throughout relatively short stories or on occasions in longer articles. Used excessively, such writing will bore the reader.

Simple Language

Simple language can be forceful language. Some teachers advise, "Write as you talk." That does not mean that a young writer should try to emulate the hemming and hawing, bad grammar, undue use of fragments, and ambiguity that normally occur in speech. It might be better to suggest that, for journalistic writing, an informal, conversational tone should be used.

Short words and sentences are often recommended for journalism, but sentence variety is needed for interest, and many words of more than one syllable are well known to most readers. It is more than short words and sentences that count. Good writing depends on the way words are put together in sentences, the way sentences are arranged in paragraphs, and the way paragraphs are organized.

Clarity is all-important. How easy is the story to read and understand? Familiar words should be used—words that do not drive the reader to a dictionary or force him to try to infer meanings from context.

Simplicity is well illustrated in a Long Beach (Calif.) *Independent Press-Telegram* story by Dick Emery. Reader interest is enhanced by the simplicity and informality of the language. The story is composed of simple, homely words: "He tossed out money," "Licata declared war on the third man," "strewed paper money like a farmer scattering grain," and "The breeze rained the bills back on pedestrians." The quotations, too, are made up of simple words—the kind of words used in ordinary conversation.

> As robberies go, this one had all the elements of a Laurel & Hardy comedy.
> Perplexed police said afterward it wasn't really a robbery, anyhow. They said it was a burglary.
> Right down the main street of San Pedro the midday chase went, with pursuers whooping like Indians.
> The man being pursued used an old trick to slow the chase. He tossed out money.
> "He sure did," police said. "$4,350!"
> The noontime breeze on Pacific Avenue picked up the money—dollar bills, five-dollar bills, 10-dollar bills, 20-dollar bills, all in lovely, beautiful genuine U.S. paper currency.
> The breeze rained the bills back on pedestrians.
> "I saw a dozen people picking up money," said a perspiring policeman who arrived at the scene and found, in an alley between Ninth and Tenth Streets, Pacific and Grand Avenues, a husky middle-aged owner of a paint store sitting on the distributor of wealth, now sprawled panting face-down on the alley pavement.
> The policeman, Harbor Officer James G. Breem, handcuffed the money-man, later identified as John Jones, 21, of Los Angeles, and thanked the captor, Karl Koch, 50.
> Because money was blowing along the sidewalk in front of a Bank of America branch nearby, it seemed at first that maybe a bank had been robbed.
> Alfonso Licata, owner of a health foods store at 1111 Pacific Avenue, put an end to that rumor. It wasn't the bank, he told police; it was his store, the California Nutrition Center.
> Three men had entered, Licata said, and two of them beguiled clerks while the third rifled a moneybag in the store office.

Licata declared war on the third man, who ran to the street carrying the money-bag's contents, namely, $4,255 in lovely bills—ones, fives, tens and twenties.

Police reported after it was all over that the fleeing man, named as the Jones who was captured, strewed paper money like a farmer scattering grain, and that Licata slowed down to grab the fluttering currency.

Not the paint-store man, Karl Koch, police reported.

"Not him," said Detective Robert Kinsey of the robbery squad, who said it wasn't robbery, anyhow, but burglary.

"Koch let the money fly," Kinsey said. "He kept right on running, trying to catch the man. He got right close behind him, running hard."

Laurel & Hardy, great comics of the '30s and early '40s, could have used the lines which followed.

"You better get away from me," the fleeing man gasped over his shoulder at Koch. "I'll shoot you!"

"You better start shooting," Koch gasped back, "because I've almost gotcha!"

A tackle, football fashion, brought down the fleeing man and Koch pinned him until police arrived.

Back at the health food store, when kindly citizens had kicked-in with what they'd found, Licata counted and re-counted a great pile of currency.

"I can't figure it," he said, over and over, to policemen watching. "I come out with $95 more than I had to begin with."

The ever-suspicious detectives who booked Jones into the San Pedro jail as a burglary suspect studied figures Licata showed, and they studied certain documents from Sacramento relating to recent adventures of the man in custody.

"The extra $95 came out of his own pocket," detectives said. "And we think—we have just a mean old sneaking hunch in connection with a little old lady's purse that we know about—how he came by that $95!"

Still at large, Friday night, but eagerly sought by the night shift of policemen, were the two companions reported seen with Man Number Three in the health store as the robbery—er, that is, burglary—got started.

(Reprinted from the *Independent Press-Telegram*)

The degree of formality used in writing a story varies according to its content. A story dealing with a United Nations session would be written in a more formal tone than the burglary story just cited. But the trend is toward informality.

EXERCISES

I. Appraise the following story openings on the basis of interest

QANTARA, Suez Canal (UPI)—"Keep your cameras up and your head down," the Israeli major warned the photographer. "We can get you a new camera. We can't get you a new head."

BY CHARLES HOWE

CULPEPER, Va.—George Lincoln Rockwell, five days dead, was lying in icy limbo yesterday after a marathon "dead-in" at the National Cemetery here failed to get him buried. (San Francisco *Chronicle*)

The final buzzer sounded in Milwaukee Arena and a tall, lanky youth went bouncing off the court. His hand was clenched in a tight fist and he was waving it high—very high—in the air. To many viewers, it was a familiar scene. One they had seen for the last three years after UCLA had won the finals of the National Collegiate Athletic Association tournament. (Long Island *Newsday*)

BY TIM HOLLAND

City Controller Bernard Klein called Thursday for a change in the Michigan Law which chains Detroit's income tax exemptions to federal tax exemptions. (Detroit *Free Press*)

HONOLULU, Hawaii (AP)—"You are cordially invited to attend the extinction of the human race, summer of 1979, one performance only," the invitation reads.

FROM PRESS DISPATCHES

WASHINGTON, D.C.—The president of the United States gave top priority Friday night to his role as a father.

Instead of celebrating his 57th birthday at the White House, he flew to Northampton, Mass., to have dinner with his daughter, who was too busy studying for exams to make the trip to Washington. (Milwaukee *Journal*)

BY UNITED PRESS INTERNATIONAL

Skid row derelicts, forced off the street by one of the most severe cold waves in years, walked into a Philadelphia police station Thursday night and asked for shelter.

Eleven were bedded down in cells and others sat on benches. "The only people on the street are cops," one officer said.

II. How strong is the interest appeal in the following quotations?

The old cowboy opened the door of the 98-year-old log cabin bunkhouse he has called home the last few years. He tossed some wood onto the fire, untied his heavy leather chaps and threw them over an old chair.

"You can come in here with dirty feet. Bring your horse in here. Hell, I don't care. It don't matter none. I've ridden my horse in here more than once when I've been half shot." (Charles Hillinger, Los Angeles *Times*)

But one woman, caught in the squealing, pushing crush when the President entered the room, remarked: "My husband's never going to believe I was at a convention. You should see my black and blue marks." (AP)

Dr. Harbold also revealed that the . . . Home employed only one nurse at night to care for more than 140 patients on three floors.

"One nurse is not enough, there should be one on each floor," he testified. (Frederick P. McGehan, Baltimore *Sun*)

Davis cited problems police have in attracting officers and said that an army that paid similar wages wouldn't have much chance of obtaining enough recruits.

He said, "I suspect that many who call for a volunteer army really don't care whether or not we have one, and might just as soon that we didn't." (St. Louis *Post-Dispatch*)

He ascribed the [cinema] failure to "the filthy films that pollute the minds and bodies of people of all ages."

Ask him what he thinks of "I Am Curious (Yellow)," and he mouths the word "shmuts." That is German and it means filth. "God forbid I should tell you what I think about that film. It is senseless and stupid.

"What is happening to this country that people want to see that kind of stuff? And the people who make them should be ashamed. Anything for a dollar." (Ian Glass, Miami *News*)

III. Comment on the interest-getting techniques used in the following excerpts

BY DAVID V. HAWPE

MANCHESTER, Ky.—The days of rootin'-tootin', straight shootin' mountain buckaroos may be ended in Clay County.

There's a new judge in the courthouse and he's declared hacksaws, whisky and pistols off limits to prisoners in the county jail.

He wants convicts in their cells, not loitering on the street outside the jailhouse.

He's stopped the smoking and joking in the courtroom while court is in session.

He's declared war against the bootleggers, the truants, and the couples who get a divorce just to get on the welfare roles. (Louisville *Courier-Journal*)

And it ended abruptly when the sheriff turned a shoulder, cold as the winter wind whipping through the Sierra passes, to a Gay Lib proposal to call a town meeting to explain its threatened invasion of Alpine County to the local residents. (Max Miller, McClatchy Newspapers Service)

There's not much else to the subway, but the French have turned on the modernity; wide halls, escalators, reds, blues, grays, phony marble, aluminum, technicians in lab coats at glass-enclosed consoles, and a machine that takes your ticket, does something electronic to it, then offers it back to you because you can't get out of the subway without it. (AP)

This past summer, 938 gritty men, women, and children lined up for the race. Fathers, mothers, kids, cousins, aunts, and 60-year-old grandfathers entered. (John Arms, *Christian Science Monitor*)

BY GERALD MEYER

There they were, almost 50 of them, rolling in a chartered bus from St. Louis to Washington and what they expected to be a day of marching. They were students in the unofficial denim uniform of the New Left, suburban housewives in their camping clothes, teachers and ministers in a hodgepodge of the warmest things they owned. At a rest stop in Indiana they discovered that their driver had the headlights on.

It was an annoying discovery. Daytime headlights, which not long ago were simple pleas for safe driving or signs of an over-charged battery, have become in this era of improvised political symbolism an emblem of support for certain Government policies. (St. Louis *Post-Dispatch*)

Freddie's philosophy was quite simple. His theory: "You take a little kid and throw him into eight feet of water. He learns to swim, right? Same in pro basketball. You learn by doing, baby. When they throw you in there, things start happening."

The bouncy rookie from Mount St. Mary's spent a little time getting his feet wet. He was hardly an instant success as a starter. He can remember nightmarish evenings like the time in Philadelphia when Monroe was thumbed out in the first six minutes and he was the only bona fide guard left. Greer went wild, scoring 38 points while Carter made only 3 of 18 shots.

"You can't say I wasn't scared," said Fred between morning and afternoon workouts at the opening of training camp here today. "An established star can go into Madison Square Garden and act real cool playing before 19,000 people. But I tell you, I was shaking a bit." (Alan Goldstein, Baltimore *Sun*)

Near the entrance to the performance site is a pile of wrecked cars and a mass of twisted metal with a broken wheelchair topped by a pair of crutches.

The conglomeration is entombed in a heavy layer of dull white paint. The label reads, "Freeway Cha-Cha-Cha."

A collage of broken and battered household appliances is just around the corner with a sign asking: "Too old to ride the range?"

Television sets with "live better electrically" painted on the screens are nearby.

The junk art is part of an ecology "circus" sponsored by the University of Hawaii. The exhibit is titled "Hawaii Shibai." Shibai is Japanese for "farce." (AP)

Litzsinger's face is tanned and his stomach bulges gently over his belt. He is a modest man with an easy smile and affable manner. (Patrick Strickler, St. Louis *Post-Dispatch*)

IV. Compare the following two leads based on the same story

BY ALTON BLAKESLEE
ASSOCIATED PRESS

NEW YORK—Two pioneers in sex research say they believe they have developed a method to prevent many thousands of marriages from breaking up over sexual problems.

NEW YORK *TIMES* NEWS SERVICE

BOSTON, Mass.—Two leading experts on human sexuality have developed an intense two-week therapy for sexual inadequacy. The therapy relies on education and rapid psycho-sexual reorientation for the patients and differs from traditional time-consuming psychotherapy in that it makes no attempt to correct deep-seated neurosis.
(©1970 by The New York Times Company. Reprinted by permission)

V. The first example that follows was a news release a number of years ago. The second example was a rewrite of it by the San Francisco Chronicle *staff. Compare the two on the basis of interest.*

If you have any delusions about life not beginning until 40, you can get rid of them in a hurry, for the latest word of science is that old age begins to set in at the age of 26.

A study made by Dr. M. Bruce Fisher, professor of psychology at Fresno State College, in collaboration with Dr. James E. Birren of the United States Public Health Service, shows you begin to lose your strength at the age of 26.

The study, published in the current issue of the Journal of Applied Psychology, was made through measurements of hand strength of 552 men industrial workers.

The original work was done when Dr. Fisher was a senior psychologist at the Naval Medical Research Institute in Bethesda, Md. . . .

Strength increases, it was pointed out, up to the middle 20s and then gradually decreases. The decrease is gradual but becomes a little sharper as age continues. At 60, the average loss of strength is 16.5 per cent.

The psychologist explained the same trend holds true for women. He also explained other measurements of ability, including mental agility, decrease after the middle 20s.

"This does not mean a man is not effective as a thinker after 25," Dr. Fisher said. "Because of accumulated knowledge it may be easier for an older man to get a lot more from a particular set of facts than it would be for a man 25 years old. New material is absorbed most readily in the 20s, however."

He explained mastery of a new subject comes most easily between the ages of 20 to 30.

FRESNO—Life begins at 40?

Unh-unh; old age begins at 26.

For that, take the word of Dr. M. Bruce Fisher, professor of psychology at Fresno State College. Writing in the current issue of the Journal of Applied Psychology, Dr. Fisher says he found out about it . . . when he was senior psychologist at the Naval Medical Research Institute in Bethesda, Md.

In collaboration with Dr. James E. Birren of the U. S. Public Health Service, he ran tests on 552 men and found they began slipping after 26.

Measurement of their hand strength, he found, disclosed that such strength hit its peak at 25 and then began gradually fading, with the rate of fall increasing with age. By the time a man reaches 60, his strength has fallen off 16.5 per cent.

If you think exercise might slow down this senescence, you're wrong. All subjects in the test were industrial workers, exercising plenty every day.

If you think the old bean might tick over faster while the hand is losing its strength, you're wrong again. Even in the mental agility department you start down hill at 26.

And if you're a woman—don't start smirking because the tests were for men only. A woman, too—says Dr. Fisher—starts getting old at 26. The psychologist offered some consolation to the old, old man of 30 or 40. While his mental decay may prevent him from grasping new subjects as fast as he used to, he has acquired a fund of information which makes it easier for him to use what he does soak up, Dr. Fisher said.

The ideal time to master a new subject, Dr. Fisher says, is between the ages of 20 and 30.

VI. *Would the opening paragraph of the first example in the preceding exercise have been improved if it had been broken into two sentences and paragraphs?*

If you have any delusions about life not beginning until 40, you can get rid of them in a hurry.

The latest word of science is that old age begins to set in at the age of 26.

Chapter 12

FEATURE WRITING

*The two most engaging powers of an
author are to make new things familiar
and familiar things new.* —Thackeray

The primary responsibility of a newspaper is to inform readers. This is done through news stories and a wide variety of feature articles. A feature story usually depends for reader interest on the way in which the facts are organized and presented rather than on the reader's interest in the facts themselves. In the news story, the reader's primary interest is in the facts.

The news story is more direct, more immediate, than the feature story, which has more embellishment in the way of examples, instances, and particulars and details.

The subjects of feature stories are almost unlimited. They may deal with society's problems—health, environment and modes of living. They may deal with human achievements—cultural, scientific and technological. They may discredit commonly accepted beliefs. They may deal with persons, both prominent and undistinguished.

Writing the Feature Story

Because the news story sticks to facts, the occasion, for example, of a new adult education class in physical education for women would be worth only a couple of paragraphs as a news item:

> A new physical education class for women will be opened by the Marysville Adult School Tuesday at 7 p.m.
>
> Those interested should attend the opening meeting in the Marysville High School girls' gymnasium. The class will be offered Tuesdays from 7 to 9 p.m. The tuition will be $2.

Most features, on the other hand, are born with an idea. A conversation with a teacher might enable a reporter to write this feature out of the preceding news story:

> Women can acquire more glamor from a little exercise than from a barrelful of cosmetics and reducing pills.
>
> This is the advice of Mrs. Mary Jones, who will teach a women's physical education class to be offered Tuesday evenings in the Marysville High School girls' gymnasium. Those interested should attend the opening session Tuesday at 7 p.m. The tuition will be $2.
>
> Mrs. Jones said exercise is better and healthier than diet in holding down the waistline.
>
> "Exercise reduces waste fat on the body and it provides a splendid emotional release for the mother who becomes exasperated keeping Sally and Johnny out of mischief all day," she said.
>
> "Not only does exercise make a woman more glamorous, but, if taken regularly, it can add 10 to 20 years to the average life."

The question facing the newsman is whether or not the feature story warrants the additional space. If he faces a space shortage, a city editor might order that the feature be rewritten as a simple news story.

Writing a feature story, in many cases, requires more skill than writing any of the simpler types of news stories. Suppose a business executive tells a reporter that the community they live in is suffering from a serious shortage of secretaries. This gives the reporter an idea for a feature story, but the information provided by the one man is inadequate.

The reporter will probably call on half a dozen or more other business leaders and then the major employment services in the city. If the first man's statements are corroborated, the reporter may decide to go ahead with the story.

He will undoubtedly have far more information than he can use in the story; consequently, he must sift out the least significant data. But data, though necessary, provide only the substance for the story. The reporter must organize his material in an interesting fashion.

The opening often sets the pace for the remainder of the story, so the reporter concentrates on his lead. He may start with the general impression he wishes to make on his readers:

> Springville is facing a serious shortage of secretaries.

This statement would be merely an expression of the writer's opinion if it were not attributed to someone, so the reporter supplies the attribution in the second paragraph:

> This is the lament of more than a half dozen business leaders in the community. The shortage also is verified by the city's employment agencies, which are unable to come up with the number of secretaries needed.

But the reporter might decide that his lead is too dull and rewrite it:

> The biggest headache Springville business executives have today is not a lack of business—it's a lack of secretaries.

Or he may decide on a two-paragraph lead:

> Springville's business executives are having a headache over secretaries.
>
> No, it's not the secretaries that are causing the headaches—it's the lack of secretaries that's creating the problems.

However the reporter decides to open his story, he is likely to rely on examples, incidents, details and quotations as he follows up his lead:

> One business executive said he has hired, in the last six months, three women in succession to replace a secretary who quit and he had to fire each in turn.
> "They were inexperienced and only created problems instead of being of help," he said.
>
> ———
>
> A sales manager for an industrial firm complained that many of the secretaries hired by his company are married and have to move with their husbands when they are transferred.
> He told of one case in which he had hired a woman with years of experience. She worked for the company two months and had just become familiar with the office procedures when her husband was transferred to Florida.
> "She gave us two days' notice before leaving," he groaned.
>
> ———
>
> A personnel manager for a large department store spoke longingly of the good old days when a secretarial job had some prestige.
> "Today most of the high school girls who can spell go on to college and expect loftier things than being a secretary," he said.
>
> ———

The manager of a manufacturing concern told of one secretary he hired.

"When I came in the morning after she was hired, I suggested she dust my desk each morning," he said.

The woman went for her coffee break that morning and never came back.

"She wrote later asking us to send her check to her," he commented.

There is no formula for writing a feature story—much depends on what the reporter has to say and the purpose he hopes his story will serve. Notice the simplicity with which a San Diego *Evening Tribune* story by Guy Ryan is told:

Invitation to read on	COLORADO SPRINGS—As Colorado mountains go, Cheyenne Mountain, a few miles southwest of here, hardly rates a second glance—just another mountain overshadowed by its famous neighbor, Pike's Peak.
	But there's more here than meets the eye—both inside and outside the mountain.
	Cheyenne, the great lizard-dragon of Indian legend, could well be the most important mountain in the world to 225 million people of the United States and Canada.
	Their very survival is tied up in the military installation hidden away deep inside the mountain.
Basic facts	This is the nerve center of the North American Air Defense Command (NORAD), an underground city of highly trained men and sophisticated machines maintaining a constant watch against an aerial attack and providing the means for directing a defense against it if it comes.
Particulars and details	The mountain serenity has barely been disturbed by the mighty installation. The entrance is hardly noticeable and, except for a sentry booth and a couple of air policemen, there's nothing to attract attention.
	From the entrance, a paved underground road runs about four blocks up to a pair of 30-ton blastproof doors held in place by 17-foot concrete collars.
	Behind these doors is where the action is—or will be if some unfriendly country decides to lob a few missiles in the direction of the two nations.
Particulars and details	High up on the side of the 100-million-year-old mountain and looking down on the "command post for survival" is a shrine to the late Will Rogers, built by the people of Colorado Springs. The voice of the sage old philosopher lives again here, and visitors can hear the recorded Oklahoma twang of Rogers as he comments on political and social situations of the early and mid-30s. There's a bust of the humorist and entertainer up here, too.
	The hockey arena here is where teen-aged Peggy Fleming perfected the form that would win her an Olympic gold medal and other honors which launched her professional skating career.

Cold-weather vacationers flock to the ski runs above the hotel during the winter months for relaxation and sport. Before the snow flies, visitors come to play on the two 18-hole golf courses, wander through the Cheyenne Mountain Zoo with its colony of giraffes, or, in the fall, watch real cowboys risk their necks in the Pike's Peak or Bust Rodeo.

Introduction to legend, followed by narrative

If you look southwest from Colorado Springs today, you can see Cheyenne Mountain, which the Indians called the lizard-dragon, "Thirst." With a little imagination you can see that the dragon is still there, its head pointing toward the west and the tail toward Pike's Peak.

The legend is still here, too.

The Indians told it that when a flood covered the earth eons ago, this lizard-dragon was turned loose. He had an insatiable thirst and drank the floodwaters in great gulps, night and day. So, the water receded and the mountains grew higher and higher as the great beast drank up the water.

Fears arose that the lizard-dragon would drink up all the earth's waters, so the Indian God, Manitou, ordered "Thirst" to go back to where he came from.

But by this time, the dragon's body was so waterlogged he was unable to fly, as dragons are wont to do, and he crashed back to earth.

Manitou wasn't taking any chances that Thirst would drink up the rest of the water on earth, so he turned the great dragon into stone.

Appropriate ending

It's a perfectly logical story about the formation of Cheyenne Mountain.

At least to the Indians.

The words in a feature story should flow easily for the reader. Notice the simplicity with which the following Detroit *Free Press* story by Andrew Mollison is told:

Enticing lead

Richard Pinkston sometimes has trouble flagging down a cab in Detroit.

He thinks it's because he's under 30 and is black.

Supplementation

And it's especially galling to him because he is general manager of City Cab Co., an association of 58 Negroes who own 72 of Detroit's 1,310 cabs.

The 72 City cabs, three Exchange cabs and 10 Checker cabs owned by Negroes are only a small portion of Detroit's fleet, but unofficial estimates of the racial balance among drivers indicate that more than half of them are black.

Basic information

The stereotype of the white cab driver is that he is extraordinarily racist.

But there seems to be more than simple racism involved.

Many drivers who admit discriminating against black customers claim that fear is their main reason. They are afraid of being robbed.

Supplementation	"Why are you going to pick up a man you're scared is going to rob you?" asked Pinkston, who says he has seen 10 or 12 cabs pass him by before a driver recognizes him and picks him up.
Basic information	The law requires drivers to pick up all "orderly" passengers, but it can be evaded easily. A driver can claim that he is on his way to answer a radio call, or that he failed to see the person hail his cab.
Supplementary details	Some drivers simply avoid black areas of the city, and refuse to respond to radio calls in those areas.
	If no cab driver offers to answer a radio call after 15 minutes, the major cab companies simply stop putting the number on the air and the customer never knows why no one picked him up.
	The companies are protected because a loophole in the city taxicab ordinance requires only drivers, not the companies, to give service to anyone who asks for it.
Basic information	Black areas of Detroit used to be served by City Cab and other Negro companies which received cab licenses—known as bond plates—under explicit racial quotas.
Supplementation	"They used to be called colored cabs, and they served the colored market in Black Bottom, along Hastings and on the west side," said Pinkston. "Now with white customers willing to use black cab companies with black drivers we have to serve the whole of Detroit."
	The result is that fewer cabs are serving the black community.
Basic information	Thomas Turner, president of the Detroit chapter of the National Association for the Advancement of Colored People, said:
	"It's very difficult to get some cabs, particularly after dark. And if some people look in any way suspicious, cab drivers even pass them up in the daytime."
	He said the NAACP had received numerous complaints about poor cab service for black people.
Supplementation	"We hope that in the not too distant future we can compile enough evidence to discuss the problem with the powers that be," Turner said.
Basic information	He plans to approach the mayor, Common Council, the police commissioner and executives of the cab companies.
Supplementation	He observed that it was not only young black men who complained about poor cab service.
	"I'm talking about people in every walk of life," Turner said. "We've received far too many complaints for this to be ignored."
Basic information, followed by details	A young Negro who works in a downtown office kept a diary for two weeks, at the request of the Free Press, in which she recorded her observations of cab service.
	Here are some excerpts from her report. . . .

The organization of a feature story—basic information followed by supplementation—is somewhat similar to the organization of an opinion interview story, which is based on major points followed by specifics, usually in the form of direct quotation. But the supplementation in a feature story typically uses all the rhetorical devices: direct quotation, background, examples, incidents, narrative, and particulars and details. A feature story may end with the supplementation of a basic point, as does the foregoing Detroit *Free Press* story, or it may have a separate, planned ending, as in the Cheyenne Mountain story.

In learning how to approach a feature-writing assignment, the student can perhaps profit most by examining diverse examples of the subjects and purposes of feature stories.

Social Problems

Readers are interested in social progress, and, when social retrogression takes place, they want to know about it, too. There is often disagreement over what is progress and what is retrogression. Controversy over legislation introduced by a state legislator is the subject of the following feature by Dennis J. Opatrny:

Attractive lead	SACRAMENTO (UPI)—One woman calls Sen. Anthony C. Beilenson a "people-hater," while another views him as a near saint.
Supplementation	They are assessing his legislation to remove all restrictions on abortions in order to provide the operation on demand.
Basic information	The topic generates more emotional responses than nearly any other issue and Beilenson's mail reflects it.
Background	The controversial bill is scheduled for hearing today before the Senate Judicial Committee, but hundreds of Californians have already made their feelings known.
First example (unfavorable)	A Burlingame woman reminded the Beverly Hills Democrat that "many of the greatest men in history came at the tail end of large families and many a genius was the 7th or 8th child."
	She ended her letter by criticizing the lawmaker for his "filthy, degenerate ideas . . . you are a people-hater and need a psychiatrist."
Second example (unfavorable)	A clergyman from a Palm Springs church asked Beilenson to withdraw the measure "before you have the blood of countless innocent unborn infants on your hands.
	"The awful thought strikes me," the reverend added, "that if the forebearers of Senator Beilenson had been moved by the same spirit that prompted the offering of the

216 *Reportorial Writing*

<table>
<tr><td>Third example (unfavorable)</td><td>above mentioned bills, California could possibly have been the loser of an able, sophisticated lawmaker."
A Costa Mesa couple doubted whether the world is really threatened by unchecked population growth.
"Malthus, himself, had not even thought of overpopulation problems until he found himself burdened and embarrassed by the heretofore unsuspected fecundity of his many mistresses," they said.</td></tr>
<tr><td>Fourth example (unfavorable)</td><td>But a student in a Roman Catholic school in Santa Ana decided to register her protest in the form of a poem with a familiar opening:
"Violets are blue, roses are red, we need your bills, like a hole in the head."</td></tr>
<tr><td>Basic information and background</td><td>On the other side were letters from proponents who heartily endorsed Beilenson's attempt to scrap existing restrictions. Presently, a woman can get an abortion only if her health is endangered or when pregnancy results from rape or incest. The only provisions in the proposal are that a physician perform the operation before the 20th week of pregnancy.</td></tr>
<tr><td>First example (favorable)</td><td>"Hooray! You're at it again," wrote a Santa Barbara housewife, referring to Beilenson's authorship of the 1967 liberalized abortion law.</td></tr>
<tr><td>Second example (favorable)</td><td>Another woman from his hometown of Beverly Hills told the lawmaker that she has been circulating a petition to put the unrestricted abortion question before voters.
"Every person I asked for a signature was most happy to give it to me. Even elderly and very conservative people agreed with legalized abortions. I believe the climate is changing."</td></tr>
<tr><td>Third example (favorable)</td><td>And from Los Angeles another woman praised Beilenson for his past and present efforts in removing abortion restrictions.</td></tr>
</table>

The organization of the article is exceedingly simple. The opening paragraphs introduce the subject—the response to a senator's bill. The story follows with examples of responses, unfavorable and favorable, to the bill. The examples make the story.

Many of society's problems are being reported in depth by newspapers today. We shall see the dimensions of this coverage in greater detail in the next two chapters.

Science

The American people are naturally curious about the spectacular achievements the United States has made in science and technology. Before the astonishment and anxiety that resulted from the channeling of nuclear energy could be calmed, men had done the seemingly impossible and traveled to the moon.

Only recently, polio has been licked, hearts have been transplanted, and life, generally speaking, has been lengthened. Engineers have designed planes that, in a few hours, can take persons distances that would have taken weeks to travel 50 years ago.

The task of the journalist has been to translate scientific terminology into a popularized kind of language. In so doing, he has had to guard against the danger of distortion.

Timely achievements in science and technology are reported in the general news column. Many news stories stem from reports made at scientific meetings. Others come from press releases made by the officials of scientific groups.

The lead of the following Miami *Herald* story by Al Volker indicates that the information came from a press release issued by a scientific agency:

News lead based on timely agency report	Two Miami oceanographers have established with the aid of a computer that Antarctica was once attached to the southeast coast of Africa, the Environmental Science Services Administration said today. In the 200 million years since they separated the two continents have drifted 2,000 miles apart, say Dr. Robert S. Dietz and Walter Sproll of the Atlantic Oceanographic and Meteorological Laboratories here.
Remainder of story based principally on studies and theories developed by two scientists	According to their theory, there once existed a single continent, which they call Pangaea, 80 million miles in area. For reasons they do not understand, the land mass began to break up, like an ice flow. Dietz and Sproll believe that the split between Africa and Antarctica was one of the first to occur. Both scientists believe that the continents are drifting at a rate of an inch a year in the earth's mantle, that part of the earth's interior that is sandwiched between the surface crust and the molten central core. Dietz believes that the pre-rift outlines of the continents are to be found in the submerged continental slopes at the 6,000-foot depth-line in the oceans. The theory that Africa and Antarctica were once part of a super continent is not new, but Dietz and Sproll say they have achieved a "remarkably good" fit in the area where the continents were once joined. The ESSA oceanographers say their computerized fit revealed that a 1,200-nautical-mile-long, S-shaped portion of the Antarctica coast fits a similar profile along the southeastern coast of Africa. According to this fit, Antarctica's Princess Martha coast was connected in part to what is now Portuguese Mozambique, while the Weddell Sea margin joined Africa in the

Indian Ocean sector where the city of Durban is now located.

There was a discrepancy of only about 17,500 square miles, an area slightly larger than the state of Maryland.

The same misfit will always remain, they stressed, because of geologic changes that have occurred since the ancient supercontinent split up. Rocks now at the bottom of the sea, they speculate, are the debris from erosion and account for much of the misfit.

"While the geology of the undersea regions is too poorly known for us to propose any specific geologic explanation for these discrepancies," they stated, "we believe that the fit is sufficiently good to indicate that these two were actually joined along this line."

(Reprinted from the Miami *Herald*)

The previous news story is based on the timely announcement of a scientific discovery. The following feature article has a "come on and read" type of lead that is less immediate and less direct than the lead in the news story.

Enticing lead	SACRAMENTO (UPI)—Twelve-year-old David Scott is "thrilled" that he is now as tall as his 8-year-old sister, Daphne. Four months ago the Sacramento youngster had no chance of catching up to Daphne. Because of a pituitary hormone deficiency, he was destined to be a dwarf—to be no taller than 4 feet at age 21.
Basic information	But last Jan. 10 he began receiving shots of a pituitary growth hormone under a research project at the University of California at Davis Medical School.
Supplementation	The result has been an almost 3-inch growth to a height of 3-feet and 9¾ inches. "I don't like the needles," admits David, "but it's worth it." "He's thrilled now," says his mother, Mrs. James Scott. "He couldn't play Little League ball and do all the things other kids do, and now there's hope for a normal existence," she added. Mrs. Scott said the growth hormone "is the difference between a normal life and—I don't know what his life would have been without it. "We had to pull him out of public school because children treated him unmercifully."
Basic information	The growth hormone injected in David three times a week is extracted from the pituitary glands of dead humans, then purified and distributed by the federally financed National Pituitary Agency. Use of the limited quantities of the hormone is restricted to such research.
Supplementary explanation	A child may need the extracts from two or three persons in one week. In a year, he may need extracts from 70 to 100 glands and he will need the hormone for several years.

> The hormone is injected for eight months, then stopped because the body's defenses begin to produce antibodies that reduce its effect. After a four-month pause, injections are resumed for another eight months.
>
> When given to a child like David, the hormone has a general effect on metabolism. But its main impact is on the growth of long bones.
>
> UC Davis doctors said that of the 3 per cent of all children who are abnormally short, 15 per cent have a shortage of pituitary growth hormone in their bodies.
>
> David's father is an Air Force major. . . .

The feature article provides scientific information that is made vivid in the reader's mind by a strong human interest appeal. The information, though not new in science, is no doubt new to many readers.

The story does not have the immediacy of a news story, but David's successful medical treatment gives an impression of timeliness, even though the story could have been told some time earlier or later without attenuating the element of interest.

The organization is a simple one. A strong element of interest is introduced in the early paragraphs and is followed by supplementation. A mid-story scientific explanation is offered, and it is followed by more specific information about the hormone that has meant so much to David.

Education

Parents and grandparents in particular and Americans in general have a stake in the education of the young. They are interested in knowing what schools are doing and how much children are learning. They have a right to know about new approaches to the teaching of English, mathematics and science. They particularly want to be informed about the many controversies in education, all of which lend themselves to feature coverage.

Is kindergarten just a place where children are sent to get them out of their mothers' way? This question is answered in a Fresno (Calif.) *Bee* feature story.

Story's central idea in capsule form	Kindergartens are not operated for baby-sitting purposes —instead they perform an important function in the education of children. Any of the city's kindergarten teachers will tell you this and if you wish to miff one of them just tell her how good a baby-sitting job you think she does.
Purpose introduced by question	What then is the purpose of the kindergarten? The teachers generally concur:

Reportorial Writing

Specifics

First, the child who goes to kindergarten gets used to acting in a group. He learns to listen, think, and act. As one veteran teacher, Mrs. Grace Heisinger of the Homan School, explains it:

"A child may get individual instructions at home and follow them, but when you put him in a group and give instructions to the group, he has problems. You can't say all the class and Johnny will do this—he has to be one of the group."

Question introduces major points

What about reading, writing and arithmetic? The kindergarten teachers will tell you that the 5-year-old child gets the foundation for all these, although formal instruction is not offered at the kindergarten level.

Reading readiness is stressed in the kindergartens.

Supplementation and elaboration

Mrs. Lucille M. Freeman of the Heaton school, another veteran teacher, describes it this way:

"We enrich the youngster's vocabulary. Every day he learns new words and the meaning of them. We have the youngsters tell about experiences—things they are interested in. Some are hesitant to talk before a group but when they are asked to tell about things that are close to them, they become expressive.

"Then we sit together and write their ideas. The children learn that writing is one way of telling something to others. They also learn that to read is to learn what others say.

"We put much emphasis on sounds. As we discuss the different sounds, we have the children point to objects with names starting with those sounds. We also have the children bring to school things with names starting with those sounds."

For the letter "P" the children may come up with all sorts of things ranging from popcorn to a puppy.

The children learn, however, that sounds and words alone will not enable them to express themselves, so they must put the words into sentences.

Some of the teachers use sound shelves for objects starting with the same sound.

In arithmetic, the children do considerable counting and learn numbers. They count the days in a month, the stars in the Flag and the number of small milk cartons needed to take care of all the youngsters at snack time.

Mrs. Lorraine A. Jones of the Manchester School, who also has had years of experience, explains:

"Mere counting or reciting of numbers as such has no meaning to the child of 5 years of age. But when he counts the number of pupils in a group, the beads on a string, or other objects, the counting takes on meaning. In the same sense, when we take several members out of a group, the child learns the meaning of subtraction."

The child is first introduced to fractions in the kindergarten. Large quarter blocks, for example, are used and the youngsters learn the meaning of halves and quarters. Other objects are counted in halves and thirds.

Different shaped blocks also help the children to learn the meaning of triangle, square and other shapes.

Basic information, followed by details
The sciences, social studies, geography and other subjects also are introduced informally into the kindergarten. A small girl's rubber doll starts an inquiry into how rubber grows and where it comes from. Insects, minerals, animals and fish are the basis for study and discussion of science. . . .
(Reprinted from the Fresno *Bee*)

It should be noted that the general statements in the article, such as "Reading readiness is stressed in the kindergartens," are fortified by evidence—specifics such as examples, particulars and details, and quotations.

Business

Large newspapers cover detailed business and financial news in a separate section. But business news of general interest, such as price changes, increases in the cost of living, attempts to curb inflation, and new products, often appears in the general news columns.

And the opportunity exists to offer readers a variety of features that deal with such subjects as shoplifting, merchandising trends, consumer reactions and inflation.

A representative example of the business feature is this *Christian Science Monitor* story by Diane Lansing on trends in toymaking.

Inviting introduction
NEW YORK—A new game is headed for toy shelves. The object as in Monopoly isn't to capture the Boardwalk. Instead, the winner is the first player to get rid of his pile of trash.

The "relevant" toy is just one new trend in the burgeoning $2-billion-a-year toy industry.

More toy astronauts and aquanauts, programmed dolls that respond to voice commands, pollution and conservation games, toy computers, more authentic model racing cars—this is what industry officials see for the future.

Supplementation
"There will be increasing emphasis away from toys that do things to toys that stimulate the children to do things," forecasts Henry Coords, president of Fisher-Price Toys, Inc.

The industry has thrived on miniaturizing the adult world for the young, whether the products be dolls or cars.

But more emphasis on education is likely, with social problems and causes playing greater roles in games and toys of the future.

In addition, the industry is looking to the adult population as a new market for games and crafts. "Crafts will grow faster than any other segment of the toy industry,"

	forecasts Charles Diker, president of Aurora Plastics Corporation.
Basic information	The toy industry has been growing at 7 to 8 per cent a year for the last decade with no slowdown in sight.
Supplementation	With size comes heightened sensitivity. Refer to toys as playful trivia, and you'll get a verbal dissertation on toy research and development—including a head count of child psychologists, engineers, and technicians at the company headquarters.
	The current boom, however, is still in the stars—either in space travel or the newest fad, astrology.
Basic information	Toymakers keep pace with space technology. Before man traveled to the moon, space toys were mostly rockets to get the information on the moon. Now that man has landed on the lunar surface, toys deal with lunar exploration, interplanetary travel, and, of course, getting back to earth.
Supplementation	Moon-walk and space-travel games, space stations, lunar vehicles, space suits (complete with life-support systems and air filled shoes to simulate weightlessness) are filling the toy shelves. For extra excitement toymakers give more rein to science fiction with a variety of robots and monsters from outer space.
Basic information	Most of the industry's growth has been based on expanding present lines of toys and formulating more elaborate versions of existing ones.
Supplementation	The desire to imitate mother has already put little girls into junior laundry-kitchens with working washing machines, driers, dishwashers, stoves, and refrigerators.
	Now their brothers can have the same advantages with motorized cars, dune buggies, short-haul trucks, and snowmobiles which whiz along at 4 or 5 m.p.h. . . .
	(Reprinted with permission from the *Christian Science Monitor*)

What is new in toymaking? This is the question the writer strives to answer. The idea for the feature could have been suggested by many sources or by observation. It could have come from a parent, a toy manufacturer, a toy store manager or a salesman. It could have come from observing children at play with toys, from observing toys displayed in a store window, or from visiting a department store. Sources of information could be toy manufacturers, toy buyers or retail store managers.

Religion

The coverage of religious news was once limited to times of services, special religious ceremonies, occasional sermons and church social functions. Most coverage was run in a church section or page.

Wider participation by clergymen in social progress and reform movements, greater liberalism in religious doctrine, and reform movements among religious denominations are but a few of the factors that have broadened the scope of religious news and feature coverage.

A front page Fresno (Calif.) *Bee* feature by Charles McCarthy tells of the role played by a Roman Catholic priest in a five-year strike against California grape growers.

Invitation to read on	The highway between Fresno and Delano has become a commuter-way for Msgr. Roger Mahony during the past five years of grape strike and boycott.
Information presented in chronological order	Soon after the first "huelga" cry sounded in the grape harvest season of 1965, the tall, soft-spoken director of Catholic social services in the Fresno Diocese found himself involved. Groups of growers and workers, saying they were "good Catholics," came to Bishop Aloysius J. Willinger, each seeking his support for their side in the dispute.

Bishop Willinger, who has since retired because of advanced age, had his young, newly appointed social services director sit in on these meetings.

"Nothing came out of these talks except the makings of a very big battle," Msgr. Mahony observed.

With Bishop Willinger's permission, Rev. Mahony went to Delano and began two years of talking to both sides in the growing dispute, driving sometimes daily from his office in Fresno.

"I was anxious to find out from them how they saw the whole thing and trying to share with them the church's concern for the rights of the farm workers to form their own associations."

Both sides treated him cordially, Msgr. Mahony said, but he realized that "tremendous emotional" pressure was being brought to bear on Bishop Willinger. And as he spoke out at public meetings defending the right of workers to organize, pressure also increased on Mahony.

"I began to get all kinds of nasty letters," he explained. "I still get plenty of those, but none since the signing the other day."

When Bishop Timothy Manning, now archbishop of Los Angeles, took over the newly divided diocese in 1967 after the retirement of Bishop Willinger, the new bishop asked Mahony about the grape strike.

"I told him I felt that if the church was going to have a role in this, it had reached the point where he (Manning) was going to have to take an active role in it himself," Msgr. Mahony said.

Shortly after this Bishop Manning and Msgr. Mahony met separately with growers and workers in Bakersfield and Delano. During Cesar Chavez' fast to emphasize nonviolence, Bishop Manning went to Delano and pledged his support to the principle of nonviolence, while emphasizing his neutrality in the dispute itself.

"When the boycott started, we got blamed for that," Msgr. Mahony mused.

But in the national Catholic bishops' meeting of 1968, Bishops Manning and Hugh Donohoe, then leading the Stockton diocese, led the effort to have the church neither endorse nor condemn the boycott but to seek ways for active conciliation.

Msgr. Mahony wondered "if the strike was ever going to end."

Soon after the hierarchy meeting, Bishop Manning went to the Los Angeles archdiocese and Bishop Donohoe took over the Fresno diocese, which includes Delano in its jurisdiction. Under the new bishop, whose credentials include a Ph.D. from Catholic University in economics and a dissertation on labor-management relations as well as experience in mediating Bay Area labor disputes, talks soon began which led to the accord in the long grape strike. . . .

This article was a related feature and some of the background of the strike was given in the main story. The story related by the priest lent itself to a chronological organization. In presenting the information, the writer alternated incidents, background and indirect quotations with direct quotations to maintain the thread of interest.

One of the accomplishments of the story is that it assembles many of the fragmentary occurrences of the five-year strike. It also shows the role religious leaders played in helping to end the strike. Chronological order was a simple means of holding the story together.

Historical Significance

Historical occurrences take on timely significance on anniversary dates. A Richmond (Va.) *News Leader* story by Dean Levi, for example, related for its readers the disastrous collapse of the House of Delegates building 100 years before:

Introduction lures reader to read on	Obscured in Virginia's history is the astonishing plan contrived by members of the Senate and House of Delegates to level Thomas Jefferson's classic Capitol and build a new one.

Luckily—and obviously—the plan came to naught.

But during those late April days a century ago, confusion, mourning and mass burials came out of one of the worst calamities ever chronicled in Richmond's long history.

Shortly before 11 a.m. on April 27, 1870, a large crowd had gathered in the old House of Delegates to hear the

Feature Writing

Chronological order with narrative style

opinion on a case which had come before the Virginia Court of Appeals.

The gallery, the corridor and the lower floor of the House—a temporary courtroom—were packed.

With the suddenness of a bomb exploding, there was a loud report followed by another.

To the horror of all, the gallery gave way and then the main floor went down. The disaster killed 63 persons and injured about 260.

Timely tie-in

This week marks the 100th anniversary of that calamity.

Why were so many Richmonders intent on hearing a decision rendered by the Court of Appeals?

Virginia had been readmitted to the Union following five years of federal government military rule.

There was the happy hope of a new era. The end of Negro and carpetbag government was at hand and there was the giant task of reestablishing state government.

Chronological order with narrative style

The General Assembly met Feb. 8 and dived into the task, which included passage of Virginia's "Enabling Act."

That act empowered Gov. Gilbert C. Walker to appoint a new Richmond City Council. The governor displaced all military appointees in the council and placed in power (requested) nominees submitted by the city.

The new council then elected H. K. Ellyson mayor. On March 16, Ellyson notified George Chahoon, the mayor appointed by the Northern military commander, that he, Ellyson, would take over the office of mayor on the following day.

Chahoon failed to yield his position and would not recognize the authority of the council to elect a new mayor.

To resolve the impasse, which also included street violence, the case finally was brought before the Virginia Court of Appeals.

On April 20, after the case had been argued, the court took the matter under advisement, with an opinion as to who was Richmond's mayor to be delivered on April 25.

For some unknown reason, the date was changed to April 27.

The mood of the crowd which packed the old House was happy, though eager to hear the decision.

Two of the judges had taken their seats. They awaited the arrival of the remaining judges in the case.

It was shortly before 11 a.m.

The portion of the room where the judges sat did not give way, thus many were saved.

But there was the stifling cloud of dust from the collapse of the gallery and the main floor. Many spectators clung to doors and windows.

The bell tower sounded the fire alarm. The dust pouring from the Capitol windows was so thick, many witnesses thought the building was on fire.

226   Reportorial Writing

	Fire companies responded, and the square was filled with Richmonders.
Reference cited	The book, "Richmond, Her Past and Present," by W. Ashbury Christian, described the disaster:
Details	"The scene beggared description when they entered into what was once the house of Delegates and saw the tall yawning walls which looked down upon them, the confused mass of broken timbers, twisted iron, smashed furniture, covered with plastering, and beheld underneath this rubbish hundreds of bleeding and suffering citizens, many mashed beyond recognition. . . ."
	Every vehicle that could be used was rushed to the Capitol. They were turned into temporary ambulances. Rescuers worked for hours until every person was taken from the debris.
	Killed were state senators and delegates, attorneys, policemen, city and state officials, a newspaper reporter and a federal marshal.
	Sadness and mourning settled over the capital city like the disaster's heavy coating of dust.

The historical feature is the product of research. Books, reference texts and old newspapers are some of the sources from which information can be obtained.

The feature writer reveals a source of information—a book—in telling the story of the Richmond disaster. The chronological order brings many of the facts together. It can be particularly effective when used with a narrative style, which leans heavily on actions. The rich use of incidents in the Richmond story includes the gathering of the crowd, the two judges taking their seats, the spectators clinging to doors and windows, dust pouring from windows, and the response of the fire trucks.

Timely Occasions

Special days, such as Valentine's Day, Father's Day and Columbus Day, often inspire timely features. Mother's Day prompted the following one.

Introduction invites reader to read on	HENDERSON, Ky. (AP)—Mother's day has a special meaning for residents of this northwest Kentucky community.
Basic information	Why? They claim that Miss Mary Towles Sasseen, a Henderson native, was the real founder of Mother's Day 83 years ago.
Background	Anna M. Jarvis of Philadelphia is generally credited as the first to celebrate Mother's day.

Supplementation	Miss Jarvis, a spinster and one of 11 children, sent 500 carnations to St. Andrew's Methodist Church in Grafton, W. Va., on May 10, 1908, to honor her mother, who had died three years before.
Basic information	Henderson residents, however, point to Miss Sasseen as the first to actively work for a special day for mother.
Supplementation	They say Miss Sasseen was a teacher here and in 1887 began the observance in her classroom.
	Some years later she visited a sister in Springfield, Ohio, and introduced the idea in the public schools there.
	Then in 1893, Miss Sasseen published a pamphlet which set her goal. After that she began traveling across the country, speaking before education groups in an effort to have her day more widely observed.
	Miss Sasseen quit teaching in 1900, married and moved to Florida. She died six years later, still endeavoring to promote a nationwide day for mothers.
Basic information	In 1914 President Woodrow Wilson signed a resolution making the second Sunday in May a "flag holiday" to be known as Mother's Day.
Supplementation	Neither Miss Sasseen nor Miss Jarvis ever experienced the thrill of being honored on the day they had worked so hard for.
	Miss Sasseen had no children after her marriage and Miss Jarvis never married.

This type of feature resembles the <u>historical feature</u> in that it usually recounts past events.

Advice from Specialists

If an epidemic were to take place, health officials would come forth with suggestions for checking the spread of disease. Stories of their comments would be timely news.

Stories that offer advice from experts, however, are not always based on anything so timely, and sometimes they are more feature than news stories. Specialists, for example, may advise parents not to try to force left-handed children to become right handed, or they may offer helpful hints for detecting handicaps among the young, such as hearing and visual deficiencies. In any case, the purpose of the advice-offering feature is to <u>help the reader to</u> solve common problems.

A Fresno (Calif.) *Bee* story offers expert advice on pet selection from officials of the Society for the Prevention of Cruelty to Animals:

Story's central idea	Personnel at the SPCA Animal Shelter urge would-be pet owners to give up the notion of exotic pet ownership and try a dog or cat or even a tank of goldfish instead.

	Experts who know the problems discourage the practice of taking exotic animals into private homes as pets and are alarmed over the number of these animals caught in this snare.
Supplementary reasons	Exotic animals do not adapt successfully to a domestic home situation, they say. The person who adopts such an animal, no matter how well meaning and loving, is still usually faced with often insurmountable difficulties.
	Wild animals, they warn, are just that; they have not been domesticated. Veterinarians are usually not schooled in their care. It takes an expert and great expense to assure an adequate diet.
	An exotic animal which has been raised as a pet until it grows up and becomes unmanageable faces almost certain death. It cannot be returned to a natural state, because it has no experience in protecting itself or seeking food. Such animals are adaptable to life only with other animals in captivity and few zoos can accept them, even as gifts.

The *Bee* feature is relatively simple. Advice attributed to experts is followed by supplementing reasons. The following feature, because its subject is more complex, needed greater development.

Consumer problem presented	NEW YORK (AP)—Many a motorist has been tempted by the lower prices of gasoline sold at independent stations. But he passes on by to get his fuel at a name brand pump despite the fact he probably will pay four cents a gallon more.
	His fear: "inferior" gas sold at the independent stations might damage his car. How valid is this fear?
Opinion of an authority	"I don't think there is any evidence of physical damage to a car from use of unbranded or private brand gasoline," says Bryce Cedil, assistant marketing director of the American Petroleum Institute, whose 8,000 members include representatives of every phase of the petroleum industry from technology to marketing.
Opinion of another authority	Gerry Ferrara, executive director of the New Jersey Gasoline Retailers Association, adds that if the motorist is dealing with the honest businessman, independent or name brander, most of his fears are unfounded. The association represents some 2,500 service station owners, chiefly "big branders."
Supplementary reasons	For one thing, the gasoline sold by independents may be made by the same major oil company supplying the name brand station down the road. It also could come from one of the small independent refineries which produce for the unbranded market.
	Moreover, there is a great deal of commingling of gasolines.
	Big companies buy raw crude from each other, and the extra bargeload of refined gasoline a major oil company has at delivery time may wind up in an independent's tank.

	None of the major companies supplies independents directly, but they do sell to "jobbers," middle men who resell the gas to independents.
Opinion of another authority	Max Victor, executive director of the New York State Association of Service Stations, which has a membership of about 2,000, says the main difference between buying gas from an independent and buying a major brand is that the big brand may offer special additives—such as detergents or anti-rust and anti-stalling compounds for improved performance.
Basic information	This is the key problem facing the economy-minded motorist: finding the right gasoline for his particular car. And spokesmen in both the petroleum and automotive industries concede "the only way is by the trial and error method."
	Whether a particular gasoline is right for a particular car depends not so much on the name of the gasoline in the tank as on the car itself, when and where it's being driven and by whom.
Supplementation	"If you have a car with a high-compression ratio you can do serious damage to the engine if you use a gasoline that is of too low a grade," according to David Staiger, manager of publications for the Society of Automotive Engineers.
	"And if you're a hot-footed driver, you need a good premium or you'll blow the motor," he adds. "If you're the 'little old lady' type driver, on the other hand, you can probably get along on a lesser grade."
Another authority introduced	Adam J. Rumoshoski, marketing director for API, suggests that shopping for gasoline is just like shopping for anything else.
Supplementation	"You can judge by [the dealer's] reputation, the premises—almost by instinct," he says. . . .

The Debunking Feature

Unfounded beliefs, fallacies, misconceptions and misunderstandings are sometimes the targets of feature articles.

A feature writer might present the views of dietitians on food fallacies. Are raw foods more healthful than cooked ones? Is rare meat better for a person than well-done meat? Will food left open in cans spoil?

One reporter questioned two university deans of women on this oftentimes expressed view pertaining to women: "Beautiful but dumb." Here is the lead to his story:

> NEW YORK (AP)—Two of the nation's outstanding women educators concur in the declaration that the expression "beautiful but dumb" is passe, hors de combat, non compos mentis, and a dastardly lie.

The belief that western gunfighters were heroes or at least courageous is debunked in a story by Robert Musel.

Engaging introduction	LONDON (UPI)—The western gunfighter went for his six-shooter and shot his enemy—in the back. In the back? Well, that's the way it often happened in real life and if you prefer the stand-up heroes of television, don't read Joseph G. Rosa's new deep study of the old west, "The Gunfighter: Man of Myth?"
Basic information	Back in those old cowtowns they didn't approach each other stiff-legged on main street, hands clawed for a lightning draw as they do in "Gunsmoke" or "The Virginian." They sought to obtain what Rosa, who loves the era and has spent most of his adult life studying it, understates as "an element of surprise."
Incidents	So Wild Bill Hickok, one of his heroes, was shot in the back by a hired gun who didn't know his famous quarry's eyes were so dimmed by disease he would have been safe to approach head-on. Jesse James was shot in the back. Billy the Kid was shot from ambush. And the great Ben Thompson was gunned down in the gloom of a theater in Austin, Tex., in 1884.
Background on source of information	Rosa is a member of the English Westerners Society, whose members have found a good deal of original material bearing on life in the old west.
Elaboration	"The story of the American gunfighter is comparable to Europe's Robin Hood and knights in shining armor. Their common bond being lone crusaders fighting evil in order that good might prevail. The legendary gunfighter is beyond reproach, gifted with phenomenal reflexes enabling him to draw and fire a six-shooter with incredible speed, and the ability to hit his man with great accuracy. "But the real gunfighter was never such a paragon of virtue. A few men, notably Hickok and Bartholomew (Bat) Masterson, emulated some of their legends but the majority only achieved heroic status long after they were dead. "I traced the word 'gunfighter' back to the 1870s but it did not become prominent until 1907, when Masterson publicized the word in a series of articles in 'Human Life.' From then on it was eagerly exploited by novelists, moviemakers and others to whom the character suggested some sort of demigod." The romanticization of later years, he said, has tended to blur the fact that Jesse James was paranoiac, Billy the Kid subnormal, John Wesley Hardin a pathologic killer who died in a saloon brawl, Doc Holliday a dangerous drunk with an ungovernable temper detested by those who knew him. "When they went into action," Rosa said, "they had the gun already in their hands."

Usually the reporter does not do the debunking—he is only the narrator. An authority is cited—he is the one who corrects the unfounded belief, and the exposure of the sham is only as valid as the exposer is authoritative.

The preceding story has a London dateline because the authority wrote his study there. The dateline is of little importance in most debunking features. Authorities may pop up in Mukilteo, Wash.; Oshkosh, Wis.; or Skowhegan, Me.

In a typical type of debunking feature written years ago by Charles Honce, the writer did his own research and served as the authority.

Reader challenged	NEW YORK (AP)—It's dollars to doughnuts you cannot correctly name the man who made the following statement: "Everybody talks about the weather, but nobody does anything about it." Mark Twain, you say? No. A thousand times no!
Basic information	Mark never even came near such a declaration, although for years he has been widely credited with uttering it. The real author was Charles Dudley Warner, a humorist of parts during the latter part of the last century.
Elaboration	The writer has heard the remark hung on Mark Twain three times in recent days—on the radio, in a book and in a news story. That seems to give the matter sufficient currency to warrant an attempt to try to set the business right. It is not likely, however, any such thing will happen. It is to be presumed Mark Twain still will be called the author of one of the most widely known quotations of modern days. It is difficult to arrive at any satisfactory explanation why Warner was deprived of the credit. The nearest approach to a solution is in the fact both Warner and Twain were humorists, once lived near each other in Hartford, Conn., were close friends and collaborated on a book.
Background	Warner, who was born in Plainfield, Mass., in 1829 and died in Hartford in 1900, was a sort of great champ of polite letters near the turn of the century. Warner worked up a considerable reputation as an author, editor, critic, traveler and homespun philosopher, first coming into literary notice with a book, "My Summer in a Garden" (1870), made up of articles originally contributed to the Hartford Courant. A critic proclaimed it "placed Warner in the front rank of American humorists."
Basic information	Occasionally another well known statement is attributed to Twain: "What this country really needs is a good 5-cent cigar."
Elaboration	More people, however, know the father of that one was the late Vice President Thomas R. Marshall. He said it while presiding over the United States Senate during a debate on the needs of the country.

People

There are many reasons individuals are singled out for feature stories: their interesting backgrounds, their achievements, their experiences or adventures, or their personalities.

Knight Newspapers published a copyrighted story by Vera Glaser and Malvina Stephenson on Wernher von Braun, a man who has achieved much prominence in America's space program.

Attention getter	WASHINGTON—Rocket-genius Wernher von Braun has shaved off his beard to help "sell" Congress on President Nixon's slimmed-down space program.
	The 58-year-old glamorboy of space, recently transferred to Washington, said in an interview that his facial foliage might have been viewed by the lawmakers as a "rebellious demonstration" against cuts in the 1971 space budget.
Basic point	Von Braun, whose Saturn booster put a man on the moon, has been trying to keep out of print until his formal "unveiling" Tuesday at a news conference at NASA, where he is settling into a newly created top planning post.
Elaboration	He said he has been "batching it" at a local hotel this month while waiting for his family to move from Huntsville, Ala.
Basic point	Cornered outside a House committee room where he was due to give secret testimony, the handsome, hefty von Braun displayed charm while claiming the United States has not abandoned its ambitious space goals.
Elaboration	"But the rate at which we can attack them is slowed down," he conceded. "It is a great tragedy that we are so deeply involved in Vietnam."
Basic point	As a living legend, von Braun will have a problem not overshadowing such space VIPs as NASA Chief Thomas O. Paine.
Elaboration and background	Some say von Braun himself would head the NASA now were it not for his German birth. The son of a baron, he directed Hitler's V2 rocket program in World War II, then joined the Americans and became a U.S. citizen in 1955.
Basic point	Von Braun's position is sticky. As a NASA official, he has to back the President's space budget while wishing it were fatter.
Elaboration	Rep. James G. Fulton of Pennsylvania, ranking republican on the House Space Committee, has warned, "If we don't use our astronauts, they'll look like the Smith Brothers on the cough drop box by the time they get near a space vehicle."
Basic point	Von Braun is viewed in some quarters as a showman and super-salesman as much as a technician. His unofficial contacts with the powerful here are expected to influence long-range space plans as much as his public appearances.

Feature Writing   233

Elaboration	His pretty wife, the former Maria Louise von Quistorp, whose picture he carries in his wallet, could be helpful. She is von Braun's first cousin, 16 years his junior, but is known to be shy. The fact that she was not keen on Huntsville may have influenced his decision to move. Mrs. von Braun was scheduled to arrive this weekend preparatory to occupying their newly purchased home in suburban Alexandria, Va. The von Brauns have three children, 22-year-old Iris; Margrit, 18; and Peter, 9. Von Braun's brother, Magnus, works for the Chrysler Corp. in Detroit. Another brother, Sigismund, is ambassador to France from the Federal Republic of Germany.
Basic point	Von Braun consistently has rejected fat offers from industry, one reportedly for $250,000 a year, to make his talents available to the nation which gave him haven. His present salary is $36,000.
Elaboration	He believes the United States is at a critical juncture in its space program. The Soviets are actively supporting their space effort, he warned, and "if we rest on our laurels, the United States may be surprised by another Sputnik." (Reprinted with permission)

The writers have divulged how much of the information for the story was obtained: von Braun was "cornered" outside a house committee room. But a lot more information was needed to fill in the crevices. Some no doubt came from the observations and backgrounds of the writers themselves. And clippings in a newspaper library are always valuable sources of information.

Even though the story is based on an interview, the article goes considerably beyond the scope of the usual interview story. The article is broadened by information not obtained in the interview and by views other than those of von Braun.

The article borders, in spots, on interpretation, as in the paragraph:

> As a living legend, von Braun will have a problem not overshadowing such space VIPs as NASA Chief Thomas O. Paine.

Personality and exploits rather than prominence or achievement prompt many feature stories.

Persons who overcome some of the limitations of physical handicaps are also occasionally the subjects of features. An example is this article by Charles Kershner in which personal courage, not prominence, captures the reader's attention:

Inviting lead	SOUTH BURLINGTON, Vt. (UPI)—Charles "Chuck" Leonard, 38, is an electronic design engineer who skis and plays pool. So what? Leonard is blind.
Background	Leonard, who works at the General Electric plant here, lost his sight—but not his nerve—about four years ago.

As an undergraduate at Williams College in the early 1950s, Chuck, as he prefers to be called, took up skiing as "a large portion of my life and motivation."

He raced for Williams and took skiing vacations in Argentina, Chile, Austria, Switzerland and France. He skied the most famous trails and glaciers in the world.

Chuck joined the ski patrol at Mad River Glen in 1951, a membership he still holds on an honorary basis.

"I figured statistics were against me when I traveled the 280 miles each way between Binghamton, N.Y., and Mad River every weekend," he said, "so I looked around for a job in Vermont."

Basic information

After a routine medical checkup at the GE plant in September, 1964, he was told he was a victim of retinopathy, a progressive, nonreversible complication of the diabetes he had developed at the age of 10.

Supplementation

Chuck confronted the problem of blindness by taking a 16-week course in rehabilitation at St. Paul's Rehabilitation Center in Newton, Mass. He later found Braille and typing too slow for his rate of production, so he had developed a magnetic tape recorder with a specially adapted "wire tap" for telephone work.

"I still ski," he said, "but now I need the aid of a sighted partner wearing a throat mike so his hands are free as he radios me directions."

Chuck wears a small radio receiver and an earphone to get directions as he makes his way down the trails. He also wears a bright orange sign with black lettering on his parka that reads: "Danger—Blind crossing," a touch of humor.

Basic information

Chuck is experimenting with an ultrasonic guidance device invented by Dr. Leonard Kay of the British University of Birmingham.

Supplementation and elaboration

Kay's invention looks like a flashlight with a wire leading to a tiny earphone. The pitch of sound in the earpiece lowers as the user approaches an obstruction.

Chuck is trying to improve the sensing device for his own use in skiing and for other blind people.

To play pool in his basement he has attached a photocell to his cue. This, with a tiny "beeping" device, he said, allows him to "zero in" on the penlight his partner holds above the ball he is to hit.

"I listen for the ball to drop in the pocket," Chuck said. "And it does. My device is accurate to one-half inch in eight feet."

In addition to skiing and pool, Chuck sails his own boat and putters around at golf during the summer.

Basic information

Leonard was named Vermont's engineer of the year last week. . . .

Hobbies

Hobbies that are unusual or that have wide interest can be the subjects of feature stories. Old automobiles have attracted the interest of many, and a family that made a hobby of restoring old cars was the subject of this *Christian Science Monitor* feature by John Bunker:

Story's central idea	Restoring old cars is a family hobby for the Petersons of San Diego, Calif.
Supplementation	Husband Joe, wife Alita, and the five Peterson children have all had antique cars of their own and shared the fun of old-car meets and cavalcades.
Basic information	For Mrs. Peterson this hobby was just something that messed up the garage and tracked oily spots into the house —until the time that son Gary asked her to come out to the garage and hold a light while he worked on a Ford Model A transmission.
Supplementation	"First," she recalls, "I just held the light. Then I was passing wrenches. First thing I knew I was loosening a nut and getting my hands all oily. I was 'hooked.' It was a family deal from then on."
	She soon graduated from being a wrench holder for the men to buying an old car of her own, a 1930 standard Ford coupe. She is now driving her fourth restoration, a snappy 1931 deluxe Ford roadster that would have been the envy of any "Joe College" back in the early days of Rudy Vallee and Kate Smith. It took her two years, with the help of the men, of course, to restore it to mint condition, complete to the deep-throated "cay-ooga" of an original 1931 Ford horn.
	Roadsters and phaetons are very scarce and are much prized by antique car buffs.
	Mrs. Peterson fell in love with this car when she saw it on a freeway and followed it for 10 miles before she could flag its young driver to stop and offer to buy it on the spot.
	Most of her nights and weekends for the following year were spent crawling over and under this prize, scraping off coats of old paint, taking every bit of the car apart for inspection, cleaning, repairing, and replacement.
Basic information	You don't restore an old car overnight, she explains. It takes long hours to disassemble and renovate, not to mention the difficulty of obtaining the needed authentic parts from dealers, at swap meets, or by correspondence with other Model A fans all over the country.
Supplementation	The Petersons have a garage full of Model A parts purchased from hobbyists and collectors.
	"If you have a 'thing' for old cars," she says, "you learn to live in a house full of horns, clutch assemblies, fenders, transmissions, steering wheels, extra headlights, wire-spoke wheels, starters, and other parts. Model A fans prize them

	more highly than Rembrandts and Van Goghs. They collect wherever and whenever they can and hoard them against the day when they may need to swap for a much needed piece of body or engine."
Basic information	The Peterson cars have won many prizes at southwest Model A meets.
Supplementation and elaboration	Restoring the car is only part of the fun. Hobbyists wear period clothes to meets and get-togethers because judging in Model A contests requires that contestants drive in authentic clothes of the Model A era, the late '20s and early '30s.
	Mrs. Peterson scours secondhand shops and classified columns, attends swap meets and estate auctions. During the past few years she has accumulated several closets full of tassled dresses, pin-stripe suits, white flannels, knickers, blue blazers, straw hats, bowlers, and some 20 pairs of men's and women's shoes.
	"The payoff to all this time and effort comes," she says, "when you pull up to a stop light and a big car pulls up alongside. A middle-aged man looks up very wistfully and says, 'What a beauty, lady, what a beauty. I had one just like that when I was in college. Wouldn't like to trade me, would you?' " (Reprinted with permission from the *Christian Science Monitor*)

Short Features

Many opportunities for short features present themselves to the alert reporter. An uncommon cent prompted the writing of the following article.

Invitation to read	NEW YORK (AP)—If someone offers you a penny for your thoughts—ask to see the coin.
	If it's a 1799 United States copper penny, start talking and do not stop.
Basic information	The coin might be the one of that vintage which brought $10,500 at auction last night in a Manhattan coin dealer's headquarters.
	The penny was sold to Richard Picker, a rare coin dealer of Albertson, Long Island, N.Y.
Background	The coin was minted in Philadelphia using the die for a 1798 penny with alterations to change the last numeral in the date to 9.
Elaboration	A similarly dated penny made with a 1799 die sold for $10,000 in 1959.

Editors sometimes like to run a humorous story to offset their newspaper's many serious stories. Here is a good example of a short feature whose only purpose is to bring a smile to the reader's lips:

Initial incident	MUSKEGON, Mich. (AP)—Police Sgt. William Hicks, presiding at a recent meeting of women school crossing guards in the basement of City Hall, expressed concern about whether women would be able to find the meeting site.
Chronological order of incidents	The women had no trouble, but Hicks remained worried. "If any of you ladies have any trouble finding your way out," he announced, "just use one of these telephones, dial zero, and we'll have an operator come down and help you out."
Surprise ending	Hicks then opened the door and walked into a closet.

EXERCISES

I. Questions for Discussion

1. What are the differences between a news story and a feature story?
2. What is meant by the statement, "Most feature stories are born with an idea"?
3. Which requires more skill, the writing of a news story or the writing of a feature story?
4. What are some of the embellishments that are frequently used in feature articles?
5. Is there a standard type of organization for feature stories?

II. Determine which of the following story openings introduced news stories and which introduced feature articles

1. Desperate arthritis sufferers spend between $300 million and $400 million a year on useless cures dispensed by quacks—far more than is spent to research the disease, according to Dr. Herbert Kaplan of the University of Colorado Medical Center.

    Dr. Kaplan called for a debunking of misconceptions in arthritis treatment in a Friday speech—"Quacks vs. Facts in the Treatment of Arthritis"—at a one-day workshop. . . . (Denver *Rocky Mountain News*)

    BY MIKE WINES

2. "Sergeant Edgar N. Kelley, the songwriting policeman," may sound like an act on the Amateur Hour, but the Jeffersontown patrolman's first record is selling as if he were an old pro in the music business. (Louisville *Courier-Journal*)

    BY BEN ZINZER

3. Dramatic relief from excruciating chest pain is now being achieved by two Long Beach heart-disease patients by a simple push-button maneuver.

Thanks to a relatively new operation performed at Memorial Hospital, these patients can switch off the agony of angina pectoris, a vice-like-pain brought on by oxygen deficit in the heart muscle. (Long Beach *Independent Press-Telegram*)

BY WALTER SULLIVAN

4. A substance widely considered to have been a key ingredient in the early evolution of life has been detected among the stars by a radio telescope atop Kitt Peak in Arizona.

    It is hydrogen cyanide, a deadly poison to higher life forms. As a gas it is used, with special precautions, to fumigate pest-ridden ships and other confined areas.

    (©1970 by The New York Times Company. Reprinted by permission)

BY JEFF NESMITH

5. By literally flipping switches, the drivers of 1,200 cars and trucks owned by the federal government will soon convert the vehicles from gasoline to natural gas.

    Then, government officials and engineers said during a meeting here Friday, the vehicles will run cheaper and air pollution from each will be reduced by up to 90 per cent. (Atlanta *Constitution*)

BY CHARLES HILLINGER

6. GUGGEY, Colo.—Charley Dell, 66, woodchopper, mountaineer and lifelong bachelor, hung his long johns on the clothesline outside his log cabin.

    The stubborn backwoodsman, whose only concession to 20th-century living is driving a pickup truck, is "sore as hell." (Los Angeles *Times*)

7. MADISON, Wis. (UPI)—A University of Wisconsin scientific team, headed by a publicity-shy Nobel Prize winner, has artificially created a gene. The breakthrough could lead to the eventual creation of life by man.

    The announcement by Har Govind Khorana, who won the 1968 Nobel Prize for work in deciphering the genetic code, was made at a meeting of UW scientists yesterday.

BY JAMES M. NAUGHTON

8. CLEVELAND—The man who came to dinner here last night to arouse the passions of 1,400 listeners and nearly as many demonstrators left in the rain today without a peep and with scarcely a spectator.

    He was Vice President Agnew, the hottest property the Republican party has had on its banquet circuit since the party first trotted out an elephant. Since Feb. 1, he has raised more than $3-million in campaign funds by raising his voice at banquets from coast to coast. (©1970 by The New York Times Company. Reprinted by permission)

BY ROBERT C. BLETHEN

9. Wolf Jakubowski, 20, a junior at the University of Washington, spent most of his higher education studying the sciences. He wanted to become an oceanographic engineer.

   Last year he began feeling that maybe this wasn't his "bag." He decided to experiment in an economic venture. (Seattle *Times*)

BY NEAL STANFORD

10. WASHINGTON—For decades—for centuries—population has been like weather: everybody has talked about it but didn't do much about it. Now that's changing. In fact population this past year has ranked right up there with environment, crime, and Vietnam for governmental attention. (*Christian Science Monitor*)

III. List the sources of information you would consult to get information for feature articles on the following

1. Shoplifting
2. Unemployment
3. Fire hazards
4. Child care centers
5. Mentally retarded children
6. Nursing homes
7. Credit cards
8. Thefts by hotel patrons
9. Use of narcotics by school children
10. Crowded court calendars

IV. Critical Questions

1. Is attribution needed in the ninth paragraph of the story about a Sacramento, Calif., boy who is being saved by science from becoming a dwarf?
2. Is the word "luckily" used subjectively in the second paragraph of the historical feature on the collapse of Virginia's House of Delegates?
3. Is adequate attribution used in the feature advising persons not to select exotic pets? In the same story, should SPCA be spelled out in the opening paragraph?
4. Are the words "said in an interview" needed in the second paragraph of the Wernher von Braun story? In the same story, is the sentence in the 13th paragraph listing the names of the von Braun children parallel?

Chapter 13

REPORTING THE NEWS

IN DEPTH AND IN BREADTH

*That there should one man die ignorant
who had capacity for knowledge, this I
call tragedy.* —*Carlyle*

Any new communications medium, if it is successful, has an impact on the other media. Over the years, television has had an impact on newspaper coverage of the news. The emphasis on spot news has been modified, for example, with more and more attention being given to reporting the news in depth and in breadth.

That does not mean newspapers are not doing a good job of reporting spot news. Newspapers have an advantage over television in that they can go into more detail than can be accomplished on the average news telecast. It does mean that newspapers are providing background for the news and reporting in far greater depth than they used to.

Gene Sherman of the Los Angeles *Times* once told an amusing story at a seminar for teachers conducted by his newspaper:

A cub reporter was assigned to cover a party held by a wealthy set of nudists in the swank home of one of the colony's members. When the reporter returned to his desk to write the story, the editor asked how he got along with the assignment.

The reporter answered that soon after he had rung the bell, the maid, naked, opened the door. The editor asked how he knew it was the maid and the reporter replied:

"Well, I knew it wasn't the butler."

Sherman cited this as an example of the opposite of reporting in depth.

What is reporting in depth?

As the term implies, it is digging far below the surface. A college student, for instance, takes a survey class in literature and covers a lot of breadth but goes into little depth. He gets a smattering of Chaucer, Shakespeare, Dryden, Pope, Cowper, Wordsworth, Scott, Tennyson, Arnold and others.

The wide coverage provides breadth, but not depth. Later the literature student digs beneath the surface in separate courses in Chaucer, Shakespeare and others, or he takes courses on literary periods. Then he begins to study some of the literary figures in depth.

Both the survey and the more specific in-depth courses are important. Newspaper articles that cover the news in breadth and those that cover it in depth are both important, too.

Most, but not all, in-depth articles found in newspapers today are exhaustive composites, with ample background, of what has already been reported in spot news stories. Most are expansions of the feature story, with considerable elaboration in the way of facts, incidents, examples, quotations from "experts," and particulars and details.

The term "in depth" implies deep digging—search, research, inquiry, investigation and exploration. An interview with one or two persons may end up as an interesting story, a worthwhile one, but it can hardly be called in-depth reporting.

In his seminar, Sherman gave an example of in-depth reporting:

> The essence of in-depth reporting is *thoroughness,* which has no relation to the length of a story when it appears in print, nor does it have any relation to the time spent in developing a story. A good example of reporting in depth for those of you who read the *Times* . . . was the series of stories on last year's Bel Air fire that ran some months after the spot news of the fire itself. Hank Sutherland and Howard Hertel thoroughly researched the background, the cause, the human interest and all the collective factors of the disaster. At the time of the fire you wanted to know *what* was burning, but after it was all over you wanted to know how it happened, the total impact of the fire, the magnitude of it in human terms. That's reporting in depth, a thorough presentation of all available facts. . . . One-dimensional news reporting no longer is acceptable—facts must have meaning.

How much time is required to report a subject in depth? That depends on how specific the subject is—the extent to which the subject has been narrowed. It can be hours, days, weeks or months.

How long should the article be?

That also depends on how much the topic has been narrowed. It should be long enough to cover the topic thoroughly.

The subjects selected for in-depth stories are usually of public significance, although reporting in depth is not necessarily limited to problems of timely social concern.

In-depth stories have been written about narcotics, the generation gap, law enforcement and crime, the penal system, civil rights, minorities, racial oppression, desegregation, the population explosion, pollution, mental illness, education, slums and poverty.

It is conceivable, however, that Disneyland, mink farming or some wonderland of nature—topics not of serious public concern but still interesting—could be the subject of in-depth reporting.

A newspaper's format and the size of its staff largely determine how much in-depth coverage it can carry. The philosophy of the editors is also a factor. A small newspaper with a limited staff may not feel that it can afford to free a reporter to do the research necessary for in-depth articles. It may rely on some local feature coverage and use in-depth articles supplied by the wire services.

The survey story, partly because of its length, is sometimes confused with the in-depth article.

The in-breadth story, like the in-depth article, may be a composite, with added background, of what has been covered in spot news stories. Often, too, it is based on subjects of deep public concern. Its purpose may be to give the diverse views of many persons on a controversial subject already reported in the news.

In-depth and survey stories differ from the typical feature in that they develop their subjects more thoroughly.

As television has encroached on the news function, newspapers in turn have invaded the general magazine field. In-depth and survey stories, because of their intensive or extensive development, resemble the magazine feature article that strives for mass reader appeal rather than appeal to special groups.

Some editors, because of space limitations in an issue or because of an aversion to having a large block of gray type, prefer breaking in-depth stories into series rather than using single-story play.

Wire services and large newspapers with many correspondents generally cover vast topics or geographical areas in depth and in breadth, but the medium-sized newspaper is likely to restrict its efforts to its service area.

Getting the Information

One of the first things a reporter embarking on an in-depth or an in-breadth story must do is to note all the sources of information available on the subject, starting with his newspaper's own past coverage. Other sources are myriad.

Do local organizations or agencies have an interest in the subject or information about it, and, if so, are officials of these organizations available for comment? Have any reports or investigations been made?

Public officials, politicians, lay leaders, college professors or teachers, professional men, clergymen or students might be knowledgeable about the subject.

Two college students working on an in-depth reporting project on California's freeway problems first reviewed clippings on the subject in the local newspaper's library and then talked with several local officials who were familiar with the subject, including a highway commissioner.

Trips followed to the state capital, Sacramento, and to the San Francisco and Los Angeles areas. In each place the students reviewed clippings in newspaper libraries and talked with newspaper reporters who had written stories dealing with the freeway problems.

In the state capital, they talked with the governor; the chairman of the State Senate Fact Finding Committee on Transportation and Public Utilities; the chairman of the State Assembly Committee on Natural Resources, Planning and Public Works; the director of the State Department of Public Works and chairman of the State Highway Commission; the president pro tempore of the State Senate; the speaker of the State Assembly; the state highway engineer and chief of the Division of Highways; and the executive secretary of California Tomorrow, a private organization interested in planning.

In the San Francisco Bay area, they talked with the chief administrative officer of the city of San Francisco; an official in the city's planning office; the assistant state highway engineer, San Francisco district; the general manager of the San Francisco Bay Area Rapid Transit District; a former official in the transportation division of the state chamber of commerce; and an official of the University of California Institute of Transportation and Traffic Engineering.

In the Los Angeles area, they talked with the district highway engineer; the executive director of the Los Angeles Metropolitan Transit Authority; an official of the state highway division, Los Angeles district; the assistant state highway engineer, Los Angeles district; and an official of Los Angeles Beautiful, a private organization interested in planning.

Among others interviewed were the executive secretary of the California Citizens Freeway Association and the executive vice president of the California Roadside Council, private organizations interested in freeway problems.

The students attended hearings of a joint legislative committee on freeway proposals. Reams of reports and brochures came from public officials and representatives of private organizations, all of which were studied.

The final research on a topic for a survey story should be done in news clippings, recent magazine articles and books. The process then usually becomes one of multiple interviewing.

Much depends upon the point from which the reporter starts. The two students started from scratch, but a reporter may have acquired considerable background from spot news coverage before taking on an assignment to do an in-depth story, a series or a survey article.

Writing the In-Depth Story

One of the first things to be decided when a reporter embarks on an in-depth reporting assignment is whether one article will suffice or a series should be written. This decision is usually made in consultation with the city editor or the managing editor, or both.

Extended columns of gray type are not particularly attractive or inviting. It may be better to run several relatively short articles than one long one. The editor must decide whether or not the newspaper can afford to give enough space for complete coverage in a single issue.

Before he even begins to write, a reporter has usually collected far more information than he can put into his story. He must therefore decide what to include and what to omit.

A simple method is for the newsman to make a skeleton outline—to jot down the main points that are needed to tell the story. His next task is to select the material—quotations, examples, incidents, particulars and details—he feels will best supplement the main points. If there are conflicting opinions, they should be given.

The following Los Angeles *Times* article by Charles T. Powers offers a good example of how an in-depth story should be written.

Enticing introduction in narrative style	TAOS, N.M.—The Grateful Dead presides over the valley at dawn, and the stoned occupants of the three-room ramshackle adobe stagger into the sunlit yard.
	The music of the Dead sounds right. Rasping from a portable record player in the house, it adds the perfect touch of crazy religiosity to the weirdness of an acid-crystalled morning.
	Incredible, the way the mountains leap out, all pine forested and patched with snow. It's like being hit in the face with beauty.

Don stands there, reeling a little as he scratches at a month's growth of beard and a year's length of wispy hair. "Whew," he wheezes, grinning. He shakes his head, pops his eyes open in his comic mock double-take. "Outrageous," he says. "Stoned again."

Or stoned still and coming down. The day will float along in slow motion, the flashes of the night will be bobbing to the surface like apples in a barrel. "This is it," someone had said then, standing in the center of the room under the glaring light bulb.

A FAR-OUT PHILOSOPHY

"This is all you need. Your dope, your friends and a warm place. All you need in the world."

Transitional paragraph

It rang like the truth of the ages.
But then, not everybody in Taos was there to agree.

Background

The country around Taos has always been poor, and for generations it has been populated by Mexicans scratching a living out of the rocky soil, two or three silent Indian pueblos and a few hardy whites who enjoy the peace, the mountains and the money from the tourist trade. Together, they make up the old, more or less native Establishment of Taos.

Beginning with the summer of 1967, the new people came, hiking up the road from Santa Fe with their pasts wrapped in bundles and battered suitcases, or in bright painted buses from San Francisco, rollicking and roaring into the desert and mountains where they set the roots of a new culture.

ESCAPE FROM COMPLICATIONS

The reasons for their coming were almost as varied as the length and color of their hair. If there is a common denominator among them it is probably that they came from the cities, where the complications have become, to them, overwhelmingly depressing. To many, the wilderness was an escape; to some a place to hide.

In any case, to most of them, material wealth means little—at least for the present. Most bring only the necessities: rugged clothes, a sleeping bag, perhaps a prized book.

For them, life can be simple—simple as nature, requiring food, shelter and love. Anything more is trimming. Dope, of course, helps, because dope simplifies; it is the strongest bond between them and the broadest cultural foundation.

For some it is easier than for others. The middle-class work ethic, the idea that one must constantly be striving for some goal (A bigger house? A faster car?), doesn't die easily. But for those who began to reject it, Taos seemed a good place to be.

So groups like the Hog Farm left behind the hostile vibrations of Los Angeles County and set up camp 20 miles southeast of town. The communes of Morningstar and New

Buffalo and others came and their solid adobe buildings, after the fashion of Indians, rose on the mesas. In a way they became a new Establishment.

POPULATION PROBLEM

To the natives, it was a strange one, to be sure, but the new long-hair residents (often called "Hips" by old-timers) stayed mostly to themselves and got along well.

It was almost too good to last.

As time went on, it was too good not to attract more and more of the new people. With the people came problems. And a quiet hostility that now and then surfaces.

Basic information

Today, with 1,500 to 2,000 long-hairs in the area, there is a sense of impending crisis in both the hip and native communities. There is a mutual fear that spring and summer will bring more people, more than either the small town or the communes that surround it will be able to absorb.

Background and supplementation

Already, most of the communes are overcrowded. Food and water supplies were stretched to the limits; the teepees and adobe buildings are packed with transient heads who came looking for pastoral spaciousness and found, instead, a kind of ghetto in the wilds.

Disease, though not running wild, has become a problem. Persistent "staph" infections, dysentery, hepatitis and a resistant strain of gonorrhea keep Free Clinic doctors busy.

Even grass and acid, which form the most solid cultural foundation and bond, are getting scarce, simply because money is scarce. Marijuana and LSD dealers will sometimes trade their dope for food stamps (still another cultural foundation), but without food stamps, meals become modest and far between.

Most of the communes hope to develop crops and gardens, both for the satisfaction of taking their food from the soil and to live more economically. But few of them are into it heavy enough to support themselves, particularly in the long, high-altitude winters.

Those who support themselves best are hunters and trappers, but the biggest game is generally rabbit and squirrel. Deer is occasionally shot, but then the hunter is constantly in danger of running afoul of the game laws, and poaching, in New Mexico, is not taken lightly.

In all, communal living is not an easy way of life. Those who arrive—and expect to survive—must know or learn quickly how to take care of themselves. As one Hog Farmer said, "Some of these chicks can't cook on their mama's gas range. How do they expect to cook on an old wood-burning stove."

Basic information

The fears for the coming months stem generally from a plan, widely promoted in the hip press, to develop an

"Earth People's Park" this summer in northern New Mexico.

Supplementation

The plan calls for people to donate money to a group which will purchase a large plot of land (70,000 acres is the figure most often cited), probably in the vicinity of Taos or Santa Fe. When the land is obtained, a vast "earth warming" party will be scheduled. Many envision the celebration as a cultural event whose magnitude will dwarf the Woodstock festival of last September.

At the festival's conclusion, the land will be "freed" for the people to live on in the life style of their choosing, free of cops and the troubles of urban society.

It would, no doubt, be the weirdest land rush in history, but few of the scheme's promoters fully understand the problems it would bring. Woodstock, according to most who were there, was a peaceful, three-day sharing of mud and music. But no one attempted to extend it for weeks or months.

Basic information

Despite its scenic wonders, New Mexico is harsh country. It is cold in winter, arid in summer. Most of its back-country roads are rocky, rutted and treacherous, passable only in a four-wheel-drive vehicle.

Supplementation

Water, where it is available to the communes, comes from mountain-fed streams, many of which become polluted as warm weather approaches. In the dead of summer, most run dry. Heads who have been around a while note with alarm that mountain snowfalls have been light this winter. The streams, they say, will dry up early.

Sheer physical survival is only a part of the problem. Today, within a 25-mile radius of Taos, there are more than a dozen communes, some whose names are widely known in the area and others guardedly remote and accessible only to those who were party of the original settlement.

BUT STILL PLEASANT

Basic information

Already, a certain heaviness has crept into a few communes that once, in their beginnings, seemed to radiate good feeling and welcome. At least one is dominated by a group of young heroin addicts.

Supplementation

However, on the whole, the scene around Taos—at least for those firmly established—is still pleasant. There are merely glimmers, distant fears of what might become a colossal bummer, a 70,000-acre Haight-Ashbury in the desert. Everyone remembers that the Haight, before the speed freaks and muggers came, was a nice place, too.

Basic information

Of course, not every head who comes to Taos goes to a commune—or, more precisely, not every commune is made up of an elaborately organized large group of people. Some people who come take up residence in out-of-the-way houses, heated with wood-burning stoves and rented for

Supplementation

$15 a month. They become, in the sense that everything is shared, household communes.

Brian, Bill, Jeff and Don came to Taos last fall and found such a house, about 25 miles from town on the edge of a national forest preserve. It was a wreck and soon to be torn down, but it made a suitable home for the winter.

Soon they were joined by Greggo and Kathy, who moved down from Wyoming—forced to leave because Greggo was caught trapping beaver in a national park.

Then Tina came from the Hog Farm, fed up with disease, the "unbelievable outdoor john" and the general lack of direction.

Suzanne, a beautiful girl of 18, moved in from Sausalito. Terry, a 20-year-old Colorado girl, wandered in, absorbed in her leatherwork, and moved into Brian's bed. A few days ago she split, for parts unknown.

By then Jeff had already gone, staked by Tina to a journey to Nepal, where, it is hoped, he will score a hashish deal that will set them all up for life. Now, in the meantime, life goes on in fairly organized fashion and the members of the household feel themselves getting more together as time passes.

Though they seem to have fallen together almost randomly, they have known each other for years. Don, who is 20, and Brian, 21, estimate they have taken more than 100 acid trips together. Some unbreakable bonds have been forged.

"We're acid freaks first, hippies second and hunters third," says Don, who seems to provide the comic looseness the group needs to get along through difficult times—for it is unavoidable that nerves and patience are occasionally rubbed raw.

Patience is not one of Brian's strong points. He comes from a wealthy Bel Air family and, someone in the household occasionally (and good-naturedly) points out, is spoiled enough to spend the group food stamps on candy if he's not watched.

Basic information

The federal food stamp program is a mainstay not only of their household, but of virtually every member of the hip community around Taos. Without food stamps, the life style would be altered drastically or killed completely.

Supplementation

New Mexico, in cooperation with the federal government, is participating in a unique experiment in which unrelated people of the same household can receive food stamps. The food stamps, "purchased" from the welfare office for nominal prices (largely as a show of good intention), may then be used to buy commodities in Taos supermarkets.

RESENTMENTS RISE

Oddly, certain requirements in the welfare laws prevent some genuinely poverty-stricken long-time residents from receiving stamps. They are usually Spanish-speaking people who own a few acres of poorly producing farmland. It is not unusual to see a Mexican woman with a shopping basket full of beans and pig kunckles glowering at long-hairs in the check stand lines who are paying for steak and butter with food stamps that are forbidden to her. The inequity is causing increasing bitterness in Taos.

To the group that Brian and Bill belong to, food stamps mean about $180 a month. They could survive without them; they have before, usually by dope dealing (which, to any head culture, is honest commerce) or by devising ingenious schemes to relieve the Bank of America of a few hundred dollars in petty cash. But New Year's resolutions have forbidden that.

Basic information, followed by supplementary specifics

Their household is a gregarious one, given to adventurous traveling and gossiping with heads from the other side of the county. The exception is Greggo, the quiet hunter in the skunk-skin hat tied with eagle feathers. Greggo, who seems to identify with the animals he shoots and traps, is the first to bed and the first to rise, and he spends his day in communion with the wilderness.

Tina, in a way, is a loner, too. But she likes to get out and tour the scene, trading news and opinion in equal portion, as on a recent visit to the Hog Farm, where she used to live.

CRUDE, DISORGANIZED

Basic information —commune introduced

The Hog Farm is probably the most widely known commune in New Mexico. It also may be the crudest and most disorganized commune in New Mexico. But the vibrations are good, largely because they are comic; Hog Farmers have a reputation around Taos as the stoned-out clowns of the New Mexico head movement.

Supplementation

For example, few people there are likely to forget the time, a few weeks ago, when two Hog Farmers returned from a run to Texas with enough peyote to keep most of Taos County out of its skull for a week. The Hog Farm became a popular place, with heads from 50 miles away trekking in to help dispose of this incredible surplus.

"Things were really weird at the Hog Farm for a while," one visitor recalled. "People up there were howling at the moon for days."

The Hog Farm of today is not quite the same Hog Farm that gained some national fame for providing a sort of underground police force and field kitchen at the Woodstock celebration. The old leaders, Hugh and Bonnie Romney, have departed in a bus with other veterans.

Known now as "Wavy Gravy," Romney puts on shows and festivals around the country. Last time anyone heard, the Romneys were somewhere between Oklahoma City and Miami, Fla.

CRASHERS A PROBLEM

Even earlier, the Hog Farm turned up at the 1968 Democratic Convention in Chicago, providing Abbie Hoffman with the hog, "Pigasus," the Yippie candidate for president. Pigasus is still at the Hog Farm, happily rooting in a pen.

"The problem at the Hog Farm now," Tina says, "is that so many transients are coming in. They drain the energy of the place. People come and crash and expect someone to take care of them."

Sitting in the cluttered yard of the kitchen house, Tina argued cautiously with one of the four or five girls (as opposed to about 15 men) present on the farm.

"I'm just sorry you feel that way about it, Tina," said Michelle, who was rolling herself a cigaret. "I mean, it seems to me that part of the trip is letting people have a chance to get their heads together."

"Well, I'm sorry, too," said Tina, "but I just don't dig staph infections. And nothing ever seems to get done around here. The A-frame isn't finished. And the vibes in that kitchen! And that john!"

Basic information —another commune introduced

A few days after Tina visited the Hog Farm, Don and Suzanne set out northward to see Morningstar, a commune originally from Sebastopol, Calif., that has been in Taos about two years. It is a long distance, and the car barely manages to climb the mesa where the commune, the largest in the area, has established itself on land purchased by a wealthy New York head.

Supplementation

Possibly because of its isolation, short-term visitors at Morningstar seem welcome, and are greeted by people eager for news or dope. It is something of an occasion, as if an overland stagecoach had just arrived at a frontier outpost. But the atmosphere at Morningstar is odd.

On the whole, the people seem unusually young and articulate—like the bright junior class of a hip high school kidnaped and transplanted in the desert. But some of the guys are running from dope peddling or draft evasion charges, which lends an intense quality to the style of life there. To some, Morningstar is a refuge and a kind of last stand.

About 15 people gather in one of the dugout rooms. Among them are two teen-aged girls, one of them pregnant; and a gray-faced fiftyish man who looks like a bookkeeper turned freak. They talk as Don rolls joints.

"We got 80 people here," someone explains. "Too many."

"Yeah, we get more food stamps than any commune in Taos."

When the smoke gets thick, one of the group leads a tour to the communal kiva, an ingeniously complex underground meeting room, entered from above by a ladder carved from a pine pole.

Inside, a black chick and a white guy are necking listlessly. The guy announces with an air of authority and grim significance that there will be a "meeting" that night. Later it is learned that someone is to be told he is no longer welcome in the commune, and why. It does not promise to be a festive gathering. Don and Suzanne leave before suppertime.

Basic information—third commune introduced

The next day, Don and Brian (who wears his huge buffalo hunter's hat) spend the morning on a trip to the Reality Construction Company, a commune located on the north edge of the mesa occupied by Morningstar.

Supplementation

While the first snowflakes lace the wind, Hawk, a friendly cat who is shivering in the cold, talks about some of the heaviness at Reality. He says some Chicanos from Santa Fe are there. Two of them are strung out on "smack." Not long ago, they ran a magazine reporter off the place at the point of a gun. Days later, armed with high-powered rifles, they opened fire on a Taos County deputy sheriff.

"That's pretty heavy stuff," Hawk says. "The cops are liable to come back here with an army." The teepee is secured and the group heads for the commune for some hot tea.

SEVERAL CHILDREN

Another commune introduced

By afternoon the sun is out and the chill has subsided. At New Buffalo, 10 miles away, most people are inside, busy with winter projects.

Supplementation

There are about 40 people there, along with several children, including one eight- or nine-year-old experienced dope smoker, who gets stoned, then cuts out around the commune on his bicycle.

In one room, a rare luxury, a record player is working, and people are happily stoned, listening to the new Rolling Stones album, sewing, reading, making leatherwear.

Later, when warm weather arrives for good, there will be more activity. New Buffalo members are farmers. They don't eat meat and today they are celebrating the birthday of a yoga saint.

ONE'S "LORD BYRON"

Still another commune introduced

Easily the most visible communal group in the area is the Family of Taos, which runs a general store, an information center, a free clinic and a monthly newspaper, all operated out of a single building at the south end of town.

Supplementation

Members of the group affect names like "Lady Celeste" or "Sir Lawrence" or "Lord Byron," who, in an easy democratic way, is head of the family.

They live together—46 adults and 8 children—in a small, four-room house a few miles away. A dozen people, at least, sleep in each room on handmade bunkbeds. Despite living conditions that would be intolerable to many people, they are a happy and together group, and their house is full of music.

252   Reportorial Writing

"It gets worse every day," Lord Byron says.

In the house, two girls are chopping lettuce for the night's meal. "Veggies," they explain.

"Veggieburgers" don't sound very appetizing to Don and Brian, who are meat eaters. Once, when they were out of everything else, they shot a raven and ate it, and, as Don explains, "You've got to be into meat pretty heavy to eat a raven."

And besides, there is a treat at their own house tonight. A big roast.

Ending   They head for home, where, at least for the present, there are only seven people to crowd around the table.

(Reprinted with permission from the Los Angeles *Times*)

The preceding article flows smoothly, easily. Its structure is simple and effective. A narrative introduction followed by background on the hippie movement to New Mexico, the fear of many more arrivals, the concern over plans to develop an "Earth People's Park," the harshness of the New Mexico country, the "heaviness" that has crept into some of the communes, the hippies who live in out-of-the-way places, the food stamp program, and the various communes—these are the basic points developed through the use of supplementary details.

Supplementation is enriched by the use of incidents and examples. Telling much of the story through an "out of the way" group whose members traveled to various communes helps to achieve unity in the story.

The Survey Article

A survey article's information may be spread out more thinly than that in an in-depth or an in-breadth story, but the structure is frequently the same in all three types: basic information followed by supplementation.

The following Louisville *Courier-Journal* article by Bill Peterson exemplifies the survey type of article.

Enticing introduction   LEXINGTON, Ky.—That old alma mater where the college administration was the parent away from home is undergoing a quiet revolution.

Gist of article   Campus administrators aren't quite ready to pronounce their parental roles—"in loco parentis," they call it—dead yet.

But the signs of change are unmistakable whether you're here at the University of Kentucky, where upperclass women no longer have to return to their dorms at an appointed hour, or at Alice Lloyd College in Pippa Passes, Ky., where an old rule requiring female students to wear look-alike white uniforms was abolished this year.

	The changes are in attitudes, rules and student lifestyles. They vary from campus to campus in the state. But wherever they occur, administrators say the changes reflect the general social upheaval of the 1960s and the demands of a new breed of students.
Supplementation	"The kind of student we get today has a broader view of the world and his rights than he did 10 years ago," says Jack Hall, UK dean of students. "He's grown up in front of the television set. He's more concerned about social issues: Vietnam, race and environment. He's serious about these things."
Basic point	This may offer little comfort to the old grad returning to campus for the first time in 10, 20, or 30 years.
Supplementation	"What disturbs them (returning to old grads) the most is to come into the Grill (a snack bar in UK's Student Center) and see the kids with their grubs on, their long hair and the girls with no bras," says Frank Harris, Student Center director. ("Grubs," in youthful parlance, means dirty bluejeans and other grubby attire.)
Basic point	If the old grads looked further, they would find even more basic changes in the way college administrators across Kentucky view students and campus life.
Specifics, including examples	A sampling of colleges around the state shows that: — Bellarmine-Ursuline College in Louisville sought a license to sell beer on campus—something unthinkable just a few years ago. The school was turned down by the state Alcoholic Beverage Control Board. — There is relaxation of rules governing student residences on most campuses. Rules on who has to live in dormitories and when they must come in at night have been liberalized almost everywhere. — Georgetown College, where there once were restrictions on how many letters students could write home, is sticking by its decision last year to allow dancing on campus and is liberalizing other student conduct rules. — At Centre College in Danville, juniors and seniors have keys that enable them to get into their dorms at any hour; drinking is allowed for students over 21 in the dorms; and two nights a week are set aside to allow men and women students to visit one another in their rooms. — While some colleges have gone further than others, there has been a general liberalizing of student-conduct rules. "What we're trying to do is operate with as few rules as possible," says James A. Keown, dean of students at Western Kentucky University. "We're very open-minded these days about everything from what course a freshman takes to smoking," comments a Berea College spokesman. The changes—ranging from whether colleges should allow cigarette machines on campus to what to do about drug offenses—vary from campus to campus. . . .

MOST IN LAST FIVE YEARS

Basic point — Most of the changes that can be seen have come in the past five years.

Supplementation — "Our rules have changed greatly the last few years, simply because we hadn't changed up to that point," comments Katherin Nichals, dean of women at Centre College.

Students at Centre and most of the other colleges have taken part in the changes by "working in the system," as they put it. At UK, for instance, a group worked almost daily from last March surveying campus opinion, holding meetings and pleading their case to get women's dormitory hours changed.

Basic point — UK approved their well-documented proposals in December. Since the beginning of the current semester, upper-class women have no restrictions on when they have to be in at night. Freshmen now must be in their dorms by midnight, instead of 10:30.

Sara O'Briant, one of the leaders of the women's hours push, says it's too early to assess the change. However, she maintains that many co-eds are coming in earlier than they used to.

Supplementation — "Before, there was the psychological hangup of watching the clock," she says as she sits behind her desk in the UK Student Center. "You knew you had to be in at 3 a.m., so you knew darn well that's how long you'd stay out."

Basic point — Do this and other rule changes create problems?

Supplementation — "I don't think so," continues the brunette West Virginian, who is president of UK's Student Activities Board. "The girls who are going to be promiscuous were and are promiscuous. I don't think that the system of when they have to come into the dormitory has anything to do with it."

UK student government president Tim Futrell, a senior from Cadiz, agrees. . . .

(Reprinted from the Louisville *Courier-Journal*)

The purpose of the article is not to go into great detail about the relaxation of rules at any one college or university, but instead to give an overall impression that changes have been made.

The theme of the article is not that colleges and universities, generally, are relaxing their rules, but that all of Kentucky's higher educational institutions are easing their restrictions on conduct.

The gist of the article is given in the introduction. Basic points, with supplementation, follow. A sampling of changes made in colleges and universities around the state provides examples and some specifics on what has been taking place.

No article can be composed entirely of specifics—some generalizations or basic points are needed for organizational purposes. Specifics take on meaning when they are classified into "categories." The categories in this case are the basic points.

Where did the information for the article come from? The writer discloses his sources of information at the institutions.

Direct contact with all information sources is not necessary in gathering information for the survey article; the telephone may save considerable time and travel expense. Small newspapers are likely to concentrate their efforts on their service areas and let larger newspapers and the wire services take care of the in-breadth stories that cover wide areas.

Appropriate subjects for local survey stories are the views of educators on school discipline, the opinion of law enforcement officials on a rising crime rate, the attitudes of a number of citizens on a proposed park site, and the reactions of civic leaders to an announcement that an historic building will be razed, to name just a few.

Problems of deep public significance and concern provide the meat for many in-depth articles. The articles do not promote causes or pass judgment—they do not praise or condemn. They simply present the facts and let them speak for themselves.

Depending on the circumstances, the facts may or may not be so evident that a foregone conclusion can be expected of the reader. Ample specifics—examples, incidents, and particulars and details—are provided for the reader to give him a clear picture of the situation.

The following Los Angeles *Times* in-depth article by Jerry Cohen is a thorough and fair presentation of the marijuana controversy, and leaves it up to the reader to decide, after reviewing all the facts, whether or not the use of the narcotic should be banned.

Interesting introduction to controversy	Pot's bad; it'll wreck you. Pot's good; it'll turn you on, unchain your mind and transport you "into the gates of paradise."
	Pot's evil. A society which tolerates it is sick.
	Pot's great. So what if society's sick? Pot can cure us all. "It could bring," rhapsodizes a pro-pot writer, "a quick end to a part of the American way (presumably the bad part) once and for all."
	Whoa, now. What's going on here?
	What's going on just may be a major philosophical revolution, generated by what once was an ultimate sin, smoking marijuana.
	At the very least, the happening is a wholesale change of attitude toward a subject which, less than a decade ago, was spoken about in hushed, embarrassed language—if at all.
Controversy	Now suddenly—almost overnight—two sharply divergent views regarding marijuana are on collision course, and almost everybody has something to say about the matter.

Supplementation	"Marijuana," observes Los Angeles Police Chief Tom Reddin, "is rampant."
	And so are public utterances about it. The good of it—if there is good in it. The bad of it—if it is truly bad. And even the harmlessness of it—if indeed it is harmless.
Background	Atty. Gen. Thomas C. Lynch released figures showing an absolutely fantastic upswing in marijuana use among juveniles. . . .

REGARDED AS VALID

For want of a more absolute indicator (who knows how many kid smokers are caught?), Lynch's figures can be accepted as a valid measure of marijuana's current popularity with youth, the generation most tuned in on the drug.

Lynch called the statistics "appalling," a sentiment shared by most in law enforcement. But not quite—and that's part of the dizzying phenomenon.

General view on controversy	About the same time the California public was digesting the Lynch figures, a Los Angeles deputy district attorney specializing in narcotics told a State Senate committee he thought marijuana may damage society less than liquor and that laws against it are unrealistic.
Supplementation	"There's a fantastic relationship between alcohol and crime. The same cannot be said of marijuana," said Joe Reichmann, adding: "It seems unfair to have harsh penalties for drugs that are no more harmful than alcohol."

CALLS FOR REPEAL

Another voice in controversy	At the same committee hearing, a former Santa Barbara prosecutor, Thomas J. Sammon, went even further: Repeal laws against possession and use, he urged.
Supplementation	More people than ever are smoking pot despite "outrageously severe penalties" and "extremely vigorous methods used by police to enforce the law," Sammon claimed.
Another view expressed	A Reichmann counterpart in Santa Barbara, Boyd E. Hornor, simply up and quit as a deputy District Attorney, saying he thought too much police and prosecutive effort aimed at enforcing marijuana laws could better be expended on more serious crime.
View from judiciary	The judiciary also raised its exalted voice, and, for one of its members, the result was a bad trip.
	Los Angeles Superior Court's presiding juvenile judge, Joseph A. Sprankle Jr., said he believed marijuana should be legalized for adults and its use left to the individual's "good judgment." Minors, he added, should be limited by the same restrictions placed upon alcohol.

NOT SERIOUS PROBLEM

Supplementation	Evidence presented him "over the years," said Judge Sprankle, left him with the sense that "use of marijuana is

no more serious, no more of a public danger or a danger to the user, than alcohol."

Consequences   A week and a half later, Judge Sprankle no longer presided over juvenile court; he was not even a juvenile judge. Chief Superior Judge Donald R. Wright said Sprankle's remarks had "destroyed his value" as a juvenile judge and shifted him to civil court.

Another view   Another Superior Court judge's comment shortly after invited no repercussion, even went virtually unnoticed. Yet it probably more closely reflects the sentiment of jurists confronted daily with increasing numbers of downy-cheeked defendants who, at worst, are tempted to experiment with pot solely from curiosity.

Judge Mark Brandler's comment came as he presided at the trial of Gridley Wright, a high priest of hip. . . .

Judge Brandler . . . said he was "disturbed" by "harsh" and "savage" prison sentences dealt smokers "merely for privately using or having possession of the drug. . . ."

Supplementation   He noted that possession of just one cigaret constitutes a felony, a blemish which faults the possessor for life. Judge Brandler suggested the Legislature "re-examine the issue of punishment . . . to afford the trial court judge some discretion. . . ."

Then Judge Brandler found Wright, a onetime stockbroker attacking the constitutionality of state and federal marijuana laws, guilty of possession.

Major point   That the utter boldness of Wright's legal assault and his open admission to being a user stirred no public outcry testifies to the temper of our sophisticated times. . . .

Supplementation   Into its orbit have vaulted professors and social theoreticians, medical men, ministers and criminologists. . . .

Major point   A sense of the rocketing challenge toward the traditional concept of pot as a global menace could be felt in the very courtroom in which Wright was tried.

Supplementation   Some of the large number of his hippie followers monitoring the trial exhibited signs of the euphoria commonly associated with marijuana intoxication.

Transitional paragraph   Then, these other developments occurred in California, either a few days preceding or following the Wright trial:

List of events   — In little Nicasio, north of San Francisco in Marin County, the elementary school principal kicked up a pot ruckus heard 'round the nation.

Mrs. Garnet E. Brennan, 58, in an affidavit taken by an attorney sparking a Northern California bid to overturn marijuana laws, boasted she had smoked pot "almost daily since 1949." The school board suspended her.

— In Monterey, delegates to the State Bar Assn. convention adopted resolutions urging that judges be given discretion to treat marijuana offenders as misdemeanors.

— In Sacramento, California's capital, State College students, in a campus-wide vote, favored legalization. . . .

MANY OTHER EVENTS WERE LISTED

Major point —prestigious view expressed	Then came an unexpected eruption on the national scene, a surprising declaration emanating from no less a person than the boss of the U.S. Food and Drug Administration.
	Because of his position in so sensitive a post, Dr. James L. Goddard's voice probably was the most forceful, certainly the most prestigious, supporting relaxation in severity of punishment.
Supplementation	Dr. Goddard said, while he did not favor legalization, he "didn't happen to think" marijuana is more dangerous than alcohol and he favored removing all penalties for its use, keeping only those for distribution.
Major point	During the same month's time, the marijuana debate breached the national borders, as the reading public learned that pot was big with our fighting men in Vietnam. But how big?
Supplementation	John Steinbeck, IV, 21, son of the novelist, just returned from the war front, claimed in a magazine series that three fourths or more of the GIs in Vietnam use the drug. This large a figure met with a skepticism that was not mitigated when young Steinbeck was "busted" a short time later himself. . . .
Generalization	Among those who hew to the hard line, the concept of marijuana as a doomsday drug is more fiercely held than ever.

HARD LINE BY ENFORCEMENT MEN

Specifics	This is especially true of the career narcotics officer, from the federal level down. And even more particularly, the medical and professorial people who support police with figures and observations directly contrary to those cited by colleagues in the medical and academic crafts who take a soft view of marijuana's use.
	It's tough to find policemen who openly will admit that the evil they preach about marijuana is overstated—though some hippies will tell you they've run into "plenty of bright young cops" sympathetic toward them.
Generalization	They probably have a point.
Specifics	A 30-year-old narcotics officer in Pasadena, where marijuana arrests increased 214% in the last three years, said he favored legalization "because it would eliminate the criminal aspect and reduce the ability of users to go to harder drugs."
	He said he had interviewed 650 persons arrested in the last 3½ years and had yet to find an instance of violence associated with an arrest. . . .

Reporting the News in Depth and in Breadth

Generalization	But his is the minority view, by far, among law enforcement.
Specifics	Far more typical is the stance taken recently by the California Narcotic Law Enforcement Officers Assn. at its recent Lake Tahoe convention, a meeting addressed by U.S. Narcotics Commissioner Henry L. Giordano, an ex-Californian and an implacable foe of marijuana law easement.
	Convention delegates took note of the almost overnight upsurge of marijuana use. . . .
	The convention adopted a resolution. . . .
Background	Federal laws, the pattern for state statutes, followed a spate of fright stories about pot leading to crime, rape and general misbehavior, including outright looniness, Harry J. Anslinger, Giordano's predecessor, generally gets credit for being a prime mover behind the tough marijuana laws.
Generalization with example	Oversimplifications are easy—such as this offered by a teen-age hippie: "I just like to get high." Certainly, however, it's not an invalid explanation when considered as part of the multicolored whole.
Generalization	So many reasons suggested embody a truth.
Reasons	"It's part of the whole scene—the increasing permissiveness of society, the relaxing of our morals, the weakening of the church and family," said a suburban policeman.
	"We're too affluent, we're living too fast. Parents don't spend enough time with their kids; they don't know what their kids are doing. They're too busy keeping up with the Joneses. Dad works, so does mom. Too many divorces. . . ."
Basic information —opposing views stated	"A new philosophy rears its head," a grim Commissioner Giordano told delegates to the Lake Tahoe narcotics conference, "one which suggests that when an individual or group feels a law is unjust they have no obligation as citizens to obey it."
	Or, if you look at it from the other side: the "new philosophy" is a breath of fresh air, sweeping away on happy clouds of pungent smoke hypocrisies that have been an All-American hangup.
Specifics	Nor, in seeking an explanation, should one overlook the contention of Joseph Oteri, persuasive attorney in a celebrated pre-trial challenge to Massachusetts marijuana laws —a claim widely subscribed to—that:
	"The hazards of marijuana are a myth."

INDICATES DISILLUSIONMENT

Echoed Bob Schmidt, a student leader at Sacramento State:

"It is indicative of the entire disillusionment, the entire frustration of our generation against what we feel have been the lies told us . . . on marijuana as well as other issues.

	"We have been told it is an addictive narcotic, told it leads to the use of heroin, told it is physically destructive. We found these were lies."
Related subject introduced	As for sex and immorality? Again, it depends on whose logic you follow.
Supplementation	Antimarijuana spokesmen say this frees uncontrollable urges which produce rape and orgy.
	But users claim it only sweeps away hangups, freeing both procreative and creative urges and gifting the smoker with greater self-awareness. It doesn't lead to rape or orgy, just as it doesn't lead to violent crime, they say, because it soothes the user's baser instincts. . . .
Major point	Police blame what they consider pro-pot statements by members of the academic and medical communities for what's happened. To a lesser degree, officers are critical of news media for disseminating them.
Supplementation	Los Angeles Superior Judge Arthur L. Alarcon, who would appear to be a moderate of the Brandler persuasion on the subject . . . pointed a finger at no single segment, but he observed at the Lake Tahoe meeting:
	"In almost any daily newspaper or magazine you can find an article in which a college professor, a medical doctor, a school principal and even elected public officials claim that marijuana should be legalized because it is harmless, or no more dangerous than tobacco or martinis."

POLICE OPPOSE PUBLICITY

Major point	Some policemen just plain think the news media should leave unpublicized such remarks, no matter the stature of the maker or the basis for them.
Elaboration	Chief Reddin, while not among them, thinks "all the constant talk about pot being good" has popularized it among youth. But he concedes:
	"One place law enforcement has been remiss is that, for a long time, we argued against education in schools where drugs were concerned—we thought it would do more to stimulate than control their use among the young. In the light of what's developed, this was not a proper position."
	(*Following paragraphs, here deleted, dealt with the controversy over whether marijuana has spread in usage from the bohemian scene to wide numbers of middle-class Americans*)
Major point	Though the drug has been known and used for hundreds of years by man, "expert opinion" is based on personal observation and anecdotal evidence, not scientific experimentation.
Elaboration	What scientific evidence exists comes from nations such as India, where hashish is used. And hashish, while derived from the same hemp plant as marijuana, is to pot, observed one writer, "what an extra dry martini is to a short beer."

So these foreign studies are of little worth to the American issue.

Supplementation
"Unfortunately," as Judge Alarcon noted, "there has been almost no medical research in the United States as to the harmful effects of the use of marijuana. Certainly the self-serving claims of individual marijuana users that its use has no harmful effects are of little scientific value."

But the same argument works the other way, too.

(Many paragraphs followed giving conflicting views on whether or not marijuana is harmful)

Chief Reddin says he's perfectly willing to "let the scientists and lawmakers take over, and when they find the total answer, we will do as they say."

Appropriate ending
Until then, he said, policemen must enforce the law as it's written now. And he added:

"Based on the findings of men I've spent most of my adult career working with, men who have worked with the marijuana problem, I have to conclude the drug should be outlawed. In the absence of scientific proof otherwise, I couldn't change my mind."

(Reprinted with permission from the Los Angeles *Times*)

Months of research and investigation provided the information for the story. Its extensive background rounds up into one package what has appeared in numerous news stories and feature articles. All the information was selected on the basis of its pertinence to the general subject, the controversy over marijuana.

The Los Angeles *Times* devotes many columns to reporting the news in depth, far more than a small newspaper could afford to do. Much depends upon a newspaper's size and philosophy. The Fresno (Calif.) *Bee* covered the subject of marijuana in a series of seven articles that required nearly a month of research and investigation. One article in the series was devoted to the controversy over marijuana.

The writer of an in-depth article starts with a timely topic and then collects all the available information to develop the subject. The writer of an in-breadth article, likewise, starts with a timely topic. But he relies less on research, developing his article mainly from information obtained from his survey. Some background in the subject is usually helpful.

The writer of a survey story often draws comparisons and contrasts —similarities and dissimilarities are likely to occur in the expressed views of sources of information and in situations.

The following New York *Times* article by Enid Nemy illustrates how the survey method can be used in writing an in-breadth article dealing with a social problem.

Lead starts with
Mrs. Verta Mae Grosvenor is a woman of commanding presence, imposing height and black skin. She is an author,

introduction of one of persons surveyed	a musician and a mother whose daughter recently had a book of poems ("Poems by Kali") published.
	One afternoon Mrs. Grosvenor was waiting for an elevator in the Stuyvesant Town housing complex. A white woman, also waiting, turned around "in a friendly fashion" and said, "You're going in rather late today, aren't you?"
Incident	"I said, 'I'm not a maid . . . my daughter is visiting a classmate here,'" Mrs. Grosvenor said. "And the woman replied, 'Isn't that sweet! We do get a lot of good ones here.'"
Quick summary	Mrs. Grosvenor requires no feat of memory to recall the daily indignities, the patronizing attitudes, the assumptions and the pinpricks borne by most of her race like scars that never heal.
Supplementation—view expressed	"You go along thinking you're an American citizen like everyone else," Mrs. Grosvenor said, "and then—boom—something happens or something is said because you have a black skin."
Basic information —summary of views	Most black men and women, concerned and absorbed in major issues of education, housing and employment, try to shrug off the smaller humiliations. Most of them find that shrugging off the humiliations suffered by their children is a more difficult matter.
Supplementation— incident told	Mrs. Grosvenor remembers her daughter Chandra's first experience hearing the word Negro applied to herself. Chandra was barely 6 during the summer of the Newark riots and some white children in the neighborhood (East Village) held aloft a knife and shouted 'the Negroes are coming.'
	"I ran into the house and got a butter knife," Chandra said. "My mommy asked me why, and I said, 'The Negroes are coming.' She said, 'Do you want to see a Negro?' and held me in front of the mirror."
Retrospect	Chandra, her sister Kali, and her mother laugh over it now, but they haven't forgotten, nor will they. Nor will Kali, 10, easily forget being called "dirty."
	"I really felt bad," Kali said. "I said I wasn't dirty and that I had taken a bath in the morning."
Other news sources introduced	Mr. and Mrs. Ellsworth Wright of New Rochelle have encountered degrees of prejudice all their lives. Their experience doesn't make it easier when their 10-year-old son, Mark, returns home and tells them he has been called "nigger." They can only take some cold pride in his reaction to the incident.
Supplementation— incident	"I rang the doorbell of the boy's house and told his mother what he had said," Mark said. "She told me to go away and not bother her. That wasn't very nice."
Another source introduced	For adults such as Sharon Riley, director of special projects for Richard Clarke Associates, a personnel concern that concentrates on recruitment of minority groups, reac-

Reporting the News in Depth and in Breadth   263

	tion to humiliations "depends on your personal mental framework at the time."
Supplementation—views	"In the South, you know where you stand. Here you are accepted on the surface. The white liberals are overfriendly and try desperately hard to come to your home and have you to theirs, to eat and drink together.
	"The overfamiliarity, the overfriendliness, the overpoliteness—it gets to a point where it's sickening."
Another source introduced	"It's the constant disrespect, the little subtle things," said Phillip A. Walls, a 25-year-old involved by day in the school educational program of the Addiction Service Agencies and, at night, in mental health counseling at New York Medical College's department of psychiatry.
Supplementation—views	HYPOCRISY WORSE THAN HOSTILITY "I'd rather (encounter) out and out hostility, people to be for-real, to be their true selves, rather than 'Some of my best friends are . . .' " he commented.
Consensus	Singled out by many as evidences of the "little subtleties" that Mr. Walls had referred to were such remarks as "You are a credit to your race," being asked for suggestions on a job and then having the ideas brushed away without thought ("Pacifying us like children") and, no matter what the economic or social status, being asked whether they knew anyone who might be interested in doing housework.
Another source introduced	"It's an indignity to be dealt with just as an entity, rather than as a person," said Major David J. Travis, an Army career officer who has completed two tours of duty in Vietnam.
Elaboration —views	Major Travis and his family live in East Orange, N.J., where most of their friends are black. White friends are limited, he said, "because I'm tired of getting into a social situation and having the conversation eventually turn to race."
	He hopes that by the time his 8-year-old daughter and 5-year-old son grow to adulthood, the situation will have changed and that they will be treated and considered as individuals.
	"Now, in many instances, you are expected to be a spokesman for your race and you are center stage when you don't want to be."
Other sources introduced	Mr. and Mrs. Frank Hercules, who have developed a "psychological immunity to the kind of pinpricking people attempt," have noted a form of leveling that they call "malicious."
Supplementation—views	Mrs. Hercules, principal of Public School 133 at 130th Street in Manhattan, recalled a number of occasions where she said something, in social conversation, and was answered with, "My maid told me. . . ."
	"There's a putting you in your place," said Mr. Hercules,

whose books, among them "I Want a Black Doll" and "When the Hummingbird Flies," have been published here and abroad.

WORDS THAT ANGER HER

As one of the "more minor irritations," Mrs. Hercules mentioned the number of times "halfway attractive black women" are immediately compared to Lena Horne. She said she felt slightly more strongly about certain words: "Think of blackmail and blackball," she said. "They are racist. They are pinpricks."

Another source introduced

Words like "blackie" and "black popcorn" are of the more immediate concern to W. Harmon Brown, an insurance broker and bail bondsman. They were addressed to Leslie, his 11-year-old daughter, by a classmate at St. Hilda's and St. Hugh's school.

Incident

"I got really huffed up at first," Leslie said. "I was going to call things back to him, but decided it was a waste of time and not worth it."

Mr. Brown considers the matter, on principle, more seriously.

"I brought it up with the school authorities and was told, 'Oh, well little boys.' There was no attempt to reprimand the child." He is transferring Leslie to the Calhoun School for the fall term.

Cutback

Major Travis occasionally finds a slight advantage in white bigotry.

More views

"You'd be amazed at how many times I have a subway or bus seat all to myself," he said. "I'm the last person a white will sit next to. All black people notice that whites won't sit next to them unless the other seats are filled."

Another cutback

Miss Riley has noticed being followed by store detectives.

"We're made aware of it," she said. "And our credit is usually checked even when we cash a small check at a bank in which we have an account."

Another source introduced

Mrs. Edward White, a daily houseworker, voiced a common plaint about service entrances.

Supplementation— views

"I don't mind using the service entrance or the service elevator in a building if the white houseworkers also have to use it," she said. "But I don't like to use it just because I'm black."

(©1970 by The New York Times Company. Reprinted by permission)

The basic organization of survey stories similar to the preceding one usually consists of an interesting lead, then sources of information and the views of those sources. Cutbacks were used in the article to avoid undue delay in introducing other sources of information.

One of the biggest temptations to the youthful journalist in writing a survey article is to attempt to deceive the reader into believing that the coverage is much broader than it is. A reporter for a campus newspaper, for example, may talk with five or six students and then, in writing his story, try to make the reader think that the reporter talked with many more students than he did. Or after talking with perhaps a dozen students he may permit himself to lead the reader to believe that the story reflects student opinion on the campus. On any level—local, regional, national or international—such practice is dishonest.

Investigative Reporting

One of a newspaper's most important functions is to serve as a watchdog for the public—to safeguard the people's interest. Corruption, graft and even legal official actions that are not performed with the best public interests in mind would be much more prevalent were it not for the constant scrutiny of newsmen and the would-be culprits' fear of publicity.

The following New York *Times* story by Martin Tolchin is an in-depth account of increased public spending for private consultants in New York City.

Introductory paragraphs give gist of problem	The city has vastly expanded its use of private consulting contracts, which are awarded without competitive bidding and are usually unknown to the public.
	City budget officials estimate that former Mayor Robert F. Wagner authorized less than $8-million in consultation fees in 1965, his final year in office—mostly for architects and engineers, with only $40,000 for management consultants.
	By contrast, City Controller Abraham D. Beame has estimated that the city spent $68-million last year on consulting contracts, not including per diem consultants, which would bring the figure above $75-million.
Two sides presented	Lindsay administration officials say that the use of consultants has expanded because of a "middle-management crisis" in the civil service, which is losing the talent it attracted during the Depression years and is unable to attract high-caliber personnel today because of low wages. Lindsay officials also say that they are much more concerned with "rational planning" than were their predecessors.
	Critics of the expanded use of consultants, including Mr. Beame, say that many competent civil servants were driven out of the city's employ because their functions were delegated to consultants, who are characteristically young men from Ivy League schools with limited experience.
Elaboration	Mayor Lindsay, informed that the Times had spent three weeks preparing an article on the city's use of consultants,

was expected to announce reforms concerning the use of consultants.

Questions raised

Who are the city's consultants? How are they selected? What is their impact on the city? How does the city justify this expenditure when it says it lacks sufficient funds to pick up the garbage in Brownsville? Are management consultants less effective than clubhouse bureaucrats because they propose management solutions to problems that are basically political?

Questions answered

The wide range of city consultants includes the following. . . .

BREAKDOWN IS GIVEN

Summarization

Mr. Beame's breakdown of consultants showed $31.5-million for architectural and engineering services, and $38-million for other consultant services not approved by the Board of Estimate, including $23-million in consulting fees for manpower training and $9-million for management consultant fees.

Elaboration

Mitchell I. Ginsberg, the Human Resources Administrator, said yesterday that the city's job training programs had led to job placements for 10,089 people during a 10-month period.

George Sternlieb, author of a highly regarded $250,000 study on rent control, said that "A very great part of consulting work consists in detailing the obvious—it's a back-stiffener for painful political decisions." He was selected by the city to do the study which was paid for in Federal funds.

"Consultants are entirely client oriented," says an employee of McKinsey Associates, a concern that received $1.5-million in consulting fees last year.

City Council President Sanford D. Garelik says that authorizing a study is sometimes a way to create "the illusion of activity" and that a $100,000 study of the Police Department "didn't tell us anything we didn't know."

Transitional paragraph

Among the situations that have developed because of the city's use of consultants are the following:

Specifics

—Carter Bales, the 32-year-old director of urban programs for McKinsey, was also assistant budget director of New York City last year when the Budget Bureau awarded McKinsey $1.5-million in consulting contracts. Mr. Bales was unpaid by the city, and said that he received the position to expedite his consulting work.

—Frederick O. R. Hayes, the budget director, said that he was negotiating for a job with consulting concerns that had done business with the city, because "they're a natural place to go after you're worn out by government."

Basic information

Officials of the City University have unsuccessfully sought consulting contracts that they say would help both the university and the city.

(Seven paragraphs of supplementation, both pro and con, followed)

Basic information

Deputy Budget Director Grossman, citing the value of some studies, estimates a $200-million-a-year saving in the acceleration of capital projects that resulted from a management survey.

Supplementation

He credits a Rand study with doubling the capacity of the city's fire engines. "That alone has paid for the city's investment in Rand," he said.

Basic information —contrary view

On the other hand, Milton Musicus, the new Municipal Services Administrator, found "relatively worthless" several studies on Consolidated Edison, and added: "The old studies, frankly, don't mean very much."

Supplementation

A $150,000 transportation study of the Bronx . . . is 75 pages long and has detailed descriptions of the history of the Bronx, the topography of the Bronx, and the traffic patterns of the Bronx, the thrust of which is . . . traffic tends to move toward Manhattan in the mornings and away from Manhattan in the evenings.

Basic information

Many of the consultants concede that they were awarded their contracts because they knew the right people.
(Supplementation followed)
(©1970 by The New York Times Company. Reprinted by permission)

The preceding article differs from an in-depth story only in purpose. In presentation and organization, the two are similar. The purpose of an investigative article is to explore situations, frequently concerning government, which may be adverse to public interests.

The investigative story should be based on facts. All sources of information should be tapped and a fair presentation of evidence made. The story does not evaluate; it simply tells what the situation is and lets the reader form his own judgments.

Investigative reporting requires more patience than most other types of news gathering. Anyone whose actions, if exposed, would be subject to criticism, condemnation or incrimination is going to try to put every possible obstacle in the way of the reporter seeking information.

Getting the necessary documentary evidence for an investigative story may take weeks or months, depending upon the circumstances. Records sometimes disappear, associates can be sworn to secrecy, many persons are averse to what they call "squealing," and hearsay testimony is not valid evidence. The reporter must find ways of overcoming such obstacles.

Frequently, the idea for an investigative article comes through a tip. Whoever gives it usually insists on anonymity, but he may be able to suggest ways of getting information and he may know the names of others who could help the reporter find the truth.

EXERCISES

I. Questions for Discussion

1. What are the advantages of using a series instead of a single article to report news in depth?
2. What has been the evolution of the in-depth story?
3. What is the basic difference between the in-depth and the in-breadth article?
4. How does the in-depth article differ from the conventional feature?
5. What is the difference between the in-depth story and the investigative article? Which would it be easier to get information for?

II. Comment on the following introductions to in-depth articles

BY JURATE KAZICKAS

You can bet Dad's old raccoon coat that when he and Mom were in college:

—They didn't live next door to each other in a coed dorm.

—The school doctor didn't give her a box of pills every month.

—The girls didn't pass the hat in the cafeteria to help pay for a classmate's legal abortion.

—No one tacked a sign in the dorm proclaiming "Make Love, Not War" or "Make Love, Not Babies."

They do now, all over. So there's a sexual revolution on campus and elsewhere among the young, right?

Yes.

And no.

No because the real revolution may be only beginning.

(Associated Press)

BY ANGELA TAYLOR

BERLIN, Md.—His name is Charlie Brown. He has mischievous little eyes, chatters a blue streak and is an expert pickpocket. He wears a honey-brown coat of the world's rarest mink and, because he is so appealing and mild-mannered for his breed, he has been allowed to keep it. Charlie is a 3-year-old Kojah mink.

Unlike his 10,000 Kojah cousins and 20,000 other minks of various mutations at Regal Farms here, Charlie is not likely to become a mink coat because he is the special pet of Yayne Naarup, who runs the 80-acre farm. Mr. Naarup is a partner in the operation along with. . . .

(©1970 by The New York Times Company. Reprinted by permission)

BY LUCIA MOUAT

ST. LOUIS—Needs of a supermarket bargain hunter: one free afternoon, an advanced degree in mathematics, and an iron determination not to be impressed by the size of the package.

This puts the case rather strongly—but so do a number of housewives. It has been estimated that collectively the dollars they "waste" in guessing wrong on economy choices run into the billions every year.

(*Christian Science Monitor*)

BY JAMES R. POLK

WASHINGTON (AP)—The nation is afflicted with a growing medical crisis that has no known cure: The cost.

From childbirth to deathbed, in sickness and in health, Americans are paying more, much more than ever before for medical care.

BY BILL BOYARSKY

From the sidewalk, the building at 14401 Ventura Blvd. looks like another of Los Angeles' well-appointed auto agencies. Bright colored cars fill the salesroom. Salesmen smoke cigarets and stalk customers.

But the glass-front building holds more than this year's Cadillacs. It is also an important center of city politics. It contains the office of Martin Pollard, the agency owner and one of the wealthy men who quietly supply the dollars for increasingly expensive Los Angeles political campaigns.

In the blunt language of politics, they are called "fat cats."

(Los Angeles *Times*)

III. Where would you get information for in-depth stories on the following topics? The stories would be community based.

1. Housing costs
2. Medical costs
3. Ecology
4. Business failures
5. Urban problems

IV. Critical Questions

1. Are the words "well-documented" used subjectively in the sixth from the last paragraph of the article on the relaxation of rules at Kentucky's colleges and universities?
2. Are the words "requires no feat of memory to" superfluous in the fourth paragraph of the article about the indignities suffered by black persons?

Chapter 14

THE SITUATION STORY

*Enlighten the people generally, and tyranny
and oppressions of body and mind will
vanish like evil spirits at the dawn of day.*
— *Thomas Jefferson*

After riots broke out in the Watts District of Los Angeles in 1965 and in Newark, Detroit and other cities in 1967, some persons raised the question: "Why weren't we warned about the situation?"

For years the press has covered increases in juvenile delinquency, crime and divorce in spot news stories. Newspapers have published stories about hotel fires, prison riots, student protests and the oppression of members of minority groups.

The problem is that spot news stories at times evoke a moan, a groan or even a mild yell, but the reader soon relaxes and returns to living as usual.

A new type of journalistic effort has come forth as a consequence. It is what some journalists refer to as the situation story.

The form is usually that of the feature or the in-depth article. The purpose, however, is to warn readers about trouble spots in society, and its success depends upon the extent to which the story overcomes public apathy.

Strictly factual, the situation story is a positive type of journalism in that it may stimulate the prevention or correction of undesirable situations.

Warning Flags

Seattle newspapers and the major wire services gave heavy play to a Seattle hotel fire that caused 20 deaths. No doubt many readers in Sacramento, Calif., were momentarily shocked by the news. Unquestionably, they would have been more shocked had the disaster happened in their own community.

The occasion, however, prompted Bob Taylor of the Sacramento *Union* to write a situation story warning Sacramentans of the potential dangers in their city. The editors prefaced the story with the following:

> *"At least 20 persons were killed Friday in an arson caused hotel fire that drove residents screaming from their rooms. . . . Many crashed through glass, leaping from flame-filled windows."* Associated Press story of Mar. 21, 1970, Seattle disaster.

The story, which follows, issued a clear warning to readers in Sacramento that a similar disaster could easily happen in their community.

Warning issued	Sacramento has been lucky. A score of older hotels in the downtown section of the city are similar in character to the one that was destroyed in Seattle. In the past three years, five hotel fires in the downtown area have resulted in minor damage, no injuries and no fatalities. But Sacramento hotel residents may be living on borrowed time.
Authority cited	Deputy Fire Marshal Donald St. John said, "We've got many firetraps and some are in atrocious condition."
Newspaper initiated survey	And Fire Marshal Louis Cassaglia, after conducting a survey of 26 downtown hotels at the request of The Sacramento *Union,* found at least four multi-story dwellings substandard, deteriorating and providing "no positive protection at all," but housing more than 350 persons.
Details	Cassaglia reported many fire safety violations in the hotels—no sprinklers in hallways, open stairwells and transoms which would send smoke to upper floors, hot plates in rooms. All are potentially deadly, especially to older or handicapped persons living on upper floors. "On several occasions we have had to issue violation notices to some (hotel owners) who have not maintained proper housekeeping," Cassaglia said. He also said inspections in these older buildings were being increased from two times a year to four. But when asked who has responsibility for the enforce-

Basic information, followed by supplementation	ment of safety code violations, Cassaglia said that was the obligation of the building inspection department. Section 203 of the 1967 Uniform Building Code, passed last year by the City Planning Commission and the City Council, clearly spells out the powers of enforcement. . . . (*Three omitted paragraphs listed specifications of the code*)
Basic information	Officials in both the fire department and the building inspection department explained that the hotels met fire safety standards when they were constructed more than 50 years ago.
Supplementation	As Cassaglia puts it, "All we can do is attempt to stay on top of these things, because the laws are not retroactive." Otto Steinbrenner, the city's chief building inspector, says, "It's been our policy to maintain minimum requirements when we are called in (to hotels) or are given a reason to go in. "We can go in if some official sticks his neck out and says there's a hazard, but it almost takes a small fire to show some of these owners that a potentially bad fire could occur."
Basic information	The problem runs deeper than the matter of enforcement. Many of the hotels house retired persons, transients, and others who simply cannot afford to live anywhere else.
Elaboration	Adding to the difficulty is the fact that, in many cases, the hotels are owned by absentee landlords who ignore making improvements with an apparent "out-of-sight, out-of-mind" attitude.
Basic information, followed by supplementation	The problem of replacement housing is called "a very severe, perpetual one" by Walter J. Slipe, assistant city manager for community development. . . . (*Four paragraphs of supplementation followed*)
Basic information, followed by elaboration	In an attempt to reduce the high risk of a really bad hotel fire in this city, Cassaglia has suggested several steps for owners and managers of hotels and apartment houses. . . . (*Steps suggested by Cassaglia followed*) (Reprinted from the Sacramento *Union*)

It is not difficult to recognize where the writer of the preceding story got his information. The sources are listed in the article: the fire marshal and the deputy fire marshal, officials in the building inspection department and the assistant city manager for community development. The article also mentions that the newspaper initiated the survey of 26 downtown hotels.

The organization of the story is similar to that of a conventional feature article. The introduction issues a warning, authorities are cited, and basic information is interspersed with supplementation.

No exhortation appears in the story, although newspaper editors frequently follow up such a story with an editorial suggesting corrections for the problem. And some writers emphasize the lack of public protection in a concluding paragraph or cite the corrective suggestions of information sources in the article.

Human Plight

The hardships and misery that many human beings face have provided the contents for a variety of situation stories. Poverty, unemployment, substandard housing, ghettos, slums, racial oppression —all these might easily go unnoticed by those not enduring them if reminders were not provided by the press.

This type of journalism performs a significant and much-needed innovation in the field of mass communications.

The following article by UPI Senior Editor Louis Cassels is a good example of the kind of situation articles being provided by the wire services.

Words of warning	"Black Americans today are more bitter and frustrated than ever before. The situation is very dangerous. The right spark could set off racial violence in any city in the country."
	Those words were spoken by Thomas Bradley, a Negro city councilman in Los Angeles. They summarize expressions of anxiety and despair that are widespread in the black communities of the United States.
Background for story, followed by basic information	During the past six weeks, I have traveled more than 10,000 miles to talk with—and more important, listen to —black people of all ages and income levels, in all parts of the nation. From Harlem in the East to Watts in the West, from Detroit in the North to Augusta in the South, I found them angry, resentful, cynical about white intentions, bitterly critical of the Nixon administration, determined to gain equality by whatever means necessary.
	The vast majority of blacks whom I interviewed oppose any repetition of the rioting that brought many U.S. cities to the brink of chaos during the 1960s. They don't see any future in burning down their neighborhoods.
Supplementation	"But riots don't break out because black people consider them a good tactic for bringing about social change," Bradley said. "A riot is a spontaneous explosion of rage. And black rage is at an even higher pitch now than it was in 1965"—the year in which the Watts section of Los Angeles erupted in a week-long riot that cost 34 lives and more than $50 million in property damage.
	"There's a greater sense of bitterness now," said Lewis Robinson, who helps manage a development program in

the Hough area of Cleveland. "People had hopes after the riots, because all those promises were made. . . ."

Cleveland's popular and respected Negro mayor, Carl Stokes, said black people are well aware that if they resort to violence, "it will be met by overwhelming counter-violence."

"But they've tried peaceful demonstrations to appeal to the white man's conscience—and that didn't work. . . ."

Basic information, followed by supplementation

It is a measure of the racial gulf that exists in America today that many whites will be surprised, and some irritated, by the news that black people still feel put upon. Many white people cherish the myth that blacks have made tremendous progress in recent years. . . .

(*Two paragraphs of supplementation followed*)

Basic information, followed by supplementation

The list of black grievances could be lengthened indefinitely but the bitterest gall in the Negro's cup is the conviction that he is now fighting his battle alone. The federal government, which he so long counted as his ally, now seems to him an enemy. And the white liberals who once espoused his cause have turned their attention to Vietnam, campus strife and air pollution. . . .

(*Eight paragraphs of supplementation followed*)

Basic information

The revolutionary organization that gets the most publicity and stirs the strongest fear reaction among whites is the Black Panther party. A recent Harris poll showed that two out of three white people regard the Black Panthers as "a serious menace to the country."

Supplementation

The Panthers I interviewed were delighted to be taken so seriously. But it is my impression that the actual strength of the party is considerably less than the commonly quoted official estimate of 2,000 members nationwide. Aside from having a knack for inflammatory rhetoric that gives whites the shudders, the Panthers are important mainly as a symbol of armed black resistance to white police power. There is widespread sympathy for them within the black community, but it seems to stem primarily from a belief that they have been subjected to murderous persecution. "Frankly, the police raids are keeping the Panthers in business," said a Los Angeles sympathizer.

Basic information, followed by supplementation

The more serious black revolutionaries operate with greater secrecy and sophistication than the Black Panthers. They also have stockpiles of arms, but they have no intention of using them "prematurely" in sporadic shootouts with police. They are understandably wary of discussing their plans with white reporters, but if assured of anonymity some will speak vaguely of a new type of urban guerrilla warfare, employing bombs and arson to disrupt vital public facilities such as electric power plants.

"The more industrialized a society, the more vulnerable it is to sabotage," said a young black in Cleveland.

Black moderates—meaning those, however militant, who

Basic information, followed by supplementation	are still committed to working within the system—say the advocates of armed revolution are still a relatively small minority, probably under 10 per cent of the total Negro population of 23 million. But they are concerned about the growing acceptance, especially among the young, of the idea that the Negro's choice lies between violence and a retreat into docile acceptance of second class citizenship, which burgeoning black pride will no longer tolerate.
	(*Five paragraphs of supplementation followed*)
Basic information	It will take more than words to convince black people that their problems are getting the right priority from the national administration. But even words from the White House could have a healing effect.
Supplementation	"It would help a great deal if the President would show some understanding of and concern about the black community," said Longworth Quin, editor of Detroit's black weekly, the Michigan Chronicle. "I wish he'd just let people know he cares."

The preceding in-depth article, run in June 1970, tried to alert the public to a critical morale problem. The reporter mentioned how much time and effort he spent seeking information.

Large newspapers devote considerable space to situation stories. Nick B. Williams, executive vice president and editor of the Los Angeles *Times,* had this to say about the situation story:

> The Los Angeles Times very strongly believes that it has an obligation to those in its circulation area to alert them to any serious situations developing in our society. Although these situations rarely are indicated by individual spot news stories, we believe it is our function to go far beyond the spot news article in reporting such developments. If the country is going to heaven, or hell, I don't think we should wait until it does.

How does a newspaper like the *Times* keep itself alerted to serious situations? Williams replies:

> The answer is just about the same as to spot news coverage. The first requirement is a highly intelligent and alert metropolitan editor. The second requirement is a staff of intelligent and alert reporters so stationed in various strata of the community that they not only know what has happened but can with some assurance forecast what is going to happen.

The *Times'* performance in reporting disturbing situations is reflected in an article by Lynn Lilliston on the plight of aerospace workers. It was prefaced by the following editor's note.

> Being poor in the midst of plenty is no longer reserved just for minority groups. In Southern California, it's happening to aerospace families whose breadwinners are

among the best-educated and most highly skilled workers in history.

Unemployment in Los Angeles last month reached 4.9%, compared with 4% at the same time last year. Another comparison, made just before that, showed national unemployment at 4.2% at the same time the figure was 4.7% in Los Angeles.

The local jobless rate is considered "moderate" and would have to reach 6% (like Seattle) to be called "substantial." At present, the State Department of Human Resources Development reports, Los Angeles has a score of C on a jobless scale running from A to F.

The thousands of aerospace workers being laid off have swelled these totals to an undetermined extent. Rarely has so much talent gone begging.

Here is the story:

Incidents told in narrative style used as introduction	Mrs. Marie Jones closes the front door on her $40,000 ranch-style home in Thousand Oaks ("half-acre lots, zoned for horses"), skirts the semi-circular driveway and hurries down the road to her job at a hamburger stand.
Basic information	She is glad to get the $25 a week for three hours work daily. Her husband is an out-of-work aerospace engineer whose unemployment insurance has run out, and it is their only income. They have nine children.
Elaboration	"From $290 a week to $65 (unemployment) to $25," mused her husband, John, a test equipment engineer who graduated from Purdue University. "We've found that $25 a week won't feed a family of 11. I've cashed in one of my life insurance policies. I have two more policies with a little cash value, some savings and then that's it."
Background	The Joneses have built up five years' worth of equity in their home and their one car, a 1965 model with 100,000 miles on it, is paid for.
Elaboration	"I have worn out two sets of tires looking for work," said Jones, who was laid off from his $15,000-a-year job last September at International Telephone & Telegraph Corp. aerospace division. Of 285 men working on his project, about 260 lost their jobs when a large contract was canceled.

BENEFITS RUN OUT

"They set everything up and rushed us out," he said. "We went from table to table. It was like being inducted into the Army in reverse."

When he was unable to find another position and 26 weeks of unemployment benefits ran out, Mrs. Jones got her behind-the-counter job at a neighborhood crossroads restaurant.

Basic information	She made a cheerful thing of telling how the family gets along on a budget so devoid of income that they must dip into their final resources every day or so.
Elaboration	"We had soup and hamburgers for supper last night and we're having tuna salad and French fries tonight," she said. "The children's school lunches consist mostly of bologna sandwiches, cookies and fruit.

"I never buy anything that isn't on sale if I can help it. I pay 59 cents a pound for hamburger but can't afford hot dogs at 89 cents a pound."

MILK BILL

"There was a sale on toilet tissue at 10 rolls for 60 cents and I bought several packages. I wish I could have afforded more."

The family's milk bills are $8.80 a week for eight gallons.

The milkman, also a laid-off engineer, told Mrs. Jones he appreciated being paid. "Some people aren't paying," he said.

Basic information	The children, six boys and three girls, range in age from 17 to 3. Jones worries about what will happen if one of them is ill or injured. His company medical insurance ran out after a month and he cannot afford new policies.
Supplementation	"If one of the kids has to go to the hospital, they get to keep the kid," he said.
Basic information	Looking on the bright side, Mrs. Jones said, having a large family means that they already have self-discipline and few extravagances.

BETTER SHAPE

Elaboration	"Even before this happened, our idea of a Saturday night out was pizza or a drive-in movie," she said. "On birthdays, only the birthday child got taken out anyway."

"We are in better shape than we might be because we never bought anything until we had put money aside for it," her husband added.

Basic information	Jones, who has sent job inquiries all across the country, says he has not been able to get a single offer "despite the fact that I've widened the area I'm willing to move to."
Elaboration	He pays $205 a month mortgage on his home, $80 a month property taxes "and I thought I had quite an equity built up until the real estate people came out and told me how much they thought it would sell for," he said. The figure was $7,000 less than he had estimated. Although the mortgage and tax payments are coming out of his dwindling savings, Jones says it probably wouldn't be wise to sell the home—if he could sell it.

"I don't know where else we could get housing for 11 people for only $285 a month," he said.

ONE SOLUTION

Solution suggested

Jones believes that the country is experiencing "a depression in the middle of an inflation." His solution?

Elaboration

"There used to be a joke in the aerospace industry that NASA was the professional man's WPA," he said. "The government has all these brains available and ought to put them to work on something—ecology, for instance. Maybe we could help our environment and pull ourselves out of this hole we're in at the same time."

Basic information

Many miles away in La Habra, Mrs. Helen Morgan also is the sole source of support in the household of an engineer laid off by North American. She works in a department store from 6 p.m. to 9:30 p.m.—and on Saturdays—and has to leave her four children just as they are settling down for the evening.

HELPING OUT

Supplementation

"My girl, 11, has to do the dinner dishes, and my little boy has to get himself ready for bed, but they make out all right—they have to," Mrs. Morgan said.

Basic information

Her husband, Robert J. Morgan, a veteran of 17 years in the industry, was a quality control engineer. He had a premonition.

Supplementation

"Christmas Eve, after we didn't get the F-15 contract, I looked at the tree and the thing that ran through my mind was that I ought to take some of those gifts back," he said.

Basic information

Morgan made $14,600 a year. He pays $134 a month mortgage on his home and owns two cars, a 1965 and a 1962, which are paid for.

He is now in his 11th week of collecting unemployment insurance of $65 a week. Mrs. Morgan earns less than $40 a week.

Elaboration

"It's not much, but it puts groceries on the table," Mrs. Morgan said. "We can't afford as much cereal as we used to buy and I'm using imitation milk now for everything. It's 37 cents per half gallon compared with about 54 cents for regular milk.

"We have pancakes a lot. Eggs came down 20 cents recently and that was a big saving. I can buy day-old bread if I get to the market first thing in the morning. Is it a chore to have to be at the store at a certain time? Yes, but the saving is really great.

"My two teen-aged boys used to be fussy about their school lunches, but they just can't have the cold cuts and boiled ham they're used to. They certainly are sick of peanut butter and jelly, though.

"When my husband was first laid off a friend fed us for a couple of weeks and the church sent food boxes. I remember one week when a good box came I thought, 'Oh boy, I can use the grocery money and buy toothpaste and detergent.'

"I make about $40 a week. My husband used to give me $60 a week for groceries."

GOOD ABOUT IT

Basic information, followed by elaboration	The children understand what has happened, Mrs. Morgan said. "They've been real good about it. They don't ask for things—a toy, a coloring book, the things they see advertised on TV—the way they usually do.
	"I've told everybody we just have to make do with what we have. Not everything can be postponed, though. Last week I had to get tennis shoes for my little fella and the boy who's a Sea Scout had to have a special $3 shirt, and we managed.
	"At work, I wear the same four or five things by changing them around. I had to buy one $20 dress and that really hurts when you only make $40."
Basic question, followed by elaboration	Asked if she had given up any luxuries such as having her hair done, Mrs. Morgan replied, "Silly as it sounds, I have to have my hair done now, where I didn't worry about it before I went to work. I used to have my hair done maybe every other week. Now I consider it a necessity because they wouldn't let me in the store if I did it myself. I have very fine hair that I can't handle myself."
Basic information	In the past, Mrs. Morgan and her husband had occasional nights out at a favorite neighborhood inn and frequently would take the children "for rides in the car when we would stop somewhere and eat.
Elaboration	"We used to see friends a lot, too," she said, "but now we don't because our situation gets to be the whole conversation."
Basic information	Her husband had some surprises when he attempted to act in good faith toward the family's creditors. He wrote letters explaining his situation and stating that he would try to pay off his balances at $10 a month.
Supplementation	"Apparently none of my letters got through the computers," Morgan said. "The next month I got the usual bills and demands for payment with more interest added on."
	Nevertheless, all he can budget is the mortgage, utilities and "food on the table."
Basic information, followed by elaboration	Morgan has averaged one to two job interviews a week since he lost his job Feb. 6, and usually finds there are 100 to 150 applicants for every job he hears about. He spends his time reading newspaper ads and phoning friends hoping to hear of openings.
	He can't imagine staying on unemployment much longer.
	"I've got to do something this week or next," Morgan said. "I just can't hack this." One of the ironies of his position, however, is that if he took a job in a local store for $1.75 an hour, he wouldn't have any time for seeking an engineering job.

280   Reportorial Writing

Appropriate close

Neither family—the Joneses in Thousand Oaks or the Morgans in La Habra—has thought of appealing for additional assistance.

"I've heard of a lot of people who are worse off," said Jones.

(Reprinted with permission from the Los Angeles *Times*)

How did Miss Lilliston locate the two families she wrote about in the article? Why, of the many aerospace families hurt by unemployment, did she select these two? Here are her answers:

The Joneses of Thousand Oaks and the Morgans of La Habra were chosen for the story because they were the out-of-work aerospace families I located who were willing to be interviewed and photographed.

In April, 1970, when the story appeared, the aerospace layoffs were a fairly new development and many of the families were embarrassed and felt there was some stigma attached. Now (months later) I wouldn't expect to have any difficulty at all in locating many such families because it has become all too common.

I heard about John Jones, the engineer with nine children, from a fellow reporter who heard about him from a woman friend at a party. I telephoned the woman friend and she agreed to call Mr. Jones and ask him to talk with me, but she didn't think he would cooperate. He was so desperate, she said.

In a day or so, however, the woman called back and said the Joneses were quite agreeable.

A close relative is vice president of an aerospace company and was able to put me in touch with men who knew of other layoffs, but I wasn't able to get any other names or phone numbers this way. None of several possibilities worked out. The public relations departments of the big industrial aerospace companies were not cooperating at all.

Finally, I heard of a man who was setting up an office to unionize aerospace workers so that this type of disaster couldn't ever happen again. I phoned him and he put me in touch with Robert Morgan immediately.

I was happy with the way the geographical locations developed, but it was strictly by chance. The Joneses live in Thousand Oaks in Ventura County, far to the northwest of Los Angeles, and the other family lives in La Habra to the southeast.

How long did it take for Miss Lilliston to complete the story? Here, again, is her answer:

The assignment took about two weeks to complete. I could have done it faster, probably, if I had been working on it full time, but I usually have half a dozen stories coming along at different stages.

Some of Miss Lilliston's time was consumed getting the figures on unemployment used in the prefatory statement.

She explained she could probably "have beaten the bushes and come up with several additional subjects if I had felt we needed more persons for variety or contrast. In this case, no contrast was present: they were all miserable about the situation!"

The Plight of the Cities

America's large cities have been plagued by problems for years and as metropolitan districts grow older the situation becomes more serious. Physical deterioration, financial deficits, racial division, housing deficiencies and slums, concentrations of the poor, mounting crime—all these, authorities say, are leading the way to impending crises.

City officials are increasingly speaking up about the problems confronting metropolitan areas. New York City Mayor John Lindsay, for example, complained at a National Municipal League conference in Portland, Ore., that the federal government is not doing its share in helping the cities stem environmental crises.

Spot news stories have related the outcries of urban leaders. The press has followed up such spot news stories with situation articles that more fully describe the portent. An editor's note preceding an AP story by Ken Hartnett, written in June 1970, summarizes the situation:

> Summer is here, and America's cities are sicker than ever. The problems are so immense that serious and scholarly men are saying cities are doomed. In this dispatch, an urban affairs specialist surveys the bleak situation and reports, too, on the few bright spots he found.

At first glance, the story may seem to be of the survey type. Closer study, however, reveals that it synthesizes the common problems of the cities rather than surveys the varied problems of different cities. The article, which follows, is an example of reporting in depth rather than in breadth.

Gist of article	WASHINGTON—A little older, a little poorer and a little more desperate, the nation's cities are steaming into another summer still awaiting relief.
	The major cities are sicker than ever, and top Nixon administration officials and urban experts agree that massive help is at least a Southeast Asian peace away.
Supplementation	"It hasn't been possible under the circumstances to mount an attack that begins to reduce the magnitude of the problem," said George Romney, secretary of Housing and Urban Development—the federal arm most concerned with the quality of city living.
	Slums and blight are spreading, Romney said, and now represent "a more serious problem than they have at any previous point."

Basic information	In fact, the deterioration of the cities has reached a stage where some serious and scholarly men are saying the cities are doomed.

PROTOTYPE

Supplementation	"Newark, N.J., may be an advanced prototype," said George Sternlieb of Rutgers University in discussing one of the more melancholy of American cities. "Newark isn't just an aberration. It's a foretaste of things to come."
	If Sternlieb is a pessimist, Wilbur Thompson of Wayne State University in Detroit is an optimist. Yet Thompson, a pioneer in urban economics, paused an uncharacteristically long time as he tried to tick off the positive signs he reads in the current state of the cities.
	The short term outlook seems bleak.
Basic information, followed by supplementation	Unemployment, which hits the major cities hardest, is deepening and some experts are afraid a prolonged economic slump could sharply erode the marked economic gains made by Negroes in the past decade.
	(*Two paragraphs of supplementation followed*)
Basic information	The housing problem is worsening, particularly for the urban poor.
Supplementation	"Crisis is an understatement," said former New York housing administrator Jason R. Nathan. "Disaster may be more appropriate."
Basic information	After 20 years of urban renewal and a federal financial commitment of $8.2 billion, the physical erosion of cities continues unabated.
Supplementation	"As long as you are moving in terms of acres instead of square miles, you don't have a chance to arrest blight," said Milwaukee Mayor Henry Maier. "There's no program big enough and significant enough to arrest it."
Basic information	Crime, if no longer advancing in quantum leaps, is still surging and its handmaiden, hard narcotics, has hit epidemic levels in some cities. And federal officials say there are indications that more and more young people are carrying guns.
Supplementation	"It's a curious thing how the Black Panthers and the National Rifle Association have a common ground on this thing. They both argue there is a constitutional right to keep a gun and they practically use the same language to justify it," one Justice Department official said.
Basic information, followed by supplementation	The big-city schools, once a bulwark of urban stability, remain deeply troubled. Now a new affliction is besetting them—the rising tide of pupil absenteeism. On an average day in New York City's strife-torn system last year, 4 out of 10 students were absent.
Basic information	Despite the growth of a now-substantial Negro middle class, the number of husbandless families is also growing.
	Arson rates have skyrocketed in some cities. Attacks on police and firemen are becoming more common.

Basic information, followed by example	The cities themselves are getting into deeper financial trouble as their social and physical problems mount. Detroit adopted a city budget with $21 million deficit. Now Mayor Roman Gribbs is hoping the state legislature will help the city raise the additional revenues.
Basic information, followed by supplementation	Paradoxically, despite the gloom, many see daylight ahead once the nation extricates itself from Indochina and wins the domestic war against inflation. *(Four paragraphs of supplementation followed)* The cities are not all poverty, slums and failure.
Basic information	Despite great concentrations of the poor, only about 14 per cent of the nation's central-city population is classed as poor. *(Five more paragraphs of supplementation followed)*
Basic information	In the face of white wariness, there are signs that alienation among young blacks is growing.
Supplementation	"It's a different kind of alienation and in a way it's deeper now," said John Gardner, former secretary of Health, Education and Welfare and now chairman of the Urban Coalition. More and more people are using the firebomb to communicate. *(Four paragraphs of supplementation followed)*
Basic information, followed by supplementation	Abandonment and unchecked deterioration are taking a fearful toll in existing housing stock—in New York alone abandonment is running 30,000 units a year. At the same time, soaring costs of material, land and labor and prohibitively high interest rates have stopped new building programs in their tracks. It cost less than $16,000 to build a single family house in San Francisco in 1959. The same house cost almost $31,000 to build a decade later. Only 69 single family houses were built in that city last year. Only 14 were built in St. Louis. *(Four more paragraphs of supplementation followed)*
Basic information	The most persistent fact of all is poverty.
Supplementation	Urban affairs adviser Daniel P. Moynihan told President Nixon in his controversial "benign neglect" memorandum that "Nowhere in history is there to be encountered an effort to bring a suppressed people into the main stream of society comparable to the public and private initiatives on behalf of Negro Americans in recent years." The results, said Moynihan—who refused to be interviewed for this story on the current state of the cities—have been dramatic. A substantial Negro middle class—one of every three Negro families now has an income of at least $8,000 a year—is emerging. . . . Yet, it takes three working members in a Negro family to achieve the $7,724 median income of a white family with just one breadwinner.

284   Reportorial Writing

	And even with two or more working, a Negro family isn't automatically out of poverty.
	(Six more paragraphs of supplementation followed)
Basic information	For millions of the nation's ghetto dwellers, the prosperity of the Sixties was a sweepstake ticket held by someone else. The payoff passed them by.
Supplementation	Today, despite undeniable gains, statistics from federal and state agencies show that if you are black, not only are you almost twice as likely as a white person to be unemployed, you are better than three times as likely to be poor, four times as likely to belong to a household headed by a woman.
	If you are 25, your life expectancy is five years below the 49 additional years of life a 25-year-old white man can expect.
	(Three more paragraphs of supplementation followed)
Basic information, followed by supplementation	Adding to today's apprehension is the widespread belief among urban experts and city officials that the Nixon administration is anti-city.
	(One paragraph of supplementation omitted)
	"The national leadership has not been such as to confirm Negro hopes and constructive possibilities," said the Urban Coalition's Gardner. "The main problem is a lack of deep commitment to the urban problem. . . ."
Basic information	Housing expert Sternlieb maintains that what is happening to the cities is simply the exercise of the laws of the marketplace.
Supplementation	He noted what he considers almost the universal failure of the American industry to succeed in new ghetto enterprises, including enterprises carried out with the highest of bopes and the best of intentions.
	Even were the cities' racial problems suddenly solved, the city would still not survive because the city is "an antiquated form of social organization," Sternlieb said.
	(Six deleted paragraphs presented the opposing views of Sternlieb and Cleveland's Mayor Carl B. Stokes, the first Negro to be elected mayor of a major U.S. city)
Basic information	But there's general agreement that economic forces will shape the city of the future, for either better or worse.
Supplementation	Continuing prosperity will assure a closing of the income gap between white and black, said poverty expert Levitan. He noted that between 1960 and 1969, the median income of white families with both husband and wife working rose 25 per cent. The median income of black husband and wife families rose 55 per cent.
	(Three more paragraphs of supplementation followed)

With their many bureaus, the press associations have the machinery to cover widespread sources of information. Most newspapers concentrate on their service areas. But some of the largest newspapers, such as the New York *Times,* which operates its own news service, have bureaus and many correspondents scattered across the country.

Ecology

The press deserves credit for its part in warning the public about the despoilers of nature and for its role in arousing human concern over what man is doing to his environment.

Spot news stories have told of water and air pollution, of the destruction of wildlife, of the depletion of natural resources, and of the desecration of areas of natural beauty.

Such coverage has been followed by situation stories that have delved into the problems of waste disposal, litter, oil slicks, pesticides, smoke and fumes, noise, mercury poisoning of water and many other forms of environmental devastation.

The following Seattle *Times* story by Jerry Montgomery describes the despoiling of nature.

Then and now	Devil's Elbow once was the big dip on the road to Newcastle, a great spot to pick wild blackberries but otherwise untouched because it was too far from Renton. Today the canyon has two ugly scars inflicted by man: a gravel pit where an 11-year-old boy recently was smothered under an unstable cliff of sand and a wooden glen which is the neighborhood's unofficial garbage dump.
Supplementation	The dividing line is the sharp bend—called Devil's Elbow—in the narrow county road which crosses Honey Dew Creek. South of the crossing is the gravel pit. The garbage area to the north will become part of a major Forward Thrust park later this year.
Basic information	Seclusion is the canyon's major asset. On the bluffs around it are Renton neighborhoods where some of the canyon's polluters live.
Supplementary details	The canyon is marred by rotting mattresses, rusting automobile hulks, tons of ordinary household trash scattered about and a number of neatly sealed green plastic sacks of garbage.
Basic information	Richard Sodergren, an environmental health specialist for the Seattle-King County Health Department, said most of the garbage comes from residents in the immediate area, primarily from the Renton Highlands neighborhoods.
Supplementation	"It is one of the worst areas around," he said. "Persons in the area dump the trash. They don't drive too far. They wouldn't drive from Seattle. . . ."
Basic information	The mess has created a great "rat potential," he said. "The creek provides water for them and there is lots of undercover."

286   *Reportorial Writing*

Supplementation	Rats so well cared for won't stray far. But the neighborhood is only a few yards up the hill. The situation creates a health hazard for the neighborhood, he said.
Basic information	The county parks department will have to spend additional funds to clean it all up before work on a park can begin.
Supplementation	The park area will include. . . .
Basic information	The county will finish acquiring all the undeveloped land of the park area this year.
Elaboration	The area "will be kept as much as possible in its natural state," a park department spokesman said. Pollution has made the creek unsafe, so drinking fountains will be installed when comfort stations, picnic areas and trails are constructed, he said.
Basic information	Dumping trash on someone's land is a crime. Sodergren said his men have had a difficult time enforcing the law.
Supplementation	"We would have to have someone up there almost 24 hours a day because we have to see someone dumping the garbage," he said. Sheriff Jack D. Porter has decided to have his deputies make a special effort to write tickets for littering violators. (*Two paragraphs of supplementation followed*)
Basic information, followed by supplementation	But garbage isn't the canyon's only problem. It has steep, unstable cliffs of sand in the gravel pit just south of Devil's Elbow. (*Four more deleted paragraphs reported the name of the company that owned the gravel pit in which the boy was smothered by a sand slide and then told how the gravel company's operations were halted on the ground that zoning requirements for fencing had not been carried out. A boxed paragraph at the end of the story told of a forthcoming public hearing on the gravel pit operator's application for a six-year, nonconditional use permit.*)

Among the things that could have prompted the story were the death of the 11-year-old boy, information coming from an official of the county health department, a complaint from someone who disapproved of the littering, or the gravel pit operator's application for a nonconditional use permit. Alert reporters have a way of learning what is going on.

An AP story by James O. Clifford warns that man may be polluting himself to extinction but that first he is exterminating wild animals:

Gist of story	SAN FRANCISCO—If man is really propagating and polluting himself out of existence as many scientists say, he is pushing hundreds of species of animals over the edge into extinction first.
Basic information	The federal government estimates that 76 kinds of mammals, birds, reptiles and fishes in the United States alone

are either threatened with extinction or reduced to a perilous fraction of their once-vast numbers. Conservation groups estimate the number worldwide at more than 800.

Supplementary examples

They include such familiar animals as the American alligator, the Eastern timber wolf, the giant California condor, the grizzly bear, the whooping crane, several varieties of whale, and even the national emblem, the bald eagle.

There are less than 100 California condors still in existence, and less than 70 whooping cranes left in the wilds.

Only a few hundred grizzlies still roam the mountains of Colorado, Idaho, Montana and Wyoming. No one knows how many alligators are left, but poachers in the Florida swamps are killing them off at a perilous rate.

Heavy hunting has reduced the Eastern timber wolf to Minnesota. Pesticides kill off animals since man took over their habitat. Ranchers shoot the bald eagle, mistaking it for the golden eagle, a threat to livestock.

About 50 years ago the last passenger pigeon died in a zoo, and bison were reduced to a few hundred stragglers. The species was brought back from the edge of oblivion by a concerned public.

Basic information

David Brower, president of the militant conservation organization, Friends of the Earth, says worldwide the number of species . . . known to be in danger of extinction is 861, and 131 have become extinct in the last 300 years.

Elaboration

These wild creatures face many problems: the loss of space to live, death through pollution and hunting, capture of specimens for zoos, the pet market and large scale research.

"If you add into this already unbalanced equation the incredible demand for skins, fur and feathers, prompted by the fashion and interior decorating market, the outlook for wild creatures is very grim indeed," Brower said.

Basic information

In the interest of saving these imperiled creatures, some of America's most fashionable women have sworn off furs in a pledge drive started here recently by Brower's group.

Supplementation

More than 1,500 persons have signed the pledge to stop buying the thousands of fashion and home products made from the skin, fur, feathers and horns of wild animals.

They include such names as actresses Lauren Bacall and Tammy Grimes, model Mimi London and Mrs. Jacob Javits, wife of the senator from New York.

"We feel strongly that wildlife is of immense importance as part of the ecological community," said Joan McIntyre of Friends of the Earth.

"By cutting off the demand for wild animal products at the point of sale, we may achieve the time necessary to evaluate the world wildlife picture."

Sources of information for an article such as the preceding one could be many, including government reports, zoo officials and conservation groups. Much literature is available on the subject. An official of the

Friends of the Earth organization obviously provided much information for the story.

The article would have required more effort and development had the author decided to broaden his subject to all the animals on earth that are nearing extinction. It was more practical to narrow it to wildlife in the United States.

The subject could have been narrowed further. The article, for instance, could have been narrowed to the inroad on animal life brought about by fashion—the use of skins, furs and plumes in clothing.

A Los Angeles *Times* women's section article narrowed the subject of a story on wildlife extinction to the dangers to reptile life caused by the snakeskin fashion fad. The information—much of it, at least—cane from the curator of the Los Angeles Zoo's reptile collection and the president of the Greater Los Angeles Zoo Association, a volunteer support group.

The reader was warned that the disappearance of reptiles could cause a serious imbalance of nature. It was pointed out, in the words of the curator, that reptiles feed on rodents and that the extinction of snakes would leave rodent population out of control.

EXERCISES

I. Questions for Discussion

1. Would the story on the plight of aerospace workers in Los Angeles have been improved if more families had been interviewed? What did Miss Lilliston mean when she said even if more had been interviewed there still would be no contrast?
2. How can contrast be used effectively to introduce a story?
3. How can the "then and now" introduction be effected?
4. Must situation stories always present the negative aspects of conditions?
5. How much credit do you feel the press deserves for the growing concern of Americans about their environment?

II. Discuss the following introductions to situation stories

BY WARREN L. NELSON

WASHINGTON (UPI)—For some antiwar militants, buildings occupied on campuses by an enemy called Rotsy have become prime targets of attack. More than 30 have been firebombed this term.

Rotsy is the pronunciation given to ROTC (Reserve Officers Training Corps) and the antimilitary uproar on campuses frequently centers on it.

The defense department is concerned about it.

BY ARTHUR EVERETT

His uniform is the same shade of blue, the metal of his badge the same quality. But when a policeman's skin is black, his problems tend to multiply. Often, he is the man most in the middle—either because of his color or his badge.
(Associated Press)

BY LANDT DENNIS

NEW YORK—A sudden upsurge of young people fatally entrapped by drug addiction—people from all economic strata—has New York City officials groping for some crash preventive measures.
(*Christian Science Monitor*)

BY JEFFREY D. ALDERMAN AND VICTOR L. SIMPSON

When an 84-year-old Oswego, N.Y., woman died recently, she left three daughters, two sons, 39 grandchildren, 62 great-grandchildren and a pair of great-great-grandchildren.

To population experts, such a family tree is dangerous. For the experts say that the world population will double to seven billion human beings by the year 2000—only 30 years away.
(Associated Press)

BY ROY REED
NEW YORK *TIMES* NEWS SERVICE

NEW ORLEANS—Government investigators have found potentially dangerous levels of mercury in lakes and streams in 14 Eastern states during the last two months.

Most of it appears to be from industrial wastes.
(©1970 by The New York Times Company. Reprinted by permission)

III. Assignments

1. Search your local newspaper for situation stories and report on what you find.
2. List subjects for five stories that could be written by narrowing the content of the article on the bitterness and frustrations of black Americans.
3. Select five topics that could be used for situation stories in your community.
4. List the sources of information you would contact to get data for the topics you selected in the above assignment.

IV. Critical Questions

1. Do you object to the use of nicknames in bylines, such as Bob for Robert and Ken for Kenneth?
2. If you had been the author, would you have made a change in the placement of attribution in the 17th paragraph of the June 1970 wire

story on the plight of America's cities? (In your paragraph count, include the deleted paragraphs.)
3. Do you have any objection to the word "less" as it is used in the fourth paragraph of the story, datelined San Francisco, on man's pushing animals into extinction?

Chapter 15

INTERPRETATIVE WRITING

There is no Heaven but clarity,
No Hell except confusion.
　　　　　　—Jan Struther

Objectivity in news presentation became a generally accepted standard on most American newspapers before World War I. After the war, critics argued that merely presenting the bare facts did not convey to the reader the full significance of the news. They believed that causes and effects were needed to give the facts meaning.

The result was that a new emphasis was placed on the interpretative (or interpretive) article. By midcentury, the use of interpretative writing by newspapers had grown considerably, but not without opposition.

The subject came under heated debate at meetings of the Associated Press Managing Editors and the American Society of Newspaper Editors. Opponents charged that interpretation would inevitably lead to subjectivity. Proponents argued in turn that, instead of subjectivity, interpretative articles provided objective judgment or appraisal.[1]

One of the proponents, Lester Markel of the New York *Times,* said:

> Interpretation is an *objective* judgment based on background, knowledge of a situation, appraisal of an event. Editorial judgment, on the

[1] See Hillier Kriegbaum, "Background for Today's News," *The Quill,* June, 1968.

other hand, is a *subjective* judgment; it may include an appraisal of the facts but there is an additional and distinctive element, namely emotional impact.

Opinion should be confined, almost religiously, to the editorial page; interpretation is an essential part of the news. This is vital and it cannot have too much emphasis.[2]

Quite a different criticism of interpretative writing, made more recently by writers in the field of mass communications, is that it encourages readers to accept predigested decisions instead of reasoning for themselves.[3] Yet, despite opposition, interpreting the news continues, particularly on large newspapers.

It is wholesome, nevertheless, that this type of writing should continue to have the surveillance of skeptical editors.

The American Newspaper Publishers Association reported some findings of a recent study:

> 1. The writer of the interpretative story injects his own opinion more frequently than does the writer of a straight news story.
> 2. The writer of the straight news story also frequently injects his own opinion but to a lesser degree.
> 3. The interpretative story tends to be longer, to contain more background and more extensive explanation.
> 4. The subject matter of the interpretative story more often relates to race relations, education, the local community and its problems, and transportation.[4]

The ANPA report cited a study made by John De Mott of Northwestern University. Three coders were engaged to make a content analysis of 184 stories. The study indicated a considerably higher frequency in the injection of the writer's opinion in interpretative articles than in straight news stories.

Among the words used by the coders to identify the reporter's reactions to events were "critical," "crisis," "crucial," "menacing," "vital," "successful," "dramatic," "surprising," "ironic twist" and "profound impact."

Professor De Mott said that finding a greater injection of opinion in interpretative stories "appears to support the contention of critics who argue that interpretative reporting leads to opinion inevitably, and appears to refute the counterargument of interpretative reporting advocates who argue that such reporting is no less objective than other reporting."

---

[2] *Bulletin,* American Society of Newspaper Editors, April 1, 1953.
[3] See Charles R. Wright, *Mass Communication, A Sociological Perspective* (New York: Random House, 1959), pp. 20–21.
[4] *News Research Bulletin,* No. 18, Oct. 7, 1970.

What Is Interpretative Writing?

Sometimes in-depth stories are confused with interpretative articles, but the two differ in structure and in purpose. News stories, features, and in-depth and in-breadth articles assemble the facts to let the reader know what is going on. Essentially, they answer the question of *what*. True, any one of these types of journalistic literature may provide some explanation and background, but the purpose of each is to add to the reader's store of knowledge.

The interpretative article is primarily explanatory, and its purpose is to answer the question of *why*. The interpretative article puts the news in context—background is used to tell what led up to the news event, evaluation is used to describe its significance, and probable results are given to complete the context.

An in-depth story puts the news components together—it synthesizes many facts. An interpretative article, on the other hand, analyzes the facts—it dissects them.

Writers of news stories, features, and in-depth and in-breadth articles sometimes present the evaluations of other persons—experts and authorities—but they should not inject their own appraisals. If they do, they are guilty of writing opinion stories.

The interpretative writer, supposedly an expert because of his training, experience and knowledge of the subject, often makes his own evaluations. This has become the point of controversy.

The interpretative writer supposedly bases his evaluations on his wide background and knowledge of the subject just as a physician bases his diagnosis and prognosis of a disease on his training and knowledge of the subject.

The task of the interpretative writer is to help the reader to understand the full import of an event, but he should not attempt to mold public opinion. That is the editorial writers job.

Unless he has expert knowledge about a subject, a reporter should not try to interpret it. It would be ridiculous, for instance, for a reporter who has never covered city hall or the local political machinery to write an interpretative article on local politics. It would be equally ridiculous for a reporter who has never covered the schools to write an interpretative article about the troubles of school finance.

It is conceivable, though still unlikely, that a reporter who has covered neither beat might be assigned to write an in-depth article on either subject, for his assignment in that case would be to get the facts, assemble them, and present the evaluations of others; his own judgments would not be involved.

Writing the Interpretative Article

Basically, the interpretative article is composed of a reference to a recent news event, background, the significance of the event and the probable consequences. Explanation is interspersed.

Background should provide the reader with an understanding of why an event took place. The writer does not necessarily have to rely on his own evaluation of the significance of the event. He can quote authorities. Frequently, some form of general attribution is used, such as, "Many Washington political leaders believe the measure will increase inflation instead of curb it."

Often, too, the predictions of authorities other than the writer can be used to indicate probable consequences.

The following New York *Times* article by Harold M. Schmeck, Jr., reveals some of the qualities and peculiarities of interpretative writing.

> WASHINGTON—Doctors who treat more than a million adults with mild diabetes face a problem this summer *that most cannot solve independently.*
>
> *Many of the patients have been worried by fragmentary reports on the same subject.*
>
> Reference to news
>
> At issue is whether or not the doctors should continue to give their patients oral antidiabetes pills to help keep the disease under control. *Most doctors who face that question do not have the facts to decide the issue for themselves. They must accept, largely on faith, one or two sharply divergent points of view.*
>
> Background
>
> One holds that the pills do no real good and may, over the years, actually shorten the lives of some patients.
>
> The other holds that the pills are safe and effective.
>
> Both the American and British Diabetes Associations have issued cautious statements indicating that the evidence to date does not warrant changes in practice by doctors using the drug.
>
> *Fortunately it is not an immediately urgent problem. There is no suggestion of any short-term danger from the drugs; only a question of their usefulness and safety over many years.*
>
> Expert quoted
>
> One expert has called them drugs of convenience.
>
> Explanation
>
> The pills are an unquestionable convenience in helping mild diabetics control their blood sugar level without the need for injections. Furthermore, many diabetics find it difficult to maintain proper diets. *Thus, the pills have served a real purpose for those diabetics not dependent on insulin.*
>
> But the pills have often been prescribed simply on the ground that they cannot do any harm and may be doing some good. Both of these points are now subject to serious question.

Explanation	The drugs, of which tolbutamide is the most common, have been in wide use here and abroad for more than a decade, primarily for mild adult cases of the disease in patients who find it difficult to keep their condition properly under control by diet.
Background and explanation	The new uncertainty has arisen because of a major study that has cast serious doubt on the drugs' usefulness, and because the conclusions of that study have been attacked. The problem is sharpened for the average doctor because the full report of the study is not yet available. Furthermore, the argument often turns on complex points of statistics far removed from the ordinary concerns of medical practice.

(Another paragraph of background followed)

Background	The issue came to a focus a week ago at the annual meeting of the American Diabetes Association in St. Louis, but many participants said later it was not likely to be resolved in a way useful to the average doctor, or his patient, for months, perhaps for years.

The study, conducted at 12 university medical centers and clinics, began almost 10 years ago when the oral antidiabetic drugs were relatively new.

The study is called the University Group Diabetes Program. More than 800 patients have been involved, most of them for more than eight years. The purpose was to test whether the oral drugs or insulin could help prevent the long-term complications that are the main hazard for mild diabetics whose disease appears in adulthood. These are blindness, heart disease and other disorders of the circulatory system.

Background	*It was not expected at the outset that the study would reveal any differences in death rates among patients treated with the oral drugs and otherwise,* but such differences did appear after the study had been in progress for several years. The statistics showed that patients who had been taking tolbutamide, the earliest of the oral drugs, were not doing as well as patients who were using insulin or were merely dieting.

The study group found significantly more deaths from heart and circulatory system disease among those who had been using tolbutamide than in any of the other groups of patients. The difference was so marked that the 50 doctors involved in the huge study decided to halt use of that drug last year. The rest of the study is continuing.

Explanation	The present sharp debate has arisen over the significance of the study group's findings. *For doctors the issue is complicated because the facts are available to most only in fragmentary form and from sources that might be suspected of bias.*
Background	Tolbutamide, marketed by the Upjohn Company as Orinase, represents over half of the oral antidiabetes drug mar-

	ket at more than $50-million a year. Upjohn has made a major effort to make known dissents from the study group's findings. Some doctors say pressure from the concern has been extreme.
	A spokesman for the company denied that there had been any such pressure.
Background	On the other side, the Food and Drug Administration has accepted the university group diabetes program's principal conclusions, *but many doctors tend to be suspicious of the government agency in situations like this one.*
Explanation	*Doctors using the oral drugs for diabetes for years with apparent benefit to their patients find it hard to believe that there might be hidden drawbacks that escaped their notice. On the other hand, doctors in the university group program have an equally compelling commitment to work that they have been doing for nearly a decade.*
Background	Other reports to the same session of the diabetes meeting suggested that tolbutamide was useful, *but none of these studies was comparable in scope or design to the university group project.*
Background	Questions from the floor were often sharply critical of the group's report. A spokesman for the Joslin Clinic, a diabetes center in Boston, said that the university group's findings were contrary to the clinic's own experience over the years.
Conclusion	*But the kind of problem that seemed to emerge from the group's statistics would be extremely difficult to detect without a major comparative study of the type made by the 12 university teams.* (© 1970 by The New York Times Company. Reprinted by permission)

Certain words, phrases and sentences were italicized to point out some of the appraisals made by the writer of the article. No one who was not well acquainted with the background of the problem would have been capable of writing such an article.

The concluding paragraph sums up the objective judgment of the writer.

The article could hardly be called subjective, for the author refrains from bias in presenting the two sides of the argument. He uses ample background to enable the reader to understand the cause for the controversy.

A news story on the subject would have been limited to the views expressed at the annual meeting, and a feature or an in-depth story would have given the views of leading contenders on each side of the issue along with some background and ample attribution. The attribution in the above interpretative article is sparse.

Length is not a factor in the interpretative article—the subject, the needed analysis and the required background determine length. As far as organization is concerned, background and explanation are to the interpretative article what supplementation and elaboration are to the in-depth story.

The Political Scene

Interpretative reporting can be practiced on many subjects: the adequacy of school facilities, discrimination in employment, requirements for voting eligibility, welfare problems and housing needs, to list only a few.

Politics has provided the incentive for many analytical articles. What are the motives behind a piece of legislation? What is the significance of certain political maneuvers? What political strategies are being used in some quarters?

Instead of emphasizing spot news, the *Christian Science Monitor* provides its readers with features, in-depth stories and many interpretative articles. It does a good job of backgrounding and explaining the news.

The evaluation of a senate action stands out in sharp relief in the following *Monitor* article by Richard L. Strout (again, italicized passages indicate reportorial appraisal).

Reference to news	WASHINGTON—*Nobody in Washington really knows what the Senate's approval of the Stennis amendment to the school-desegregation bill means. There are hopes and fears. But nobody knows.*
Explanation	The amendment seeks to have desegregation guidelines applied uniformly to segregation by law in the South and segregation by housing patterns in the North.
	What stands out in the extraordinary situation is the purposeful ambiguity of the White House, the humiliation of Senate Minority Leader Hugh Scott (R) of Pennsylvania, the elation of Southern segregationists, and the equal dejection of civil rights forces.
	There are also political consequences.
	Mr. Nixon's careful planning to win the South over to the Republican Party has run into friction with certain Northern leaders of his party who are put in a difficult position by the so-called "Southern strategy."
Background mixed with appraisal	*This fissure has been growing* as Attorney General John N. Mitchell *castigated* the Ripon Society (the Massachusetts-centered organization of young Republican liberals); as Health, Education, and Welfare Secretary . . . met various rebuffs at the White House on desegregation; as Vice President Spiro T. Agnew attacked black quotas for college admission used by many Eastern colleges and universities. . . .

Taken by itself it is agreed here that the Stennis amendment, supported by Sen. Abraham A. Ribicoff (D) of Connecticut, is merely a statement of policy without immediate legal binding effect (*though it might affect deliberations of courts as an instance of congressional viewpoint*).

Explanation mixed with appraisal	Again, the Stennis amendment hasn't passed the *ambush* of the Senate-House conference where *the conferees seem antagonistic*. And it must finally get the approval of the house itself.

From this point of view the matter can be dismissed as of little importance or, as some call it here, an optical illusion.

Explanation	But some see it as of historic importance—a marker showing the turning of the tide; the high point of civil-rights support that signals the ebbing of momentum 16 years after the Supreme Court's public school desegregation decision.
Background	It came to a head on the floor of the Senate Feb. 18 when Minority Leader Scott said he had a letter from the White House ending once and for all any doubt over President Nixon's position.

The letter came from Bryce N. Harlow, counselor to the President, saying that Mr. Scott's alternative to the Stennis amendment was in "administrative language, preferred in existing circumstances over the original or amended Stennis proposal. . . ."

Background mixed with appraisal	But then Senator Stennis himself rose and by quoting other passages from the same *carefully balanced epistle argued so forcefully* that it supported him that he ultimately prevailed. When the *innocuous* Scott substitute came up for vote, a majority of Republican senators voted against him, 18-22.
Background	Then the original Stennis amendment was added, 56-36, with Republicans voting 27-to-12 for, and Democrats 29-to-24 for.
Appraisal	*It would be hard to find a controversy that goes deeper into the racial issue in America.*
Background	Since the Civil War there has grown up a code in the South by which schools are segregated under the color of law (de jure). *Theoretically* the Supreme Court struck this down. Congress has passed civil-right enforcement acts, frankly designed to apply primarily to Southern states.
Explanation and appraisal	But simultaneously in the rest of the country residence requirements have produced another kind of segregation (de facto).

Senator Stennis *innocently* said that this was just a simple expression of piety whose generalization could hardly be opposed save by the hypocritical. *President Nixon in effect supported Senator Stennis, either by ambiguity or silence. A strong White House statement almost certainly would have changed the vote.*

Opponents of the Stennis amendment say that it has a big hook in it and is making dupes of Northern supporters. True, they acknowledge, there is hypocrisy in areas outside the South. But in Senator Scott's racy language, it "opens up the largest can of worms in a long time."

<small>Background mixed with appraisal</small>

Ending segregation where it is forbidden by law is one thing; combating it where it is a matter of economics and residence is another. Senator Scott called it "an open and overt move to dilute the enforcement of the law by the addition of types of desegregation not yet ruled on by the Supreme Court so as to render virtually impossible the enforcement of existing law."

The Senate seems confused by what it has done. Next day, 49-30, it killed a Southern amendment to ban any federal court from ordering busing of schoolchildren to change a school's racial composition.

However, the House on Thursday adopted additional amendments which would prohibit federal support of bussing for integration and would require Health, Education, and Welfare Department acceptance of freedom-of-choice desegregation plans. *It appears unlikely that these House amendments will survive a later Senate test.*

Where Mr. Nixon stands on the Stennis amendment, however, what the Stennis amendment actually means, and where the Senate goes from here, nobody really knows.

(Reprinted with permission from the *Christian Science Monitor*)

Erwin D. Canham, the editor in chief of the *Monitor,* has been a longtime defender of interpretative writing. In his book *Commitment to Freedom,* written in 1958, he said:

> In the face of every problem of life, a first necessity is information. . . .
>
> The second tool comes with explanation of the information. The newspaper's task of digging deeper into the news, giving perspective to events, relating today to yesterday and tomorrow, is a role pioneered by the [*Christian Science*] *Monitor.* It, too, is more urgent today than ever before, as the modern world grows more complex and filled with voices. The meaning of the news is sometimes the most important news of all. To understand it gives the citizen the means of action.[5]

In answer to some of the doubts expressed about interpretative writing, Canham wrote:

> Some of the readers, however, have wondered and occasionally criticized the idea of interpretative writing. The very word is a misnomer. Interpretation suggests editorializing. That is not the fact or purpose of *Monitor* coverage. The word "explanation" is better, or "clarification."

---

[5] Boston: Houghton Mifflin, 1958, p. 436.

The value which the *Monitor* must add to all possible copy is the value of placing the news in its proper perspective and context. It calls for much greater digging, not for less. The task is essentially reportorial. The writer must consult files and sources, in order to show the real meaning of today's news events. He must write objectively, not simply out of his own opinions. He must not obscure the news, but clarify it.[6]

A significant difference between the quotations used in straight news stories and those used in interpretative articles is that quotations in news stories are usually current, fresh, whereas those used in interpretative pieces may have been made sometime in the past and serve the purpose of providing background.

Economics

Business and finance, directly or indirectly, affect the lives of most persons—business owners, stockholders, bondholders, employees and consumers. Some subjects that are of general interest are employment and unemployment, prices and inflation, labor contracts and strikes, and governmental controls and taxes.

Business and finance have provided the subject matter for many interpretative articles. A good example is a Los Angeles *Times* article by John F. Lawrence, the financial editor, on the 1969–70 stock market slump.

Reference to news	The stock market has come tumbling down. Some would call it a crash.
Background	The Dow Jones Industrial Average, which measures the stocks of 30 of the nation's biggest and oldest companies, has dropped 10% in a single month. Tuesday it hit the lowest level since August of 1963. Stocks in younger companies generally have dropped more sharply, some more than 50% since last November.
Pertinent questions	What does it mean? Another 1929? And what caused it? *What it means, in terms of immediate effects on American life, is not very much. So far, except for a mild economic recession which probably wasn't caused by the stock market, people are still buying cars, planning vacations and even adding to their savings.*
Explanation	The best explanation the experts can offer for the relative calm with which the general public has taken the market's plunge is that somehow most people learned the lesson of 1929. This time the money they put into the market was money they didn't figure they'd ever need to buy the groceries. A good many people planning on retirement

[6] Canham, pp. 335–336.

Interpretative Writing 301

may have been badly hurt. But as one elderly Los Angeles executive put it:

"If I had to sell my stock today, I'd be in trouble. But as long as I don't need the money, I don't care. And I think most people were in the market on that basis."

One thing that has saved many persons is a rule that grew out of the crash of 1929—a rule limiting how much stock can be purchased on credit, or "margin" as the brokers call it.

Explanation	In the '20s, you could put almost nothing down to buy stock, so when it went down in value, the banks were quick to sell out the margin buyer.
Explanation mixed with appraisal	In recent times purchasers have had to pay 80% of the price of a share of stock in cash. *Hence, investors were less likely to get into such a hole when stock prices dropped.* (*Apparently to stimulate investing,* the government Tuesday cut the cash requirement to 65%.)

REASON FOR DROP

Pertinent question	But if the general public hasn't panicked up to now, just why are stocks dropping so fast?

The economists wag their heads sadly and blame the failure of the government to stop the spiraling cost of living, the high interest rates on money, and the economic recession. Now there's Cambodia.

But those are the external causes. Far more significant is an internal illness of the market that began long before tight money. It has been given a name: The Performance Cult.

Explanation mixed with appraisal	The Performance Cult comprised a sizable band of professional money managers, men who made the investment decisions for scores of mutual funds. *They were bent on beating each other at the game of seeing how quickly they could rack up fast stock market profits for their funds.*

"PLAYING" THE MARKET

Unfortunately, the race didn't go just to the wisest. It went to those clever enough to find ways to "play" the market, which is to say they managed to talk themselves and everybody else into believing a stock worth $10 could be worth $100 before the end of next month.

While everybody was a believer, the cult had a field day. Unknown companies gained stock values that exceeded those of even some old-line companies that had paid dividends every year since time began.

Even the managers of some of these older companies came to believe it. They had to. As the young companies' stocks reached such high prices, the youngsters were in a position to buy out the oldsters. In short, as one Wall Street leader put it, "company presidents got more interested in what their stock was selling for than in what their plants were turning out."

WARNING IN 1967

Background

As far back as May of 1967, William McChesney Martin, then chairman of the Federal Reserve System, which governs banking, made a speech in which he warned, "Given the large buying power of the institutions, there is an obvious risk that speculative in-and-out trading of this type may virtually corner the market in individual stocks.

"In any event," Martin added, "activity of this kind tends to create undesirably volatile price fluctuations. I find this trend disquieting.

"However laudable the intent may be, it seems to me that practices of this nature contain poisonous qualities reminiscent in some respects of the old pool operations of the 1920s."

Those "old pool operations" involved secret agreements, no longer legal, among groups of wealthy investors to deliberately buy and sell a stock in a way which tended to drive it up and to convince the public to jump on the bandwagon. Once the poor suckers were on, the pool members would quietly get off, pocketing a huge profit and leaving the small investor with a stock worth a fraction of what he paid for it.

Appraisal

In a sense, the Performance Cult, that 40% or so of the mutual fund industry which engaged in rank speculation rather than long-term investment, did much the same thing to the little investor. In this case, however, the institutions as well as the little guys got caught when prices collapsed. There were no suckers big enough to sell to.

In sum, the late 1960s saw a speculative binge unparalleled since the 1920s.

Background

The president of one major New York-based mutual fund, a fund which climbed only part way into the performance game, saw the situation this way:

"We're now reaching the climactic phase of the market decline where the Performance Cult will be washed out. Every time there's a market run-up, it's a new group of people doing it. The tools they find that work eventually work to excess. Then, the tools are never used again."

Explanation

Not everyone, however, is optimistic that the cult is being washed out for good. The cultists themselves—some of them, at least—still defend their right to drive up stock prices just as quickly as they can—within the limits of the law.

Now, an old word in investment circles is beginning to replace "performance." That word is "values"—referring to shares in companies that make things or perform services that people want—and have a record of making money at it.

It means getting back to where a stock certificate in American business is not a stack of chips on a roulette table.

(Reprinted with permission from the Los Angeles *Times*)

The author of the article posed two questions: What did the stock market slump mean to the American people, and what caused the slump? Then he analyzed the situation and came up with answers. The italics indicate his appraisals.

Foreign Affairs

Straight news stories of summit meetings, talks among foreign ministers, and agreements and treaties between nations are often meaningless to readers without some explanation and background.

Americans rely heavily on newspapers, magazines and broadcasting for their knowledge of what is going on in foreign countries. Press associations, making use of correspondents with an accumulation of background and knowledge, provide, along with spot news stories, interpretative articles in order to clarify the facts and give them perspective. Some large newspapers also have foreign correspondents who interpret news.

Consider the following article by John Lawton.

Reference to news	LUXEMBOURG (UPI)—The Italian lira, French franc and West German deutsche mark will be replaced by a common currency by 1980 if plans now under consideration by the European Common Market bear fruit. It is proposed that the margins of fluctuation between these and other Common Market currencies be progressively abolished, starting Jan. 1, 1971, as the six market nations move towards full economic and monetary union.
Possible results	*If realized, this ambitious scheme would take Western European nations one step nearer to a United States of Europe, and create a rival to the U.S. dollar on the international money mart.*
Background	The Common Market, or European Economic Community (EEC), links West Germany, France, Italy, Belgium, the Netherlands, and Luxembourg in a prosperous trading club. Britain, Ireland, Norway and Denmark are trying to join. Eleven months ago, the heads of governments of the six market nations commissioned a study on transforming the trading bloc into an economic entity. The result is a 31-page report drafted by financial experts from the six market nations, on development of full economic and monetary union within the community by 1980. The experts' proposals were unveiled Oct. 26, at a meeting of the market's ruling Council of Ministers in Luxembourg. They now are being discussed by the governments of the six market nations. The so-called "Werner Report," named after Pierre Wer-

ner. Luxembourg's premier and finance minister who headed the drafting committee, is described by market officials as the most important document produced by the community in recent years.

Besides calling for the creation of a common currency, with perhaps a common name, the report also proposes:

—Setting up a supranational "decision center" to control the market's economic policy.

—Creation of a central bank system to administer the market's monetary affairs.

—Strengthening the political powers of the European Parliament.

Explanation

National governments would be responsible to the community "decision center," with which they would have to discuss budget proposals before submitting them to separate national parliaments.

The "decision center" would be politically responsible to a strengthened European Parliament. This would imply replacing the existing system of appointing national parliamentarians to the Strasbourg-based legislature, by universal elections.

The central bank system, modeled on the Federal Reserve System of the United States, would control interest rates, lending policies and the community's monetary reserves as a whole.

The proposals for achieving all this, said Werner himself, probably would create controversy, *and it already has.*

Hardly had he spoken when cries of protest began from French Gaullists, *who hotly oppose surrendering national powers to the community.*

Another problem is phasing new market members into the economic and monetary union process.

Background

Britain, which would endow the community with an international currency—sterling—has said it will go as fast and as far as the Six in developing economic and monetary union should it join the market.

But, like France, Britain is opposed to diluting its political sovereignty.

The UPI writer has placed heavy emphasis on background and explanation, and lighter emphasis on evaluation.

To distinguish interpretation from straight news stories, some newspapers call articles that deal in evaluation "news analysis," "news commentary" or even "opinion."

EXERCISES

I. Questions for Discussion

1. What are the basic differences between the straight news story and the interpretative article? What are the differences between the in-depth story and the interpretative article?
2. Do you consider the words "critical," "crisis," "crucial," "menacing," "vital," "successful," "dramatic," "surprising," "ironic twist" and "profound impact" to be subjective? Why or why not?
3. Do you believe that interpretative writing inevitably leads to opinion?
4. What difference, if any, is there between objective judgment and opinion?
5. Do you consider the appraisals in the article on the Stennis amendment to be objective?

II. Assignments

1. Search your local newspaper for interpretative articles and report on your findings.
2. Compose a list of at least five local subjects suitable for interpretative articles.
3. Contrast the article on diabetes pills with the story on New Mexico's hippie communes in Chapter 13.

III. Critical Questions

1. Is the expression "whether or not" wordy in the third paragraph of the story on pills for diabetics?
2. Would the word "toward" be better than "towards" in the second paragraph of the Common Market story?
3. Is the expression "in recent years" wordy in the eighth paragraph of the stock market story?
4. Is "cries of protest" wordy in the fourth from the last paragraph of the Common Market story?

Chapter 16

THE BACKGROUND STORY

What can we reason but from what we know?

—Pope

The background story has some kinship with the interpretative article, but the two are far from being twins. They cannot even claim as close a relationship as cousins. To say that the background story is a second cousin to the interpretative article would be a more accurate way of describing the relationship.

The background story has one thing in common with the interpretative article: it provides, as the name indicates, background for what has been reported in the news. It also explains. But from there on the similarity ends. It is not the purpose of the background story to appraise or to indicate probable results or consequences.

Writing the Background Story

The background story is simpler to write than the interpretative article. Its method is to refer to a recent news event and then turn to background and explanation, which usually accounts for almost all of a background story's content.

The background story is not new. It has been used for years. A good example of this type of journalistic literature is a Copley News Service story by Paul Corcoran, written after the severe earthquake in Southern California in February, 1971.

> LOS ANGELES—It doesn't take a giant earthquake to cause large-scale losses in lives and property. What counts most is where the earthquake is centered.
>
> That is a big part of the story of the Newhall earthquake which recently caused severe damage in Southern California—particularly in the Los Angeles area.
>
> There are three major conclusions that can be reached on the basis of the Southern California catastrophe:
>
> No. 1—The fact that the quake—6.5 on the Richter scale—was centered near a heavily populated area made it far more destructive than it might have been in a rural sector. Had an earthquake of the intensity of the Alaska temblor of 1964—which registered 8.5 on the Richter scale—occurred in the same geographic location there would have been structural damage over about 100,000 square miles, or the entire Southern California area.
>
> No. 2—Structural damage was limited largely to old buildings constructed before 1933. That was the year of the Long Beach earthquake, which killed at least 120 persons, injured thousands, and caused $40 million in damage. Donald E. Hudson, professor of mechanical engineering and applied mechanics at the California Institute of Technology, said the earthquake led to structural restrictions on all buildings built subsequently.
>
> "As a direct consequence of the great damage to school buildings in the Long Beach earthquake," Hudson wrote, "the (California) Legislature, through the Field Act, assigned to the State Division of Architecture the authority and responsibility . . . to approve or reject plans and specifications and to supervise construction of all school buildings."
>
> Also, as the result of a survey of the special Seismology Committee of the Structural Engineers Association of California in 1960, Los Angeles and San Francisco have virtually the same earthquake building restrictions.
>
> No. 3—Despite all the research in this country and abroad, no one can predict when an earthquake will occur. And, like cancer, the fear of earthquakes—of the unknown—is so acute that the human reaction to one of major intensity is panic. Telephone connections with the nation's third largest city were overwhelmed with calls from persons concerned about the safety of their relatives and friends. It was very difficult to make a call into Los Angeles on the morning of the quake.
>
> Dr. Charles Richter, perhaps the best-known seismologist of recent years and the designer of the Richter scale, is one of those who has said for years that a major earthquake in

California was inevitable. The only question was at what time.

There will be more, Richter believes. Hudson concurred in an article in Engineering and Science Magazine five years ago in which he explained that about 80 per cent of the world's earthquakes occur in a relatively narrow belt circling the Pacific Ocean.

As for California, Hudson comments:

"One cannot 'run away from earthquakes' in California by locating structures far from known faults; there are too many faults distributed throughout the state. A common opinion now is that perhaps the whole of California should be considered to have approximately the same earthquake risk."

Hudson also explained why seismological instruments near the scene of earthquakes do not always register the intensity.

"If a strong earthquake should occur near the station, the instruments would read off scale, or might even, as in Tokyo in 1923, be thrown off their bases onto the floor."

Earthquakes are not rare; there are perhaps 1 million true earthquakes each year. But fortunately, as Hudson notes, "only" about 100 are of a size sufficient to cause severe damage, and most occur far from any man-made structures.

Commonly described by their magnitude on Richter's scale, many of the most destructive in terms of property and lives were seismologically "moderate or small." Richter, in arbitrarily applying yardsticks to judge earthquake intensity, has said a temblor of 4.5 or greater is potentially dangerous in a populated area.

The Santa Barbara (6.3) and Long Beach (also 6.3 on the Richter scale) earthquakes were relatively small, yet they killed hundreds and caused many property losses.

How massive were the earthquakes in San Francisco (about 8.3) in 1906 and Alaska in 1964?

One analogy is that the Alaskan quake—plus 12,000 aftershocks—released energy equal to 100 underground nuclear explosions of 100 megatons each, or 200 times the power of the largest man-made nuclear blast.

Still unanswered is the question of earthquakes damaging skyscrapers. Although the most recent temblor was near Los Angeles, it was 35 miles to the north and too far to make it possible to evaluate what would happen if the epicenter was within a few miles of downtown San Francisco or Los Angeles.

The first paragraphs refer to the news event; the remainder of the story is devoted to background and explanation.

As is often the case in writing background stories, some research was necessary. The writer mentions one article that provided considerable information. It is general practice in doing research for the writer to resort to newspaper clippings, magazines, encyclopedias and other reference volumes.

Background and explanation are used in practically all types of journalistic literature, but the background story is *based* on them.

The following Long Island *Newsday* story by Arthur Hill contains background in no small amount, but it is essentially a news article, as indicated by the italicized passages.

HOUSTON—The lunar dust brought back by the Apollo II astronauts *was reported today* to be extremely ancient —at least 4.6 billion years, which is the generally accepted age of the solar system.

The age was one of the major findings *disclosed as the 142 principal Apollo scientists from nine countries gathered here to present the results of experiments conducted over the past several months* with some of the material collected last July 20 by astronauts Neil Armstrong and Edwin (Buzz) Aldrin as they completed man's first stroll on the lunar surface.

The age of the dust, based on measurements of the radioactive decay of uranium and thorium into lead, *was reported by Mitsunobu Tatsumoto and John N. Rosholt of the U.S. Geological Survey, Denver, Colo.* Similar results, based on another method of atomic age dating, *were reported by Dr. G. J. Wasserburg of the California Institute of Technology.*

In a preliminary examination, conducted before the samples were distributed to the scientists, the lunar material from the Apollo II landing site in the Sea of Tranquillity has been found to be at least 3 billion years old. That, however, was a type of dating that established only a minimum age. Even so, the lunar rocks and dust *were proven* to be older than the oldest rocks, at 3.5 billion years, ever found on earth. That does not prove that the moon is necessarily older than the earth.

The age *reported today* was based on the fact that a radioactive element, such as uranium, gives off atomic particles at a known rate, until an atom of uranium is transformed into a stable atom of lead. Thus the amounts of lead and uranium remaining in a given sample provide a clue to the ultimate age of the material.

A mineralogist from the University of Chicago, Dr. J. V. Smith, *presented a theory on the formation of the moon* that explains why the side of the moon that faces earth has smooth flat areas know as "seas," while the side away from the earth is considerably more cratered and rugged. *According to the theory proposed by Smith and his co-workers, Alfred Anderson and Robert Newton, the rocks at the Apollo II site indicate* that the moon now has a solid core although it was liquid more than 4 billion years ago. *Smith said* the lunar rock and mineral samples examined indicate that water and other volatile substances boiled away from the original glob of molten moon material. Then, as time passed, *Smith said,* heavy liquids rich in iron sank toward the center to create a core. A thin crust then formed at the surface and the moon began to cool.

The lunar highlands, or mountainous terrain, *Smith continued,* began their existence from surface cooling. They thickened because light minerals floated upward through the molten interior and were incorporated into the crust. The crust was thin enough then to be broken by either internal processes or meteoroid impacts. Breaking of the crust, *Smith proposed,* would release the molten magma, rich in titanium and iron, to the surface, where it solidified into the rock with the composition that was found to be high in those elements at the Apollo II site.

In other words, it was the flowing magma released from just below the crust that flowed onto the surface and the seas. On the side away from earth, there was no magma layer and therefore no formation of seas. *"The last liquid on the moon was drawn to one side by attraction from another planet, probably earth. This explains why there are seas only on the earth side of the moon,"* Smith said. The Chicago scientist acknowledged that his theory would be controversial but it was based, he said, on the examination of the lunar material and the way in which some rocks on earth have formed containing a high percentage of titanium and iron.

The theory was derived after studying the rocks, dust and numerous glass spheres in the Apollo II material with X-rays and an electron microscope. *The glass spheres, Smith said, have depressions* that appear clearly to be the results of small meteoroids striking the lunar surface. *"The glass spheres are formed as a fiery rain falling back onto the moon after a meteorite melts and splashes rock off the surface,"* Smith said. Some of the microscopic-sized spheres "look like golf balls, they are so covered by dimples," he added.

(Reprinted with permission from *Newsday*)

Better Perspective Is the Goal

The purpose of the background story is to give the reader a better perspective of selected news events.

It may provide perspective by revealing causal factors, as in the earthquake story. The background article, on the other hand, may provide better understanding by giving historical parallels; it is frequently used to provide more thorough political coverage than the news story can provide.

The following Miami *Herald* story by Saul Friedman lends perspective by listing the historical events leading to a current situation.

Reference to news	WASHINGTON—Here is how the Nixon Administration guide to school desegregation came about.
Background	More than six months ago, White House sources said, the President himself felt it necessary to issue a document for use within the government setting forth the administration's policies on school desegregation.
Explanation	Nixon's promises to southerners at the 1968 Republican Convention, talk about a "southern strategy," and the political tug-of-war between North and South and Attorney General John Mitchell and Health, Education and Welfare Secretary Robert Finch brought confusion within the administration as well as outside.
	As a result, the President, with the help of civil rights aide Len Garment, began putting together an administration policy statement.
Explanation	Meanwhile, administration actions on civil rights seemed ambiguous, at best. There were many, including some Republicans, who accused the administration of backing down on civil rights in general and school desegregation in particular in order to woo the South.
	The administration actions which stirred questions included the Supreme Court nominations of Clement F. Haynsworth of South Carolina and G. Harrold Carswell of Florida; apparent support of amendments by Sen. John Stennis (D., Miss.) to weaken enforcement of school desegregation guidelines; the dismissal of HEW's civil rights chief, Leon Panetta; the appeals by HEW and the Justice Department to delay school desegregation; and the creation of a committee under Vice President Spiro Agnew to oversee desegregation.
Background	In February, Presidential Aide John D. Ehrlichman, in charge of domestic policy for the White House, was vacationing in the Rocky Mountains. While reading the local press, he was dismayed to find that the President's views on desegregation seemed misunderstood, he later said.
	Ehrlichman recommended that the presidential statement, intended for internal use, be made public. Garment argued to the contrary, unless the statement was unambiguous and pledged more money for schools, which it did.
	At about the same time, Senate Republican Leader Hugh Scott of Pennsylvania, a civil rights liberal with a large black constituency, urged the President to make a clear public statement on school desegregation.
	And other northern Republicans, uncomfortable over administration court nominees and civil rights policies, grumbled aloud for something from the White House that they could talk about back home.
Background continues	Republican Edward Brooke of Massachusetts, the Senate's only Negro, denounced the administration for retreating on civil rights two weeks ago. And that night he pointedly boycotted a big Republican fund-raising dinner.
	Goaded by pressure from Republicans as well as Dem-

ocrats, and possibly by the sudden outburst of antibusing violence in the South, the White House decided to make a public statement.

Garment, speechwriter Ray Price, and the President had help from academics, including Yale Law Professor Alexander Bickel; James P. Coleman, of Johns Hopkins; White House Aide Daniel P. Moynihan (whose memo on "benign neglect" heightened the pressure on the President); and 35 black appointees within the administration.

Although the President had help in drafting the document, White House sources said, like other statements which he considered of crucial importance—the State of the Union message and his Nov. 3 Vietnam speech—"it was uniquely his own."

(Reprinted from the Miami *Herald*)

The *Herald* used a boxed label for the article which read: "Fills in the Background." The author is with the *Herald's* Washington bureau, and obviously much of the information came from his own observation and store of knowledge.

Part of a Series

Sometimes one of a series of articles on a particular subject is devoted to background. Such was the case for the following Newark *Star-Ledger* article by Robert J. Braun.

Subject introduced	The two-year college concept is not new—it is many years old.
	And the idea is not a product of the thinking of New Jersey educators. This state, before 1962, was one of only nine that did not have a system of junior colleges.
	But since the concept's formal introduction with the passage of the County College Act in 1962, the idea has become a reality of concrete and aluminum, of temporary facilities—for some 9,000 students in six community colleges.
Background	According to the American Association of Junior Colleges, the first two-year schools devoted primarily to liberal arts and privately operated were opened in the 1800s.
	In 1901, the first publicly supported two-year college was opened in Joliet, Ill. Now some 1.5 million students are enrolled in 900 junior colleges, 600 of which are community-based, publicly supported schools offering a wide range of technical and vocational training as well as conventional liberal arts programs.
	The call for the establishment of the inexpensive and close-to-home community colleges in New Jersey dates back to 1930. In that year, the now defunct State Board of Regents noted in its annual report:

"The establishment of junior colleges would provide broad and differential courses for large numbers of the youth of New Jersey. Such schools would assist materially in providing courses for many persons who might otherwise seek to enter fields for which they are not fitted.

"Many young people are financially unable to attend college. Junior colleges, if provided in the state, should be built from public funds and be supported in part by tuition and by state aid."

The Regents repeated their call for the junior colleges in 1931 and again in 1939. In 1950, a study committee . . . pointed out that a "serious need" existed for community colleges.

Two more studies were made in 1956 and 1957—but still no community colleges. . . .

The final impetus to the drive was obtained through a unique coalition of education, citizens and industry. . . .

But in 1954, local citizens joined the struggle. In that year, a citizens committee was formed in Atlantic City— they demanded the construction of a community college.

Background continues

Four years later, the Bergen County College Needs Committee, another citizens group, reported it had "tangible evidence of the interest of numerous organizations and individuals throughout Bergen County and adjacent counties in a low cost, community-type college."

In 1962, the voice of New Jersey's burgeoning research and industry was heard in another report issued by the State Department of Education.

A study . . . pointed to the shortage of manpower for the research and technical needs of the state's industries. The needed manpower could come from a system of community colleges.

"Industry," the report explained, "particularly research industry in New Jersey has difficulty recruiting personnel with adequate technical training, and favors the development of post-high school technical programs in the state."

The increased momentum brought the community college to the doorstep of the Governor and the Legislature. . . .

The wheels began to turn almost immediately. By May of 1963, the New Jersey Education Association reported that nine counties were planning community colleges. Four months later, the State Board of Education gave its first approval to a county college—Ocean County College. . . .

In 1964, colleges were proposed for Middlesex, Mercer, Morris and Essex counties. A year later, formal plans were initiated for schools in Camden and Bergen counties.

September 15, 1966, marked the opening of the first community college as Atlantic County College began operations. Within a few weeks, colleges in Middlesex, Cumberland and Ocean counties started classes.

Summary close

In the fall of 1967, Mercer and Camden Community Colleges opened. With six colleges operational, and another six scheduled to open by September, 1969, there are now more than 9,000 full- and part-time students in the schools. (Reprinted from the Newark *Star-Ledger*)

Many sources of information are usually available for articles like the preceding one. Specifically, the author cited the American Association of Junior Colleges as providing information about the first two-year colleges in the United States.

Public records should be helpful. Early reports may be found in school or community files. Treatises dealing with local history may be available in libraries. Clippings in a newspaper library are frequently used as sources of background information.

Historical societies function in many communities. Old-timers are usually ready to share information with reporters. Many institutions, including schools and educational organizations, compile histories of their own.

Reporters do not need to have encyclopedic minds, but they should know where and how to get information.

Opportunities Are Many

A reporter does not decide on the spur of the moment to write a background story. There must be an appropriate occasion for one—a news peg to tie the story to. When an occasion does arise, though, a reporter should be able to recognize the opportunity. And a well-organized staff is alert to situations other than those that are likely to occur on the regular news beats. A background story can grow out of almost any news item.

Community progress dictates the razing of an historic building, for instance. A tip may come from persons inside or outside the newsroom. A background story is in order.

A dog-leash ordinance comes under attack. What prompted the law in the first place?

A new type of fire truck is about to replace older models. What changes have taken place in fire-fighting equipment through the years?

A longtime business establishment in the community is going to be dissolved. What story lies behind it?

The opportunities for background stories are virtually unlimited.

EXERCISES

1. Compare the following background story, written after the Alaskan earthquake in 1964, to the one about the Southern California earthquake.

BY ROBERT M. ANDREWS

WASHINGTON (UPI)—Earthquakes like the giant one that hit Alaska are nature's way of relieving the tremendous stresses and strains that build up below the earth's surface.

Sometimes they are centuries in the making. Then suddenly, with little or no warning, they strike with the force of thousands of atomic bombs, producing the most awesome spectacle known to man.

Every year, a million quakes jar and shake the planet. Most are too slight even to be noticed. The United States alone experiences 700 quakes a year that can be detected.

No one can see it happen, but the earth's crust still is cooling and contracting, creating wrinkles on the surface that humans know as mountains and valleys. Great, sluggish currents in the bowels of the earth, constantly rising and sinking, help push mountains higher. Some "grow" at the geologically fast rate of several inches a century.

Evidence of the great pressure these infinitesimal changes can produce was seen in upper Assam and neighboring Tibet in Asia in August, 1950. One of the strongest earthquakes ever recorded devastated a vast area, leveling hills, throwing rivers off course, destroying villages and bridges and twisting miles of railroad track.

Scientists saw the Assam-Tibet quake as a symptom of "growing pains" in the mighty Himalayas, which have been reaching higher and higher for 40 million years.

Alaska is at the upper end of one of the world's most active "earthquake belts," or weak areas in the earth's crust. The belt rings the eastern edge of the Pacific from the Aleutian Islands south along the North and South American coasts.

Another major quake belt runs from the Atlantic Ocean through the Mediterranean into southern Asia. A smaller one extends from Mexico into the West Indies.

As the world's mountain chains keep growing slowly, enormous strains are put on masses of rock that support them under the earth's surface. When a rock mass is strained beyond endurance, it breaks or slips. The result is a massive jolt felt sometimes around the globe.

Most of the slippages occur 10 to 30 miles below the surface, although some go as far down as 400 miles. A shift of only an inch by a slab of rock hundreds of miles long is enough to start an earthquake.

These pressures produce cracks—or faults—down

through the earth's crust. Great rocks on one side of the crack, under severe pressure, may move tens of miles against the other.

The movement of rock masses may be triggered when the earth's crust adjusts itself to the varying pull of the sun, the moon or other planets.

The U.S.'s most famous internal crack is the San Andreas Fault, which runs 600 miles from Mexico into western California. After 100 years of increasing strain, this fault's rock masses shifted horizontally 21 feet in 1906. The result was the great San Francisco earthquake, in which 450 persons were killed and fires consumed the city.

Friday night's quake in Alaska measured greater in intensity than the San Francisco quake.

A University of California seismologist said the Alaska quake was "equal in magnitude to the most powerful quake ever recorded in North America," which also occurred in Alaska in 1899.

The National Geographic Society says probably the greatest earthquakes ever to jar the U.S. occurred in 1811–12, about 80 years before effective seismographs were available to record them. Alaska was not then a state of the union.

These quakes wrenched enormous areas in the Mississippi Valley, destroying the town of New Madrid, Mo., and creating a lake by dropping the northwest corner of Tennessee.

II. Questions for Discussion

1. How does the background story differ from the straight news story?
2. How does the background story differ from the interpretative article?
3. What is meant by saying that a background story is tied to a news peg?
4. What is the purpose of the background article?
5. What is one of the principal differences between the quotations used in spot news stories and those used in background stories?

III. Assignments

1. Search your local newspaper for spot news stories that suggest occasions for background articles.
2. Give some possible sources of information for background articles suggested by spot news stories in your local newspaper.
3. Assume that impeachment proceedings are being taken against a federal judge. Prepare an outline of the information you might use in a background story and list your sources of information.

IV. Critical Questions

1. Do you think a subjunctive verb in the last clause of the last sentence in the California earthquake story would improve the paragraph?

2. Do you see any objection to the use of "Health, Education and Welfare Secretary Robert Finch" in the third paragraph of the story on the Nixon administration's guide to school desegregation?
3. Would you have chosen a different word for "academics" as it is used in the next to last paragraph of the same story?
4. Would "dates from" be better than "dates back to" in the sixth paragraph of the community college article?
5. Do you have any question about the use of the word "unique" in the 11th paragraph of the same story?
6. Is the word "they" used correctly in the 12th paragraph of the same story?

Chapter 17

THE HUMAN INTEREST STORY

The same heart beats in every human breast. —Matthew Arnold

A newspaper executive recently commented that there has been a growing trend for newspapers to provide more entertainment. "We must make the reader laugh, cry, feel good, sad," he said, adding that it is the "show business" aspect of television rubbing off on all forms of communication.

Whether or not that is true, the human interest appeal was used in reporting the news long before the advent of commercial television. Human interest is often injected into straight news stories in small or liberal doses, but the subject of this chapter is the human interest story —a type of article based on emotional, rather than mental, appeal.

The human interest story is sometimes placed in the category of news that provides immediate satisfaction, rather than future reward, for the reader. That means the effect of the human interest story on the reader is ephemeral, adding little or nothing to his knowledge for future reference.

A typical example of the human interest story is one that touched the emotions of Los Angeles *Times* readers in the early 1930s. It follows:

Clowns may have to laugh when they feel more like crying, and all that mawkish sort of thing, but they're no different in that respect than anybody else.

But consider the case of Edmund Rosko, who tried to go on acting like a man when he was only a midget and who finally became so distraught with his discouraging prospects that he begged Superior Judge Trabucco yesterday to put him in jail that he might get away from it all.

Yes, he had passed some bad checks, here and in Oakland, but most of them were just midget checks and he was desperate when he did it, he said.

Judge Trabucco looked twice when the defendant, standing only a few inches higher than a yardstick—3 feet 6 inches to be exact—was brought before him.

"This is a Juvenile Court case, isn't it?" asked the court. "How old are you my boy?"

"Twenty-eight," was the astonishing reply.

When the situation had been explained, Judge Trabucco was nonplussed.

"I don't like to send you to San Quentin," he said after the miniature defendant had pleaded guilty. "I'll think it over. Appear Wednesday for sentence."

"I don't want to wait any longer," said Rosko. "I want to be sentenced right now. Can't you send me to jail or something?"

Even Prosecutor Joseph Garry was moved to curiosity by this insistence.

"What's wrong? How did you come to pass bad checks?" he asked.

"Well, I just don't care any more," said the little man. "I'm out of my element and I can't seem to get back into it."

Then he told his story—a novel, if anybody cares to write it.

He was a wire walker with a troupe of midgets that has passed through here several times. In love with a midget girl of the troupe several years ago, he was married to her despite the protest of her parents, who wanted her to marry a normal man that the offspring might be normal.

A baby came—a much smaller baby than people usually have. They watched it and did everything they could to make it grow up like other children. But it was only a midget baby and nothing they could do was of any avail.

The dissatisfaction of the girl's parents grew more pronounced. Their censure so worked upon her that she decided a year ago to leave her husband forever. She took the baby and went home to Germany.

After that Rosko's wire walking act was not so good. He left the company and tried other work in an effort to forget. But when thousands of strong men are out of employment there is little occupation for a midget.

Rosko attempted to pawn his clothing, but found even less demand for midget's apparel. Then he began cashing checks and was caught at it. He said he would go back to the troupe if he could, but that it is now somewhere in Idaho.

"Well, I'll tell you what I'll do," said Judge Trabucco. "I'll sentence you to a year in the County Jail. Meantime, if your troupe swings around this way again and will take you back, I'll suspend your sentence and you can rejoin it."

It was so ordered.

(Reprinted with permission from the Los Angeles *Times*)

The situation for the story, which resembles today's human interest stories, took place in a courtroom, but an appropriate subject can pop up almost any place—a school ground, a zoo, a shack by a river, a mansion or practically any street. A good reporter recognizes human interest elements wherever he runs across them.

There are no age limitations on human interest stories, but the young and the old usually make a stronger appeal than those of in-between ages.

Had the preceding story been told in straight news fashion much space could have been saved but much interest would have been lost. Consider the following rewrite.

Edmund Rosko, 28, a midget circus wire walker, was sentenced yesterday by Superior Judge Trabucco to a year in the county jail for forging checks.

Rosko aroused the curiosity of the court when, after Judge Trabucco said he would take the sentencing under consideration, the midget asked to be sent to jail right away.

Rosko explained that, after his wife had left him, his act deteriorated and he left his troupe and sought other employment but couldn't find it.

He said that he forged the checks in desperation.

Judge Trabucco said he would suspend the sentence if the circus troupe should swing this way again and was willing to take Rosko back.

Press associations frequently compress local human interest stories before putting them on the wire. The Rosko story might have been put on the wire in the following condensed form:

LOS ANGELES—Edmund Rosko, 28, is a midget but his story made a whale of an impression in a courtroom here.

Rosko had pleaded guilty to passing bad checks, but Superior Judge Trabucco was hesitant about sending the miniature defendant to San Quentin Penitentiary.

The judge postponed the date of sentence.

That's when it all started. Rosko protested:

"I don't want to wait any longer. Can't you send me to jail or something."

Both the judge and prosecutor appeared puzzled. The judge asked Rosko how he happened to pass bad checks.

Rosko related the following story.

He had been a wire walker with a troupe of midgets. He fell in love with a midget girl member of the troupe and married her over the protests of her parents. They hoped she'd marry a normal man so that she might have normal children.

When a baby arrived, it was a midget. The parents' protests grew and the girl left Rosko and returned to her home in Germany.

Rosko's act deteriorated after that and he left the company to seek another job. With many big men out of work, Rosko found little opportunity for a midget.

In desperation, he started passing bad checks.

Judge Trabucco sentenced Rosko to a year in the county jail but told him that, if his troupe should swing around that way again and would take Rosko back, he would suspend the sentence.

Writing the Human Interest Story

A feature style is used in writing the human interest story. Short, straightforward sentences are best. Staccato is useful. Understatement is more forceful than overstatement. Restraint is important. Pathos can be a strong factor, but bathos never is. The facts and incidents should speak for themselves: it is through the selection and presentation of facts and incidents that the writer communicates an emotion, a mood, to his reader. Chronology and suspense—presenting incidents that lead up to a climax—can move the entire story or they can animate its parts.

The organization of the human interest story is practically the opposite of that of the straight news story. The former is indirect—the reader must move into the story to get the full import. The latter is direct—it gets to the point immediately.

Study the following human interest story by Aldo Trippini.

Story starts with quotation	MADRID (UPI)—"You will write about me and my photo will be published on every front page," boasted 16-year-old Mariano Garcia two years ago. "I will be a great bullfighter one day."
	This was his dream and the theme he returned to time and again during our 200-mile drive from Saragossa to Madrid.
First meeting with boy	It was . . . in the outskirts of Saragossa that Mariano had asked me for a ride.
Boy tells of his dream	"I want to go to Madrid and start a career as a bullfighter," the boy said in the accents of his native Mancha.
	Mariano's was a classic story of Spain: the eager youth deserting the misery of his sun-baked village with its whitewashed walls for the danger and glory of the bull ring.

Incident during conversation	When he learned that I was a newsman, Mariano pulled a pencil stub and sort of calling card out of his pocket. The card bore an amateurish sketch of the Virgin Mary and Jesus. Across it he scrawled his name in bold letters.
Conversation continues	"The Virgin and the Christ are my protectors," he said. Then he talked with wide-eyed dreaminess of how the bull paws the ground with his left forefoot when excited, of his sudden charges, of the secrets of the matador's cape-work and of the "pata, rabo y orejas"—the hoofs, tail and ears of the bull—the highest honors the fickle Spanish can pay a matador.
Chronological order	For two years, Mariano tried to get a start on the road to fame and fortune. It came not in Madrid, but at San Martin de Lavega. The bull he met Thursday was six years old, fat, limping, and the sharp tips of his horns had been clipped. But the old bull could be dangerous. He had survived the ring once and remembered well how the matador evaded his charges and the hooking of his horns.
Incidents leading to climax	Mariano made three or four passes with his cape. But the bull was old and the boy was young and the fickle crowd was bored. "Just a meletilla," some shouted, just a beginner. Another matador stepped in to divert the bull. But the animal had his eyes fixed on Mariano. Suddenly, he charged the boy and knocked him down. Then the old bull drove his blunted left horn into Mariano's skull.
Climax	It was a quick kill, as the good matador's sword should be quick. Mariano Garcia's mother and father carried his body in a blood-stained sheet to the local cemetery. And today I wrote the story Mariano promised I would write.

The story was told objectively, as it should have been. The author did not say it was a sad story about a boy with a dream, but the incidents, as he narrated them, implied as much.

The article resembles a short story, but newspaper space does not permit the development most short stories need. Then, too, the writer of a human interest article must deal with facts. The short story writer is limited only by the extent of his imagination.

The above story begins with a quotation, moves quickly to the conversation between the boy and the reporter, and lists in chronological order the events leading to his opportunity to enter the ring. From there, the writer moves swiftly to the climax. The last sentence provides an appropriate close.

There is no prescribed way of opening a human interest story. Sometimes direct quotation is used, although other methods are called upon more often. The initial incident can be used for an effective opening, as in the following paragraphs.

> Fred Dewey walked into the backyard of his Woodstock District home to get a breath of fresh air.
> He inhaled deeply.
> "Humph!" he muttered. "Smells like gas."

At other times, flashback or cutback can be used:

> Mary Jones is resting comfortably in Mercy Hospital today, trying to forget her ordeal of the last 48 hours.

The story would then go back to relate the ordeal, probably in chronological order.

The lead is most frequently of the "come on and read" type, which encourages the reader to go further to find out what has happened. The two short examples above fit into this category. But this type of lead can vary considerably, as the following examples indicate.

> Joseph Brown has deplored for years the fact that he is a light sleeper.
> Last night for the first time he was thankful about it.

> Karen Smith knows what it means to be broke in a large city.

> Mary Black may wear glasses with thick lenses, but that doesn't mean much when it comes to spotting something unusual in her home.

> Frank Rogers has a smile that has bewitched practically all the nurses on the fourth floor of Franklin Hospital.
> But Frank, who is 2 months old, cannot see the faces of those he's bewitched.

> Sara Lent has always boasted about being an unemotional woman, but she's having a hard time keeping tears out of her eyes these days.

Ordinarily, inspiration for the lead of a human interest story comes from the facts and incidents to be told. If a writer runs into difficulty in coming up with an interesting lead, he can usually resort to starting with the initial incident or the single impression he wants his story to make on the reader.

An initial incident was used to begin the following story.

Incident on which story is based	SAN ANTONIO, Tex. (AP)—A 13-year-old boy complained to police that a 12-year-old knocked him down and took his tennis shoes.
	When the 12-year-old was arrested, he told this story:
Culprit's story	His shoes were only leather tops; the soles were the bottoms of his feet. When he went to school barefooted, class-

	mates teased him. So he dropped out a couple of days each week.
	The principal warned he must stay in school or be expelled. So the boy became a robber.
Incidents follow in chronological order	Sgt. Jerry Gutierrez and detectives P. R. Gonzales and Jimmy Cuellar chipped in to buy a new pair of tennis shoes. The 13-year-old's stolen shoes were returned and the new shoes were given to the 12-year-old.
	The three officers contacted friends and relatives for clothing to take to the youngster's home. They learned he is one of 13 children of a cab driver who earns $300 a month.
Policemen's summarization	He's had previous brushes with the law, the officers said, but they're impressed with his determination to stay in school.
Appropriate close	They checked later to be sure he was there. He was, in his new tennis shoes.

Using an initial incident is one of the simplest methods of starting a human interest story. It is effective in getting the reader's attention because it suggests that a story is coming.

Another simple means is to start the story with a statement of the general impression the writer wishes to make on the reader, as in the following example. It, too, encourages the reader to read on.

General impression	HOLLAND, Mich. (UPI)—Because a little girl turned her back on Santa Claus, a high school "problem student" has found himself.
Chronological order begins	A 16-year-old, unidentified high school senior, described by his teacher as a "problem student," was assigned last week to guide a group of kindergarten children through an art show at Holland High School.
	Santa Claus was on hand, went through his usual routine and got the usual response from the children—all except one, a cute, 5-year-old girl, also unidentified.
	She turned her back on him and refused to talk to him. She couched her disapproval in words that indicated that, for two Christmases past, Santa didn't come through with generosity.
	"Actually, she comes from a home of five children where both of the parents work," explained Lincoln Grade School Principal Ivan Compagner. "But there appears to be a certain amount of neglect and a lack of attention to the child."
	The "problem student" was struck by the little display.
	The student told his father of the incident in passionate words and said he would buy her a special doll she wanted. The son will pay for it out of earnings or allowances. The father told school authorities the child can have whatever she wants for Christmas.
	Mrs. Jean Visscher, who described the benefactor as a

"problem student," remarked yesterday, "he apparently has found himself this year and has improved considerably."

Appropriate ending

Perhaps next week will tell whether the kindergartener reaches a similar conclusion about the man in the red suit.

Attaining a Single Effect

The appeal of the human interest story can be intensified by creating a strong, single impression on the reader. That is what is meant by "single effect."

How does a writer attain a single effect?

Partly through his choice of words. Words can express gaiety or gloom. Joy or sorrow. Hope or futility.

A single effect can be enhanced by avoiding any extraneous facts or details. All the components of the story should contribute to the impression the writer wishes to leave with the reader.

This method is used in the following UPI story, written by Milton Richman shortly after the death of prizefighter Barney Ross.

NEW YORK—Barney Ross *wasn't a fighter, he was a lover.*

He loved everybody in the whole world and it was mutual because *everybody loved him.*

They'll tell you he was one of the toughest little guys ever to lace on a pair of burgundy-colored boxing mittens, but that's a bald-faced lie because *he was the softest touch you ever saw.*

Barney didn't have very much left in the way of material things when he died in a Chicago hospital Wednesday at the age of 57. Maybe that was because *he could never say no and was forever trying to help others.*

"He had this habit where *it was impossible for him to pass a beggar on the street without giving him something,*" says Sol Gold, who knew Ross more than 30 years and served as his eastern representative during his fighting days.

"In later years," Gold recalls, "I'd see him *give his money away to bums and beggars* and I'd say to him, 'You got nothing yourself, why are you giving away the little you have?' He'd always answer the same way: 'I can get it. They can't.' "

Ross wasn't merely sympathetic to lost causes, he embraced them. Some deadbeats knew that and actually lay in wait for him.

One of the things that made you love this *perpetually smiling* gray-haired little man who once held the welterweight, lightweight and junior welterweight titles was that *he never put on. He was always himself* whether he was fighting back to conquer the dope habit in 1946 or whether he was being welcomed back as a national hero with the Marines three years before that.

Barney loved his country.

He loved it so much that he got down on his hands and knees and kissed American soil in San Diego when a hospital ship landed him there from Guadalcanal on Feb. 25, 1943.

Barney loved not only his *religion,* but also the other fellow's.

He never forgot his orthodox Hebrew *upbringing* and frequently conducted services in synagogues. Yet he used to play the portable organ in the Pacific for the Catholic chaplain, Father Gehring, when Mass was said.

Ross had friends from all walks of life and he never forgot them.

One fellow, a bartender, was stricken with cancer and removed to Welfare Island, where they hospitalize indigent cases.

Barney was managing a local restaurant at the time. Every day, rain or shine, *for nearly a year he visited his friend until the day the fellow died. Barney never came empty-handed, either.* He'd bring his friend a steak, a bowl of soup or whatever he could from the restaurant.

Then he'd tip the orderlies to take good care of his friend and sit around telling stories to all the patients.

It is something of a tradition in boxing that fighters and managers split up and go their separate ways as soon as the pay days end.

It says something for Barney Ross and also for the men who managed him, Sam Pian and Art Winch, that they stayed together and *remained warm friends until death.*

Barney always used to claim he was no saint.

Maybe not, but he came as close as anyone can get.

The italicized words obviously create the desired impression, which the headline emphasized: "Sport's Toughest Soft Touch." Some variation on the word "love" is used five times, and "friend" or "friends" appears three times. The word "sympathetic" is used twice. Also notice how the phrases "softest touch," "perpetually smiling," "never put on," "always himself" and "never forgot" are distributed in the story.

Used thoughtlessly, repetition can bore the reader. But in able hands the repetition of words or ideas can create a strong effect.

Conflict

Conflict means struggle. The three basic types of conflict are man's struggle against the forces of nature, man's struggle against other men, and man's struggle within himself.

Sometimes the element of conflict can be presented in a human interest story. Here are some topics of wide interest:

The struggle of man, lost in a wilderness, to get back to civilization.

A child's fight to overcome a paralyzing illness.

The struggle faced by a family evicted from the house it had lived in for years.

An ex-convict's struggle to regain acceptance in society.

The element of conflict is present in the following Miami *Herald* human interest story by Jean Wardlow.

Introduction to conflict	WASHINGTON—The road back. Every wounded veteran must take it. And every wife who loves him.
	It's beginning now for determined 24-year-old Ted Bridis of Miami who, two legs amputated, his right hand gone from a mortar explosion, was brought to Walter Reed Army Hospital here Friday. And it's beginning for his 24-year-old wife Sallie, who flew to his side for an emotional reunion.
The struggle	"I think the worst is over," Sallie said. "I think he'll make it all right."
	There were few words about the "future" Saturday. Who can make plans before the healing?
	But the road back was quietly beginning Saturday, even as Ted, eyes brighter, quietly voiced quips to ward buddies.
	"You don't have to worry about Teddy," one told Sallie. "He's got guts. He'll make it. His morale is high."
	He was lying on his side, much as he had been the night before when Sallie had given him an alcohol rub during her first visit.
	"I'm so proud of you," she had told him. And, lying there in near sleep, he had replied: "I don't want you to be proud of me. I just want you to love me."
New beginning faced	It was a new beginning, too, for Sallie, even as she walked from her hotel room across the street from the hospital grounds—past Walter Reed's red brick buildings, its beds of tight tulips, its flowering trees standing in pools of dropped blooms from the day-before rain, past the huge, heavy sounding fountain in front of the hospital building.
	She'll be going there every day now.
	"I can't think of leaving," she said. "I want to stay with him every day as long as they'll let me stay." The night before, she told Ted, "I'll be here when you open your eyes in the morning."
Problems ahead	"Somehow, I've got to stay here. My problem is bringing the baby (Teddy, 2, now with her parents) up here. I'll have to have someone with me," she said. Ted's cousin, Rose Garcia, with her now, will be returning to her Miami job soon.
	"Maybe I can space people out," she said of potential friends and relative visitors.

"The worst is over," she repeated.

Reader identification

Theirs may be a more dramatic road, perhaps. But it is the story of hundreds of Vietnam veterans returning home.

The questions ahead stay the same, no matter the wound: What will our future be? Where do you start again? Or pick up? How long will it take things to heal? Adjust? And the deepest question of all—the one no man voices, seldom to himself: Can I make it?

The talk is far from serious, usually, in Ted's ward. There's a big sign posted just outside labeling it "The Pit." And inside the room, where beds are set in groups, there's a big basket filled with stuffed animals—fake snakes, like the ones on teenagers' beds. And around a pole, stuck up in their midst, one has been deliberately coiled, looking down nonvenomously at the group below.

Incidents and details

When Sallie first entered his room Friday night, the nurse had preceded her with, "Look who's here." Ted had been talking with a buddy, who hastily wheeled himself out.

A patient farther over in the room who couldn't leave his bed had turned up his TV set in the kind of code of the boys in the ward to say that they weren't listening, just couldn't leave.

Ted had been due for a pajama change and after their first few private moments, the nurse came back and flung a pair of pajamas at Sallie with a cheery, "Here, want to help your husband?" and left immediately.

"You know," Sallie said later. "That pajama thing I think is what pulled us both through that time. I think that nurse knew exactly what she was doing."

For it gave both Sallie and Ted the opportunity to perform a task together—easily and naturally—with his new body.

"Once I jiggled him around," she said of the pajama maneuvering. "When you do that, you find he's not that fragile. He's tough. Then you, well, you just get going," she said. "That's it."

She added later, "When you love someone, nothing changes, no matter what."

More incidents and details

Most of the talk was light and teasing—not forced teasing—that first time. Even when Ted told her he had received the Bronze Star for valor, "I teased him at first," she said. For it had been a surprise to Ted, he told her. They came to the hospital to present it to him, and he didn't have a pajama top on, "so there was nothing to pin it to." A top was hastily found, and Ted received his star.

"That'll go to little Teddy, won't it?" she asked. And Ted said, "Yes."

She kidded him about a new mustache—"now that I'm here, that's got to go," she said. Tentative plans were talked about for a Saturday mustache disappearance.

"He didn't look as bad as I had thought he would from what I had been told of his injuries," Sallie said thoughtfully later.

"I was really surprised at his back. I thought that would have a lot of scars. But when I turned him over to massage his back, it was smooth."

She was surprised, too, that he had a suntan. The hospital at Saigon had wheeled him out for sun.

"His color is good, and his eyes are so bright," she said happily. "And that big toothy grin." Sallie smiled thinking about it.

She stayed at the hospital long after visiting hours. "I just hated to leave" and was so excited afterward, had only a cup of hot tea, no supper. "I'll eat a big breakfast," she said.

After 1 a.m., she was still talking contentedly about Ted. She sat on her hotel bed in a pink gown, her knees pulled up under her chin, the brown eyes thoughtful.

"I have such a feeling right now. I don't want to cry. I don't want to stomp my feet. I think I just want to push time on. I know it's all just a matter of time, and I just want to hurry it as fast as I can.

"I knew we were close. But I didn't know how important we were to each other. You take people so for granted, then when they're almost taken away, you think, 'Wow!' What are we going to do?

Looking ahead

"I'm really looking forward to our life. Ted is, too.

"You can't really plan ahead at a time like this. Everything depends on getting well, getting fitted. It will take time. Ted thinks it will be a long time at the hospital. But we don't know. I think he said that because one man in his ward has been there for 28 months. Of course, he gets to go home for periods of time."

She spoke of Ted's methodical "engineering way" of doing things.

Future uncertain

"Ted's a very orderly person. He doesn't clutter his mind with a lot of useless things at one time. Right now he's not thinking about getting a job immediately, because the first thing has to be getting out of the hospital—getting his limbs. He hasn't even seen any yet, and he seemed very pleased that I had already found out something about them and had seen some. He asked me all kinds of questions about them.

"He was pleased that Mr. Rogers, the man from the Miami engineering firm holding a job open for him, had written him about the job. But I don't think he has made any definite plans when he'll be taking a job yet.

"He still lacks 15 hours for his master's. I think he'll probably get that. Probably at the University of Miami. But I don't know. That hasn't been decided, either. He might even want to get his doctor's degree.

330 Reportorial Writing

	"The thing is, this just isn't the kind of thing you can really decide yet."
Conflict summarized	The talk ahead, but inability to make plans. The wanting to get the healing business over with. The sense of urgency to get on with this beautiful business of living. All part of what every family of every wounded veteran feels.
	"We'll just live from day to day for a while. See how things go. The important thing is Ted now," Sallie said. "Now that he is home and we're together, things will work out.
	"I know it."
	(Reprinted from the Miami *Herald*)

The writer has broadened the possibilities for reader identification by using comments such as "it is the story of hundreds of Vietnamese veterans" and "All part of what every family of every wounded veteran feels."

The Young and the Old

Human interest has no age limitations, but reader appeal seems to be strongest in situations involving the young and the aged. Why? Perhaps because of greater relative helplessness or because of a feeling of protective instinct for the young and the old.

The human interest appeal of the young is depicted in the following AP story by John Armstrong.

Story starts with incident	IVANHOE, Calif.—Tears fell from little 2-year-old Mary Flake's one eye last night—she saw Santa Claus.
Element of suspense introduced	But doctors say the chances are 50-50 that she will never see Santa again. Golden haired Mary has retinoblastoma, a cancer which is prevalent among children.
	Her left eye was removed last month. According to her physician, Dr. Max Goldstein, she will lose her right eye unless treatments are successful.
Chronological order	Several weeks ago Mary made out her Christmas list. She asked for only three things: a doll, a ball and the sight saved in her one remaining eye.
	Santa gave her the doll and ball and a truckload of presents last night.
Background	Mary lives with her parents, Mr. and Mrs. James Flake, and two small sisters. Mounting medical expenses cut into the Flake budget so much that the children were told Santa might not be able to drop by their home this Christmas.
Community response	Then the people of Ivanhoe and other nearby communities took over. Santa, sponsored by the Ivanhoe Chamber of Commerce, paid a visit to the Flake residence last night, bringing presents for Mary, her sisters and parents.

Mother's reaction	"It's fantastic that people have such warmth in their hearts," said Mrs. Flake. "Our family truly felt the spirit of Christmas this year. I'm too thrilled for words."
Cutback to community response	More than 400 Christmas cards have been delivered to the Flake home, many of them containing money. More than $3,000 has been raised through the efforts of civic groups in the area, high school students and private citizens. The Ivanhoe Chamber of Commerce has set up a Mary Flake Fund . . . which will help to pay medical expenses.
Girl's prospects	Dr. Goldstein has one encouraging word for the parents. "With each passing month the chances the cancer will not spread grow better."
Parental reaction used for climax	"If our child does lose her other eye," the father said, "we will always be grateful that Mary's fondest wish was fulfilled. She got to see Santa Claus."

The story starts with an incident—a little girl's tears on seeing Santa Claus—but not the initial incident, which was the removal of one of the girl's eyes.

Instead, the story starts with what would have been a final incident if a strict chronological order had been followed. From there, it moves on to fill in all the gaps, and ends with what was told in the first paragraph, the realization of a girl's dream—seeing Santa Claus—as her father related it.

The simplicity with which the story is told—simple words and simple sentences—adds much to its forcefulness. And the girl's age weighs on the reader's emotions throughout the story.

The human interest appeal of older citizens is perhaps of equal strength, as this UPI story by Robert Crabbe demonstrates:

Suspenseful opening	LOS ANGELES—Bunnie Burns is a frail, wispy woman in her sixties. She seldom left her 8-by-10 room at the run-down Northern Hotel in downtown Los Angeles. Bunnie had her reasons. "God told me in 1964 never to set foot out of this hotel," she explained. "He told me to keep my room like a living garden, in witness to the Lord, and that people would come to me."
Initial incident	Tuesday they came—11 county officials and a 76-year-old blind man named Burt Wilson, who was one of Bunnie's few close friends.
Background	Their job was to evict Bunnie. The Northern Hotel, wearing its 56 years badly, had been condemned in an urban renewal project. Bunnie had lived there 17 years. Since April 26 she had been the only tenant in the 180-room hostelry, resolutely refusing to go. Her tiny room was furnished with a dresser decorated with assorted flowers and plants and a bed.

Chronological order	The job of leading the eviction party had fallen to a kindly sheriff's inspector named Joe Brady. For the last few days he had been telephoning Bunnie regularly, trying to convince her to move on her own.
Brady led blind Burt Wilson and the rest of the party up to Bunnie's little room on the eighth floor.
For an hour Burt and Bunnie chatted animatedly, while the others stood around.
"It was just the Lord speakin' through each of us," Burt said. "Waitin' for the good word."
Finally came the moment of truth.
"It's time to leave," Joe Brady said.
Bunnie took the proffered arm of a woman deputy sheriff, and walked slowly to the elevator.
The party walked one block to another hotel, newer and in better condition than the Northern. Bunnie got two $10 bills out of her purse and paid a week's rent.
With a sigh she surveyed the third-floor room officials had reserved for her.
Appropriate close	"It's so lonely and bare," she said. "But I'll have it decorated with all my pretty flowers and other living things—and it'll be like a garden again."

As in most human interest stories, understatement rather than overstatement is used. And of course simple sentences composed of simple words lend force to the story. Three short sentences form the first paragraph.

The writer expresses no opinion. Facts and incidents are interwoven to make one major impression on the reader—a resigned woman moves from what she considered to be a "living garden." With her goes her determination to make her new home resemble her old room.

Animals

The number of American families that go to zoos each year, the number of people who own pets, the number of veterinarians who cater to pet owners, the number of pet hospitals and cemeteries, and even the number of pet apparel stores indicate the interest of many Americans in animals.

All kinds of opportunities arise for stories about animals: spring comes to the zoo, a pet monkey adopts a dog and carries it into the trees, a dog travels 300 miles to get back to its owner, a hen adopts a brood of ducklings, or a parrot hums when a piano is played.

Sources for stories about animals are numerous. Most owners are more than willing to talk about their pets. Zoo keepers, breeders, humane society officials, veterinarians and managers of stores that sell pet paraphernalia are potential sources of information about animals.

It is not difficult to determine where the information came from for the following article, but it might be hard to approximate the year the story was written.

> CHICAGO (AP)—Hair isn't good enough for the fashionable town dog's winter coat this year.
> When it snows he will have a fur coat of Siberian wolf. When it rains he will wear a raincoat and leather boots.
> Yes, fur coats in black, white, tan and gray; raincoats in bright colors and pawgear of stout leather (they look like baby's booties) are displayed by up-to-the-minute canine shops, catering especially to pooches that live a hot-house life in a town apartment.
> But that isn't all. When Fido goes motoring and there's a bit of glare, special goggles may be had to protect his eyes.
> In addition to fur coats and rain coats, the smartly groomed dog may be togged out in gaily colored sweaters and blankets. . . . Some of the blanket coat styles have small patch pockets to the left stern in which tiny hankies may be tucked.
> This season there's a wide assortment of colored collars and leashes to match the dog owner's costume. Also there are swanky Scotch plaid leather collars for the scotties. Canine cosmetics include special new "defleaizers," deodorizers and perfumed shampoos.

The narrative is far from profound, but it is amusing. Even people other than pet owners can enjoy it. And the trademark of the human interest story is present—simplicity. Today's reporter might well learn from this 1935 article.

Zoo officials are good sources for many stories. An elephant is born. A gorilla suffers from a strange malady. The first koala bear arrives from Australia. A polar bear pines for a dead mate.

Children are among the most fervid zoo fans, but that does not mean the reporter can appeal to them alone. He must try to appeal to all readers. With that in mind, consider the characteristics of the following Washington *Post* special by Phil Casey. How would readers react to it?

> WASHINGTON—Adelaide is a hard girl to like.
> For one thing, she is jumpy. She is always in motion and is hard to pin down. And when you do, she bares her teeth. She has a lot of those.
> She is largely a despondent gray. Her eyes are moist and beady. Her toes are black. She is nervous and uncommunicative. She has a great tail. It must be a foot and a half long. All of her is at the Washington National Zoo.
> But, compared to her consort, Frazier, she is a tower of strength. She appears in public and she has guts. She is not even very afraid of newspaper or TV photographers. This is a feat, even for humans, and Adelaide is not human.
> She is a wallaby, which is sort of a tiny kangaroo, and

so is Frazier, who stayed in the wings, unable to face all that humanity. Frazier is even more nervous than Adelaide, which is hard.

No one at the zoo seems to know whether this is the way with wallabies—that the females are braver than the males—but it was agreed that, if wallabies are anything like humans, it might be so. Anyway, it was clear on a recent visit that Frazier is someone Adelaide cannot lean on, even if he would, or could, stand still.

If Frazier has been out there in front of the crowd at the zoo, he'd have been climbing the walls. There would have been chaos. If people think Adelaide is fast, they should see Frazier. He does not adjust easily.

Americans are largely unacquainted with wallabies, which may be good or bad, depending on how you feel about a wallaby after you meet one.

When you do meet one, you find that she is, like the kangaroo, which she resembles in miniature, a marsupial (which means, in part at least, having a pouch to carry her young. No one seemed to know what the male wallaby carries his young in).

Adelaide and Frazier are two rare, young Parma wallabies presented to the zoo by John S. Foster, director of research, development and engineering in the Defense Department. Foster got the wallabies as a gift from Sir Allen Fairhill, former minister of defense for Australia.

The Parma wallaby story is complicated, but here goes: They are about two feet long, with tails 18 inches long. The tails are terrific. Wallabies can sit on them, like shooting sticks, or propel themselves with them for a fast getaway.

There are only 62 Parma wallabies on exhibit in zoos around the world. The Washington National Zoo had no wallabies until Adelaide and Frazier showed up.

How did they get those names?

"Adelaide and Frazier are very good Australian names," explained Mrs. Foster.

Australian Ambassador John Keith Waller was on hand to witness the ceremony in which the two wallabies from New Zealand were given to the zoo, and there were a lot of lights and cameramen and reporters.

Adelaide just kept hopping and jumping around. Then she got competition from a female orangutan that had just returned to the zoo after being raised for months by a zookeeper's family.

The orangutan, named Manis (which means "beautiful" in Indonesian and is a lie), had long auburn hair, a pale, flat face, a flat nose and a lot of teeth. She seemed phlegmatic and dull compared to Adelaide, who was still jumping, but the photographers loved her. Manis is, despite her faults, better looking than Adelaide.

Zoo officials hope Adelaide and Frazier will slow down long enough to provide the zoo with more wallabies, but

this is uncertain. There may be, after all, the problem of tranquilizing Frazier enough for him to notice that Adelaide is more than just a blur.
(Reprinted with permission from the Washington *Post*)

A staccato style is used for effect early in the story (notice particularly the first three paragraphs). The writer devotes many paragraphs to describing the animals and their actions. A "come on and read" type of introduction is used, and the name of the animal is withheld until the fifth paragraph.

Human interest stories, as indicated by the examples in this section, do not have to communicate pathos. They can be light and amusing. But their appeal is always emotional rather than mental.

EXERCISES

I. Questions for Discussion
1. How does the organization of the human interest story differ from that of the straight news story?
2. Since human interest stories usually provide only immediate reward to the reader, do you feel that newspapers are justified in providing space for them?
3. Under what circumstances might a story handled locally as straight news be sent out by a press association as a human interest story?
4. What are some of the ways of starting a human interest story?
5. How does a writer achieve a single effect?

II. Assignments
1. Rewrite the following story, starting with the initial incident and using a chronological order.
    RALEIGH, N.C. (UPI)—For the first time in the two years of his life, little Walter Strickland faces Christmas without a mother, a father or any relative—unless someone comes forward.
    Walter was brought to a day nursery here Oct. 7 by a shabbily dressed woman who said she wanted to leave him for the day. When she walked out the door, she also walked out of his life.
    Thirty minutes later, a cab pulled up to the nursery and left a small suitcase, a bag of toys and a note.
    "I have a tumor on the brain," read the note, apparently written in desperation. "The doctors have given me a short time to live. Find Walter a good home."
    Mrs. Gladys Lanier of Pam's Play School still remembers that day.
    "She wanted to leave the bag of toys for the little boy but we

insisted that she not since we have our own play things and the boy's toys could have been broken," she said.

"Her actions were more or less routine," recalled Mrs. Lanier. But she said somehow she felt the woman wanted to hug Walter tightly.

While police continue their search for relatives, Walter, a brown-haired, brown-eyed waif with the normal happy, curious and sometimes sad moods of any child his age, lives in a rural home with an affectionate foster mother.

While he never mentions his mother, he still sometimes says "daddy" and likes to hug the legs of men he sees on the street.

"But when you mention grandmother, he begins to cry," she said.

Among the clothes left in the suitcase was a small T-shirt with "grandma loves you" stenciled on the front.

2. Assume that you are working for a press association. Rewrite the following story.

Leapy is back home with the James Quillen family at 7052 S. East Ave. after a seven-month absence and an extraordinary coincidence.

Leapy is a starling, but not an ordinary one. Starlings often are considered pests, but since the spring of 1968 Leapy has been a household pet.

She joined the family by flying to the patio where Darren, who then was 8, fed the young bird bread. When Darren's father appeared, Leapy flew to his arm, was carried into the house, and hand-fed on a diet of hard-boiled egg yolk, mulberries and strawberries.

Within three weeks, she was feeding herself, but remained around the property.

Certain patterns became established. Inside the house, Leapy would perch on a curtain rod above the kitchen sink, watching Mrs. Quillen work.

The bird learned that special food treats were kept in a turtle food box to which she would fly.

A starling's natural song consists largely of squeaky notes, but Mrs. Quillen said Leapy learned to speak a few words that the family—at least—could understand.

Leapy delighted in taking a warm bath in a dog's dish placed in the bathtub, then flying to a living-room lamp to dry by the heat from the bulb.

Outside, Leapy stayed in a flight cage. The bird could squeeze through the cage rungs, but never did.

That is, until last April when the family went away for the day, forgetting to put Leapy inside the house. The night turned chilly, and when the Quillens returned the cage was empty.

Early this month, Mrs. John M. Steele of 7159 S. East Ave. noticed a bird around the property. It ate from the dog's dish, played in water put out for the duck and did not fly away when chased by 2-year-old Nathan.

Steele farms 20 acres. To him, starlings are pests. He tried to scare the bird away, but it remained day after day.

"Then I opened the back door to go out," Mrs. Steele related, "and the bird flew right into the house. It sat on our wine rack like it was a perch. It didn't act wild."

She put it in a gunny sack. Her husband suggested they call the neighbors, the Quillens, who they knew used to have a bird.

Yes, the Quillens were interested in having a bird again. As Mrs. Quillen and her daughter, Alisa, 7, began talking to the Steeles, the bird began making noises inside the sack. The Quillens said it sounded like Leapy talking. They took it home.

Mrs. Quillen said she took out the turtle food box. The bird flew to it, opened it with its beak, and began eating.

She filled the dog's dish with warm water and put it in the bathtub. The bird splashed in the water, then flew to the living-room lamp to dry.

Leapy was home. (Fresno *Bee*)

3. Rewrite the following story, cutting its length in half.

OAKLAND (AP)—Helena Yorro is happy—very happy—because at last she has ears that stick out like any other 7-year-old girl's.

Helena was born without ears in a remote Otomi Indian village 200 miles northeast of Mexico City.

There weren't even any openings where her ears should have been.

"Several tribesmen told her parents that they should kill her," says Miss Vola Griste, a missionary of the Wycliffe Bible Translators who has spent 27 years among the Otomis.

"But her mother had been converted to Christianity, and she told them she couldn't do that, that the Lord gave her to them for some purpose. Right then and there, I pledged to help that little girl."

When Helena was old enough last year, Miss Griste took her to Oklahoma City, where an ear surgeon had offered his services.

"When the doctor finished he told me he didn't think he had done her any good," recalls Miss Griste. He was wrong. After a postoperative period, Helena could hear. Miss Griste considers it a miracle.

Helena began to learn to talk, but Otomi girls wear their hair long, pulled back off the ears, and if Helena couldn't do that she wouldn't have much of a future.

Executives of Realastic Industries, an Oakland firm that makes cosmetic restorations, heard about Helena and offered to help.

Money for the trip was raised through the efforts of James Santos, a United Auto Workers member employed at Realastic. A few weeks ago Helena was brought here to be measured for artificial ears.

This week she came back, a sober little girl with her black hair combed straight down, hiding ears that weren't there.

She walked out radiant, her hair pushed back behind her new ears in proper Otomi style.

"She was all giggly," said Miss Griste. "Kept looking at the mirrors around her and taking her hair, a strand at a time, placing it behind her ears."

The plastic ears are attached with a special adhesive.

Helena will stay with Miss Griste until she can be taken back to her home in Mexico.

III. Critical Questions

1. Do you object to the use of "different than" in the first paragraph of the story about the midget who cashed bad checks?
2. Is the third paragraph of the Barney Ross story subjective?
3. Is there a superfluous word in the expression "get the healing business over with" in the third from the last paragraph in the story about a crippled war veteran's return?
4. Are all the words necessary in the expression "one remaining eye" in the fourth paragraph of the story about the girl whose dream of seeing Santa Claus came true?
5. Are both words necessary in the expression "private citizens" in the 10th paragraph of the same story?

Chapter 18

RELATED STORIES

Float double, swan and shadow!
—*Wordsworth*

The word "sidebar," once used to denote a bar or sidepiece placed on a saddle or carriage, has considerable significance in a newsroom as a term meaning a story related to another. It is sometimes referred to as a "with" story.

The sidebar can be a news story related to another or it can be what is often called a side feature. If he so wished, the editor could incorporate the sidebar into the main story to which it is related, but to do so would be to deemphasize it by burying it.

The News Sidebar

The purpose of the sidebar differs from that of multiple story coverage of city council meetings and conventions. A sidebar is used to elaborate on certain aspects of another story. Multiple story coverage is used to report on different topics stemming from a single source.

The following excerpts, for example, were taken from a Chicago

339

Tribune story, written by Edward Schreiber, on Mayor Daley's reaction to a study group report on police activity at the Democratic National Convention.

> Mayor Daley gave the city's police department his unqualified support yesterday for actions during the Democratic national convention which led a government study group to charge there had been a "police riot."
>
> His superintendent of police, James B. Conlisk Jr., rejected the summary of the study group's report and said he was confident "the overwhelming majority of Chicagoans will agree. . . ."
>
> Asked at his press conference if he would have handled the situation which prevailed in the city in the last week of August any different now than he did then, Daley said:
>
> "Who handled it? What do you mean? Do you have me out there responsible for an individual policeman?"
>
> Daley denied reports that Hubert H. Humphrey or any other prominent Democrats had asked him not to hold the Democratic national convention here.
>
> "The problems of the convention were worked out by many agencies, and there was no hard line," he said. "There were no police riots."
>
> Daley said he took exception to the entire summary of the report. The study group was headed by Daniel Walker, 46, Chicago corporation lawyer and president of the Chicago Crime Commission.
>
> Walker has said he stands behind the report and the summary.
>
> Daley also denied a report that he and the justice department disagreed on the question of negotiating, in advance of the convention, with leaders of the thousands who gathered in Lincoln park and in Grant park to demonstrate.
>
> Conlisk, in his first public statement on the study group's report and the charges against police, said he disagreed with conclusions expressed in the summary by Walker.
>
> (Reprinted by permission of the Chicago *Tribune*)

The following sidebar by Ronald Koziol was run beside the foregoing story.

> A staff member of the National Commission on Violence told The Tribune yesterday that the ad which appeared in a California student newspaper soliciting anonymous statements charging Chicago police with brutality during the Democratic convention was paid for by the commission.
>
> Miss Kathleen Courts, 22, secretary of the task force on demonstrations, protests, and group violence to the commission, with headquarters in Berkeley, Cal., said the ad was prepared by John Hoskins, a law student at the University of California, in an effort to "attract attention."

> The advertisement stated: "Are Chicago police really brutal fascist pigs? You can help us document the answers to this question. You will remain anonymous."
> Miss Courts, Hoskins, and an undergraduate student at the university were employed by the Chicago study team, headed by Daniel Walker, assigned to investigate disorders during the convention. Miss Courts said the $120 for the ads was paid for out of commission funds.
> Walker earlier had denied that the advertisement was placed by any members of his staff. He told the Tribune on Monday: "This really shocks me. I would like to know who was responsible for this."
> When informed yesterday of Miss Courts' statement, Walker said, "This is news to me but I certainly will investigate it further."
> The advertisement ran for four days in October in the Daily Californian, a paper distributed to 41,000 students at the University of California Berkeley campus, the scene of violent disturbances led by student activists for months.
> According to Miss Courts, the advertisement drew about 20 students from the Berkeley campus who said they were in Chicago during convention week and wanted to give statements about police brutality here.
> Miss Courts said she conducted five interviews and the remainder were handled by Hoskins and the undergraduate student. "All of the interviews were then forwarded to the study team in Chicago," she said.
> Miss Courts, who has been employed by the commission for two months, said that interviews of witnesses to the disorders were conducted on 30 college campuses across the country.
> "And from what I've been told, some of the advertisements in other college papers were a lot rougher than the one we placed in the Daily Californian," Miss Courts said.
> In the Chicago area, newspapers at the University of Chicago and Northwestern and Roosevelt universities carried only mildly worded advertisements on three different days in October. The ads in this area stated:
> "Witnesses and participants in the convention disorders, come forward and tell your story."
> (Reprinted by permission of the Chicago *Tribune*)

At least part of the sidebar could have been injected into the main story by using a cutback or switchback something like this:

> Meanwhile, a staff member of the National Commission on Violence told The Tribune yesterday that the ad....

Had that been done, however, the information would have lost much of the emphasis it achieved as a separate story and the main article would have been much longer.

Eyewitnesses

A plane crashes, a hotel burns, a church wall collapses during services, or a bus flops over a bridge—survivors or eyewitnesses may be able to provide interesting details that can be used for a side feature.

A Seattle hotel fire, for instance, killed many persons. The Seattle *Post-Intelligencer* used a follow-up or second-day story and two sidebars the day after the fire.

The main story by Rick Anderson dealt with an investigation:

> Fire marshals and police detectives were questioning five persons yesterday as possible suspects in the tragic early morning arson fire that killed 20 and injured 14 at the Ozark Hotel, at 2038 Westlake Ave.
>
> It was the most casualty-strewn hotel fire in the city's history and financial loss may run as high as $125,000.
>
> Fire Marshall Stephen MacPherson told The Post-Intelligencer:
>
> "We are questioning five people immediately. And we are talking with anyone who has any knowledge whatsoever of the fire—all the survivors, witnesses, anybody."
>
> MacPherson said a recent disturbance, possibly involving threats at the hotel, was being checked out.
>
> "But," he said, "I don't know if this enters into the picture at all."
>
> It was first theorized that the explosive ignition and quick spread of the fire was caused by a flammable liquid.
>
> But MacPherson said he now thinks it "may well have been ordinary combustible material. This, however, remains to be proved."
>
> The fire was set in two separate locations—at the main, north, stairwell and the rear, south, stairwell.
>
> It roared up the stairs and in minutes completely engulfed all exits, except for windows and a fire escape in the 60-year-old structure.
>
> Most of the dead were trapped in the five-story steel-and-concrete building. At least one died in a fall.
>
> Fourteen were injured by the fire or during escape and eight were unharmed.
>
> The hotel housed many long-time residents and some transients. Some were invalids.
>
> MacPherson, who didn't want to speculate on motive, said he is uncertain whether the arsonist may have been the same man who set a number of apartment fires on Capitol Hill in the past year.
>
> "I really don't have any idea at this point," he said. "We have a line on that arsonist, but haven't caught him yet.
>
> "This hotel fire is a unique fire—that is, it takes a 'special' kind of person to do it."

Somebody, he said, probably bent on death and destruction.
(Reprinted from the Seattle *Post-Intelligencer*)

A related news story told of the problems confronted by firemen and of the casualties:

> The first firemen to arrive at the Ozark Hotel fire early yesterday were confronted by a roaring inferno and people jumping from the building, Fire Chief Gordon Vickery said.
>
> "Somebody jumping from the building almost landed on the fire truck," Vickery said. About half a dozen residents were forced to jump.
>
> One woman slipped on a fire escape and fell to her death.
>
> The first-arriving unit had to come only three blocks, Vickery said. It had been working on a small fire in a garbage container that was also . . . set.
>
> It has not yet been determined if that small fire was related in some way to the hotel blaze.
>
> Vickery said the downtown blaze was the city's worst hotel fire and the largest fire-death toll in 10 years.
>
> Twenty bodies were recovered, hours after the fire, which broke out at 2:42 a.m.
>
> Vickery said identification of the dead may take days.
>
> Forty of the 62 hotel rooms were occupied.
>
> Firemen, under a canopy of water from high-pressure hoses in the street, carried most of the survivors down ladders. Some escaped down outside fire escapes. Some died in leaps.
>
> More than 100 firemen and 20 units, responding to three alarms, fought the raging fire for 50 minutes.
>
> Two hosemen were injured, one suffering a dislocated knee, another cuts and burns.
>
> The fire roared up the middle stairway to the top floor in minutes. The roof caved in and the fire moved to the outside walls and worked back down.
>
> There were only two ways out, down the fire escape or out windows.
>
> The coroner's office said the victims died from burns, smoke inhalation or injuries sustained by jumping.
>
> All bodies were taken to the county morgue.
>
> Chief Vickery said the Ozark Hotel was on the department's "high hazard" list. He said it had been checked six times since Feb. 6.
>
> Vickery, who said Seattle has the most intensive hotel fire inspection plan in the country, stated the Ozark had been checked out as recently as six hours before the fire.
>
> "It was arson, no doubt about it," Vickery said.
>
> "The fire initially engulfed the lobby and main stairway.

"There was another fire going on the rear stairway at the same time. There was no way the two could have connected—one started by the other. They were set."

An unidentified man, one of 10 survivors who escaped with only minor injuries, said:

"I heard a great boom. I saw a huge cloud of black smoke rolling out the first floor windows.

"Somehow, I got out. But I lost all I own."

The injured were taken to four Seattle hospitals. Five were listed as serious; one critical.

Many of the survivors were transported—without charge—to the YMCA and YWCA and to other hotels.

The Ozark is owned by. . . .

The worst previous high loss of life in a Seattle fire was on Oct. 17, 1929, when 10 died in a fire at the old Portland Hotel.

(Reprinted from the Seattle *Post-Intelligencer*)

Another sidebar, a feature by Robert M. Cour, related the tales of horror told by survivors:

There was this fire that roared a deadly thunder in the black of the night, killing 20 and leaving 14 severely burned survivors to tell of their terribly close brush with death.

Some could tell about it through blistered lips, wheezing out particles of smoke. Some could not. Their burns and injuries were so severe they were in intensive care units of three hospitals.

Harry Currie, 60, occupied Room 315 at the Ozark. He said from his bed at Harborview Medical Center:

"The heat of the flames woke me up. The flames roared at the door. I put on one shoe and a pair of pants—nothing else. I went out the window and clung to the ledge. I was afraid to let go.

"It (the fire) seemed to come with such rapidity and flames licked at my face. Boy, did I ever take in smoke."

Currie was spotted by a ladder truck and firemen picked him off the ledge. He said:

"I was lucky. They say I'll be OK. But my eyes, my eyes . . ."

Currie wore bandages over both eyes and he coughed to rid his lungs of smoke. A doctor told him:

"You'll be coughing for two or three days."

Delvin Dieterle, 33, was asleep in Room 501. He said:

"I heard this loud, rushing noise and awakened. I saw fire at the transom. I went to the door in my pajamas and opened it. Flames burst at me from the hallway.

"I put up my hand to shield my face. That's why the hand is burned so badly, but I saved my face.

"I closed the door. I knew I didn't have a chance that

way. I went to the window. I heard a woman scream. People were calling for help."

Dieterle went out a window. A police car spotted him. He said:

"The officers kept a spotlight on me until firemen took me off on a ladder. I stood on that narrow ledge a long time.

"If anyone had ever told me I could do that for 15 or 20 minutes I'd have told him he was crazy."

A floor below Dieterle—in Room 401—was James Donahue, 68. Yesterday at Harborview they were in the same room. Donahue said:

"The fire, the noise, woke me. I heard a woman screaming nearby. I'm 68 and I've got a bad right arm. I called for help. I started to dress—I don't know why.

"The flames came into the room and I started out the window.

"I was there a long time with flames whipping at me; that's why my back is so burned. The fire took all my clothes off. My money, my food stamps—everything is gone. I don't even know if I have a hat."

Firemen plucked Donahue from his open window with an adroitly placed ladder.

As lucky as any of those trapped in the fire was perhaps James Williams, 29. He told an officer:

"I don't remember anything. I was in bed and I woke up in the hospital."

Joseph Smith, 36, told a poignantly tragic account. He was roused from sleep by another hotel tenant, Maureen Emmons, 37. He said:

"We went out my window after finding the corridor so full of smoke we could not see. I got out and climbed onto the fire escape. Then I reached back to help her. It's a little jump."

Miss Emmons leaped for the fire escape, her hands grasping Smith's.

She slipped, and for a few horrifying moments dangled in mid-air. Then, she fell to her death. Smith said:

"There was no way I could hold her . . . no way . . . I tried."

The words were of sad dejection of a terrible experience—a moment among hundreds for survivors of Seattle's worst fire in 27 years.

(Reprinted from the Seattle *Post-Intelligencer*)

The story, followed by a short, boxed item telling of Red Cross assistance, is filled with human interest and drama.

In contrast, Professor Walter Steigleman of the University of Iowa, in the Sept. 28, 1957, issue of *Editor & Publisher,* lampooned editors for trying to find a "hero" for every disaster:

Newspapers still insist that every disaster must have a hero. Most times this honor is conferred upon any person who retained consciousness or regained it first. An airliner heading for Miami lost its landing gear and a motor conked out. It landed its passengers with only a jar and a shaking up. Press services hailed a hostess as a "heroine." Her knightly gesture consisted of walking up the aisle to tell passengers to tighten their belts. The ordinary person, lacking in reportorial imagination, would presume such action was part of her duties. It would have been news only had she grabbed a parachute and leaped with a farewell: "So long, suckers."

The "heroine" of a hotel fire was a telephone operator who kept open the switchboard. The next day she deflated her own acclaim by admitting she did not know the hotel was burning. . . .

Steigleman went on to take editors to task for always needing "eyewitnesses":

> Disasters, too, must have their "eyewitnesses." A man or woman who has a front row seat at a disaster and can talk intelligently about it deserves space. But most "eyewitnesses" tell nonsensical stories such as this farmer talking about an airliner that crashed in a ravine across from his land:
>
> "Me and Jed were in the barn milking. I heard a plane and it sounded funny. I said to Jed: 'I bet that plane's in trouble.' Just then Martha stuck her head out the door and yelled that Bill had phoned that a plane has crashed in Stoner's Woods.
>
> "Me and Jed hustled over there. We could see a lot of smoke but we couldn't get across the gully. We didn't see any signs of anybody around the plane. I guess they were all killed. There was nothing we could do so I said to Jed: 'Lets go back and gather the eggs.'"

Superficial statements by eyewitnesses or survivors should not be quoted. The comments should be relevant and acute and should express spontaneous human reactions.

Public Reaction

Human reactions to events do not have to come from eyewitnesses. A newspaper might run a sidebar with a main story announcing a sharp rise in the price of coffee. Its sidebar might give the reactions of some housewives.

The Louisville *Courier-Journal* gave full news coverage to a Kentucky teachers' strike in 1970. Follow-up stories were used. A related feature by Bill Peterson, in the form of a multiple interview article, gave some of the public's reaction to the strike:

"The kids are just in and out. They don't know what to do with themselves," Mrs. Haskel Cox said as she leaned back in her television chair with her feet up in the air.

"I hope it will last two weeks. It's more fun to be at home than at school," a voice came from the hardwood floor beside her.

Bridgette Gail, 7, a second grader at John J. Audubon Elementary School, was speaking. "My teacher said that she didn't want to strike, but that the rest of the teachers needed more money," she continued.

Bridgette's 9-year-old sister, Kathy Sue, was on the floor beside her. Her oldest sister, Betty Lou, 15, was on the sofa across the room. All the girls had big brown eyes and straight dark hair.

"I don't like it," Betty said with the wisdom of her advanced years showing. "All there is to do is stay home and babysit. I'd just as soon be at school."

That is what it was like yesterday in the Haskel Cox home at . . . and hundreds of other homes across Kentucky.

It was the day—the first of what may be many—that the kids stayed home because their schools were closed. . . .

Mrs. Cox wasn't happy about it. She didn't like the idea of leaving the children home with Betty when she went to work at 3 p.m., knowing that her husband, a truck driver, might not be home for six hours.

(Two deleted paragraphs quoted more of Mrs. Cox's views)

Her comments and fears were doubtlessly expressed over and over in homes throughout Kentucky yesterday.

In five of them which I visited, there was little consensus about the strike. Some parents and children said that they supported the strike. Others related that they were bitterly opposed.

Like most first days, yesterday was probably a little better than those that will follow. It was more fun for the kids —they weren't bored yet. It was less painful for the mothers—they weren't tired of the kids yet.

"It will probably be next week when the kids run out of things to do that it will really sink in," philosophized Mrs. Benny Little, as she rocked in a chair in her suburban home at. . . .

Her daughter, 14-year-old Laura, a student at Butler High School, thinks it will be even sooner.

"When you really get down to it, it's no fun to stay home," she said, stroking her long strawberry blonde hair.

(Two deleted paragraphs expressed the girl's views further)

Mrs. Little and her husband said they feel education needs upgrading in the state and that "Kentucky is 20 years behind the times."

(Further comments by Mrs. Little followed)

Mr. and Mrs. George A. Williams Jr., the parents of five school children, take a different view. Said Williams:

"I'm all for the strike. I think the teachers deserve the money."

Mrs. John W. Henderson, who lives at . . . , agreed. . . .

The strike has put the Henderson kids—and most like them—in an unusual position.

They say they like the idea of a few days or even weeks off. And what kid wouldn't.

But they add that they'll probably miss their classmates, and that they don't like the threat of having to make up missed time next summer.

(Reprinted from the Louisville *Courier-Journal*)

The writer of the story makes no pretense of conducting a scientifically planned survey—he explains that he has talked with five families. What he was trying to do was to present scattered public reaction to the strike. The story supplements the news.

The *Courier-Journal* also carried a news story on a crackdown on drug peddlers and followed it up the next day with a news story on further arrests. A reporter, Paul M. Branzburg, interviewed a number of persons involved with illicit drugs to find out if they feared the possibility of arrest. The story did not run the same day as the arrest story because the reporter needed time to make his contacts.

Four days after the second news story appeared, the following related feature story ran (it was not a sidebar because it did not run in the same issue with the news story).

> Cold fear. That is what many of Louisville's illegal drug users are feeling as city police continue to arrest persons indicted last week on charges of selling illegal drugs.
>
> Among those interviewed in the last several days was a 19-year-old girl who is a small-time drug peddler.
>
> "I'm afraid to return to my apartment," she said breathlessly. "The police may be looking for me. I'm staying with friends."
>
> "I just wish we could find out who the narcs (undercover agents or informers) were who made the buys," said a worried young man who deals in drugs. "I'm laughing about it but only because I don't want to cry."

Background and reference to news

> Last Wednesday morning, the Jefferson County grand jury indicted 52 persons on charges of illegally selling drugs. Louisville police started arresting those named that afternoon.
>
> So far, at least 40 have been arrested. That leaves about a dozen not yet picked up.
>
> But, judging from conversations with members of the city's young drug subculture, far more than a dozen fear arrest.

There is no way they can know whether they will be picked up, because the indictments were "sealed"—the names being withheld from the public until the arrests are made.

Actually, the "paranoia," as long-hair drug users call it, began to set in some months ago.

On a bright sunny morning in early June, a blond long-haired young man sat in his apartment in south-central Louisville, flipped through a sketch pad on his lap, and said quietly:

"I think I am going to get busted. A guy came in here a while ago and asked for some grass. I sold him some. I don't know why I did—he was a stranger. But I sold him some. And now I think he might have been the Man (police)."

Last Wednesday night the fellow was arrested.

There was paranoia, too, in the drug group that met nightly at the north end of the amphitheater parking lot in Iroquois Park.

Hippie types told highly imaginative tales of how electronic "bugs" had been placed in the trees so that narcotics detectives could listen to the conversations below.

There was tension when one fellow openly accused another of being a "narc."

For some of the younger and less cautious drug dealers —called "twerps" by older and wiser dealers—last week may have been the first time they knew real fear.

Many "hip" kids who have started to sell drugs in the last year are from respectable middle-class homes, and the idea that they could be arrested is beyond their comprehension.

They talk about "busts" and "narcs," but deep down they really don't believe it can ever happen to them.

For many of Louisville's more experienced dealers, last week's bust was a confirmation that caution is the best policy.

The veterans won't sell to strangers. They do not trust a person just because he is young and has long hair or a beard.

They prefer to wholesale drugs—sell to dealers who retail it on the streets—than to retail it themselves.

A veteran dealer dislikes the idea of buying a pound of marijuana and selling it in "nickel bags" or "dime bags" ($5 or $10 packets). That way he has to sell at least 50 to 100 bags. He prefers to buy 10 pounds and sell one pound to each of 10 retail dealers.

In view of these practices, it isn't surprising that the older hip dealers seem the least paranoid. Less than 48 hours after the arrests began, two wholesalers were already discussing new purchases, new sales.

They had heard about a television interview in which Capt. Jack Green of the Louisville vice and narcotics squad said many of those arrested were retailers.

"I guess that means they'll go after wholesalers next," joked one dealer. "Suppose we'll have to start retailing."

"Yeah," said a friend, "either retail or hightail."

They all laughed a bit nervously.

(Reprinted from the Louisville *Courier-Journal*)

The advantage the sidebar has over the follow-up feature is its closer identification with the news occurrence as related in the main story.

The advantage of a follow-up feature, such as the preceding example, is that it allows more time and therefore more opportunity for thoroughness. The sidebar feature is more likely to appear with a second-day than with a first-day news story because of the time factor.

Similarity to Other Events

When disasters occur, newsmen often draw parallels to similar occurrences of the past by writing either sidebars or follow-up features.

Following are the introductory paragraphs of a second-day news story on the plane crash that killed a number of Wichita State University football players.

SALT LAKE CITY (AP)—Twenty-three Wichita State University football players flew home in silence and sorrow today, a day after their coach and 13 teammates had been killed in a plane crash.

They were aboard a second plane when a crash near Silver Plume, Colo., killed 13 players, Coach Ben Wilson, Athletic Director A.C. "Bert" Katzenmeyer and 14 other persons. Eleven persons survived.

Wichita State was to have played Utah State University at Logan today.

The trip back for those aboard the second plane was interrupted today when the bus carrying them from Logan to Salt Lake City broke down and a substitute bus was pressed into service.

When the bus arrived at Salt Lake International Airport the players walked with heads bowed directly from the bus to the plane.

Accompanying this story was a sidebar that reviewed some of the plane accidents of the past in which sports figures were killed.

BY THE ASSOCIATED PRESS

Ten years after his California Poly at San Luis Obispo football team was decimated in a plane crash, the former coach, Sheldon Harden, recalls that the tragedy has had lasting effects.

Harden, 49, spoke after learning of Friday's crash in

Colorado that killed 13 members of the Wichita State University team.

On Oct. 29, 1960, 16 players on the California Poly team were among 22 persons who perished when their chartered plane went down in fog near Toledo, Ohio.

"The 1960 crash has had a long-standing effect on the school and the town, even today," Harden said. "The question still remains: Whose responsibility was it when we took off under questionable conditions in the fog—the pilot, the tower, or whose?"

Harden, the only one of the 48 persons aboard not hurt or killed, was assistant coach at the time. He later became head coach.

For a year after the accident—caused, the Federal Aviation Administration later said, by an overload and poor condition of the plane—the school scheduled no games.

"Then we started scheduling within the boundaries of California so we didn't have to fly," Harden said. The California squad has flown only twice since the resumption of air trips in 1967.

Air crashes have taken the lives of many sports figures over the years.

Eighteen members of the United States figure skating team were killed when their plane went down in Belgium on Feb. 15, 1961, as they were heading to the world championships in Czechoslovakia.

Former heavyweight boxing champion Rocky Marciano died when his small plane crashed near Newton, Iowa, on Sept. 1, 1969.

Rafael Osuna, the Mexican tennis star, was one of 79 persons killed three months earlier in a crash near Monterrey, Mexico.

Golfer Tony Lema died in a crash in 1966, and Chicago Cubs second baseman Ken Hubbs died in a 1964 crash.

Sports figures of an earlier era who died in plane crashes included Notre Dame football coach Knute Rockne in 1931 and France's world middleweight boxing champion, Marcel Cerdan, in 1949.

(Five more paragraphs followed listing other sports figures, both American and foreign, who died in air mishaps)

The sidebar should be identified early with the main story to which it is related, but the writer should avoid any unnecessary repetition of information given in the principal story.

Multiple Sidebars

Emergencies that affect many people are frequently covered in a number of related stories. Floods, hurricanes and other natural disasters are among these emergencies.

The wire services sent out numerous sidebars when an earthquake struck Los Angeles in February, 1971. One California newspaper in a city more than 200 miles from Los Angeles used the following stories, which were related to the main news article:
1. A pledge of state aid for the Los Angeles area
2. State disaster office dispatched rescue workers
3. Damages suffered
4. Highway damages
5. A key state water project escapes damage
6. Loss of utility services
7. A scientist says an eclipse of the moon caused the quake
8. Delay of highway traffic
9. A dam in Central California escaped damage
10. Four held by police for investigation of looting
11. Most homes had no insurance
12. State legislators get plea for catastrophe insurance
13. Rescue efforts
14. Small likelihood of quake in newspaper's circulation area.

EXERCISES

I. Questions for Discussion
1. What are the advantages of using a sidebar, compared with putting all the information in one story?
2. What are the advantages of the sidebar over the follow-up feature? What, in turn, are the advantages of the follow-up feature over the sidebar?
3. How did the writer of the Seattle hotel fire sidebar telling of the horrors suffered by survivors locate his sources of information?
4. What are your reactions to Professor Steigleman's criticism of some eyewitness stories?
5. Were enough families interviewed for the story on public reaction to a Kentucky teachers' strike?

II. Which of the following news stories would warrant sidebars or follow-up features?
1. School officials have notified more than 100 teachers that their services will not be required for the next school year. The district is facing financial squeezes and, although the next year's budget has not been started, officials stated that the educational code makes it mandatory that any teachers who may be dismissed be notified by Mar. 15. It is expected that other than personnel cuts may save the teachers' jobs and they will be rehired if they do not find other positions before.

2. A wire service report says that the number of arson cases in the state has increased 87 per cent in the last three years.
3. A wire service report says that the number of jobless in the state has reached 7 per cent of the number of persons available for employment.
4. Three persons were killed when a private plane ran into a mountain side. One person survived.
5. Local school bus drivers have walked off their jobs in a demand for higher pay.
6. Six were killed in a chain of accidents on a nearby freeway during dense early morning fog.
7. More than 100 families will be evicted from their homes following condemnation proceedings to acquire more property for the expansion of a junior college.
8. A test case is challenging the legality of a new ordinance on pornography.
9. A 13-year-old boy saves two youngsters, one 9 and the other 11, from drowning in a lake. Another boy, 8, drowned.
10. A family of seven is left destitute by a house fire.

III. Compare the following Seattle Times *follow-up feature to the Seattle* Post-Intelligencer *sidebar on the survivors of a Seattle hotel fire.*

BY MARTY LOKEN

Grace Chambers stared, blinking, at names of the dead.

Burned badly, cut, fractured and swollen, she is the small, frail woman who refused to die in the Ozark Hotel. Still in serious condition at Harborview Medical Center, Mrs. Chambers was desk clerk when the hotel burned a month ago in a still-unsolved arson fire which killed 20 occupants. Today is her 75th birthday.

Grace Chambers knew all of the residents, and most of the temporary guests. She knew the dead, but, until this week, she was not sure who had died.

"Oh, Doris Symes . . . Doris Symes was lost? Archie Eagen . . . Archie Eagen was lost? Walter Berard, 63, yes, . . . Mr. Berard. Minnie Graham . . . Minnie Graham was . . . Joseph Mandt . . . Mr. Mandt was lost?

"Emmitt Kehoe and Linda Kehoe . . . that was the young couple, the nice young couple . . . Charles Cossette, yes . . . Joseph Cote . . . Oh, Mr. Cote. Mr. Cote was lost? It says he was 70 here, but Mr. Cote was older than that. Yes, he was older than me . . . Genevieve Moran. Poor Mrs. Moran—I couldn't find out from anybody if she was lost . . ."

The list went on. . . .

It is amazing that Mrs. Chambers was not on the list of dead. And it is ironic that she was in the hotel at all the night of March 20.

"I was the day clerk, you know, and I worked my shift," she told a visitor. "It ended at 6 o'clock, but the woman who worked at night was a crippled woman (Mrs. Lula Vossos, who leased the hotel).

"She asked if I could take it over for her that night because she couldn't. She was about halfway crying, and she said, 'Grace, will you stay?' And so I stayed . . ."

She "closed up" at 11 p.m., locked the elevator at the second floor, slipped a large brown envelope with the day's money and paperwork under Mrs. Vossos' door and retired to a vacant room, 211.

The last sound she heard, before flames engulfed the hotel 3½ hours later, was a tenant on the second floor.

"I talked to the man when he came in. He was, you know, inebriated, but he wasn't a man who was drunk all the time or anything. Then I heard him say to the man next door, 'Wake up, Bud, it's your neighbor.' He perished, poor man."

When the arson fire erupted, Mrs. Chambers grabbed her heavy, leather purse, made her way to the window through dense smoke and broke the glass with her purse. She then tossed the purse to the ground, where it apparently was stolen.

"I could feel the fire coming up behind me," she said. "I had my head out the window, and I was all smoked up, but I could see the police, the fire trucks and the ambulance . . . I could see the ladders running up, and I can remember reaching, reaching.

"Then I felt the boards going out under my feet, and I was reaching out trying to get hold of that ladder . . ."

That is the last thing she remembers. In severe pain from the flames, she either jumped or fell through the window. One fire fighter recalls being struck in the head by Mrs. Chambers' foot as she fell.

(Three deleted paragraphs contained Mrs. Chambers' comments about the hotel and previous fires)

Today, slowly healing from the burns, surgery and cuts, Mrs. Chambers sits in her hospital room, thinking about the fire. Friends from the hotel visit, and doctors, nurses and interns wave cheerful greetings as they pass in the hall.

Each morning she is taken to therapy. . . .

"Oh, I just hope I'll walk . . ."

Does she have plans for the future—after release from the hospital?

Mrs. Chambers hesitated.

"All I want to do is live. Just live."

IV. Critical Questions

1. Would you prefer "Fire Marshal Stephen MacPherson said" to "Fire Marshal Stephen MacPherson told The Post-Intelligencer" in the third paragraph of the main story about the Seattle hotel fire?
2. Do you object to the idiomatic usage "died from burns" in the 15th paragraph of the news sidebar on the Seattle hotel fire story? Was an unnecessary word used in the expression "on Oct. 17, 1929" in the last paragraph of the same story?
3. Could the placement of attribution have been improved in the first two paragraphs of the story on the Kentucky teachers' strike?
4. Have you any objection to the use of the word "decimated" in the first paragraph of the Wichita State University sidebar written by the Associated Press?

Chapter 19

THE COLOR STORY

*Bright is the ring of words
When the right man rings them.*
—*Robert Louis Stevenson*

The color story attempts to depict the psychological and physical environment surrounding certain occasions and special events. The writer's job is to blend realistic and picturesque detail into a total picture or impression.

The occasion may be a parade, a festival, a celebration, a circus or almost any suitable event. Crowds are usually involved, but not necessarily so. The story might depict a particular setting, such as Arlington Cemetery on Christmas Eve.

Color, as it is used in this sense, means vivid, lively description. Many types of articles contain some color, but the principal purpose of the color story is to capture the atmosphere of a particular occasion.

Writing the Color Story

The color story is one of the most difficult types of journalism to write. It is one thing to record facts, quite another to report on observations, particularly when the scene is conglomerate.

A sports writer, for example, may be assigned to cover a football game. His concentration, he well knows, must be placed on a contest between two teams. If he is alert to his surroundings and if the occasion warrants it, he may inject some color into his story, as these paragraphs demonstrate:

> As Kelly squatted to receive the ball and Jorgenson stood poised for the field goal attempt, a hush descended over the thousands of partisan spectators.
> Then came the pass from center, the kick—it was good.
> The crowd suddenly turned into a shouting, screaming, arm-waving mass of delirious fans.

Suppose, however, that the game represented a strong, traditional rivalry, and that a city editor decided to assign a reporter to write a color story. The color story would then be a related story that would concentrate on the prevailing atmosphere rather than on the contest, except to tell how individual plays affected the attitudes of the spectators. The score would probably be repeated in the color story, but the description of the fight between the two teams would be left to the sports story writer.

The color story writer presents a point of view, but that point of view should indicate what any attentive person would have observed had he been in the same place. The reporter appeals imaginatively to the reader's senses.

Visually, he would describe such things as colored banners, paper streamers, card stunts, pompom girls, colorful apparel worn by any of the spectators, and any unusual cavorting in the bleachers.

An auditory appeal could be made by describing the cheers, boos, gasps, shouts and roars of the crowd and the catcalls of individuals. An individual description might be:

> One man kept blowing a trumpet intermittently. At times it sounded in single blasts and at other times, when the crowd was exploding, it only added to the deafening din.

The smell of popcorn, hot dogs and coffee might permeate the air.

The fans might feel hot, as indicated by perspiring brows, removed coats and men in shirt sleeves, or they might feel cold, as revealed by earmuffs, overcoats and blankets.

It is the little things carefully put together to create an impression which make the color story interesting.

A reporter does not use imagination to fabricate or distort a story, but he often uses imaginative writing to make his presentation more interesting. Some excerpts from a Chicago *Sun-Times* story by Bob Green describing the 94th-floor observation deck of the new John Hancock Center illustrate the use of imaginative writing:

But Thursday morning it [the observation deck] was almost empty—there were only a few security guards and workmen doing last-minute duties—and a walk around the deck was like a *private 60-second stroll across the rooftops of Chicago.*

That's all the time it takes, really, if you want to do it fast. The floor area is more than one-third of an acre, and it's all carpeted and the deck is softly lighted. The huge windows are spotless, and if you start at one point and walk very quickly around in a big circle, you see all of Chicago in a minute. When it's nice out, you get parts of Indiana, Michigan and Wisconsin, too.

Up to the north, the Outer Drive *squirms* toward the suburbs, and the tall apartment buildings *scratch* the air. To the west, the flat, dark land goes on forever. The south is the *dazzling clump* of offices in the Loop, and miles of *drearier* buildings after that. The east is the lake, more of it than you can imagine.

(Reprinted with permission from the Chicago *Sun-Times*)

Used with restraint, figurative language such as that italicized above helps to make the color story more interesting.

Special events may be reported in typical news story fashion or they may be detailed in color stories, depending, in part, on how much emphasis and space are considered appropriate.

A parade is reported in news story style in the following Atlanta *Constitution* article. The first four or five paragraphs would receive considerable elaboration in a color story.

A pleasant, 30-minute parade down Peachtree Street entertained a chilly, windswept crowd Monday night to cap the first day of Atlanta's Dogwood Festival.

The parade leaned on traditional favorites with a complement of pretty girls, brass bands, floats, decorated trucks and cars.

More than the usual number of police were dotted along the route, but there were no incidents.

Bands from Hillcrest High School in Memphis, Tenn., and marchers from Litton's Music City from Nashville added a regional flair while local participants included the Gordon High School Band, Atlanta Public Library bookmobiles, the U.S. Post Office and Atlanta Fire department.

As in all parades, the kids under 10 and over 60 enjoyed the excitement more than anyone else and they were quick to applaud each unit that passed.

Featured personalities in for the twilight event included Vicki Lynn, festival queen, Miss U.S.A. (Wendy Dascomb) and James MacArthur, star of Hawaii Five-O.

Earlier Monday, the weeklong festival began on a holiday note as 1,959 gaily colored balloons sailed into bright spring skies from downtown Atlanta while the Third Army Band played "Up, Up and Away."

The annual festival, titled "Atlanta's Many Splendored Spring" this year, attracted Gov. Lester Maddox, who declared, "This is going to be a week to remember." Maddox joked and signed autographs on the sun-splashed sidewalks.

Mayor Sam Massell was scheduled to be one of the speakers at the noon ceremonies but was unable to attend due to negotiations going on over the garbage workers' strike.

The Dogwood Festival, which continues through the week, is sponsored by the Atlanta Women's Chamber of Commerce.

(Reprinted from the Atlanta *Constitution*)

The story is more factual than descriptive. It tells what took place but does not give the observations of the writer in the same way a color story does.

It is far simpler to report sequential events, such as parades, than it is to picture them in color stories. The writer of the color story must be free to select particulars and details just as a painter must be free to choose his colors.

It would be difficult to try to describe all the sequences—space would hardly permit it—and the question arises of whether it is better to describe a few of the highlights or simply to report what took place.

Length is not a prerequisite of the color story. The following Chicago *Tribune* article, though compact, provides a sharp contrast to the preceding example.

It wasn't exactly spring yesterday, but for 13 days before Christmas, it was a beautiful day for shopping.

Some people, at least those on the sunny side of the street, got the full benefit of above-normal temperature. Many donned sun glasses and opened their coats as the mercury reached into the 50s.

"I really hate shopping; I should have done this in August," said one man who was gift hunting in the Loop. "But at least it's a nice day."

It was a day when lone male shoppers wandered about department stores with an air of confusion and uncertainty.

Mrs. Helen Czaja took advantage of her husband's day off work and each of them toted large shopping bags. After 3½ hours, they had had enough.

"But I didn't get everything. I'll have to make a couple more trips," she said.

A steady stream of inquiries kept Mrs. Lee Elgin busy in one department store information booth. Where, customers wanted to know, could they find adult games, ladies' billfolds, costume jewelry, electric lather dispensers, music boxes.

"Music boxes drive me crazy," said Mrs. Elgin. "We have them in three different places."

On the crowded sidewalks, Salvation Army singers urged passers-by to "smile to make us happy . . . give now and then."

Groups of school children had a day to remember. Twenty-five kindergarten boys and girls from the Dumas school, 6650 Ellis Av., and 70 1st graders from the Anderson school, 1148 N. Monroe st., came downtown for lunch and talked to a department store Santa Claus.

The Santa Claus at the corner of State and Randolph streets noted that yesterday was "the best so far and it's going to get better."

Not everyone was buying, however. There was not a desperation, now or never, atmosphere yet.

Some people looked and still could not make up their minds.

One woman sprayed her hands with six different men's colognes, sniffed long and hard, and finally walked away without making a purchase.

(Reprinted by permission of the Chicago *Tribune*)

The writer of the Peachtree Parade story told what took place—listed the sequences of the event. The writer of the preceding story selected details and put them together in such a way as to give an overall impression of busy shoppers going about their chores on a pleasant day about two weeks before Christmas.

The writer of the color story does not rely wholly on adjectives to describe his observations. Verbs are the most effective agents in describing actions; incidents and examples help to complete the impression; and utterances portray human reactions.

The next to the last paragraph in the foregoing article says some shoppers "could not make up their minds," and the incident cited in the last paragraph vivifies that part of the overall picture.

Special Events

There are many special events for which color stories can be written. In the following New York *Daily News* story by Jean Crafton, it is backstage before the opening of the Metropolitan Opera season.

White and yellow-robed priests sip soup from cardboard containers. Robert Merrill and Richard Tucker clown it up for a photographer in Tucker's dressing room. From the stage, the sounds of hammering and of machines moving scenery depicting Egyptian temples, palaces and tombs mix with the shouts of stagehands. White-clad slave women munch Christmas goodies.

When the business is opera and there are only 15 days between first rehearsal and opening night, it's comforting to know that the production's an old standby like "Aida."

As soon as the Metropolitan Opera and its unions settled their differences two weeks ago, the cast, production crew and all the behind-the-scenes people who make an opera work set about their business to prepare the opera for tonight's opening.

Almost everybody already knew his job. The main problem was getting it coordinated and timed . . . a task that fell largely to director Nat Merrill.

Merrill's the man in the blue-green turtleneck. It's just a few hours before final dress rehearsal and he's a little upset because the weather has kept so much of the chorus away. But he's obviously trying to make the best of it, and the thinness of the chorus doesn't keep him from paying close attention to detail.

"Slaves, huddle close together. No mingling with the priests!" The direction is shouted to the right of the stage where men and women dressed in unglamorous cold-weather gear are standing on a flight of steps.

"Remember, you're waiting for a parade," Merrill explains to the people on the left of the stage. "You've been standing out here two hours waiting and you're craning your necks, wondering why the parade doesn't come."

A piano to the right of the stage tinkles out the triumphal march from the second act, and the beginning of the parade marches onstage between huge columns at the rear. They come to the front of the stage where they give out with a mighty "Gloria Egitto." That's as far as they get. Merrill raises both hands to stop them.

He calls out more directions, among them the exact position for holding the hands "with no thumbs sticking out." The chorus goes back to where it started, Merrill walking with them, talking all the while.

He demonstrates how he wants them to march, keeping time by humming the opening bars. The piano comes in. It doesn't really look much like opera with the lack of orchestra, costumes, lighting. But Merrill doesn't seem concerned.

Neither does the cast. At one point, where Merrill talks with the small group to the left, Ray Michalski, a member of the alternate cast, bursts into "I've been working on the railroad." Occasionally the chatter among the cast gets so loud that an assistant stage manager claps his hands and shouts "Quiet, please."

The stars of a production like "Aida" (in this case, Leontyne Price, Robert Merrill, Tucker and Irene Dalis) are the least cause of concern, since the work is so frequently performed by them.

Most of the extras in this production are experienced in their roles, too. John Birkner of Queens, who works for International Paper Co., is playing the part of a priest.

"I've been in every 'Aida' performance for the last ten years," he said, adjusting the plastic skull cap which makes it look as if his head is shaved.

It's dark backstage and a person has to watch closely to

keep from barking his shins on props. At a console, members of the production crew stare at two closed-circuit television screens—one trained on the stage, the other on the orchestra pit.

A voice over an intercom announces "The curtain rises in exactly eight minutes." The 1969 opera season is about to begin.

(Courtesy of the New York *News*)

The writer wove minutiae into a single piece of tapestry to leave the reader with an image. Of the many particulars and details available for selection, the writer chose those which would best give the total picture.

A rock festival is the subject of the following Miami *Herald* color story by Jay Maeder.

BITHLO, Fla.—Much to the astonishment of even the staunchest believers, the Easter rock festival here was back on its feet Saturday night.

Sheriff's deputies had predicted early Saturday that the festival, still wallowing in attempts to get moving, would quietly collapse all by itself.

But after the late afternoon go-ahead, a handful of rock bands from around the state were brought out on stage, rallying some 12,000 or 15,000 fans who were becoming visibly disappointed that none of the advertised headliners, including Grand Funk Railroad, the Grateful Dead, and Canned Heat, were present at the sprawling be-in here in the heart of Central Florida's ranch country.

By early evening the caravan of returning and newly arrived vehicles was such that state troopers sealed off the festival site. The young people parked their cars, campers, and motorcycles alongside State Road 520 as far away as two miles from the grounds.

Visitors to the festival took to hiking cross-country over barbed wire fencing and through shallow marshland to reach the stage area.

Though the festival is projected to run through Tuesday, major attractions remain tentatively scheduled for today. They include blues singer Johnny Winter, according to most reports, and there was a possibility that Britisher John Mayall would appear.

And despite earlier reports that rock superstar Bob Dylan had definitely dropped his plans to perform, a fresh wave of rumor swept the grounds late in the evening that Dylan would show up after all.

The county's reprieve saved the widely publicized festival, at least for the time being, from becoming an extravagant failure, musically speaking.

Young men and women of assorted degrees of freakiness, hitchhiking to Bithlo from Miami and Fort Lauderdale, were stranded here and there along the highways that border Lake Okeechobee, where real live longhairs are seldom seen. The local residents were having themselves a good old time.

"Hey hoe-head," comes a call from a passing truck. "Your barber die?"

"Come on, pretty boy, smile for us one time."

"Oh, 'scuse us, we thought you was a boy, lady."

"I thought we'd never get out of here," sighed Bonnie and Pat to the motorist who stops for the girls and their boyfriends. "This is really traumatic."

"I hope it gets better farther upstate," says one of the youths. "What's the name of the place again?"

"Bithlo, for God's sake," says Bonnie. "Sounds like some disease that cattle get."

A pair of Orange County deputies stand quietly at the second ticket checkpoint, politely declining to discuss with newsmen whatever special instructions they had, and past their station no officers go. In the great inner pasture, beyond the final checkpoint, dope is a taken-for-granted presence. Strange men will materialize beside one in the darkness:

"Jamaican grass, man, good stuff."

"Want to score a little hash?"

"Need downers?"

One forlorn young man, hair trimmed short and dressed in conventional clothing, tries desperately all night to score a nickel bag from someone; since he comes on precisely like one would somehow expect a narc to come on—self-consciously hip and too well scrubbed for credibility—he encounters shrugs and blank gazes instead. "I'm not The Man," he pleads repeatedly. "Really I'm not."

Vehicles continued to arrive throughout the night, cautiously and quietly, considerate of the sleepers in their lean-tos at either side of the cold roadway. Others are huddled in their small, foreign-built roadsters, still others share the seats of converted school buses. Figures are wrapped in sleeping bags atop car roofs, beneath wheel wells, between rows of tents, on the banks of drainage ditches, in the soft straw with the horses.

"I'd guess we're equipped here to handle anything up to major surgery," says Dr. Tom Kelly of Miami's Jackson Memorial Hospital, who, in 24 hours, has outfitted a complete field hospital. Dr. Kelly, along with two other physicians and a team of seven nurses, was dealing primarily with sunburn and drug overdosage and bare feet slashed by broken glass. "I think it's going to be a really beautiful scene," says Rosie, a nurse. "With any crowd of this size you'd normally expect something to happen, broken bones or something, but things have been really peaceful. I think it's going to stay like that, too."

Members of a Lauderdale commune are standing watch over the trippers who have dropped injudicious combinations of chemical agents. "We go over and check on them once in a while," Rosie says. "It's really no problem."

The existing medical facilities are sufficient to handle childbirth as well, Dr. Kelly points out. By Saturday, the only new arrivals are those delivered to a nondescript dog; she had been assisted in her labors by her masters and mistresses, who diverted pedestrian traffic around her.

The sun is up now, and the festival site awakens. "Good morning everyone!" sings the girl who is peddling fresh oranges and grapes from her station wagon. "Breakfast!"

Her oranges cost 25 cents. A young man, perhaps 15, stands back from the stall and grins sheepishly. "I don't have a quarter," he explains.

"My goodness," she smiles and tosses an orange toward him. "Enjoy your breakfast. Vitamin C is very good for you."

At the rear of the ranch, the Hog Farm has set up a free kitchen, dispensing bulk quantities of raisins, bananas, and raw carrots to all who are hungry, with a splendid disregard for fables such as the one about the grasshopper and the ant. The hog farmer, a shirtless man with a thick mane of hair and scholarly hornrimmed glasses, administers the program in no-nonsense and imperious fashion. "All right," he addresses himself to a lad whose stay at the raisin bin has become rather lengthy, "We have a lot of people to feed today, you know?" To another, who has asked for hot water to add to a dry oat and nut mixture: "You don't need water, my good fellow. You eat that just the way it is."

The multitudes begin to gather at the great wooden stage, still under construction. Many have spent the night here in order to hold on to a ringside seat; a couple in a sleeping bag stretch and yawn and bid good morning to their immediate neighbors and begin to make love.

"Oh wow," remembers Pat, stretched out on her muddy blanket. "I had this really groovy flash when I opened my eyes this morning. I mean, I looked out and all I could see were millions of freaks. Freaks as far as you can see. Out of sight."

(Reprinted from the Miami *Herald*)

Blending description, incidents and quotations, the story portrays the festival scene in a single picture.

A reporter must be alert and observant to write a story like the preceding one. Many spots were covered, including the festival site, routes of access, the fields across which visitors hiked, the sheriff's checkpoints and a field hospital.

Capturing the Mood

To the extent that a writer can, he should try to capture the prevailing mood and, by careful word selection, convey it to the reader.

A UPI writer attempted to do this in an article written after the first human beings landed on the moon:

SPACE CENTER, Houston—You sat there and watched man step into his own dream. The silent footfall on the airless moon that was the leap of ages. You sat and saw a corner-turning in the human saga.

Man left his footprints on the sands of space, and a great portion of the world sat and watched with you as the television eye stared at the audacity of the bootmarks of a civilian from Ohio and a colonel from New Jersey signing in on the register of the lunar soil.

After a million years of dreaming, guessing, wondering, wishing, questing in the mind for the impossible visit, feeling the urge of the unknown sky above, humankind had gained a toehold on the heavens.

Those two make it seem too easy. Like Joe DiMaggio in centerfield. The mark of the pro. The first moon tourists were humble. They realized, with a terrible start when the President called them, what was happening to them and to their fellow men.

Who can forget the great emotion obvious in the midwest twang of Neil Armstrong's voice when he answered President Nixon? The tremble when he spoke of "the honor for us to be able to participate today" was that of a man in high emotional stress.

But otherwise they were unbelievably eager, like kids in a schoolroom when the lesson is a stimulus. They hopped. They took their own pictures standing beside the Stars and Stripes. They romped, pranced in the elegant state of one-sixth gravity, invented a new dance of sorts which may be named the lunar hop.

They cavorted from nowhere into the middle of the television tube, like men buoyed by attachment to a rubber band strung above them.

And it must be said that after a good deal of wonderment on the part of many observers prior to the Apollo 11 flight whether Armstrong's rhetoric, when he planted a timid foot on soil truly foreign to life as known on earth, would come up to the occasion at hand—well, as they say around Wapakoneta, he done right noble with "one small step for a man—one giant leap for mankind."

He spoke it good and plain, too. For a first-class flying man, he did well in his first feature-length television show.

And as for mastery of flight, you began to realize as you looked at the absolutely level terrain when he did the panoramic shots with the television camera that you were witnessing the culmination of one of the greatest pieces of piloting ever achieved. A lesser pilot could have dumped the whole shot into the nasty situation of the crater that Armstrong avoided with the skill of his hand and brain.

From the time when the loudspeakers in a myriad of living rooms carried Armstrong's assured voice—before the camera was in use—announcing "Okay, Houston, I'm on the porch," it was obvious that a moment of history was well in hand. And in a miracle of technology, you were there.

The first picture live from the moon was upside down, and this was appropriate. Man's conventional world was getting the same treatment.

The memories . . . memories . . . memories.

The shadow of the first picture, ghostlike as if not quite true, of Neil descending the ladder. The first bounding steps, slow bounds like a man in a dream, or like an old-fashioned movie being run at funny speed.

His guiding of Buzz Aldrin down the ladder. His joyous call to Buzz when Aldrin took his first steps: "Isn't that something?"

The reverent tone of Armstrong's voice when he uncovered the module plaque and read: "We came in peace for all mankind."

The story was written in a heightened style—much connotation, figurative language, sentence variation, comparison—not suitable for many lesser events but appropriate to the occasion. The significance of the event justifies the writer's use of embellishment. Certainly the story captured the mood of many who watched the moon walk on television. And the author chose a particularly effective ending.

How do you capture a mood? First you must feel it yourself, and then you must find the right words with which to express it.

EXERCISES

I. Questions for Discussion

1. Why is the color story one of the most difficult types of journalism to write?
2. Why might a city editor prefer a news story about a parade to a color story?
3. How much time do you estimate was needed to gather the information for the Easter rock festival story?
4. Does the use of the present tense in the Easter rock festival story add to its effectiveness?
5. Do you consider the story about man's first landing on the moon to be subjective?

II. Assignments

1. Compile a list of words that imaginatively appeal to the senses.
2. Write down the topics of at least six local color stories you feel you could write.

3. Write a color story based on one of the following:
    a. An athletic event
    b. Backstage before a college theatrical production
    c. A parade, march or demonstration
    d. A balmy day on campus
    e. A day at the zoo.

III. Critical Questions

1. Would the word "persons" have been better than "people" in the seventh paragraph of the story about being backstage at the Metropolitan Opera?
2. Should such expressions as "nickel bag," "narc" and "The Man" have been explained in the Easter rock festival story?
3. Is the expression "in order to" redundant in the next to last paragraph of the same story?
4. Would you have preferred the word "put" to the word "planted" in the expression "planted a timid foot" in the eighth paragraph of the story about the first moon landing?

Chapter 20

ETHICAL AND LEGAL CONSIDERATIONS

God make our blunders wise.
—*Vachel Lindsay*

Ask a city editor, a journalism professor or a veteran newsman what the qualifications for a good reporter are and you will get many answers. Alertness, inquisitiveness, intelligence, judgment, resourcefulness, a nose for news, thoroughness—these are only a few of the many qualifications that may be listed.

These are important attributes, but they apply mainly to capability. Certainly integrity and independence are two prime requisites.

Integrity

Many journalists argue that complete objectivity does not exist in reporting the news. Reporters, it is pointed out, cannot include all the facts in any one news story. The newsman must therefore decide on what to include and what to omit.

The good reporter makes his selection of what to include honestly, using public interest as a guideline. He leans over backward to make sure that he is fair in his selection and presentation of information.

A so-called newsman who distorts the news out of self-motivation is no better than a quack in medicine, a shyster in law or a fraud in business.

The good reporter always remembers that there is more than one side to every question and that it is shabby reporting to give a one-sided view of a controversial issue. He also remembers that any man in public life who is accused of inefficiency or misconduct in office should be given an opportunity for rebuttal.

Controversy should be reported only when it is of public interest. The newsman should ignore personal squabbles and should always be on guard against the publicity seeker or the person with an axe to grind.

Independence

The newsman should be independent in his thinking and in his actions. He should be neither subservient nor suppliant to any person or group. Two of the risks to independence arise from affiliations and gratuities.

The question a newsman should always ask himself when he is invited to join an organization is whether the bid was prompted because of his personal qualities or because of his connection with a newspaper. If by joining a group he would lose any of his independence, he should not make the affiliation. Some groups seek newspapermen as members in the hope of getting more publicity.

Obviously, a reporter may be a member of a political party without jeopardizing his independence. It should not blunt his sense of fairness in writing a political story. If it does, he should be assigned to news coverage other than politics.

An important question rises, however. How active should he become in a party? It would seem that if he became a member of a state central committee his value as a political reporter might be impaired. Even if he were a paragon of fairness, as a journalist he would certainly invite distrust from persons belonging to other parties.

Similarly, it would seem unwise for a reporter to become a member of a publicity committee for any type of organization. Serving in such a capacity, how could he maintain that he would provide equality of treatment for all organizations?

One of the potential perverters of reportorial independence is the man bearing gifts. To what extent can a human being accept gifts without feeling some obligation?

J. R. Wiggins, when he was executive editor of the Washington *Post* and the *Times-Herald,* was a longtime disbeliever in gratuities. In the August 1, 1958, issue of the *Bulletin* of the American Society of Newspaper Editors, he wrote:

> The flocks of reporters who descend upon press conference cocktail party functions to munch the buffet and partake of the drinks undoubtedly persuade some envious folk into believing this is a piece of free loading. The non-professional onlooker can hardly know that nine out of ten of the reporters would a great deal sooner do their eating and drinking under more pleasant circumstances. It would be a pleasure to get the story straight, the press conference unadorned, the publicity pitch on the line, without the gustatory adornments that press agents seem to think make even bad news palatable. . . .
> Gifts and gratuities are open to reproach, where newspapermen are involved, not only on the moral and ethical grounds that concern many others, but they are objectionable because they impair either the objectivity or the appearance of objectivity in the press.
> We may be as indifferent to the persuasions of personal gifts as Carrie Nation was to the temptation of the demon rum, but still be a long way from impartiality and objectivity. Besides being a newspaperman, each of us is an individual person with a private as well as a public life. Each of us has friends who influence us and shape our judgments and appraisals. Each of us has affiliations, formal or otherwise, that lay claims upon our loyalties and inspire our dislikes. . . . The "gifts," in some ways, may be less of a menace to our objectivity and impartiality, than some other factors in the environment. Whatever their relative importance, among all the springs of bias, they have the quality of being tangible, physical and accessible. We cannot get rid of all the things that make us something less than deserving of the appellation "Fourth Estate." We can get rid of the gifts and favors and gratuities. They may not be big enough to buy our favor; but they are big enough to make a lot . . . think our favor can be bought.

Some editors would take into consideration whether passes and free meals and drinks should be accepted by the working press, meaning those involved in immediate coverage, or by other reporters.

Others would take into consideration the value of the gift. Many would point to the embarrassment of refusing to accept token gifts. Most agree that it would be a rare reporter who would be influenced by a necktie, a bottle of liquor or a meal. The ethical implications, however, are still present.

It is easier, in many respects, for a reporter to maintain independence in a large city than in a smaller one. In a large city, a reporter can walk the streets, go into a restaurant, or attend a meeting with relative anonymity. That is not true in a smaller community, where everyone knows almost everyone else. The pressure of wide acquaintance and practically no anonymity can at times provide a test of independence.

Coercion

How far should a reporter go in attempting to extract information from a reluctant news source? The question is difficult to answer without resorting to specific cases, but some generalizations can be made.

Intimidation, generally speaking, should not be resorted to. A reporter would be acting anything but professionally, for example, if he intimated that his newspaper is a powerful force in the community and that, if someone was not about to cooperate, he would be treated unfavorably in future news stories. Any threat of reprisal or retaliation should be strictly avoided.

There is a difference between coercion and persuasion. Depending on the circumstances, a reporter might say:

> You're only hurting yourself by refusing to talk. The other side is talking plenty and all you're doing by remaining silent is forcing us to say that, when asked about the matter, you refused to comment.

Or, if the occasion warranted it, the reporter might say:

> You have a lot to gain by speaking openly and frankly. You know some of the rumors that have been going around and the kind of insinuations being made. An honest statement from you could do a lot to help clarify the matter.

Deceitful methods of getting people to talk are ill advised. The following kind of persuasion is valid, if true:

> We already have some information from other sources. We'll have to base our story on it if you refuse to talk. It's rather negative. It would probably be a better story as far as you're concerned if you'd tell me what you know about the matter.

If the comment is not true, it is not only an unethical way of eliciting information, but it may also prove to be a boomerang—the person being questioned, if he fails to fall for the gag, will eventually learn that the reporter lied and his respect for all reporters may diminish as a result.

Baiting news sources is a questionable means of getting persons to talk. Baiting is the practice of using provocative statements to arouse the anger of the person being questioned and thus, by upsetting his emotional balance, getting him to say things he ordinarily would not want repeated. This comment is baiting:

> They may tell you to your face what a smart guy you are but that's not what they say when your back is turned.

A far better way to get people to talk is to win their confidence.

Reporter Identification

A reporter should identify himself on approaching a news source unless he has justifiable reasons for doing otherwise. Even in investigative reporting, identification does not always interfere with collecting information.

There is a considerable difference between concealed identification, which is sometimes practiced, and false identification.

Suppose a reporter should sleep for several nights in different flop houses to get first-hand information on existing conditions. He probably would not reveal his identification. The flop houses are public, however, in that for a fee they are open to anyone as long as all the beds have not been taken. Failure to disclose identification would hardly seem to be a breach of ethics in such a case.

Similarly, it would not be unethical for a reporter investigating a lax enforcement of gambling laws to visit, without identifying himself, places where gaming was taking place to get first-hand information.

Quite different would be a case in which a reporter disguised himself to gain admission to a private affair.

Likewise, a case would be different in which a reporter disguised himself, with police cooperation, as a jail inmate to seek information from a man being held as a suspect. Both the reporter and the law enforcement officials would seem to be violating the civil rights of an individual.

Obviously, it would be dishonest for a reporter to misrepresent himself as a public official to elicit information or for him to pose as a representative of a school system to get certain data from parents.

Eavesdropping

A reporter has the right of access to public records and the right of admission to public meetings. He does not have the right of admission to private meetings. For him to eavesdrop to get information about what takes place at a private meeting would be ethically questionable.

For a reporter to tread on private property to eavesdrop would be not only unethical but also illegal.

Does a reporter have the right to take a room in a hotel to eavesdrop on a private meeting in an adjoining room? He has a legal right as long as he does not use "bugging" devices. But what about the ethics?

If the meeting is not in the domain of public interest, it would seem to be a violation of privacy. If a reporter knows a meeting is for conspiratorial or illegal purposes, the answer would be different.[1]

News Policy

In an effort to set common standards for the handling of some kinds of news, newspapers adopt news policies. Should a set procedure, for instance, be followed in the handling of all drunken driving cases or should each case be handled individually?

Many newspapers have adopted a policy of not using the names of women who are raped. The reasons are many. Rape victims, fearing publicity, frequently refuse to make reports to the police. Stories that list names sometimes unintentionally injure innocent persons. A school teacher, in one instance, quit her job and left a community because of publicity.

Many newspapers have adopted policies on the use of the names of juveniles involved in crimes and on racial identification in crime stories.

Juvenile Offenders   Should the names of juvenile delinquents be printed when the offense is less than murder? Some states have legal restrictions but in those that do not the question today is under considerable debate.

In the 1940s and the early 1950s most newspapers had the policy of not printing the names, at least those of first-time offenders. By the late 1950s some editors as well as law enforcement officials began to question the policy.

A 1960 study by Walter Steigleman and Paul Jess indicated that during the previous five years there had been a definite tendency for more newspapers to print the names of juvenile offenders.[2]

The August 1957 issue of the publication of the United Press editors of Pennsylvania carried the following letter from Theodore Gress of the Lebanon (Pa.) *Daily News:*

---

[1] See Ira Lurvey, "Some Say It's Good Reporting: Others Call It Eavesdropping," *The Quill,* Nov., 1958, pp. 9–10, and "Eavesdropping Story Debated in New York," *Editor & Publisher,* June 26, 1965, p. 49.
[2] *Journalism Quarterly,* Summer, 1960, pp. 393–397.

> It long has been the contention of the Lebanon Daily News that publishing the names of juvenile delinquents is a constructive means of curbing hell-raising among the younger set.
>
> It is a policy, I must admit, that has met with some resistance. We expected this, of course, from the parents. But we were taken back by the bitter denunciation we received at some state and national newspaper sessions.
>
> Recent years, however, have seen many papers coming around to our way of thinking.
>
> The policy, as evolved by the Lebanon Daily news, is based on what we consider logic.
>
> Publication of the names of youths involved in minor crimes does not hurt the culprits. What it does do is point the finger of shame at the parents, which is what we want. If the parents would take more interest and show more concern over the doings and the whereabouts of their offspring they would be less likely to stray.
>
> Typical example was the woman who stormed into our office one day and gave me merry hell for publishing the name of her son in connection with some minor crime.
>
> Did she worry about the boy? Not one bit. Her chief complaint was that the story embarrassed her in front of the other women at the factory where she worked.
>
> To us, this was the perfect complaint. It proved our point. . . .

A California publisher who changed his policy in 1961 stated that he expected a barrage of protests. Of 50 telephone calls received, he said that two protested and 48 lauded his policy change.

The following comment is taken from an editorial in another California newspaper that announced in 1967 that it would thereafter use the names of juvenile delinquents.

> There is growing belief in many quarters, both in California and other states, that the publicizing of the names of juvenile wrong-doers may prove helpful as a deterrent to crime at lower age levels. It is contended that immunity from exposure for young lawbreakers breeds more contempt for the law and encourages them in wrongful acts damaging to innocent persons and the public property and welfare.

The principal objection usually given to printing the names of juvenile offenders was that the publicity made the task of correction and rehabilitation more difficult.

Two of the most common arguments for printing the names are that parents are often the really delinquent ones (and are seeking protection) and that juveniles, knowing they are protected from publicity, have no compunction about repeating their offenses.

Racial Identification Some division of opinion exists on the use of racial identification in news stories. The great majority of newspapers in the northern part of the United States do not use racial identification in news stories unless it is pertinent to the story.

The same practice is not necessarily true of southern newspapers.

The major press associations, which provide service to newspapers all over the country, have had some difficulty in pleasing all editors. The joint AP and UPI stylebook published in 1968 simply states: "Identification by race should be made when it is pertinent."

Although the greatest objection has probably come from the identification of Negroes, others are involved, including Mexicans, Indians, Japanese and Chinese.

A letter sent to the UPI by a Midwestern editor stated in part:

> My main concern as an editor is helping the reader. I believe the reader should be armed with every possible fact when he reads my paper or any other paper. The fact that a man is a Negro, or Mongolian, or white, is significant to a story. Negroes don't object to being identified in stories as a rule, I'm sure. They certainly don't object to being so labeled when they win Nobel prizes, carry home Olympic medals, win championship fights, write great books, etc. By the same token, they shouldn't mind being labeled Negroes in relation to crime news.
>
> Let's either be consistent with use of the word Negro or eliminate it. I'd vote for the former.
>
> Actually, I believe the U.S. Marine Corps has a better arguing point than Negroes. I'm sick of the stories which always identify ex-marines.
> . . .

Earl J. Johnson, when he was editor of the UPI, answered in the Dec. 31, 1964, UPI *Reporter* by quoting from a directive from one of the organization's service logs:

> We have a general policy of not stating the race, color or creed of a principal in a story unless there is a reason for it. . . . In a number of instances where we make such references they may be obvious in one section of the country while seemingly unrelated in others.
>
> For example, in the case of a man who recently rescued a child from drowning in the East we identified the hero as a Negro at the request of a Midwestern newspaper which has a large Negro readership among its circulation. To others, the identification may have seemed unnecessary.
>
> Where a crime has been committed, there seems to be no question that identification of a wanted suspect as black, white or yellow is as much a part of his description as whether he is short or tall, fat or slim.

The AP *Log* of January 10–16, 1963, ran a condensation of an article written by Franklin K. Arthur, chief of the New York bureau, for the bulletin of the New York State Society of Newspaper Editors. It read:

> This is a southern editor speaking: "I don't care particularly how other newspapers handle these stories with a racial angle, but I do know what our readers expect of us in reporting them. We therefore ask that (even parenthetically) the race angle be made perfectly clear. . . ." And this is a northern editor: "I realize that you have in your membership some editors who will play a story one way if the protagonists are white and another if they are black, but I see no need to accommodate such bias. It seems to me this kind of identification caters to discrimination."
>
> So, what is AP practice? It was defined this way some years ago in the AP Reference Book: "The practice is to name a person's race whenever such identification is pertinent to the story. It is important to remember that in some sections racial identifications affect story values." That definition hasn't changed.
>
> So, what is pertinent? There can be little argument in some cases: a race riot, a cross burning or window busting when a Negro family moves into a white neighborhood. . . . But the AP has not yet been able to come up with a solution that makes everybody happy on borderline stories. On many papers, particularly in the South, a name is assumed to be white unless identified otherwise. On many others, notably in the North, the tendency is to identify rarely, sometimes not at all. Several New York papers skip racial identification as a matter of practice. . . .
>
> It would be simpler if the only problem were to please northern and/or southern editors. But there are other groups at work—the NAACP, the Anti-Defamation League, the Commission on Human Relations, and one which may not be familiar, the All-America Union. The All-America Union protested because in six stories we identified the principals as Negroes—even though each story reflected credit on the Negro or Negroes involved. Calling American citizens Negroes, said the group's president, "is a fraud and a deception against all Americans of African descent." He said Negro is a derogatory nickname like coon or darky.

Although not acceptable to everyone, a fair policy, it seems, would be to use racial identification only when it is significant and helps to clarify a story.

News by Association   A criticism, not new, but being voiced louder today, is what may be called news by association. It is the ascribing of more significance than would usually be accorded a person involved in the news because that person's name is connected with a prominent person. The relationship may extend beyond the immediate family; sometimes it involves a rather remote association. The objection stems particularly from stories involving arrests and court actions.

In 1959, a baseball star's son was arrested and wire stories carried the star's name in identifying the youth. The baseball star had been active in organizing youth groups and in striving for the betterment of boys. Considerable criticism arose over the play the story got because of its identification with the star.

A panel debated the issue and the following excerpt from the Feb. 28, 1959, AP *Log* expressed some of the views of news executives:

> A weekend conference of editors and judges was called by the National Probation and Parole Association. All four New York City newspapers [AMs] which had first crack at the story used the name [of the baseball star]. What would have happened if the name had been withheld and, as inevitably it would, had leaked out later. This point was raised by Frank Starzel, AP general manager. "There would have been a greater hue and cry about favoring the son of a famous man than about using the name." Turner Catledge [New York *Times*] said, "We have much less to apologize for than . . . if we had withheld his name."

Many recent stories have been based on scandals involving the children of film celebrities, prominent politicians and others. Roger Tatarian made the following comments in the UPI *Reporter* of July 30, 1970:

> On both sides of the Atlantic some sentiment is evident against what can only be described as news by association. This usually has to do with court cases that are not particularly newsworthy in themselves but become publicized because the person involved is linked in some way with a celebrity.
>
> Thus two editors protested a recent UPI dispatch that reported the arrest on marijuana charges of the nephew of a close friend of President Nixon. They felt that the story served only a partisan cause. They would, I am sure, have felt the same way about a report that appeared in print this week under the headline: "Brother of Counsel to Nixon Is Accused."
>
> It is not only the reference to the president in these cases that is under criticism, but even the mention of the uncle in the first case and of the brother in the second. In other words, these critics feel the decision on whether or not to publish should be based solely on the importance of the event and of the principal, and on nothing else. . . .

The criticism is likely to continue, but, in cases involving immediate family, newspapers are not likely, for some time, to omit news by association.

The most immediate question involves the remoteness of association. How close should the relationship be for identification to be of significant news value?

Trademarks and Trade Names   Through common associations created by advertising, trademarks are often used as generic terms; Butane for liquified gas, Kodak for camera, Fiberglass for glass fiber, Novocain for pain-relieving drug, Scotch tape for cellophane tape, Thermos bottle for vacuum bottle, and Vaseline for petroleum jelly are but a few examples.

Trademarks should be capitalized. Usually, it is better to use the generic term, such as small bandage instead of Band-Aid, refrigerator instead of Frigidaire, jeans instead of Levi's, and rifle instead of Winchester. News columns should avoid any type of free advertising.

There are occasions, however, when trade names are pertinent. The name of an automobile is significant when a suspect is fleeing in one.

In cases of obituaries, hospitals prefer that "local hospital" be used rather than the hospital's name, and when suicides take place hotels prefer that "local hotel" be used instead of the hotel's name. If a newspaper does not have a policy covering such situations, it is up to an editor to make the decisions.

Legal Implications

The three amendments to the United States Constitution usually referred to in cases involving freedom of the press are the first, fifth and 14th.

The courts almost unanimously accept the principle of freedom from prior restraint or censorship before publication. Yet publishers can be held responsible for words used in articles after publication. Under the laws of libel and under growing recognition of the rights of privacy, newspapers can be held accountable for what they publish.

Libel   Slander is oral defamation, and libel is written defamation. Exposition is not the only form in which libel can occur. Cartoons, pictures, recordings and even skywriting may constitute libel.

There are two general classifications of libel, criminal and civil. The former would be a violation of whatever criminal statute a state may have adopted. The prosecution would be undertaken by a district or prosecuting attorney. Imprisonment or fine or both may be the consequence.

Criminal libel cases are rare in the United States today.[3] Most criminal actions originally stemmed from seditious statements or from com-

---

[3] See John D. Stevens *et al.,* "Criminal Libel as Seditious Libel, 1916–65," *Journalism Quarterly,* Spring, 1966, pp. 110–113.

ments that could have led to a breach of the peace. Libel against the dead, for instance, was one type of criminal libel. The reasoning was that, because of aroused emotions, admirers might seek to avenge a libeled dead person and thus bring about a breach of the peace.

Civil libel results from wrong done to an individual. It is the individual who brings the action in an attempt to get redress for wrong done to him. Three types of damages may result.

General damages may be granted to redress a person for the suffering and pain caused him by a libelous statement. Exemplary or punitive damages may be assessed if a person maliciously libels another; the damages are a punishment to the one who committed the act. Special damages are granted only when pecuniary loss can be proved.

Some words are considered to be libelous on their face, or, to put it another way, some words are considered to be clearly libelous when applied to a person. These words are called libelous per se. Some examples are "shyster," "cheat," "swindler," "whore," "quack" and "imbecile."

Some words may or may not be libelous, depending on how they are used. "Queer" and "loose" are examples.

Other words that are not libelous under ordinary circumstances may be in certain situations. To say that a wedded couple had a child would not ordinarily be libelous, but it would be if the couple had been married for only one month.

Civil libel laws come under the jurisdictions of the states and vary from state to state. The newsman should study the laws of the state in which he works.

Generally, reporters should be careful in their use of words that could possibly impute a criminal offense or immorality, hurt a person in his profession or occupation, impute a loathsome or venereal disease, accuse a person of belonging to an organization generally held in bad repute, insinuate a bad credit rating, or belittle character.

Misspelling names and identifying persons incorrectly are libel hazards. To write that A. R. Smith was arrested on a charge of vagrancy when it was actually A. B. Smith who was arrested could result in a libel action if an A. R. Smith lived in the community.

To write that John W. Jones, an architect, had filed a voluntary bankruptcy petition when the man was actually a contractor could cause trouble if there were also an architect in the community by the same name.

The careless detailing of arrests is risky. To say that Joseph Dokes was arrested for burglary would be to declare him guilty. If he is acquitted he has ground for a libel action. The reporter should write that he was arrested "on a charge of" burglary.

It is important, too, that no story be written about a person taken into custody until that person is booked. The individual might be taken to a police station and then released with no charges filed.

Corporations as well as individuals can be libeled. To say that a company sells adulterated food is libelous per se in that it accuses that company of an illegal act. To say that a business firm's credit is shaky is also libelous per se.

Defenses A publication may or may not have to pay damages if it uses a libelous statement. It depends on whether or not that publication has a valid defense. The three common defenses are truth, privilege and the right of fair comment and criticism. A publication may defend itself successfully in court and still find that the cost of doing so is considerable.

Truth Truth is a valid defense against libel in some states. In other states, truth with justifiable motives, meaning without malice, is a defense.

The burden of proving that the libelous words were true falls on the publication or defendant. It is not enough to prove that the writer or publisher thought the words were true; it must be proved that they were.

The burden of proving that statements were maliciously made falls on the plaintiff, the one bringing the action.

Privilege Certain public officials are granted legal immunity from slander or libel actions for comments made while performing their duties. This is known as privilege.

Legislative, judicial and certain other public and official proceedings are privileged.

Members of legislative bodies, including congress, state legislatures, county boards of supervisors and city councils, have absolute immunity for comments made when acting in their respective official roles. This immunity has been extended to committee meetings and to hearings.

What an alderman says at an official meeting is privileged, but not what he says when he goes to lunch.

Court proceedings are covered by privilege. The pertinent comments of lawyers, even though they may be derogatory, are immune when court is in session, but not during recess or after adjournment. Testimony admitted by a judge is privileged. Witnesses who make false statements may be charged with perjury but they are not subject to damages for slander.

Some other public proceedings, such as meetings in which the public has an interest, are considered privileged in some states. The proceedings of commissions and boards that are legislative or judicial in function are considered privileged. A local school board is an example of a board with a legislative function. The federal trade commission is an example of one with a semijudicial function.

The trend has been for courts to extend privilege to public officials for statements made about matters strictly under their administrative controls. Further clarification of this kind of privilege is needed.

The privilege accorded to legislative bodies and to court proceedings is absolute, which means that there is no qualifying provision, such as a requirement of good faith.

The newsman should study the statutory provisions for privilege in the state in which he works. The provisions often clarify the degree of privilege granted to public meetings and public administrative officials. Federal court decisions likewise should be observed.

A pertinent case involved the acting director of the office of rent stabilization in 1953; he was sued by two former employees for saying in a press release that the workers were to be fired. They sued and a federal district court jury awarded damages. The United States appellate court sustained the decision.

The United States Supreme Court ordered that consideration be given to whether or not the acting director had qualified privilege. The appellate court found he had but ordered trial to determine whether or not that privilege was forfeited by malice. Then the Supreme Court ruled in 1969 that he had absolute privilege. Malice, therefore, would have no bearing.

Reporters generally have qualified privilege to report legislative, judicial and other public and official proceedings. Malice or inaccuracy, according to most state statutes, would invalidate the defense of privilege.

Public records are privileged, but uncertainty sometimes arises over what is and what is not a public record. Most states have passed statutes to clarify the matter. There are still some gray areas, though, despite the statutes.

Is a police blotter a public record? Not all statutes are clear on this point. In some court decisions, the answer has been yes. Still, greater clarification is needed.[4]

The question sometimes arises whether court pleadings, such as civil complaints, are privileged before answers are filed or before they come to the attention of the judge.

What about a divorce complaint that is withdrawn a few days after

---

[4] See Michael J. Petrick, "The Press, the Police Blotter, and Public Policy," *Journalism Quarterly,* Autumn, 1969, pp. 475–481.

being filed? The trend seems to be that pleadings are part of court proceedings regardless of whether or not they have come to the attention of a judge. Divorce proceedings may be excepted.

The Right of Fair Comment and Criticism The right of fair comment and criticism is granted Americans by constitutional provisions protecting the right of free speech and free press. Social and cultural progress would indeed be stilted if people were not permitted to express their opinions on matters of public interest. The right of fair comment and criticism does not extend to private lives or actions.

Books, plays, art work, theatrical and musical events, and athletic contests are of public interest. So are the actions and performances of public officials, actors and actresses, musicians, artists, authors and others.

Comments and criticism should be limited to the work itself; they should never be aimed at the individuals. An actor's performance, for example, is subject to criticism, but not the actor as an individual. A public official's actions may be criticized, but extreme care should be exercised in dealing with motivations.

The facts upon which criticism is based should be accurate. To criticize a baseball infielder for frequent fumbles when he fumbled once or twice would be basing criticism on an inaccurate statement of facts.

The right of fair comment and criticism has generally been vitiated when malice can be shown.

In a significant decision in 1964, *New York Times v. Sullivan,* the U.S. Supreme Court ruled that a public official cannot recover damages for criticism, even though factual inaccuracies occur, unless he can prove malice. Malice was defined as knowledge of the falsity of a statement or reckless disregard of the truth.

In delivering the opinion, Justice William J. Brennan said:

> The constitutional guarantees require, we think, a federal rule that prohibits a public official from recovering damages for a defamatory falsehood relating to his official conduct unless he proves that the statement was made with actual malice—that is, with knowledge that it was false or with reckless disregard of whether it was false or not.

The court later broadened the term "public official" to "public figure." Some question arises over who are public figures. The best gauge seems to be that anyone involved in a public debate or controversy can be called a public figure.

Teachers, doctors, nurses and clergymen would not ordinarily be considered public figures. Let any of these become involved in a social movement, however, and they become public figures. Let a housewife become embroiled in a women's liberation movement and she becomes a public figure.

Privacy In some states, a legal right to privacy has been established through court decisions or statutes. The provisions vary from state to state. A few states have refused to recognize the right of privacy.

It is the right to be left alone—the right to the pursuit of happiness, as defined in one court decision.

Privacy violations differ from libel in that defamation is not a factor and truth is not a defense.

Wilson W. Wyatt, a legal authority, has listed four types of violations for which courts generally allow damages:

1. Appropriation to one's own advantage of the benefit of the name or likeness of another
2. Unreasonable intrusion upon the privacy or private affairs of another
3. Unreasonable publicity given to the private life of another, even though the facts are completely true
4. Unreasonable publicity that places another in a false light before the public.[5]

In the 1967 case of *Time, Inc. v. Hill,* the U. S. Supreme Court extended some of the provisions of the *New York Times v. Sullivan* case to privacy actions. In that case, the court ruled that when privacy actions are based on inaccuracies the plaintiff must prove the falsehoods to have been deliberately published or to have been published with reckless regard for the truth.

Persons who become involved in the news lose some of their rights to privacy even though their involvement may be involuntary. Included are those who are involved in court actions, accidents, public affairs, controversial issues and politics.

Prominence can be a factor. The public has an interest in actors, writers, artists, musicians and athletes.

One of the tests used in deciding if there might be an invasion of privacy is whether or not the public has an interest in the information.

Some of the areas in which caution is needed are the following:

1. Stories that put private citizens in an unfavorable light
2. Stories about persons with rare diseases
3. Stories about persons long after they have been subjects of news
4. Stories detailing private facts that might be embarrassing
5. Fictionalization.

News stories usually present no problem, but feature articles and

[5] "The 'Right of Privacy' Doctrine: A Prime Newspaper Headache," *Bulletin,* American Society of Newspaper Editors, Nov., 1967.

human interest stories can. If a reporter makes his identity known and a person gives him information, there should be no danger of violation of privacy because consent would be implicit. Giving consent waives the right to a claim of violation of privacy.

Retraction Retraction statutes have been passed in certain states. These provide some relief for a newspaper that has blundered into libel.

The reporter should determine whether or not the state in which he works has such a statute and, if it has, what the provisions are. Some questions that need answers are the following:

    1. If a newspaper complies with a retraction law, from what kinds of damage will it be exempted? Punitive probably, general sometimes, but special not likely.

    2. What are the time limitations for a libeled person to request a retraction and how soon after a newspaper receives a request must the retraction be run?

    3. What is required for a retraction to meet the requirements of the law?

    4. Does the statute state that the libelous comment must have been run in good faith?

California has one of the most liberal of all retraction statutes.[6] It provides that a person libeled by a newspaper or radio broadcast must, if he wishes to seek more than special damages, serve notice on the offending newspaper or broadcasting station within 20 days after learning of the publication. The newspaper or broadcasting station has up to three weeks after receiving notice to run a retraction. The retraction must have the same emphasis the offending article had. No mention is made of good faith.

The justification for the law is based on the haste with which news media must operate. The law provides no protection for magazines. It is generally considered that the word "broadcast" applies to television, though that would be up to a court interpretation.

The U.S. Supreme Court dismissed a constitutional challenge to the law in 1952, permitting the statute to stand.

The Right of Confidence Some states have "shield" laws, which protect newsmen from being held in contempt of court for refusing to reveal the names of news sources. These laws do not apply to litigation in federal courts.

[6] See Thomas M. Newell and Albert Pickerell, "California's Retraction Statute: License to Libel?" *Journalism Quarterly,* Fall, 1951.

The subject has been controversial. Many lawyers argue that such protection can beget injustice in some kinds of litigation.

Many newsmen argue, on the other hand, that reporters should have the same privilege of professional secrecy as that usually accorded to lawyer and client, clergymen and confessee, and doctor and patient. They also maintain that violation of confidence would dry up many news sources.

It would behoove a reporter to determine whether or not the state he works in has a shield law and, if it has, how fully it would protect him in refusing to reveal the names of news sources. Some reporters have gone to jail for contempt after refusing to reveal the names of news sources when ordered to do so by courts or legislative bodies. But their sentences have generally been mild—sometimes only small fines.

EXERCISES

I. Questions for Discussion

1. What is baiting? Should it be used to get reluctant news sources to talk?
2. Do you favor the publication of names of juvenile delinquents?
3. What policy would you recommend for the identification of race or nationality in news stories?
4. Do you consider news by association valid?
5. Under what circumstances would a reporter be justified in concealing his identity?
6. Are there any circumstances under which you feel a reporter would be justified in eavesdropping?
7. What policy would you recommend for the use of trademarks and trade names?
8. What are the differences between libel and violation of privacy?
9. In your state, is truth without justification a defense against libel?
10. What are the justifications for privilege as a defense against libel?
11. Who is a public figure?
12. How did the U.S. Supreme Court define malice in the *New York Times v. Sullivan* case?
13. Does your state have a retraction statute? If it has, what kinds of damages are exempted when a newspaper complies with the law?
14. Does your state have a shield law? If not, would you favor one?
15. What types of confidence or "professional secrecy" have generally been recognized?

II. *Do you consider the following excerpts from a story on the electrocution of Julius and Ethel Rosenberg at Sing Sing Prison in New York in 1953 to be in good taste?*

There was a rattle and a hum in the otherwise deathly still room. Rosenberg's chest strained hard against the straps that held him. His fist clenched.

His chest and neck turned red. Then he slumped visibly.

The first shock lasted three seconds. The two following lasted 57 seconds each.

Each time the straps were strained as his body pressed against them.

Again there was the seemingly long moment before the executioner threw the switch.

And again the low rasping rattle.

As the charge crashed through her body, Mrs. Rosenberg seemed to strain hard against the straps.

Her hands, which had been lying limp and open, clenched.

Like her husband, she received jolts of three seconds, 57 seconds and 57 seconds.

When it was over the current was cut, she slumped in the chair, apparently held upright only by the straps across her chest and head.

III. *Some of the questions asked Grace Kelly when she sailed from New York for Monaco to marry Prince Rainier III follow. Are they in good taste? (See Ray Erwin, "Antics of 250 Newsmen 'Scare' Grace Kelly at Ship Interview,"* Editor & Publisher, *April 7, 1956, for comments on the tactics of reporters at the interview.)*

Are you carrying a dowry to your husband?

Are there to be guests with you on the royal yacht during the honeymoon?

How many children do you want?

Is there a book of protocol to tell you how to act as a princess?

How many pieces are in your trousseau?

IV. *Problems*

1. As a political reporter, you are assigned to cover a $100 a plate fund-raising dinner put on by a political party. You estimate the actual cost of the dinner to be less than $10. The understanding was that your dinner would be complimentary. Do you feel that your dinner should be paid for by your newspaper instead of your accepting it free? Suppose it was a $10 fund-raising dinner and you estimated the cost of the dinner to be $5 at the most. Would your answer be the same?

2. As a sports writer, you interview a hunter who was the first in your locality to get his limit of ducks after the opening of the season. Before you leave, the man offers you one of the largest of the ducks. Would you take it?

3. A public relations agent has regularly supplied you with information about an industrial concern. You have used some of the information in stories. On your birthday, he brings you a pen and pencil set which you estimate cost $10. Would you take it? If instead he offers you a pen which you estimate cost no more than a dollar, would you take it?
4. You have regularly covered city council meetings. At Christmas time, one of the councilmen offers you a bottle of scotch. Would you take it?
5. As a farm reporter, you cover a cantaloupe festival. Toward the end of the festival one of the officials offers you a bag of cantaloupes. Would you accept? Suppose that he offers you a case of cantaloupes to be shared by newsmen in your office. Would you accept?
6. As a woman's section writer, you are invited to attend a dinner of one of the guilds you have written stories about. The dinner is a social affair you do not plan to cover. Each guild member pays $10 to attend. Would you accept the invitation?
7. While eating luncheon in a cafe, you hear the conversation of a group of women in an adjoining booth. You cannot see them but you assume that they are teachers. Their comments are about the increasing narcotics traffic in a local high school. One woman says that the principal is conducting an investigation. Another replies, "It's about time." You accost the principal and he denies any knowledge of dope being used by students. What would you do?
8. A political rally is held for a candidate you personally favor. Advance news stories quoted political leaders as estimating 2,000 would attend. You estimate not more than 150 attend. A political acquaintance asks you, as you cover the rally, whether you can't skip the attendance in your story and concentrate on the talks. How would you answer?
9. A strike vote is to be taken at a meeting of a local union. You want to cover the meeting but you are refused admittance. The union hall is adjoined by a vacant lot where you can stand and hear the conversation inside, since it is a warm evening and all the windows have been raised. Would this be an ethical means of getting the information you wish?
10. Your newspaper has been a strong crusader against vice of all types. You have been assigned to investigate bookie operations. You try to place a bet with a man you feel sure is a bookie but he is wary despite your assumed name and occupation. You learn of one man who has been having a hard streak of luck in picking the horses. He admits to you he knows of more than half a dozen bookies but he refuses to tell you who they are. You feel confident that if you slipped him $50 he would not only reveal the names in confidence but also help you to establish yourself well enough with some of them to be able to place your own bets. Would this be ethical?

V. Read one of the following articles and report on it
1. Mark Masterson, "The New Journalism," *The Quill,* February, 1971, pp. 14–17.
2. "Siding With Agnew," *Newsweek,* March 9, 1970, p. 84.
3. Ania Savage, "API seminar stresses facts to cool off 'ecology alarm,' " *Editor & Publisher,* January 2, 1971, pp. 7, 31.
4. "Death at the Hospital," *Time,* December 28, 1970, p. 23.
5. "Catledge finds trend to advocacy disturbing," *Editor & Publisher,* December 5, 1970, p. 13.
6. Don R. Pembern "Privacy and the Press: The Defense of Newsworthiness," *Journalism Quarterly,* Spring, 1968, pp. 14–24.
7. "Court holds reporter unprotected," *Editor & Publisher,* December 12, 1970, p. 50.

Appendix A

COPYREADING MARKS

The following copyreading marks commonly used in correcting newspaper copy may be helpful to students in going over their own copy.

Abbreviate or use figure   (Professor) Kendall . . . (nineteen)

Do not abbreviate or do spell out figure   accounting (dept.) . . . ③

Close up   a brush‿up class

Correct   The measure is ~~almost certain~~ *expected* to cause. . . .

Delete   Smith, ~~who is~~ an engineer, testified. . . .

Insertion   Actually, he said, most ∧*airline* passengers travel short distances.

Insert comma   He started for the second floor‚ but they caught him before he could get there.

389

Insert period	The education staff is in the process of moving to its new office⊙ The system. . . .
Insert quotation marks	⌒I don't care what happens,⌒ he said.
Let it stand	The ransom note demanded $25,-000 ~~in $10 and $20 bills.~~ (stet)
Paragraph	And another storm is coming, with the weatherman forecasting a chance of rain tonight and early tomorrow morning. ⌐Temperatures will continue. . . .
No paragraph	Only 256,823 persons came into the county from elsewhere during the 10-year period, the chamber said.⌒This compares to. . . .
Spelling is correct—do not alter	Charles Brackkett (ck)
Transpose letters or words	Kleith . . . he already has
Use capital letter (usually specified as three lines beneath the letter, but copyreaders often use a small z because it is quicker)	The Farm Growers association. . . . association
Lower case	the ¢ommission

Appendix B

COMMONLY MISSPELLED WORDS

Here is a list of words that are frequently misspelled.

accessibility	defendant	hygiene
accommodate	dessicate	impostor
affect (never a noun)	develop	inadmissible
all right	dietitian	incalculable
anonymous	dilemma	indispensible
asinine	diphtheria	inflammation
assured	ecstasy	inoculate
believe	embarrass	inseparable
benefited	Ecuador	insistence
buses	eying	irrelevant
calendar	feasible	irreligious
canceled	fiery	judgment
cemetery	fulfill	kidnaped
combated	gaiety	kimono
compatible	grievance	legionnaire
consensus	hemorrhage	license

liaison	realtor	strait jacket
likable	receive	stupefy
misspelled	recommend	supersede
nickel	referred	synonymous
obbligato	repetitious	temblor
occurred	sacrilegious	thorough
parallel	salable	tonsillitis
parishioner	seize	totaled
peddler	separate	traveler
Philippines	sheriff	tying
picnicking	siege	usable
pneumonia	sieve	vilify
Portuguese	signaled	voyageur
prejudice	sizable	waive
prophecy (noun)	skiing	wintry
prophesy (verb)	skillful	yield
questionnaire	stationary	
rarefy	stationery	

Appendix C

A FINAL EXERCISE

Compare the story you wrote in completing Exercise V at the end of Chapter 10 with the following story written by Melvin Mencher.

> The scientist engaged in pure research rarely knows to what use his discoveries will be put.
>
> In fact, said Dr. Serge A. Korff, a professor of physics at New York University, some of the uses come as a surprise to the scientist.
>
> Dr. Korff was in Fresno to address the local chapters of Sigma Xi and the American Chemical Society at Fresno State College last night. He spoke on the origin of cosmic radiation.
>
> Even this highly theoretical field has produced data for practical use. The physicist said cosmic ray studies have provided an explanation for the strange behavior of compasses during magnetic storms.
>
> Also, he added, cosmic ray research turned out information which has proved invaluable in dating the remains of

once living animals and plants. This is the Carbon 14 method.

Cosmic rays shower the earth constantly, subjecting its inhabitants to a type of radiation similar to that of the atomic and hydrogen bombs. Some scientists contend the natural radiation humans receive through cosmic rays should not be increased by frequent nuclear bomb testing if the human race is to survive.

But Dr. Korff refused to comment on the question.

"I am a physicist, not a geneticist," he said. "I do not know how much radiation the human can stand without damage, and, as I understand it, the geneticists differ themselves."

This unwillingness to step into fields other than his own was the reason for his declaration the scientist should stick to his laboratory and not meddle in politics.

Dr. Korff is an educator as well as a scientist, and he did express his feelings about the current crop of high school graduates.

"High school students come to college badly prepared," he declared.

He said high schools are increasingly reducing their graduation requirements and too often offer subjects which can be taught in the home.

He sees the use of school time to teach students to drive as an example of waste.

"My father taught me to drive," he commented. "It is a job for the parents, not the school."

Dr. Korff declared high schools are offering students a diet of mush when the students are capable of taking sterner stuff. . . .

(Fresno *Bee*)

INDEX

Accuracy, 8–9, 161
All America Union, 375
American Newspaper Publishers Association: study on interpretation, 292
American Society of Newspaper Editors, 291
Angles for stories, 80–93; timely occasions, 86–88; used as a wedge, 81–82; when the angle makes the story, 82–84
Anti-Defamation League, 375
Antithesis, 189
Apathy: overcoming, 270
Arthur, Franklin K.: on racial identification, 374–375
Associated Press, 16, 20; *Style Book,* 47
Associated Press Managing Editors, 291
Asyndeton, 193
Attribution, 20, 26–27, 69–73

Background, 65–66, 309
Background story, 306–314; purpose, 310–312; relation to interpretative story, 306; subjects for, 314; used in series, 312–314; writing, 306–310
Balance in news, 3
Battle of New Orleans, 3
Beats, 148–149, 151
Bernstein, Theodore, 44, 76
Blackman, Sam: on political campaign coverage, 20
Breadth reporting, 252–265

395

396 Index

Brisbane, Arthur, 4
British newspapers, 3

Canham, Erwin D.: on interpretation, 299–300
Catledge, Turner: on news by association, 376
Chronology, 105–107, 321
Cities: plight of, 281–285
City editor, 147
Color stories, 355–365; capturing the mood, 363–365; compared with news stories, 357–359; figurative language in, 357; imaginative appeal to senses, 356; occasions for, 355; special events, 359–363; writing, 355–359
Columns, 131–133
Commission on Human Relations, 375
Communications: pace of, 3–4
Confidence: keeping a, 68–69; right of, 383–384
Conflict, 326–330
Context, 18
Copy: preparation of, 153
Copy desk, 147
Copyreading marks, 389–390
Copyright, 145
County editor, 147
Crime news, 2
Cutbacks, 100–105, 323

Deadlines, 154
DeMotte, John, 292
Depth reporting, 4, 240–252, 293; getting information, 243–244; writing in depth, 252
Description: evaluative, 16–18; particularizing, 16–18
Developing news sources, 148–149
Distortion, 18–19

Eavesdropping, 371–372
Ecology, 285–288
Editorial councils, 134
Editorials, 133–134
Editor in chief, 147
Entertainment, 3, 318
Ethics, 367–377; eavesdropping, 371–372; gratuities, 368–369; independence, 368–370; integrity, 367–368; juvenile offenders, 372–373; news by association, 375–376; news policy, 5, 19, 372–377; racial identification, 374–375; reporter identification, 371; trademarks and trade names, 377; use of coercion, 370–371
Ethridge, Mark F., 2
Evaluative description, 16–18
Exaggeration, 19
Explanation, 73–76

Fairness, 8–9
Feature articles, 118–126, 209–237; about persons, 232–234; advice from experts, 227–229; business, 221–222; compared with interview story, 215; compared with news story, 209–210; debunking type, 229–231; education, 219–221; historical, 224–226; hobbies, 235–236; organization of, 215; religion, 222–224; science, 217–219; short, 236–237; social problems, 215–216; subjects for, 209; supplementation, 215; timely occasions for, 226–227; writing, 210–215
Feature writing, 209–237
Figures of speech, 54–55, 189–190, 357
Filing system for news, 149
Fire: Seattle hotel, 271
Flesch, Rudolf, 44
Foreign affairs, 303–304
Future book, 149

Gratuities, 368–369
Gress, Theodore: on naming juvenile offenders, 372–373
Griffith, Thomas: on objectivity, 13
Gruner, George F.: on meaning of words, 15

Hearst, William Randolph, 3–4
Hoaxes, 9–10
Hughes, Charles Evans, 8–9
Human interest, 2, 4–5, 89, 318–335; young and old, 330–332
Human interest stories, 130–131, 318–335; animals, 332–335; compared with news stories, 320–321; conflict, 326–330; leads for, 322–325; press associations, 320–321; resemblance to short story, 322; single effect, 325–326; suspense, 321; writing, 321–325
Human plight, 273–281
Humor, 236–237

Identification, 29–31, 62–65; reader, 195–196; by synonym, 66–68
Impressionistic writing, 192
Interest, 186–203; in news, 2–3
Interpretation, 126–130, 291–304, 306
Interpretative writing, 291–304; economics, 300–302; foreign affairs, 303–304; political scene, 297–300
Interviewee: personality of, 161–162; reactions vary, 158
Interviewing, 156–176; art of questioning, 159–161; dominating, 158–159; preparing for, 157; use of recorders, 162–163
Interview stories, 163–172; feature type, 167–172; multiple, 171–172; opinion type, 163–167
Investigative reporting, 265–267

Jackson, Andrew, 3
Jess, Paul: study on naming juvenile offenders, 374
Johnson, Earl J.: on racial identification, 374
Journalistic literature: comparisons of, 135–142; types of, 117–142
Judgment: areas of, 14
Juvenile offenders: naming of, 372–373

Kaleidoscopic writing, 194–195
Kane, George, 6–7
Kipling, Rudyard, 23

Language, 42–60; clichés, 51–53; elegantisms, 53–54; figures of speech, 54–55, 189–190, 357; gender, 57; plurals, 56–57; simplicity, 50–51; subordination, 55–56; wordiness, 44–46; word preferences, 46–49; words often misused, 49–50
Lawrence, David, 131
Leads, 23–39; brevity in, 24–26; burdensome, 23–24; dangling, 39; five Ws, 23; interesting, 35–36, 188–190; past tense, 38; question, 36; rhetorical devices, 32–34; simplicity, 34–35; suspense, 36–37; unconventional, 189; updating, 37–38
Libel, 377–383; civil, 377–379; criminal, 377–388; defenses in, 379–383; definition, 377; *New York Times v. Sullivan*, 381–382; per se, 378; privilege, 379–381; public records, 380–381; retraction, 385; right of fair comment and criticism, 381–382; truth, 379; words to watch, 378
Lilliston, Lynn, 275–281
Lindsay, John, 281
Litotes, 194

Managing editor, 147
Markel, Lester: on interpretation, 291–292
Miller, Robert, 9
Mott, Frank Luther, 13
Multiple-story coverage, 110–112

National Association for the Advancement of Colored People, 375
National Probation and Parole Association, 376
Near v. Minnesota, 8–9
Negativism in news, 6–7
News: balance in, 3; by association, 375–376; coverage, 145–154; crime, 2, 4; definition, 1–2; determinants, 4–5; future satisfaction in, 318; immediate satisfaction in, 318; negativism, 6–7; position, 14; property rights in, 145–146; relative nature, 6; reward for reader, 4, 318; selection, 5; sensationalism, 2; sources, 148–150
Newspaper: organization, 146–147; policy, 5–6, 19, 372–373
News sources, 148–150; confidence of, 68–69
News story, 97–113; compared with feature story, 118, 141, 209–210; compared with interpretative article, 126; sidebar, 339–341
New York Times v. Sullivan, 381–382
Nicknames, 151
Nova, 2

Objectivity, 12–20, 291–292, 367–368; in magazines, 13
Off the record, 68–69
O'Flaherty, Terrence, 8
Opinion magazines, 13
Organization of newspaper, 146–147
Organization of news story, 97–113; chronology, 105–107; cutbacks, 100–105; "one, two, three" order, 108–110; simple, 97–100; transition, 112–113

Parallelism, 193
Particularizing description, 16–18
Pertinent facts, 19
Policy: news, 5, 19, 372–377
Political campaigns, 20
Position of stories, 14
Press associations, 193, 284, 320–321, 374
Press conferences, 172–173
Privacy: right of, 382–383; *Time, Inc. v. Hill,* 382
Property rights in news, 145–146
Publicists, 150
Public records, 380–381
Publisher, 147
Pulitzer, Joseph, 3–4
Punctuation, 58–60

Qualifications of a reporter, 367–370
Questioning: art of, 159–161
Quiller-Couch, Sir Arthur, 68
Quotation marks, 70
Quotations: direct and indirect, 70

Racial identification, 374–375
Radio, 120, 145–146
Readability, 44
Reader appeals: sensory, 186–188
Reader identification, 195–196
Recorders: use of, 162–163
Related stories, 339–352; eyewitness accounts, 342–346; identification with main story, 351; public reaction type, 346–350; purpose, 339
Reporter: identification, 371; qualities of, 152, 367–370; responsibility, 14–15
Reporting the news in breadth, 262–265
Reporting the news in depth, 4, 240–252, 293
Research, 231, 241–244, 308–309
Reston, James, 132
Retraction, 383
Rewriting from other newspapers, 145
Rhetorical questions, 194
Right of fair comment and criticism, 381–382
Riots, 270

Scripps, Edward W., 3–4
Sensationalism, 2
Sensory appeals, 186–188
Seward's day, 87–88

Shelley, Percy Bysshe, 2
Sherman, Gene, 240–241
Shield laws, 383–384
Short story, 322
Sidebars, 339–352
Simplicity, 201–203
Single effect, 325–326
Situation story, 270–288; ecology, 285–288; human plight, 273–281; organization of, 272–273; overcoming apathy, 270; plight of the cities, 281–285
Slander, 377
Slanting stories, 15–16
Space in newspapers, 14
Spangler, Raymond, 2
Special events, 359–363
Speech stories, 174–176
Spencer, M. Lyle, 1
Staccato style, 200–201
Starzel, Frank: on news by association, 376
State editor, 147
Steigleman, Walter: on eyewitness stories, 345–346; study on naming juvenile offenders, 374
Style books, 47, 151
Subjectivity, 15–16, 291–292
Sullivan, Mark, 131
Sulzberger, Arthur Hays, 3
Superlatives, 18
Supplementation, 197–200
Survey articles, 252–265

Tape recorders, 162–163
Tatarian, Roger, 8, 20, 376
Telegraph editor, 147
Telephone: use of, 153–154
Television: impact of, 120, 240, 318
Tense, 171
Time, Inc. v. Hill, 382
Tips, 145, 150, 267
Trademarks and trade names, 377
Transition, 112–113
Truth as defense in libel suits, 379

Unconventional leads, 189
Unfair business practice, 146
United Nations, 203
United Press International, 20, 374; *Style Book,* 47

Verbosity, 44–46
Volunteered information, 149

Walters, Basil L. (Stuffy), 24–25
Warning readers, 270–273
Wechsler, James, 3
Weekly newspaper, 146
Wiggins, J. R.: on gratuities, 368–369
Williams, Nick B., 275
Wire news, 147
Words: abstract, 191; commonly misspelled, 391–392; concrete, 191; figurative, 54–55, 189–190, 357; often confused, 49–50; plurals, 56–57; preferences, 46–49; putting to work, 188–191
Writing: antithesis, 189; asyndeton, 193; elegantisms, 53–54; figurative, 54–55, 189–190, 357; fragments, 201; gender, 57; grammar, 58; impressionistic, 192; kaleidoscopic, 194–195; litotes, 194; parallelism, 193–194; punctuation, 58–60; reader identification, 195–196; rhetorical question, 194; sensory appeals, 186–188; simplicity, 50–51, 201–203; staccato style, 200–201; subordination, 55–56; supplementation, 197–200; verbosity, 44–46; word preferences, 46–49

Wyatt, Wilson W.: on privacy, 382

3